THE HEADWATERS WAR:
Conflict for the Mississippi Headwaters

W. J. RYDRYCH

THE HEADWATERS WAR:
Conflict for the Mississippi Headwaters

This is a work of fiction. Names, characters, places, and incidents are the product of the author's imagination or are used fictitiously. Any resemblance to actual events, locales, or persons living or dead, is entirely coincidental.

The Headwaters War: Conflict for the Mississippi Headwaters
All rights reserved
1st Edition, Copyright © TX000832480, 2016, W. J. Rydrych
Revised Edition, 2018, W. J. Rydrych

Cover photograph: Beaver pond near Big Sandy Lake, by author

All rights reserved, including the right of reproduction in any form or by any mechanical or electrical means including photocopying or recording, or by any information storage or retrieval system, in whole or in part in any form, and in any case without the written permission of the author and publisher.

ISBN 9781973429661
x

THE HEADWATERS WAR:
Conflict for the Mississippi Headwaters

CONTENTS

Illustration Index.............................. 4
Author's Preface 5
Chapter 1: And in the Beginning 15
Chapter 2: Conquest of Sandy Lake 33
Chapter 3: Battle of Cut Foot Sioux 69
Chapter 4: Conquest of Mille Lacs 95
Chapter 5: Dakota Campaign of 1768 121
Chapter 6: Big Marten's War 162
Chapter 7: The Saint Croix River 215
Chapter 8: Uk-ke-waus and Battle Lake 226
Chapter 9: Overtures of Peace 230
Chapter 10: Crossing the Mississippi 233
Chapter 11: Fort Snelling and Aftermath 248
Chapter 12: The Sandy Lake Tragedy 265
Chapter 13: Uprisings of 1862 277
Chapter 14: The Ojibwe Chiefs 296
Chapter 15: Big Sandy: Then and Now 328
Chapter 16: The End Game 334
Attributions and Bibliography 362
Appendix
    Treaty of 1855 367
    Treaty of 1867 375
    Dawes Allotment Act of 1887 380
    Indian Citizenship Act of 1924 387
    Indian Reorganization Act of 1934 390
    Public Law 280 (*partial*) of 1953 396
    (*18 U.S.C §1162; 28 U.S.C. §1360*)

THE HEADWATERS WAR:
Conflict for the Mississippi Headwaters

ILLUSTRATIONS

Figure 1: Continental Divides .... .28

Figure 2: Nelson River Watershed 29

Figure 3: Drainage Basins in Minnesota......... 30

Figure 4: Minnesota Lakes and Rivers 31

Figure 5: Mississippi Headwaters Lakes & Rivers ... 32

Figure 6: Big Sandy Lake (Lac du Sable) 68

Figure 7: Lakes Winnibigoshish & Cut Foot Sioux ... 94

Figure 8: Kathio Area of Mille Lacs Lake 120

Figure 9: Route of Dakota Raid of 1768 161

Figure 10: Minnesota River 214

Figure 11 St Croix River Watershed 225

Figure 12: West of the Mississippi 247

Figure 13: The Line of the 1825 Treaty of Prairie ... 263
du Chien

Figure 14: Pokegama Lake 264

Figure 15: Minnesota Territory 1849 275

Figure 16: Sign commemorating Big Sandy Lake.. 276
Tragedy of 1850

Figure 17: Chief Hole-in-the-Day the younger 288

Figure 18: Chief Little Crow IV 289

Figure 19: Chief Shakopee III 290

Figure 20 Dakota Chiefs & Villages (1862) 291

Figure 21: Sibley Campaign of 1862 292

Figure 22: Fort Ridgely (1862) 293

Figure 23: Dakota Attack on New Ulm (1862) 294

Figure 24: The Hanging at Mankato 295
(December, 1862)

Figure 25: Wooden Sandy River Dam, 1895 332

Figure 26: Big Sandy: Then & Now 333

Figure 27: Indian Cessions and Reservations 1858... 358

Figure 28: Headwaters Lakes reservations after... 359
Treaty of 1867

Figure 29: Headwaters Lakes reservations after ...360
1873 addition of White Oak Point

Figure 30: Reservations in Minnesota 2013 361

THE HEADWATERS WAR:
Conflict for the Mississippi Headwaters

AUTHOR'S PREFACE

My interest in the Mississippi River and the American Indian culture began early. I grew up in the 1930s and early 1940s in a small town in northern Minnesota bounded on two sides by an Ojibwe reservation, with the Mississippi, still a small river, only a mile or two away. The nearby reservation had no marked borders, and to those living in the area it was just like any other part of Minnesota. In fact, few even knew where the boundaries were, and as a result much of my spare time was spent hunting or fishing on the reservation with its many lakes and rivers. That was also true of my local school district, which ignored reservation boundaries, with the result that many of its students attended my school.

Why this disregard of what had once been considered a 'sanctuary' area of the indigenous tribes? That's a long story, and this revised edition includes an added chapter at the end that describes how those initial reservations, through government actions, evolved into what they had become at that time; and remain today.

Much later, when I had moved from the area and had a family of my own, we purchased a summer cabin on a lake in northern Minnesota named Big Sandy Lake. About three miles from the cabin, bordering a dirt road, was a small Ojibwe community of no more than a dozen houses located on 40 or so acres of land, with perhaps half of that swamps or ponds. There was not even a sign acknowledging its existence.

To most people living on or spending weekends at Big Sandy it was just one lake among the thousands in Minnesota, with little awareness of the lake's early history. Few realized those few acres of land and small group of homes were all that remained of the once

THE HEADWATERS WAR:
Conflict for the Mississippi Headwaters

powerful band of Sandy Lake Ojibwe, in its day a dominant force in Minnesota, or that Big Sandy Lake was known in European capitols over a hundred years before the Declaration of Independence was signed.

When we first came to Big Sandy Lake we also had no conception of its former history. All we knew was that it was an 'unusually' beautiful lake that we often drove by when visiting my former home town further north. However, one day, during one of our weekends at our lake cabin, we came across a small island toward its southern end with a sign commemorating a battle far in the past; in fact the island was named 'Battle Island'. Intrigued, I began to research the lake's early history, and gradually unearthed from musty history books and journals some insight into what Big Sandy Lake had once been.

However, researching the early days is like wandering through a fog, including why that small island bore the name 'Battle Island'. In *'Historical Highlights of Big Sandy Lake and the Savanna Portage'* (*21*), Norvis Nelson credits the name to an 1842 raid by the Dakota branch of the Western Sioux on an Ojibwe village on the island. Perhaps that is the case, but I found no records of a battle in the area in 1842. In the 1840s the primary Ojibwe village was on the north shore of the lake, but that doesn't rule out the presence of a smaller village or hunting camp on the island.

Still, perhaps Mr. Nelson was right. Even as late as 1842 raids between the two warring tribes was a common occurrence, with many small attacks whenever the opportunity arose. Such a raid could easily have taken place and escaped the notice of most. Although winter war parties were rare, it was the season when hunting parties ranged far; it could well have been a winter raid on an Ojibwe camp or settlement on the island, when it could easily be reached by crossing the ice from either the south or west. Or, in those days of much lower water, there may have been a land or

THE HEADWATERS WAR:
Conflict for the Mississippi Headwaters

shallow water connection to the west, making an attack during the normal season for war parties feasible. Neither of the above would have attracted that much attention; small raids were common.

Others claim the name results from the Ojibwe raid on a Dakota village on the peninsula a short distance away about a century earlier described by William Warren in 'History of the Ojibwe Nation' (*37, pp.176-177*). In any case, since the island was located near the probable site of the Dakota village, it is likely it at least served as a place of refuge during that earlier conflict.

While there are many 'Sandy Lakes' in Minnesota, I will usually refer to 'Big Sandy Lake' as just 'Sandy Lake', the 'Lac du Sable' or 'Lac des Sables' (*lake of the sands*) of the early French. Some say 'lake of the sands' referred to the broad sand beaches marking the lake before a dam at its outlet raised the water level, others to the 'sandy' color of the water. In the 1820s Henry Schoolcraft wrote about Big Sandy when he passed through on his way to discovering the source of the Mississippi River:

> *"the blue jay and brown thresher, the pigeon and turtle dove occasionally appeared in the forest, to enliven this part of the journey. On approaching the lake we ascended a lofty pine ridge, which forms its southern barrier, and commands one of the most charming views of this romantic little lake, which suddenly rose to our impatient sight like 'a burnished sheet of living gold' that gleamed with the declining sun"*

However, the 'romantic little lake' described by Schoolcraft was different in many ways from what it is today. The dam erected at its outlet to the Mississippi in the late 1800s raised the water level about nine feet and greatly changed its contours. Peninsulas sometimes became islands and adjacent ponds bays, and in the

THE HEADWATERS WAR:
Conflict for the Mississippi Headwaters

process most of the broad sandy shores disappeared. It was also never a 'little lake', with an area of 9,400 acres and a shoreline of over 56 miles. But it remains one of Minnesota's most beautiful lakes, with its more than 15 islands and numerous tree covered peninsulas jutting from the shores; much of the shoreline still in its natural state. Adding to its attractiveness is its relative isolation in an area not dominated by the tourist industry. Resorts are few, with its shore populated mostly by summer cabins and some year around residences, many staying in the same families for generations.

Why the importance of Big Sandy Lake in those early days? Location, location, location; it was the key to easy access to the upper Mississippi watershed by French fur traders, as well as for the Ojibwe who were in the process of migrating westward. On its eastern side Big Sandy connected to Lake Superior by a string of rivers, with a single portage across the continental divide between the Saint Laurence and Mississippi drainage basins, a trip of no more the 2-3 days. But it was also connected to the nearby Mississippi which passed by about a half mile to the west. Not only did Big Sandy provide access to the Upper Mississippi watershed, whoever held it controlled traffic on the Mississippi itself; and as the 1700s dawned that was the Dakota branch of the Western Sioux Nation.

The story this book attempts to tell is of a largely forgotten conflict between the Dakota, a branch of the Western Sioux Nation, and the Ojibwe, a branch of the Algonquin family of tribes, for control of the wild rice rich Mississippi headwaters; a conflict at the center of which was Big Sandy Lake. Not a single battle, but a conflict that raged for well over 100 years. While as the 1700s dawned a time of temporary peace reigned between the two tribes, the conflict began shortly after 1736, ending only with the intervention of the white man in the mid-1800s. Also, the story was not really 'forgotten'; parts lay scattered among various journals or

THE HEADWATERS WAR:
Conflict for the Mississippi Headwaters

books written by long-dead authors, and repeated and often modified in modern books as well. And not forgotten since it still lives in legend among the descendants of the participants.

Resurrecting the story of those early years poses a challenge since it was largely hidden from western eyes and even lacks a name; therefore, for convenience I call it the 'Headwaters War'. However, even that title is misleading. While the Corp of Engineers defines the Mississippi's headwaters as that portion north of Saint Anthony Falls in present-day Minneapolis (*see Figure 1*), the conflict was really for all of Minnesota, and involves events occurring outside those headwaters on the Mississippi's Minnesota and St. Croix tributaries to the south and east, and the Red and Rainy rivers bounding Minnesota on the west and north. In the end the Dakota were only able to maintain control of the drainage basin of the Mississippi's tributary, the Minnesota River, and the Mississippi drainage basin below the falls of Saint Anthony. Everything else either fell to the Ojibwe, or was contested.

The story begins in the late 1600s, at a time when the Dakota controlled all of Minnesota except the northern fringe along the Rainy River, which was controlled by the Cree, a tribal group related to the Ojibwe, and extends through the mid-1800s. For the first 100 years or so written records were few, and oral legends passed from generation to generation, with fragments documented by some early explorers or fur traders, the only source. But while oral legend usually contains a core of truth, it is not true history; it is colored by the biases of both the teller and the listener, and often changes bit by bit with each subsequent retelling. As time passes legend falls more into the category of historical fiction, which, according to dictionary.com is *"- narratives that take place and are characterized chiefly by an imaginative reconstruction of historical events and personages."*

THE HEADWATERS WAR:
Conflict for the Mississippi Headwaters

"*An imaginative reconstruction of historical events and personages.*" I decided to face the situation as it is and accept that anything said about the time up to the late 1700s in the Mississippi headwaters, aside from the few journal entries of early traders and explorers, IS historical fiction; finally reduced to writing in the 1850s and later. Since the core of the story takes place in the second and third quarters of the 1700s, a time of legend, I decided to frame events up to the late 1700s AS historical fiction. As a result, while Chapter 1, which sets the background of the story, is historical in nature, Chapters 1 – 6 fall back on historical fiction, using '*The History of the Ojibway Nation*' by William Warren, as the basic source. Therefore, for those chapters certain characters such as *Bi-aus-wah*, Big Marten, Shakopee, and a number of others are historical figures, and the events described are actual events they did or 'probably' participated in. However, their interactions, and most other characters as well, are of necessity fictional. As to the later chapters? There I attempt to stay within the bounds of recorded history without embellishments; sort of an extended 'epilogue'.

Other than the scanty journals of the few early French explorers and fur traders, the earliest comprehensive written source for the early period is the '*The History of the Ojibway Nation*' by William Warren, completed in manuscript form during the winter of 1852-53 and published in 1957 by permission of the Minnesota Historical Society. During his few brief years Mr. Warren took the legends and folklore of the Ojibwe among whom he lived and converted them to writing.

But what does Warren rely on? Legends and folklore. However, half Ojibwe himself, and living among the Ojibwe with numerous friends and relatives among them, Mr. Warren was able to obtain his information first-hand from tribal elders, often born only a few years or decades after the events occurred; and for the later events they themselves, or their fathers, had

THE HEADWATERS WAR:
Conflict for the Mississippi Headwaters

often been actors. While the tales Warren relates reflect both his and the teller's inherent bias, they also reflect what the Ojibwe of the early 1800s believed, or legends they wished to believe.

Yes, there were others who documented pieces of the story, but Warren deserves credit for being the earliest to create a 'written' history of the early Ojibwe and their conquest of the Mississippi headwaters. When later writers cover these early days they invariably rely on Warren.

However, since I rely heavily on Warren, anyone reading this book should understand some of the biases inherent in his work; biases arising from his background. William Warren's father, Lyman Warren, came to the Lake Superior region in 1818 to begin life as a fur trader, marrying into the family of fur trader Michel Cadotte. Mr. Cadotte's great grandfather came to Ojibwe country in 1671 and took an Ojibwe wife, as did his descendants after him.

Born in 1825, Warren obtained some education in the east, returning to La Pointe in northern Wisconsin, where his father Lyman was based, in 1841. From 1845 until his death he lived at Crow Wing in central Minnesota, where he became close to Hole-in-the-Day the younger, the principal chief of the Mississippi band of Ojibwe, and also Flat Mouth, the long lived chief of the Pillagers of the headwaters lakes of Leech, Cass, and Winnibigoshish.

While at Crow Wing, William Warren married Mathilda Aitkin, a daughter of William Aitkin (*aka, Aitken*), a prominent fur trader. Mr. Aitkin was in charge of the Fond du Lac district for the American Fur Company that included the American Fur Company post at Sandy Lake. By this union he gained many more contacts with the Ojibwe community, since William Aitkin had twenty five children by his six Ojibwe wives.

The above factors do, to an extent, explain some of Warren's biases. Most of his sources, with the

THE HEADWATERS WAR:
Conflict for the Mississippi Headwaters

exception of Flat Mouth of the Pillagers and some others, were from what would later be defined as the 'Mississippi Band' of Ojibwe, including those of the Crow Wing, Mille Lacs, and Big Sandy areas. That leads to his perhaps overemphasizing the importance of those bands in the Ojibwe conquest. The Ojibwe of the Red Lakes and the northern border lakes are largely neglected by Warren; but then those areas aren't a part of the headwaters of the Mississippi, flowing instead north through the Nelson River to Hudson Bay. I leave their story largely to others.

Both William Aitkin and Lyman Warren were typical fur traders of the time, often accused of swindling the Ojibwe by exorbitant debt claims during treaty negotiations or annuity distributions; a standard practice, with William Warren sometimes acting as translator in those negotiations. When annuity payments were due it was the practice to deduct those claims prior to distribution of the annuities themselves; often creating hard feelings between the Indians and traders. In spite of the above, the Warren history is still the best source for information on the early days.

In 1851 William Warren became the first Indian member of the Minnesota legislature, but died in 1853 at the young age of 28. After his death his manuscript was given to the Minnesota Historical Society, where it lay until it was finally published well over 100 years later.

With that warning, the Warren history does have shortcomings, such as lack of or improbable dates, the sequence of events, routes used, and village locations. Also occasionally his Ojibwe bias shows through; proclaiming a battle an Ojibwe victory when at best it was a draw or even a defeat. This is understandable since Warren chooses to relate the legends without a great deal of editing, thus ignoring the bias of the source. However, in his defense he also omits stories he considers too 'far fetched' or unrealistic.

Establishing dates and the sequence of events

THE HEADWATERS WAR:
Conflict for the Mississippi Headwaters

can be particularly difficult, and wide variation exists among sources. For example, Warren rarely attempts to assign a date by the western calendar, instead using references such as *'in the time of the great grandfather'* of the storyteller. Since to the Ojibwe of the time a generation was typically 40 years, Warren's dates are often improbably early. Another problem is descriptions of some early events are very brief, some key battles covered in half a page of text.

However, all is not lost. Some dates were fixed by journals of the early French explorers or traders, such as the nearly six decade's long peace between the Ojibwe and the Dakota from 1679 to 1736. That defines the earliest possible date for *Bi-aus-wah's* raid on Sandy Lake, the subject of Chapter 2. Warren places that raid at 1730 while Anton Treuer, a prominent Ojibwe historian and writer, places it at 1744.

As to the decisive attack on Kathio, the major Dakota village at Mille Lacs Lake, some imply it was in parallel with or even before the attack on Sandy Lake. Anton Treuer places it in 1745, although most sources place it in 1750. The year 1768 is largely accepted for the Dakota attack on the Ojibwe at Sandy Lake which led to the decisive battle of the Crow Wing; the subject of Chapter 5, as are the dates in Chapter 6, describing the raids of revenge by the Sandy Lake Ojibwe for that 1768 raid; they both are well covered by Warren.

Based on a logical sequence of events, I use 1740 for the raid on Sandy Lake and 1750 for that on Kathio. As to the battle of Cut Foot Sioux, a major factor in the later abandonment of the headwaters lakes of Leech, Cass, and Winnibigoshish, little is available. However, I place it in 1748, nearly a decade after the *Bi-aus-wah* Sandy Lake raid and prior to the Kathio raid. Warren states the battle of Point Prescott occurred shortly after the battle of Kathio, and he also states it was after the 1760 turnover of French forts on the Great Lake to the British. Whether than meant turnover of the

THE HEADWATERS WAR:
Conflict for the Mississippi Headwaters

last of those forts by conquest (1760) or official turnover by the Treaty of Paris (1763) is unimportant; it places the battle at sometime in the 1760s.

However, I don't view the exact dates and sequences as important to the story; the events were largely independent, and, except for occupation of the Crow Wing River, Long Prairie River, and Ottertail Lake areas, were largely during the 37 year period between 1736 and 1773. Exact locations are sometimes also grey, and where necessary I have picked those I consider most probable based on details listed, topography, and opinions of early and modern writers.

From the mid 1770s to the winter of 1852-53 Warren remains an important source, although other sources also abound. The French had been replaced by the British, who would later be replaced by the Americans, and the white presence was growing and more written records are available. Reliance on historical fiction becomes unnecessary, and there I attempt to tell of events as documented in early records, or as interpreted by modern writers.

I make no pretense at being a historian or expert on the Ojibwe, Dakota, or their customs, but simply an avid reader of history with an interest in those tribes and their cultures. I also admit to a bias that may, at times, focus on Big Sandy Lake and the Ojibwe rather than other participants in the events. But even so, while I class much of the work as historical fiction, that is sometimes the best (*or only*) way to remove a story from the dusty shelves of historians and pass it on to others. Perhaps, just perhaps, some knowledge of the early history of the state and its occupants will be imparted to the readers; I hope so.

THE HEADWATERS WAR:
Conflict for the Mississippi Headwaters

CHAPTER 1
AND IN THE BEGINNING:

Prior to the coming of western civilization to North America the only beasts of burden of the indigenous tribes were dogs, limiting travel by land, and making travel by water the only effective method of transport. However, continental divides directed water flow into several major drainage basins, and getting from one basin to another could be burdensome, involving portages many miles long over the dividing 'highlands'. Minnesota was divided into three basins; the Laurentian, directing the flow north to the Nelson River feeding Hudson Bay, the Saint Laurence, containing all the Great Lakes, flowing northeast to the Saint Lawrence River, and the 'Great Basin' of the Mississippi that drained the bulk of the state. Of these the Mississippi basin is at the core of this story; which, together with its tributaries, drains most of Minnesota and Wisconsin.

From their earliest presence in Canada the French had access via the Great Lakes and almost total control of the fur trade of the St. Laurence Basin, which ended just beyond the western tip of Lake Superior and, in Wisconsin, just south of the shore of Lake Superior. Initially the French were also able to compete for the fur trade of the Laurentian Basin, until expelled from their posts on Hudson Bay in the 1670s by the British. Squeezed between the American colonies and the British Hudson Bay Company, the French could only expand westward by controlling the river routes beginning at the western tip of Lake Superior, which led deep into both the Laurentian and Mississippi Basins.

The Mississippi headwaters portion of the Mississippi Basin (*see Figure 3*), encompassing most of northern and central Minnesota, remained largely

THE HEADWATERS WAR:
Conflict for the Mississippi Headwaters

untouched by the fur trade. As early as the late 1650s Radisson and Grossiers, after exploring the shores of Lake Superior, traveled south through Wisconsin to the Mississippi and then north into Minnesota. However, Minnesota and much of Wisconsin was the country of the Western Sioux Nation, an aggressive and warlike tribe largely untouched by white influence.

Who were these Sioux? One of the largest and most warlike of the tribes, the Western Sioux Nation arrived early, and by the early 1600s had taken control of the area west and south of Lake Superior. Peter Radisson was one of the first Europeans to make contact when he encountered and wintered among them in Wisconsin in the late 1650s. Sources differ on how and when they arrived in the Great Lakes area, some saying they were migrants from the southeastern states, others that they were a part of the Mississippian culture that moved north from more southern areas. But, if so, why had they left heir homeland and moved north? Perhaps it was a response to the Spanish incursions into the south and southeast in the 1500s, and the resulting conflicts.

In any case, the Sioux were initially a 'woodland' tribe, and evidence of their origination somewhere in the south was their continued use of dugout canoes rather that the light birchbark canoes typical of Algonquin tribes, and their frequent use of earth lodges. Further, tribes speaking 'Siouan' languages were common in the southeast.

The French had little direct knowledge of the Sioux, or 'Nadouessioux'. Buffered by the Iroquois and Algonquin tribes to their east, they were the powerful and fierce tribe that lay beyond. Since some consider the name Sioux derogatory, they will usually be referred to by the more acceptable names of Dakota for those four sub-tribes continuing to occupy Minnesota and Wisconsin at the time, Lakota (or Teton, eventually breaking into seven bands or sub-tribes) and Nakota (Yankton and Yanktonnai) for those who moved to the

THE HEADWATERS WAR:
Conflict for the Mississippi Headwaters

western prairies and adopted a migratory horse culture. But in the early days of their arrival they were the *Ochethi Sacowin*, the 'seven council fires', denoting the seven nations involved; *Lakota, Yankton, Yanktonais, M'dewakanton, Wahpekute, Sisseton,* and *Wahpeton.*

In time the *Lakota* moved west and developed a nomadic prairie culture based on the horse and buffalo, soon followed by the *Yankton* and *Yanktonaise* (*often referred to as Nakota*). The remaining nations stayed in Minnesota and Wisconsin and retained the name Dakota; sometimes referred to as S*antee*, or *Isanyati-'people of the knife'*. At the time of the Ojibwe intrusions the Dakota occupied all of Minnesota except the far northern border-lake area and parts of the northeastern 'Arrowhead' area; sharing the far western area of the state with the Nakota.

The invaders from the east were the 'Ojibwe', or 'Ojibwa'. As one of the largest tribes the name they were known by varied with location; in Canada they were the Ojibwe, in the United States, by an 1871 Act of Congress, they were the 'Chippewa'. Currently, however, the majority of the Minnesota bands appear to prefer use of the name 'Ojibwe' rather than Chippewa, although treaties and other formal papers involving the tribe and the federal government use 'Chippewa'.

The origin of the name 'Ojibwe' is subject to debate. Warren (*37, p.36*) interprets it as 'Ojib' for 'puckered up' and 'ub-way' for 'to roast'; or 'to roast until puckered up', reflecting the Ojibwe custom of burning captives alive. Today many read it as referring to the 'puckered' look of Ojibwe moccasins.

These invaders were a branch of the *Anishnaabe* (*Ojibwe, Ottawa, and Potawatomi*), an Algic (*Algonquin*) people of the northeast. Beginning their migration from as far away as the St. Laurence River or as far north as Hudson Bay, their initial impetus may have been the changing climate of the Little Ice Age which reigned from the early 1500s through the mid

THE HEADWATERS WAR:
Conflict for the Mississippi Headwaters

1800s. Or it may just have been overpopulation or limited resources at their original home. While the exact location of their original home is unclear, from legends it appears to have been near the eastern sea.

Or, it may well have been that both the *Anishnaabe* and the 'Nadouessioux' were fleeing from the catastrophic spread of the European diseases to which they had no immunity. By the early 1500s diseases such as smallpox and measles, brought by the early Spanish to the south and southeast and spread northward by coastal traders or along the network of well developed trade routes that laced much of North America, had decimated the densely populated northeastern and southeastern seaboards, paving the way for the early settlements at Plymouth and Jamestown.

But if such was the case, it was of little avail. Well into the 19th century epidemics of smallpox or measles, thought of as a rarely fatal childhood disease today, often proved deadly to Native Americans who lacked the inherited resistance to the diseases of Europeans. Such epidemics periodically swept westward ahead of white settlement, carried along the trade routes of the great lakes and river routes such as the Ohio River. These epidemics decimated the tribes in their path, and opened the land for later white settlement. The Ojibwe, who lived along the shores of those great lakes, were especially vulnerable.

While these diseases, new to the Americas, were a natural result of white settlement, trade, and lack of immunity of the tribes, sometimes they became a weapon of war as well, such as the distribution of smallpox infected blankets by the British during Pontiac's rebellion in the late 1760s.

Whatever the 'initial' driving force behind the *Anishnaabe* and 'Nadouessioux' migrations, later, as allies of the French, the *Anishnaabe* came in conflict with the powerful Iroquois Confederation, first allies of the Dutch and then of the British, and were driven even

THE HEADWATERS WAR:
Conflict for the Mississippi Headwaters

further west. Finally, in the late1600s, the Iroquois were defeated and driven back in a major battle.

Upon reaching the eastern tip of Lake Superior at Sault Ste. Marie the *Anishnaabe* paused for a time, until sometime in the 1500s the Ojibwe separated from the Ottawa and Potawatomi and resumed their westward march; some taking the northern shore of Lake Superior, while the larger group followed the southern shore. In the late 1650s, when Peter Radisson first encountered them, they had progressed at least as far as LaPointe (*on Madeleine Island in Lake Superior*). That westward movement brought them into direct conflict with both the Fox and the Dakota.

The French well understood the need to establish peace between the tribes if the fur trade was to flourish and expand beyond Lake Superior. To stabilize the area, in 1679 the French explorer and trader, the Sieur du Luth, arranged a peace conference between the Dakota and Ojibwe at Fond du Lac, several miles west of Lake Superior. As a result the Ojibwe, representing the French, were allowed to carry the fur trade to the Mississippi headwaters and into western Wisconsin. Soon, through intermarriage and shared hunting and wild rice harvesting, the Dakota and Ojibwe developed common interests, sometimes joining war parties against the other's enemies. However, the Fox remained a problem until driven from Wisconsin by a French inspired confederation of tribes in the early 1700s.

By the early 1700s the Ojibwe had established a village at Fond du Lac, the site of the council decades earlier. While Fond du Lac lay east of the St. Laurence Divide, Big Sandy Lake, a part of the Mississippi Basin, lay only a short distance away, separated by a series of small rivers and a six mile portage over the divide itself. With its connection to the nearby Mississippi, Sandy Lake was not only the key to access to the entire Mississippi headwaters, it blocked north-south travel on the Mississippi as well. However, Sandy Lake was the

THE HEADWATERS WAR:
Conflict for the Mississippi Headwaters

location of a major Dakota village.

While, based on the 1679 truce, the Ojibwe shared many of the resources of the headwaters, they were guests only; which must have angered many Ojibwe. However, the arrival of the Sieur de La Verendrye in 1731 with a party of about fifty at the Pigeon River on the northwestern shore of Lake Superior was a pivotal point. De La Verendrye had a dual mission; search for a water passage to the western ocean, but also expand the territory for the fur trade. That the Rocky Mountains blocked the way was still unknown.

La Verendrye immediately sent an advance party ahead to construct a fort on Rainy Lake, called Fort St. Pierre. The following spring Fort St. Charles was constructed on Lake of the Woods, where La Verendrye spent the next several years trading with the Indians and exploring westward and northward looking for a water route to the western ocean; in time establishing trading posts on the Red River, at Lake Winnipeg, and even further west. Finally the French had again gained their access to the Laurentian Basin.

However, La Verendrye faced a problem. The area near his trading posts was populated primarily by an Algic tribe, the Cree. Additionally, the most promising route in his search for the path to the Pacific was north from Lake of the Woods to Lake Winnipeg and then west; area also controlled by the Cree. An alliance with the Cree, enemies of the Dakota, was essential. As a result La Verendrye attempted the impossible; he allied the French with the Cree, hoping to continue with his Ojibwe alliance and also maintain cordial relations with the Dakota. His involvement with the Cree went so far as to allow one of his sons to be adopted into their tribe, where he was expected to, and did, join war parties against the Dakota.

While the French succeeded in maintaining their conflicting alliances for a time the situation began to deteriorate in 1734 when the Cree, accompanied by the

THE HEADWATERS WAR:
Conflict for the Mississippi Headwaters

son of La Verendrye they had adopted, assaulted the Dakota bastion at Upper and Lower Red Lakes, south of the border lake trading posts. While repulsed, the Dakota learned Frenchmen were present in the attacking party, and the revenge was devastating to French interests in the area. In June of 1736 another son of La Verendrye, accompanied by a priest and a party of seventeen, were massacred east of Fort St. Charles on Lake of the Woods; all were beheaded with their heads left on display to ensure the message was understood. Some sources say the culprits were Dakota joined by some Ojibwe, others that the Lakota were involved. Whatever the case, the blame was placed on the Dakota.

The mixed and conflicting alliances of both the French and the Ojibwe had reached a critical point, and the above massacre caused, at least temporarily, a break between the French and the Dakota. The closest and longest alliance was between the French and Ojibwe, but the Ojibwe friendship with the Dakota had also become strong over the years and the Ojibwe had to choose. Realists, they chose the French and allied themselves with the Cree against the Dakota; perhaps a decision also motivated by a desire to obtain the rich lands to the south and west for themselves.

The French were also initially ambivalent. The Dakota must be punished, but a prolonged conflict could seriously disrupt the fur trade. While the French may have instigated the conflict, the war soon passed beyond French control. In hindsight, the alliance of the Ojibwe and the Cree was a natural alliance. Both were Algic tribes, sharing many of the same totems (*clan system*), and both must have looked enviously at the rich lands held by the Dakota.

Following the massacre of 1736 the French inspired allies made ready and prepared to attack the Dakota on three fronts. From the north the Ojibwe and Cree, with the assistance of the Assiniboine, a Siouan tribe that had broken off from the Yankton years before,

THE HEADWATERS WAR:
Conflict for the Mississippi Headwaters

moved south against Upper and Lower Red Lakes, and further south against the large Mississippi headwater lakes of Winnibigoshish, Cass, and Leech. The Ojibwe of Lake Superior and Fond du Lac moved south along the Mississippi's Saint Croix, Wisconsin, and Chippewa tributaries against the Dakota of Wisconsin, and even Lake Pepin, a broadening of the Mississippi south of present day Minneapolis. They were also poised to move directly westward from the tip of Lake Superior into the Dakota heartland.

In the war than ensued the Ojibwe had several advantages, one of which was their weapons. The long alliance with the French provided the Ojibwe access to plentiful firearms, while the Dakota had only the few obtained from the border-lake posts or the few French traders who ventured into Dakota country.

A second advantage was that, while the Dakota had enemies on all sides, with the Iroquois no longer a threat, the Fox largely driven from Wisconsin, and their new alliance with the Cree to the north, the Ojibwe had allies on all sides except their border with the Dakota.

A third advantage was, that on those occasions when the Ojibwe were decimated by their conflicts with the Dakota or by epidemics of measles or small pox, their numbers were soon replenished by the stream of Ojibwe that continued to migrate westward along the Great Lakes. The Dakota, on the other hand, while they may have had some additions by in-migration from Wisconsin, were subject to the pull to migrate westward to the prairies with its plentiful game; a path pioneered by their brothers the Lakota and Nakota before them.

The fourth Ojibwe advantage was the totemic system they shared with all Algic tribes. These totems, or clans, denoted a kinship relationship and were the fundamental division among Algic people, tribal divisions resulting from quarrels or distance coming later. Since totem members were considered blood kin, independent of tribe, it created a network that could be

THE HEADWATERS WAR:
Conflict for the Mississippi Headwaters

called on for support.

While the movements south from the border lakes and Lake Superior were underway, the Dakota village at Big Sandy Lake blocked an Ojibwe move westward. That village must be removed; once Big Sandy was firmly in Ojibwe control they would not only have access to the Mississippi, but isolate the large headwaters lakes of Leech, Cass, and Winnibigoshish from the Dakota further south. The Dakota holding those major lakes would then be caught in a vice between Ojibwe advancing from both the north and the south. But the Sandy Lake village was large and powerful, and beyond the ability of the Ojibwe at Fond du Lac alone.

It wasn't until four years later, in about 1740, that the Ojibwe achieved the goal of driving the Dakota from their Sandy Lake village, when it was abandoned after a massive attack from the Ojibwe at Fond du Lac, supplemented by other Ojibwe from Lake Superior. That was followed by Ojibwe occupation; the first Ojibwe village in the upper Mississippi basin.

Squeezed between the Cree-Ojibwe from the north and the Ojibwe at Sandy Lake the Dakota villages on the large headwaters lakes of Cass, Winnibigoshish, and Leech were under increasing pressure. To counter that pressure, in about 1748 the Dakota launched a three-pronged counterattack, sending large war parties against the border lakes, the Ojibwe around Pembina, and Sandy Lake. The prong sent to the border lakes encountered a Cree-Ojibwe war party near Big Falls on the Big Fork River and was turned back after a lengthy battle, with that sent to Pembina largely petering out. The third and largest attack, against Sandy Lake, ended when the Dakota encountered an Ojibwe war party from Sandy Lake at Lake Winnibigoshish, resulting in the battle of Cut Foot Sioux. While the battle itself may have been a draw, the Dakota failure to drive back the Ojibwe led to eventual abandonment of all the headwaters lakes and occupation by the Ojibwe.

THE HEADWATERS WAR:
Conflict for the Mississippi Headwaters

By the 1750s, following the expulsion of the Dakota from Mille Lacs Lake, the Ojibwe had achieved control of all of central Minnesota east of the Mississippi, and its headwaters lakes as well. However, west of the river lay a no-man's land contested by both tribes. It wasn't until the early 1800s that the area of the Crow Wing River and its tributaries, and the areas around Ottertail Lake, finally fell to the Ojibwe. In the end the Dakota were only able to maintain control over the Minnesota River tributary of the Mississippi and areas to the south and west.

This book concentrates on the movement from Fond du Lac and Sandy Lake into central and northern Minnesota; the upper Mississippi. While perhaps equally important, the record of the movement south from the border lakes is weak, but did result in the takeover by the Ojibwe of Upper and Lower Red Lakes, as well as the upper Red River Valley, and was at least partially responsible for the takeover of Winnibigoshish, Leech, and Cass Lakes.

Warren, the primary chronicler of the contest between the Ojibwe and the Dakota, says little of the advance from the north, and unfortunately no other early author was available close enough in time to fill the blank, leaving the story to legends passed through many generations coupled with the research of modern historians. It appears, however, that about 1760 both the Ojibwe and the Dakota had substantial villages on the Red Lakes, but that the Dakota evacuated the area that year following a major conflict at Battle River. For those interested in the Red Lake area, *Warrior Nation: A History of the Red Lake Ojibwe (34)*, by Anton Treuer, provides a comprehensive source.

While the French may have instigated the conflict in the beginning, it soon passed beyond their control. Their control over their Ojibwe and Cree allies had its limits. A strong Ojibwe leader had arisen; *Bi-aus-wah*, the son of a La Pointe war chief also named *Bi-aus-*

THE HEADWATERS WAR:
Conflict for the Mississippi Headwaters

wah. Even before his rise to become war chief, and then civil chief of the Fond du Lac band, and even while still a youth, the story of the *Bi-aus-wah* of whom I speak was a legend among the Ojibwe.

The Legend of Bi-aus-wah

According to Warren, sometime in the early 1700s a party of Ojibwe was hunting about 40 miles from LaPointe (*on Madeline Island*), and their camp was attacked by a Fox warparty, with all but an old man and a young boy killed. The father of the boy, a noted warrior named *Bi-aus-wah*, later returned and found his murdered family. Seeking revenge he set out to follow the party of Fox and finally came to their village where the Fox warriors were celebrating their success. Hiding himself he set about watching what was to transpire.

As *Bi-aus-wah* watched, the old man was wrapped in flammable bitch bark and set afire. When that was finished they brought out the young boy and took him to where faggots had been burned leaving a trail of coals. The boy's fate was to walk the trail of coals until his body was consumed. When *Bi-aus-wah* saw the boy he realized it was his own son; and that he alone would never be able to rescue him by force. Rising, he walked into the village and confronted the startled Fox, according to Warren saying (*37, pp.127-129*):

> "*My little son, who you are about to burn with fire, has seen but a few winters. His tender feet have never trodden the warpath - he has never injured you. But the hairs of my head are white with many winters, and over the graves of my relatives I have hung many scalps which I have taken from the heads of the Foxes; my death is worth something to you, let me therefore take the place of my child that he may return to his people*"

THE HEADWATERS WAR:
Conflict for the Mississippi Headwaters

According to the legend the Fox released the boy and took the man in exchange, who they promptly burned. In revenge the Ojibwe gathered a large warparty from as far as Sault Ste. Marie and proceeded south and destroyed several Fox villages. Following that attack the Fox abandoned the rice lakes of northern Wisconsin and retreated to the south.

A short time later an Ojibwe leader from LaPointe gathered a group of families and proceeded west to establish the Ojibwe village at Fond-du-Lac. The exact date is uncertain, but when put in the context of the above legend and what happened later would have been in the early 1700s. Among those who went to Fond du Lac was the son for whom *Bi-aus-wah* had traded his life. When the son grew to manhood he took the name of his father, and as war chief waged a relentless war against the Fox, joining and leading numerous war parties into Wisconsin and the borderlands.

The *Bi-aus-wah* who now planned the campaign against the Dakota to the west was the above boy grown to adulthood, probably still in his 40s since he had a long future before him. While the records are silent on the subject, it appears he had largely given up life as a war chief, becoming civil chief of the Fond du Lac band; but his destiny was to become one of the most dominant Ojibwe leaders of the time, lasting until his death in the late 1760s or early 1770s, and the first of a series of 'principal chiefs' with influence far beyond their home villages.

Based at Big Sandy Lake following its takeover by the Ojibwe, through his able son, Broken Tooth, the prominence of the dynasty established by *Bi-aus-wah* extended until Broken Tooth's death in the early 1830s. Both *Bi-aus-wah* and Broken Tooth exerted influence over areas much broader than Sandy Lake itself, and were often considered 'principal chiefs' of most if not all the Minnesota Ojibwe; a title based on prestige rather

THE HEADWATERS WAR:
Conflict for the Mississippi Headwaters

than the heredity that normally established chieftainship.

Following the death of Broken Tooth the Big Sandy Lake area began its long decline, replaced in influence by the newly emerging Crow Wing-Gull Lake centers and the powerful Pillagers of Leech and the other nearby headwaters lakes.

A second, later line of 'principal chiefs' also began at Sandy Lake under Curly Head, who was followed by his adopted son Hole-in-the-Day the elder, and subsequently Hole-in-the-Day the younger. However, whether any of those later chiefs attained the prestige of *Bi-aus-wah* or Broken Tooth among their own people is questionable; much of their influence, at least of the two 'Hole-in-the-Days, resulting from their relationships with the white intruders and their ability to dominate treaty negotiations.

In the north the long-lived Pillager Chief Flat Mouth was a contemporary of all the above principal chiefs except *Bi-aus-wah*, and in the area at and near Leech Lake appears to have been dominant. His influence also appears to have spread further west to the Ottertail Lake area, where in the early 1800s he formed a new village.

And even further north at the Red Lakes? While often working with the Pillagers, as with the Ojibwe of the northern border lakes their interest was mostly on westward expansion to the game-rich valley of the Red River and the prairies further west. In time this movement led to the 'prairie' Ojibwe spreading across northern North Dakota and southern Canada, who developed a horse culture much like the Lakota. Until pushed by incursions of settlers into the rich farming lands near the Red River, and the increasing pressure of lumbering interests, the Red Lake Ojibwe largely 'did their own thing', the manipulations to the south having little impact.

THE HEADWATERS WAR:
Conflict for the Mississippi Headwaters

Figure 1: Continental Divides

THE HEADWATERS WAR:
Conflict for the Mississippi Headwaters

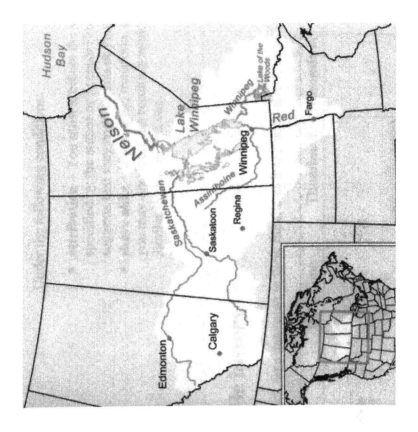

Figure 2: Nelson River Watershed

THE HEADWATERS WAR:
Conflict for the Mississippi Headwaters

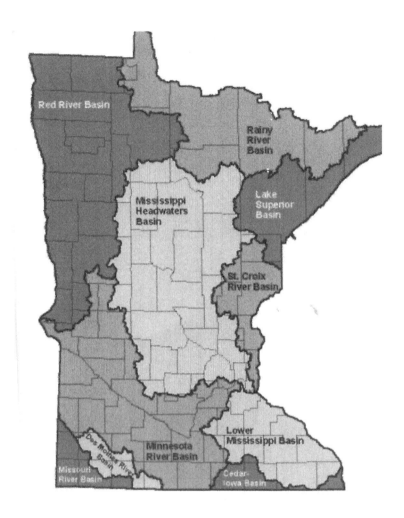

Figure 3: Drainage Basins in Minnesota

THE HEADWATERS WAR:
Conflict for the Mississippi Headwaters

Figure 4: Minnesota Lakes and Rivers

THE HEADWATERS WAR:
Conflict for the Mississippi Headwaters

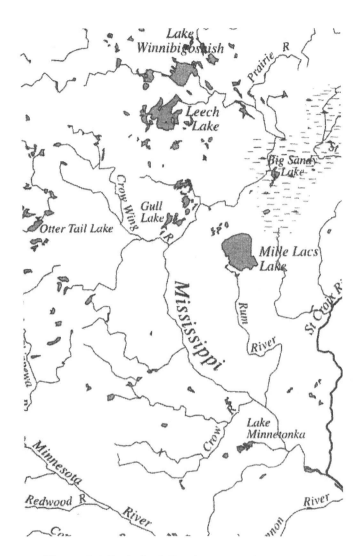

Figure 5: Mississippi Headwaters Lakes & Rivers

THE HEADWATERS WAR:
Conflict for the Mississippi Headwaters

CHAPTER 2
CONQUEST OF SANDY LAKE

To understand the importance of Big Sandy Lake one must go back to the late 1600s or early 1700s and the era of the fur trade; a time when the white man first intruded into what became the state of Minnesota. As described earlier, Minnesota was divided into three watersheds separated by continental divides; the St. Laurence, the Laurentian, and the Mississippi basins.

From their earliest presence in Canada the French controlled the fur trade of the St. Laurence basin, and by the early 1700s competed with the Hudson Bay Company for Laurentian Basin trade through establishment of trading posts on the border lakes between present day Minnesota and Canada. However, blocked by continental divides, they still lacked easy access by water to the Mississippi Basin.

Aside from traveling up from New Orleans three routes were available to the French to access the upper Mississippi. The first route was from LaPointe on Madeleine Island in Lake Superior, a long journey that involved crossing the divide between the St. Laurence and Mississippi basins, then across Wisconsin to reach the Mississippi by a series of rivers and tedious portages, then north up the Mississippi. The second was from the French posts on Lake of the Woods or Rainy Lake, which involved crossing the continental divide between the Laurentian and Mississippi basins, and involved considerable portaging. The third was from Fond du Lac at the far western tip of Lake Superior. From Fond du Lac some small rivers and a single six-mile portage over the continental divide between the St. Laurence and Mississippi basins brought them to Dakota-occupied Sandy Lake, connected to the Mississippi.

THE HEADWATERS WAR:
Conflict for the Mississippi Headwaters

To service trade in the upper Mississippi the French often utilized Ojibwe intermediaries, who under the truce arranged by the French in 1679 were allowed to enter and share in some of the resources of that Dakota-controlled area. Direct trade of the Dakota with the border posts sometimes also occurred, but was limited since the posts were located in territory largely controlled by the Cree; enemies of the Dakota. However, when the truce of 1679 was broken all three of the above routes were blocked, and the fur trade of the upper Mississippi Basin was lost to the French.

Simply reopening those routes by reestablishing the truce proved impossible as the resulting conflict soon raged out of control. The Ojibwe, who could count on French support, took it as an opportunity to conquer the entire upper Mississippi basin for their own. The conquest was not rapid, with the powerful Dakota contesting every advance of the Ojibwe and often forcing an Ojibwe retreat; it lasted over 100 years, until finally the white man intervened and the two tribes recognized the power of their common adversary. But by that time the occupation of the headwaters by the Ojibwe was largely complete.

As the conflict began, the Ojibwe of Lake Superior and Fond du Lac moved south through Wisconsin against the Dakota, and from the north the new Cree-Ojibwe alliance moved south from the border lakes, attacking the Dakota at Upper and Lower Red Lakes and the Mississippi headwaters lakes of Cass, Leech, and Winnibigoshish. Opening the route from Fond du Lac westward, and the 'heavy lifting' of conquest of the upper Mississippi Basin, was a job for *Bi-aus-wah*, and *Bi-aus-wah* began to prepare. The necessary first step was to remove the roadblock that stood in their way; the Dakota village at Sandy Lake. However, the Dakota village at Sandy Lake was large and powerful, and beyond the ability of the Fond du Lac Ojibwe alone. While they had grown over the years due

THE HEADWATERS WAR:
Conflict for the Mississippi Headwaters

to the Ojibwe western migration, they were still no match for the large Dakota presence on Sandy Lake. They would need support from the nearby Ojibwe of Lake Superior, especially the powerful Ojibwe village at Madelaine Island and the numerous satellite villages bordering Chequemegon Bay. But initially the Lake Superior Ojibwe had their hands full with the Dakota of Wisconsin to their south. There the headwaters of the wild rice rich Mississippi tributaries of the Saint Croix, Wisconsin, and Chippewa rivers beckoned.

When exactly the attack on Sandy Lake took place is arguable, but according to Warren, when *Bi-aus-wha* decided to move westward he sent his pipe and tobacco to the numerous Ojibwe villages along the shores of Lake Superior asking them to send warriors to Fond du Lac at a certain time. This was not to be a common raid; it was intended to send a clear message that the Ojibwe claimed Sandy Lake and the Dakota must leave. The other Ojibwe villages responded, and at the scheduled time their warriors assembled at Fond du Lac. While the size of the Ojibwe force is debatable, it is clear it consisted of at least several hundred warriors; very large for the time.

Several options for the attack were possible, either the canoe route, the trail from Fond du Lac to the Sandy Lake village, or both simultaneously. The canoe route up the St. Louis and East Savanna River, then the six-mile portage across the continental divide and down the West Savanna and Prairie rivers to Sandy Lake, would take no more than two-three days, while the trail from Fond du Lac would take about the same or less. However, Warren refers to the long line of warriors that "*marched against*" the Dakota, and after a severe fight forced them to evacuate the village, suggesting the land route. Since I accept Warren as the most reliable source I have accepted that the route was by land. I have also assumed the two islands offshore of the Dakota village, Battle and Moose Gut, at the time possibly connected,

THE HEADWATERS WAR:
Conflict for the Mississippi Headwaters

were places of refuge and not the location of the battle. Neither the route used nor the role of the islands in the contest are critical to the story.

The result of the *Bi-aus-wah* attack was abandonment of Sandy Lake by the Dakota, and establishment of the first Ojibwe village in the Upper Mississippi Basin, which later became *Bi-aus-wah's* base of operations for further incursions to the west and north. Warren states that initially the Ojibwe village was located on offshore islands, with no indication of when it moved to the mainland or where the first mainland village was located. If a later Ojibwe village was on the southern shore near the old Dakota village site it was soon abandoned for the western shore nearer the outlet to the Mississippi. For story purposes I have assumed it was first on the islands north of the peninsula where the Dakota village had been located, later moved to the peninsula itself near the trail to Fond du Lac, later, as the Ojibwe presence strengthened to the less secure western shore, and even later the north shore.

Only the last two of the above sites have been located. The dam erected in the late 1800s raised the water level by about nine feet and permanently changed the shoreline, but the western shore village was most probably on what is now Brown's Point near where the French trading post was later erected.

Early August, 1740 . . . .

The Dakota village near the tip of the peninsula jutting northward into Sandy Lake was teaming with people, and on the shore were far more canoes than normal. While most of the canoes were the light birch bark style they had copied from their neighbors, the Ojibwe, many were the traditional Dakota canoe hollowed from a tree trunk. While many of the people, and the canoes as well, belonged to the village, it was the time of the summer gathering and the village was crowded with visitors, nearly doubling its normal size.

THE HEADWATERS WAR:
Conflict for the Mississippi Headwaters

Within a week, possibly two, the number would dwindle as the visitors returned to their home villages, or families began to depart for their wild rice harvesting camps.

Otter and White Bird sat on the keel of the overturned canoe they would be using in the morning. It had taken them much of the summer to fashion the canoe from a hollowed out length of tree trunk, and while smaller than most they had spent many hours carefully scraping the walls to make it as light as possible. Many in the village had learned to make the birch bark canoes of their former friends, the Ojibwe, but that was something they had yet to learn. They had already assembled all the supplies needed for their hunting trip, which should last no more than a week. Now it was only a question of final packing and checking that everything was ready. The sun had not as yet set, and the heat and humidity of the day remained, with sweat running down Otter's bare back. He and his friend White Bird were discussing the best area for the hunt and had reached general agreement.

The influx of visitors was the reason Otter and White Bird would be leaving the next morning for a hunt upriver. Otter's parents, Rolling Thunder and Walks Tall, had been entertaining friends and relatives for over two weeks and food was running short. Rolling Thunder could not leave because of his other duties, so Otter and his best friend White Bird had been dispatched on a hunt. The parents of White Bird had a similar problem; their food supply was also overstressed. The supply of game near the village was exhausted, and they intended to go far upstream on the river to the east to ground not usually hunted; but Rolling Thunder's instructions had been clear.

There had been rumors of renewed fighting between Ojibwe and Dakota to the north and east, and it had been several years since any Ojibwe had visited their village, leaving a feeling of uncertainty in the air. The Ojibwe village at Fond du Lac, while not as large as

37

THE HEADWATERS WAR:
Conflict for the Mississippi Headwaters

their own village, lay only a short distance beyond the portage, an easy trip for a warparty. But so far the two villages had avoided any direct confrontation. Otter and White Bird were to stay well west of the portage to the East Savanna. All land east of the portage, and the portage itself, was claimed by the Ojibwe.

During the gathering tribe elders and other principal men of the Sandy Lake Band had held numerous meetings with their counterparts among the visitors, and everyone knew what had been discussed. The visitors from the north had asked the Sandy Lake Band to support them by sending warriors to join their war parties against the Ojibwe and Cree, or even to attack Fond du Lac; but there had been no agreement. White Water, the most important civil chief in the village, had argued strongly against upsetting the balance, arguing that while the Sandy Lake village was one of the largest Dakota villages, it was also the most exposed to attack by being so close to Fond du Lac and Lake Superior; the base of Ojibwe power. Even if the Ojibwe could not take the village itself, they could easily make living in the area difficult.

In the end White Water had prevailed, and the Sandy Lake elders had refused to endorse entering the conflict. They were confident their village was too large to be threatened by the Ojibwe, and why stir up a hornets nest? Besides, even in this time of uncertainty there were many bonds between the two villages established during the long truce, and perhaps someday that truce would return and they would again have access to trade goods without a long, tedious trip south. Even powder and shot for the few guns they possessed was now hard to come by. While Otter's father, Rolling Thunder, was one of the fortunate who possessed such a weapon, it was rarely used; the powder and shot saved for an emergency.

Both Otter and White Bird were sixteen, White Bird a few months older than Otter; but, while best friends, they could not be more different. Otter, only

THE HEADWATERS WAR:
Conflict for the Mississippi Headwaters

slightly over normal height, spare and slim, but active and athletic, while White Bird, half a head taller and thin for his size, was slow in both movement and demeanor. Only his broad shoulders forecast what he might someday become. Yet those who knew him could see beyond his appearance to an intelligent and thoughtful mind. They were inseparable, and when together there was little question that Otter was the natural leader of the two and White Bird was the follower.

Otter leaned back, brushing the hair from his forehead before standing and stretching: "I suppose we should see whether we are wanted for anything."

White Bird nodded, and also rose, putting aside the paddle he had been sanding smooth with a piece of stone. Looking over at Otter: "Do you think we will see any of the Ojibwe? I'd like to see one alone; maybe we could bring back more than just a deer."

"Don't even think about it. It would more likely be our scalps on a lodgepole," Otter responded. "It could anger the elders. Some do not wish the truce to break down completely."

All in the village were aware of the stories the visitors had brought of fighting in the north, which had begun several years earlier, and that many of the Ojibwe had joined their long-time enemies the Cree in attacking the northern villages. However; up to now their village had not been affected except by a prohibition against entering the Ojibwe held lands to the east; part of an unstated and uneasy truce between the Sandy Lake Dakota and the Fond du Lac Ojibwe.

Walking back toward the village they reached White Birds lodge and, with a nod, Otter said: "Before sunrise," continuing on to the lodge he shared with his parents and younger brothers and sisters.

That evening at Fond du Lac . . . .

The two men sat in the dim light of the flickering fire, neither finding conversation necessary.

THE HEADWATERS WAR:
Conflict for the Mississippi Headwaters

From their long relationship they knew the thoughts of the other, and now that everything was settled and the groups of warriors from east and north along the shores of Lake Superior had arrived the time for action was here. The village at Fond-du-Lac was crowded with the new arrivals, which was why *Bi-aus-wah* and Big Marten had left the village for this final meeting; they didn't want to be disturbed.

The conclave of Ojibwe chiefs held at LaPointe several years before to consider their old alliance with the Dakota, put in jeopardy by the killing of the Frenchmen at Lake of the Woods, had reached a decision. They would side with the infuriated French and make a new alliance with the Cree of the north.

Bi-aus-wah had thought long and hard on what the end of the truce could mean to his and the associated bands at Fond du Lac. Now they were free to take the rich headwaters of the Mississippi and the rice lakes of Wisconsin without angering the French. Under the old truce his people had been allowed to join in the wild rice harvest and the fall and winter hunts, but since the truce had been broken that had ended. But he also understood the large Dakota village at Sandy Lake stood in the way, and Fond du Lac by itself could not drive them away; he needed the support of the other Lake Superior bands.

When the conflict started, *Bi-aus-wah* had decided Sandy Lake must wait, and he had convinced the elders and principal men his position was best, and the reason. For now they should discourage raiding to the west and let the Sandy Lake Dakota become careless. The headwaters of the St. Croix and the other rivers further east, while smaller, were also rich in rice, also occupied by the Dakota, and the powerful Lake Superior bands of the Ojibwe lusted after them as well. First they would join the Ojibwe of Lake Superior in raids against the Dakota of the St. Croix, the upper tributaries of which were easily accessible from Fond du Lac. Later, when they decided to move against Sandy Lake, that

THE HEADWATERS WAR:
Conflict for the Mississippi Headwaters

support would be returned in full. To that end *Bi-aus-wah* had, for several years now, sent warriors led by Big Marten in support of the raids into Wisconsin.

Now he had waited long enough. There were rumors many of the French wanted to reestablish the truce, and if that were to happen the opportunity would be lost. *Bi-aus-wah* had finally made the decision to attack Sandy Lake, but what should be the goal? Should they attempt to destroy the Dakota or simply convince them to leave? *Bi-aus-wah* well understood any attempt to destroy the Dakota in a village that large could only be done with heavy losses to themselves, and the goal must be more limited. No, it was not the Indian way to seek battle when such casualties would result. Instead they would show their strength by destroying the Dakota fields and doing as much damage as they could; drive them back to their fortress-lodges and make the message clear. When their raid came it must be large enough to convince the Dakota they must vacate the area.

During the winter *Bi-aus-wah* had sent his war club, tobacco, and wampum belt of war to the scattered bands of his tribe, inviting the warriors to collect at Fond-du-Lac to 'put out the fires' of the Dakota at Sandy Lake; at the time of the Dakota summer gathering when it would be at its largest. And they had responded beyond his wildest expectations. Tomorrow at sunrise the warparty would depart, perhaps the largest in the history of the Ojibwe; at least the largest in the memory of either man. Now the time had finally come.

Bi-aus-wah was very familiar with the layout of the lands around the Sandy Lake Dakota village. His many visits during the time of peace had been useful; he knew ever inch of the land and had studied in detail how best to manage an attack. He knew how many warriors would be present, and also the number of visitors to expect to swell that count during the summer gathering. After the truce was broken he had shared what he had learned with Big Marten, and the two had developed a

THE HEADWATERS WAR:
Conflict for the Mississippi Headwaters

detailed plan.

Bi-aus-wah, of average size and build, while still in his early forties had hair beginning to show light streaks of grey, giving him a dignity beyond his years. But no one could mistake him as anything but a leader in spite of his quiet demeanor. His aristocratic face with his piercing eyes could dominate any group, and he was renowned as a speaker of power.

And dominate he had. Once reaching adulthood he had excelled in warfare, soon becoming acknowledged as the primary war chief of the Fond du Lac band. His deeds against and his implacable hatred of the Fox, who for years had dwelt to the southeast, were well known. The Fox had killed his father while he was still a youth by burning him alive, and as a result much of *Bi-aus-wah's* early adulthood had been spent in gaining his revenge. But now that had ended. The alliance of tribes put together by the French several years earlier had driven the remnants of the Fox from northern Wisconsin and they were no longer within reach.

With the Fox no longer a threat, and the Dakota still tied to them by the old treaty, *Bi-aus-wah* had abandoned the war trail and in time become the acknowledged civil chief of the band. That he had been a leading figure in the prominent Loon totem, influential at Fond du Lac, had eased the way.

As *Bi-aus-wah* sat watching the flickering coals he smiled slightly, remembering the dream his father had instilled in him; the desire to gain the rich land held by the neighboring Dakota. True, in those early days it was the rice lands of northern Wisconsin that they envied, but now in his middle years he had instead turned his eyes on the rich lands of the upper Mississippi. But during his father's lifetime and most of his own that had been beyond reach, forbidden by the truce with the Dakota. The truce was something they could not break, not without offending their friends and business partners, the French. But when the Dakota had broken that truce

THE HEADWATERS WAR:
Conflict for the Mississippi Headwaters

themselves that restraint was removed. Tomorrow they would embark on the first step of that conquest. Now was the proper time.

Glancing over at his companion, Big Marten, *Bi-aus-wah* couldn't imagine this campaign without his taking a leading place in the warparty. A huge man in his upper twenties, in appearance he was similar to what he was in battle; an almost unstoppable force with a fierce lust for battle. Almost a force of nature, like the fall storms on the big lake. But appearances also deceive; beneath what many considered a 'brutish' appearance was a quick, crafty mind coupled with an unbending loyalty to *Bi-aus-wah*. Ever since his teens he had been part of the war parties against the Fox led by *Bi-aus-wah*, and now, in spite of his youth, had risen to become the primary war chief at Fond du Lac.

Bi-aus-wah trusted Big Marten's judgment, and if it had been possible he would have put him in charge of this raid. But that he couldn't do; Big Marten lacked the prestige to become overall war chief for the many villages sending their warriors for the coming conflict. Those other bands, particularly the large contingent from La Pointe on Madeline Island and its nearby communities, led by Snake Skin, would not accept that.

But Snake Skin was also not the leader for an expedition of the type planned by *Bi-aus-wah*, and as the host village Fond du Lac had the right to name the leader. With Snake Skin needless slaughter would result, something not desired by *Bi-aus-wah*. For this one raid *Bi-aus-wah* would resume his role as war chief. Even then, once the attack began he was not sure he could control Snake Skin and the large La Pointe contingent, whose hatred of the Dakota matched that of his hatred of the Fox. He would have to arrange the attack itself to neutralize that opportunity.

Bi-aus-wah had no hatred for the Dakota, in fact many he considered his friends. He even had relatives among them, and one of his wives was Dakota, the sister

THE HEADWATERS WAR:
Conflict for the Mississippi Headwaters

of White Water, the Dakota chief at Sandy Lake. No, he had no hatred for the Dakota, not like that he had for the Fox; he only wanted their land for the Ojibwe. Besides, in a few years the truce might again be in place and there was nothing to gain by causing unnecessary animosity.

Hearing a soft crunching sound, *Bi-aus-wah* saw a figure immerge from the darkness and quietly take a seat off to the side. *Bi-aus-wah* smiled to himself; his eldest son, Bitten-by-the-Loon. Whenever *Bi-aus-wah* looked at Bitten-by-the-Loon both good and bad memories returned. The child of his youth from his first wife Pale Water, who had died giving him birth. And Bitten-by-the-Loon himself? A tall handsome man of nineteen he was destined to become chief after *Bi-aus-wah*, and even now was gaining prominence both as a warrior and one of wisdom beyond his years. His name? At the age of five he had climbed out onto a rocky point where he found a loon's nest. While attempting to steal an egg the angry mother loon, always protective and fearless, had snipped off the end of his little finger. To a five year old a mark of pride as his first battle wound; he had succeeded in obtaining the egg and proudly presented it to his father along with his bleeding finger.

The reception he had received from his father was a shock to his five year old mind. Instead of complementing him on his achievement, his father had first explained the importance of the loon to their family; it was the symbol of their totem, their clan. As such it should not be interfered with. He had been told to take the egg back and place it in the nest; one of the most frightening things in his young life, again facing the enraged mother loon. But he had done what he was told in spite of his fear. The lesson had been learned.

Even now, when Bitten-by-the-Loon had earned the right to a new name based on his accomplishments, he preferred to be known by the name he was given at the time. Some said the adventure with the loon, the symbol of his totem, was a sign of the future greatness of

THE HEADWATERS WAR:
Conflict for the Mississippi Headwaters

Bitten-by-the-Loon. Especially since the mother loon had accepted the egg without removing another finger.

The three sat a long time, *Bi-aus-wah* and Big Marten occasionally quietly exchanging short questions or comments, Bitten-by-the-Loon sitting quietly listening; his role was not to give advice, but learn from the more experienced. Eventually the sounds in the village quieted, and then died, as did the fire they occasionally had fed with the dried branches scattered nearby. Rising to his feet *Bi-aus-wah* kicked some sand over the still glowing coals, Big Marten and Bitten-by-the-Loon automatically standing also. Nothing had to be said as the three started back to the village. Tomorrow would start early, with final preparations well before dawn; something not that far off.

Two days later . . . .

White Bird and Otter pushed their canoe into the slow-moving waters of the river and let the current push them slowly downstream. It was early afternoon of this hot August day, and they were over 10 miles upstream from the lake of their village and planned to spend the next several days hunting before they returned. They had gone as far upstream as the Savanna portage before turning around, remembering their instructions to proceed no further because of the uncertain situation with the Ojibwe. So far the hunt had been both stressful and fruitless. Constantly on the alert for Ojibwe hunting parties and finding no game of any consequence.

Now, far downstream of the portage, they felt relaxed, but neither wanted to return to the village empty handed; it would be a loss of face for both. Downstream a small tributary branched off to the east into the marshes and swamps; hopefully hunting might be better there. They would spend the rest of today and most of tomorrow upstream on that seldom hunted small river and see if game was more plentiful. If they saw enough signs they might stay even longer.

THE HEADWATERS WAR:
Conflict for the Mississippi Headwaters

The sweat streaked down Otter's bare back even though they were letting the current do most of the work; the buzzing black flies, common at this time of year, an annoyance that caused him to break his stroke occasionally to slap at one that had landed, or brush one away that had made up its mind to use him for a meal. He knew the flies would be even thicker once they turned upstream into the smaller stream that joined them below. That was one reason hunters avoided that area except in the fall or winter.

Otter didn't look forward to spending the evening camped on the bank of that little river even if they could find dry land. The marshes and swamps through which it flowed were notorious for the mosquitoes that would begin to hunt as soon as the sun set. Well, at least the black flies would disappear with the sun, and the mosquitoes could be kept at bay with a smoky fire until full-dark fell, when most of them would disappear also. If not the repellant they carried would work, although he didn't want to use that unless the mosquitoes were intolerable. It might not smell good, but the repellant made from bear fat and the musk of the skunk would keep them away; and everyone else later at the village as well; at least until his mother prepared the proper materials to remove most of the lingering odor.

Otter brought his attention back from the lethargy the heat of the day brought, back to the stream they were descending and his companion White Bird in the front of the canoe. Tall, thin, and quiet, White Bird almost resembled the source of his name, the white bird often seen along the reedy borders of lakes and streams; the crane. But not for much longer, his tall frame topped by abnormally wide shoulders was finally beginning to fill out, and it was clear he would grow into a warrior of unusual size and strength. Even now, while the current pace was slow, if he applied himself he could make the canoe surge ahead. Otter accepted that he, himself, could never match White Bird in size or strength, but so be it;

THE HEADWATERS WAR:
Conflict for the Mississippi Headwaters

he would rather be what he was now. A person who could control the actions of others. At least he thought of himself that way.

As they worked their way downstream the river broadened and the adjoining land became a broad rush-filled border. But, aided by the slow current, they soon reached the mouth of the small river and headed to the southeast. Once away from the rush-filled entry the river narrowed and the land bordering the river rose and turned first to brush, and eventually to a light tree cover before again dipping down to marshy flatlands. Within less than an hour the river narrowed to where it was no more than eight feet wide, and after a couple of more hours a pair of logs, flattened on the top, appeared ahead spanning the river. They had never been this far upstream before, but the logs must be a part of the trail from Fond du Lac to Sandy Lake, now rarely traveled since the truce had been broken.

Lowering their heads to pass under the makeshift bridge, the two continued on until the land on the left began to rise to become a tree covered ridge. They estimated they were now about eight miles upstream on the tributary and in country rarely hunted. Otter, who was in back, suggested this was a good place to stop and survey the area for game, and later use for the night's camp, and when White Bird nodded his agreement, guided the canoe to the brush covered shore. White Bird stepped out and dragged the canoe part way ashore, allowing Otter to step out on dry land. Then together they dragged the canoe further into the bushes, taking care to cover any signs of landing.

Taking their bows and other belongings from the hidden canoe the boys walked up the slope and, after finding where they wanted to spend the night, sat down to discuss a plan. They decided since the afternoon was advanced they would scout the area by following the high ground inland to attempt to find a place where deer bedded down for the night. Then, if sign were found,

THE HEADWATERS WAR:
Conflict for the Mississippi Headwaters

begin the hunt at first light in the morning before the deer left their bedding area and scattered. They knew where to look for such a bedding area, low areas covered with tall swamp grass where any sign the deer left would be clear; the flattened grass and droppings.

The high ground where they landed turned out to be a ridge extending inland for quite a distance, which they followed to the end where it petered out in a shallow swampy area bordered by a fringe of meadow. Motioning White Bird to wait, Otter quietly worked his way down to examine the meadow for deer sign. In a few minutes he returned, and said to his companion:

"Deer sleep in the meadow below; at least two doe and their spring fauns. The grass is crushed from last night, and there are fresh droppings. We should leave and let them return; then in the morning set up a drive."

Pausing to examine the scene below, then pointing: "If the wind is right, if you come down from there they will smell you and follow the edge of the swamp toward the river. I can hide and wait below. But now we should leave so we don't frighten them away, and come back before sunup."

White Bird walked a distance away to examine the slope leading down to the meadow, then came back and nodded agreement, and the two started back to where they planned to spend the night, a matter of but a few minutes. Once there they started to prepare for the rush of mosquitoes they knew would arrive with the setting sun, gathering wood for a fire and green weeds to make the smoke to drive them off; the light breeze from the southwest would ensure no sign of their presence would be carried back to alert anyone taking the Fond du Lac to Sandy Lake trail of their presence. While the heat of the day would normally make it too warm to build a fire, since they needed one anyway Otter proceeded to skin the porcupine they had killed the day before. It would soon go bad, and they might as well save the dried meat they had brought; they might have to stay

THE HEADWATERS WAR:
Conflict for the Mississippi Headwaters

longer than planned if the hunt tomorrow was unsuccessful. With the hard corn bread fresh meat would be better anyway.

They needed the fire only until full dark had fallen and most of the pests had left, after which they let it die and lay down on their blankets to sleep.

The next morning . . . .

Well before sunup Otter shook White Bird by the shoulder, and the two gathered their weapons and headed up the ridge. While still the dark before dawn, as their eyes adjusted they could easily follow the ridgeline they had followed the day before. The sky was just brightening when they reached the end of the ridge near the meadow and crouched down to make final arrangements. Otter tested the wind direction with some dead grass: "The wind is from the east, but is very little; you should also make noise. Wait until the sky is brighter while I find a hiding place."

Otter moved away from White Bird and retreated back along the path toward the location he had decided the day before was best to wait. He was sure that, once frightened from their bedding ground, the deer would follow the narrow strip of land between the ridge and the swamp. Several hundred yards back Otter worked his way down the slope to the forest edge, and finding a good place of concealment lowered himself to a crouching position. This was far enough from the meadow that by the time any deer reached his position they should have lost their caution and forgotten they had been disturbed. Placing his pouch of arrows in front of him, and the bow across his knees, Otter waited silently.

In less than ten minutes the sky brightened as the sun tipped over the horizon, and Otter could hear the sound of White Bird as he called out and beat two pieces of wood together to rouse any sleeping deer. Within minutes a doe with her spring faun became visible

THE HEADWATERS WAR:
Conflict for the Mississippi Headwaters

slowly working her way in his direction, followed by a second doe also followed by a spring fawn. Placing an arrow at the ready he waited. When the first doe was nearly opposite his hiding place, less than 100 feet away, Otter rose and loosed his arrow, rapidly replacing it with another. But a second arrow wasn't needed; the doe stumbled to its knees, then fell and lay on its side threshing, its faun at first running a distance away, then returning to its mother only to fall to Otter's second arrow. By that time the second doe and its faun had bounded into the marsh and disappeared.

Otter walked cautiously to where the deer lay, an arrow at the ready. The doe still moved slightly but that soon ended. Kneeling, Otter first cut the doe's jugular to allow it to bleed out, after which he began its field-dressing. Several minutes later White Bird arrived to help prepare the faun. When finished White Bird cut a pole to which the larger deer could be tied, then, once it was secure, the two lifted the pole for the trip back to their camp; White Bird with the added weight of the faun thrown over his shoulders.

It was still early morning when the two, carrying their load, arrived at their camp of the night before and hung both deer from a low hanging tree limb; White Bird first cutting a quarter from the faun while Otter built a small fire. Here near their village there was no longer a need for caution, and some of the fresh venison would taste good before loading the canoe for the trip home.

Earlier the same day . . . .

It was just after dawn and the trail was bustling with activity. Most of the night had been spent on the trail, and now as they neared Sandy Lake the warriors were allowed to rest, eat a cold breakfast, and apply war paint for the upcoming battle. One of the advance scouts had reported back that the trail ahead was clear with no unusual activity either on the trail or at the Dakota

THE HEADWATERS WAR:
Conflict for the Mississippi Headwaters

village. Now all was ready; in less than two hours they would reach the point where the trail to the Dakota village broke off from the Kathio trail and headed north. Once at the base of the peninsula it was less than half an hour to the village.

Bi-aus-wah and Big Marten stood at the head of the line waiting until all were ready before starting down the trail at a slow trot. This was not a normal raid where they expected to attack an unprepared village when many of the warriors were away. The attack had been planned for the time of the summer gathering, and not only would most of the village warriors be present, they would be augmented by visiting Dakota from other villages as well. Further, *Bi-aus-wah* assumed they would be discovered before they arrived, but hopefully not until they were near enough to the village the Dakota couldn't fully prepare. From his previous visits *Bi-aus-wah* knew that, even in peacetime, White Water, the primary civil chief, and his war chief Black Crane, would never be foolish enough to fail to post guards to provide warning. Now, in a time of war, it was a certainty. The casualties would be great, but he would not be wasteful of Ojibwe lives.

Bi-aus-wah well knew and respected the fighting abilities of the Dakota, but he also knew he was bringing many more warriors, most with the white man's guns, which few of the Dakota owned. Further, he thought he knew how White Water and his war chief Black Crane would respond to the warning of their approach; it was exactly what he would do himself. He would send the women and children to the pair of offshore islands with the old men and some of the older warriors for their defense. To ensure no attack was also coming from the river to the east he might send some of his other warriors there as well. Then, once driven from the field, while most of the Dakota warriors would attempt to also flee to the islands, some would most likely retreat to their earthen lodges and fight to the death.

51

THE HEADWATERS WAR:
Conflict for the Mississippi Headwaters

While *Bi-aus-wah* had given instructions to his war leaders to destroy everything; the summer wigwams, fields, and those earth lodges found to be undefended, he also didn't want needless casualties. Except for blocking holes punched in the walls of the earth lodges to allow firing, his war chiefs had been instructed to leave those they found defended unmolested. Yes, in the heat of battle some would fail to heed the instructions, but that could not be helped. As for Snake Skin, whose hatred of the Dakota matched his own for the Fox? If he was foolish enough to try to send his warriors against the fortress lodges so be it; he would be responsible for his own dead warriors. There was one other instruction he would have given if necessary; not to attempt to pursue the Dakota to the offshore island. That wouldn't be necessary; he had make plans disclosed only to Big Marten. They would simply deprive Snake Skin of the means to reach the island.

Bi-aus-wah knew his old friend White Water would understand his message. The Ojibwe were coming, and even when the Dakota were at their greatest strength couldn't be stopped. If they failed to heed the message and leave the raids would continue.

On the trail . . . .

Bitten-by-the-Loon trotted along, closely following the warrior ahead. The previous two days had been at a slower pace, but today they were nearing their destination and had picked up the pace, alternating a fast walk with a slow jog; rapidly eating the remaining distance. While Bitten-by-the-Loon had been on smaller warparties before, nothing this large. In fact, his father had said this was one of the largest war parties the Ojibwe had ever raised. To get this many together had taken months of planning, but in the end warriors from as far away as Sault Ste. Marie at the eastern tip of Lake Superior and even from southern Canada had responded. Hearing of the planned attack, even some of their friends

THE HEADWATERS WAR:
Conflict for the Mississippi Headwaters

the Cree had come from far to the north. All wanted to boast of their being a part of such a major war party.

In a way, like his father, Bitten-by-the-Loon was ambivalent as to the Dakota. As his father had explained, it was only that the Dakota possessed the land the Ojibwe desired. During the years of truce they had developed a close relationship with the Dakota; not like the bitter relationship between the Ojibwe and the Fox. Perhaps someday that relationship might again be established, but only after the Ojibwe had what they wanted. To Bitten-by-the-Loon, his father was always right.

Bitten-by-the-Loon knew why his father explained such things to him, things he rarely told others. It was a lesson for the day when he himself would become chief after his father; something he never doubted. Except for Big Marten his father had said he had not explained his limited goal to any others. If they had known many would not have come to participate.

Upstream on the Prairie River . . . .

Finishing their breakfast Otter and White Bird loaded the deer and other supplies and started downstream. They had been underway for less than half an hour when White Bird raised his hand and motioned to pull into shore. Once ashore White Bird motioned Otter to listen; in the distance a faint sound could be heard which seemed to come from the trail that crossed the makeshift bridge a short distance ahead. Cautiously, remaining in the cover of the heavy brush, they headed in the direction of the source of the sound. Once in sight of the bridge they lay flat, watching, and as the sound grew louder it resolved itself into the sound of many feet pounding the ground coupled with a low murmuring sound.

They had been in position for less than a minute when, less than 100 feet away, a warrior emerged from the underbrush bordering the trail and trotted past before

THE HEADWATERS WAR:
Conflict for the Mississippi Headwaters

crossing the bridge, followed by two others. Then, within seconds a stream of warriors moving in single file followed. Otter immediately recognized the middle aged man leading the column, his face covered with war paint. It was a face he recognized; while a mere child at the time, he had seen him in their village in the company of White Water, the chief of their village. It was the Ojibwe chief from Fond du Lac, *Bi-aus-wah*; and he was painted for war.

Following closely behind was a large, muscular man, bare chested and also painted for war, who could only be the Fond du Lac war chief Big Marten, followed closely by a steady stream of warriors, all bare chested and also painted, nearly all carrying the white man's guns. After a few minutes there was a break, but then another stream of warriors, all painted for war, then the pattern was repeated. There were so many passing warriors they stopped counting. All they could do was hope they would not be seen.

While the seemingly endless procession passed Otter and White Bird pressed themselves into the sparse cover, barely breathing, afraid that if any the warriors looked to the side they would be seen. While still early, before the heat of the day had fully set in, still Otter found it difficult to keep from brushing aside the black flies attracted by the film of sweat building on his bare back. Also in Otter's mind was the fear that one of the passing Ojibwe, in crossing the bridge, would look to the side upstream to where the tip of their canoe still projected from the streamside cover. If they did hopefully a brief glance would lead them to believe it was only a log. But none did; the bridge was narrow, consisting of only the flattened trunks of two trees, and as they crossed their senses focused on keeping their footing; they had no time to look to the side. It was nearly ten minutes before the last straggler crossed the bridge and disappeared into the woods beyond. Even then the two remained silent; scouts or stragglers could be following behind.

What it all meant was clear; the Ojibwe intended to attack their village. The number of warriors was staggering, neither had ever seen such a group all gathered at once, and at the pace they were moving it wouldn't be much more than an hour before they arrived at the trail branching off to the Dakota village. Even if warned now there would be little chance to prepare; the Ojibwe would easily be able to block the Dakota from breaking out to the south, leaving only the chance of escape by water open.

While the approach of the Ojibwe warparty would almost certainly be discovered by the guards always posted at the foot of the trail to the village, providing time for the warriors present to arm themselves, there would be little time to assemble those away hunting or fishing or prepare defenses. There would also be little time to even evacuate noncombatants; most of the canoes were stored on the northeastern tip of the peninsula a distance from the village for protection from storms from the west, with few, other than those of the many visitors, kept at the village itself. What if the Ojibwe seized those stored away from the village; blocking evacuation?

After the procession had passed and the sound of passage faded in the distance the two stood listening; then White Bird broke the silence:

"Ojibwe," he said, stating the obvious. "They are going to our village. We must warn them."

Otter was silent for a moment, then responded: "How? They block the trail and we cannot pass; and there are no other trails from here to the village, and if we tried to go cross country the swamps would stop us. Only the river is open, and they will be there before we can reach them."

After a moment White Bird said: "Perhaps not. They may take time to get their warriors in position and prepare. We may be able to warn the village first."

55

THE HEADWATERS WAR:
Conflict for the Mississippi Headwaters

Adding, "If we rush."

Otter thought for a moment, then nodded: "We can try, and if we can't give warning at least we can help."

The two pushed the canoe back into the water, first unloading their kill to lighten the load, and climbing in pushed it from the bank. "We must be ready to find cover when we reach the main river. They may be coming that way also," Otter said, starting to paddle downstream.

Mid-morning, south of the Dakota Village . . . .

Each of the war chiefs had been assigned a position as, in a wide line stretching across the entire narrow peninsula, they began to advance northward; spacing between warriors becoming closer as the peninsula narrowed. Their intent was to sweep any Dakota attempting to escape by land back to the village.

Bi-aus-wah and Big Marten had been careful in their planning. Snake Skin, with the large contingent from La Point, had been given the place of honor, the far left where they would be the first to make contact with the village. Big Marten's contingent from Fond du Lac, the second largest, had the right flank. While Snake Skin accepted the assignment as an honor, only *Bi-aus-wah* and Big Marten knew the real reason for the assignment. As Big Marten advanced up the right flank he would ensure the path to where the spare canoes were stored wasn't blocked and the canoes weren't destroyed. Before reaching the canoe storage area they would turn left to attack the village itself, which would put the Fond du Lac warriors between Snake Skin and the storage area.

At the Dakota Village . . . .

The village was quiet except for women going from place to place engaged in their normal activities, with children playing or looking for something to keep

THE HEADWATERS WAR:
Conflict for the Mississippi Headwaters

occupied. From time to time a man would leave one of the bark or sod covered lodges and either go down to the shore where canoes, mostly those of the visitors, were beached, head off into the forest, or go to join one of the groups of warriors sitting in the shade. Some of the visitors were from as far north as the big northern lakes, and even some of the *Sissiton* from the western borderlands were present.

Walks Tall, the mother of Otter, was at the lake shore cleaning the last of the bowls used for the morning meal when she heard shouting from the village. Gathering her containers she hurried back to see what was happening.

Near White Water's lodge one of the sentries that had been stationed on the trail to the south was standing in front of the village chief, pointing back from where he had come. His message was clear; the Ojibwe were coming. Within minutes the village was a hive of activity, the men seizing weapons and rushing south in the direction the scout had indicated, while the women gathered what children they could find and ran north toward the beached canoes or northeast toward the canoe storage area. At White Water's order shots were fired by several possessing guns to call back all their warriors within hearing distance.

Black Crane, the Dakota war chief, joined White Water, and once he understood the situation ran south in the direction the other warriors were taking; stopping only to get his weapons from his lodge. As soon as he arrived among the gathering Dakota he began to give instructions; the warriors were to spread out and take up positions behind what cover they could find blocking the advancing Ojibwe. Use any time they had to build or strengthen their position. White Water took charge of the rest of the village, instructing the women, children, older men, and youths not yet warriors to flee either to the canoes near the village, or the storage area to the east, and evacuate to the offshore islands. Once all had been

57

THE HEADWATERS WAR:
Conflict for the Mississippi Headwaters

evacuated, some of the men and youths, and some of the stronger women, should return and wait with canoes to help evacuate the warriors if necessary.

A little later White Water stood on the shore next to Wounded Buck watching as loaded canoes left the shore and began landing on the sandbar connecting the two offshore islands, then after unloading pushing off to return.

"What were the Ojibwe doing?" White Water thought. At first he couldn't understand why they were allowing him to get the women and children to the islands where they could be defended by only a few; if it were him leading the attack he would have sent warriors by water to block any flight to the islands. It might be that other Ojibwe were coming down the river but had not yet arrived.

White Water stood contemplating the situation for nearly a minute, but then nodded to himself, and said to Wounded Buck. "It is as I should have expected. They do not come to destroy us, they come as a challenge. A statement they want this place for their own."

After a moment: "Long have I known my old friend lusted for our lake, and now he comes." Taking Wounded Buck by the hand: "If I am wrong, and some are also coming by river, we must protect those on the islands. Go there with enough men to stop a landing; build positions to repel any attack if it comes. Send a few upriver to give warning. I will stay here with the old men to guard the shore."

South of the village . . . .

Black Crane watched his warriors taking their positions as ahead he could see the line of Ojibwe, which had stopped waiting for stragglers to catch up. The sentry had been unsure as to the size of the attacking force, but now that Black Crane saw how closely spaced the Ojibwe were he knew they were outnumbered. All they could hope for was to delay the Ojibwe advance

THE HEADWATERS WAR:
Conflict for the Mississippi Headwaters

until the people were safe. If only his warriors had been armed as well as the Ojibwe he would not be as worried as he was, but they would still make them pay for every inch of ground.

Behind the lines of warriors *Bi-aus-wah* stood eyeing the scene ahead. Ojibwe warriors spread out waiting for the order to advance as the Dakota formed ahead. He couldn't help but smile to himself; no, to fulfill his dream the Ojibwe did not have to break the treaty, the Dakota had done that for them. *Bi-aus-wah* thought of his many past visits to the Sandy Lake village. Many of its leading men he considered his friends, and he admired and even liked the Dakota and did not want them destroyed. It was not like the implacable hatred he felt for the Fox, only that they must get out of their way; the peace had lasted too long and the time had come.

Bi-aus-wah's glanced over at Big Marten in the distance, who stood waiting for instructions. Yes, Big Marten had his flaws, like his inability to stand back so he could direct the overall battle. He knew, as much as he had cautioned him to keep his head, he would join the battle when it became hand to hand later, overcome with blood lust. But still, from his own years as a war chief *Bi-aus-wah* recognized his innate leadership and strategic skills. Someday, he thought, he will become a great war chief. He was exactly the instrument he needed to make his dream become fact. He would have patience and teach Big Marten all he knew.

Big Marten watched *Bi-aus-wah* for the sign to move ahead. With the warriors of the other bands positioned on the left they had enough to completely block the peninsula as they advanced, without gaps for escaping Dakota. Within minutes the order was given, and the line of advancing Ojibwe began forcing the outnumbered and outgunned Dakota back. But it was slow going; the Dakota, hiding behind cover and only retreating when about to be overrun.

THE HEADWATERS WAR:
Conflict for the Mississippi Headwaters

The fighting was fierce, often hand to hand, with sometimes dozens involved to obtain even the slightest advance. For hours the battle raged, and by mid afternoon the Dakota had finally been driven to the sparser cover near the edge of the village, some taking up positions in the small fields of still-standing corn, other using the earth lodges for cover, some retreating inside from where they could still fire through holes punched in the walls. Many of the Dakota warriors had either been killed or severely wounded, and the Ojibwe had also suffered heavy losses. But all knew that in time the superior numbers and weapons of the Ojibwe would overwhelm the Dakota defenders.

Mid-Morning, Upstream . . . .

The distance wasn't that far, but still the shallow water and deadheads slowed their progress. It took a little over two hours to reach the main river, but once there Otter and White Bird were careful to watch for cover along the shores in case they encountered Ojibwe. This near the lake the high banks had disappeared leaving the river bordered by fields of tall reeds extending to the shore. While only about a mile from the river's mouth they dared go no further until they had a better idea of what lay ahead, or whether Ojibwe were also coming down the river. Here they were invisible from any passing traffic even though near the main channel. But no canoes came, and from the lake to the west they could hear guns firing and sounds of battle; they were too late to give warning.

"What do we do," White Bird asked? Otter pushed his paddle against the reeds without answering, and the canoe moved into the slow current. In minutes they entered the lake and turned northwest in the direction of the gunfire. Soon the village came in sight; canoes sitting offshore manned by only one or two men or women, and on the shore figures behind embankments. To the north more activity was visible on

THE HEADWATERS WAR:
Conflict for the Mississippi Headwaters

the offshore islands; the sandbar between the islands and almost breaching the gap covered with other figures, canoes departing and arriving.

Otter, in the back, suddenly turned the canoe toward the offshore islands: "See, people are there. We go there first."

It took only about 10 minutes to cover the distance to the islands, where they drove the canoe onto the wide sandbar that, in this season of low water, nearly connected the two. Some older Dakota men and youths lined the sandbar, helping to ready the canoes coming and going. The situation was immediately apparent; all noncombatants had been gathered onto to eastern island, with a growing pile of fallen trees and driftwood stacked to seal the island off from the sandbar, making any Ojibwe landing on the sandbar exposed to fire from beyond the barricade. The island itself was heavily wooded, and they could also see smaller barricades being built there along the shore as well. It was clear the Ojibwe would pay heavily for any attack they attempted, even if they could find enough canoes to do so.

At first Otter stopped to talk to some of the older men, then he and White Crane headed to the barricade. First Otter wanted to find his mother and younger brothers and sisters; he knew his father Rolling Thunder, and older brother Right Hand, would be at the village. Climbing over the pile of logs they found old men, women, and youths still working to make the barricade even more secure, extending it beyond the sandbar itself into the water. Others were preparing defensive positions on the island shore as well.

It took some time before Otter found Walks Tall with several others piling brush near the shore, behind which a shallow trench was being dug. Smiling slightly, Walks Tall nodded before standing to greet Otter.

"Did the hunt go well?" she asked in greeting, as if this were just a normal day.

Otter stopped and nodded: "Yes, but we saw the

THE HEADWATERS WAR:
Conflict for the Mississippi Headwaters

Ojibwe on the trail and hurried here."

Turning, Otter asked: "Who is in charge?"

Walks tall nodded to the west toward the barricade, and answered: "Wounded Buck."

Turning, Otter headed back in the direction she had indicated to look for Wounded Buck, White Bird joining him on the way. Wounded Buck stood with a group of defenders a short distance behind the barricade watching the work in progress, but stopped his conversation as the two approached. Otter explained they had been upriver, and had encountered no Ojibwe; other than the warparty crossing the bridge. They had also not encountered the Dakota scouts dispatched upriver earlier; perhaps a good sign. While they had tried to count the Ojibwe as they crossed there were too many and they had lost count. Maybe as many hundreds as they had fingers on their hands.

After listening to them Wounded Buck thought for awhile, and then nodded to himself: "If so many the village cannot hold."

Turning to Otter and White Bird he instructed them to head for the village and look for White Water. Wounded Buck was sure White Water would need all the help he could get to cover an evacuation when needed; he was sure it would be, and maybe soon.

Otter and White Bird immediately climbed over the barricade and ran to their canoe and pushed it off from shore. The village was only a short paddle, and they soon grounded the canoe among the others lining the shore. They could hear gunfire approaching the village, but the battle itself was still to the south and couldn't be seen.

Seeing White Water standing looking toward the village they went to him and told him everything they had seen. At first he peppered them with questions, but then, after a moment of silence, he nodded and instructed them to join those preparing positions from which to defend the canoes.

THE HEADWATERS WAR:
Conflict for the Mississippi Headwaters

Mid-Afternoon, edge of the village . . . .

Black Crane disentangled himself from the Ojibwe warrior who had driven him to the ground before dying of the tomahawk wound Black Crane had given him. Getting to his feet, he called out to his remaining warriors; it was time to retreat to the beached canoes, while he and about 20 others, fortunate enough to possess guns and enough powder and shot to still use them, stayed to delay the Ojibwe. Earlier, upon receiving word from White Water as to the number of their enemy, he had passed orders to the warriors that rather than attempt to maintain the fight from the earth lodges they were to retreat to and defend the island. If not enough canoes, swim out to where they could be picked up.

Otter lay prone behind the sand barrier, his bow and a pouch of arrows at his side. Most of the gunfire had stopped, but the cries of battle were much closer, coming from within the village itself. It wasn't long before a group of Dakota warriors emerged from the cover of the lodges running toward the shore, only to be followed by others. White Water immediately called for all canoes to be pushed into the water and manned; it was time for the warriors to evacuate. Otter and White Bird immediately ran to their canoe and pushed off, exchanging their bows for paddles. As soon as the running warriors reached the shore and climbed into a canoe it paddled beyond gunshot range, that of Otter and White Bird holding two of the fleeing Dakota.

While the more heavily loaded canoes headed directly for the sandbar, Otter called to White Bird to join about a half dozen others that had stopped about 100 yards offshore to wait. If the rearguard were able to make it to the shore and swim out they would be ready. While most canoes were filled to capacity, their canoe could still hold at least one more, and others could hold on and be dragged to safety.

It wasn't long before about a dozen Dakota, led by the easily recognizable Black Crane, appeared,

THE HEADWATERS WAR:
Conflict for the Mississippi Headwaters

pursued by a large group of Ojibwe. Rushing into the water the Dakota attempted to swim to safety, but only four reached deep water and succeeded in escaping the pursuing Ojibwe, many of whom stopped to fire at any heads appearing above water; still all four made it safely to the canoes, Black Crane among them. The four grabbed the side of the nearest waiting canoe to be pulled along as it was paddled out of gunshot range. The Ojibwe, unable to follow, could do little but display their futility by ineffective firing and shouting taunts. Soon, as the canoes left for the islands, even that ended and a silence descended over the village.

It was over, Ojibwe warriors taking scalps and anything else of interest, killing any that remained alive. Those few Dakota who had taken refuge in the lodges were killed as the lodges were torn down over their heads or warriors climbed to the tops and fired down through the smoke holes, even while the more numerous bark wigwams were set ablaze. It had been as *Bi-aus-wah* had expected; since so few of the Dakota had taken refuge in the lodges his warriors were unwilling to let them remain unmolested. On the island the Dakota, safe for now, could do little but watch.

Bi-aus-wah glanced over to Big Marten and the other war chiefs who had gathered near the center of the village. Burn anything that would burn, destroy the crops, and tear down the earth lodges. Take or destroy everything of value. The message must be clear; leave or face similar raids in the future. Before dark *Bi-aus-wah* wanted to be on the trail heading back to Fond du Lac. While it would take a runner from Sandy Lake only a day to reach the large Dakota village of Kathio on Mille Lacs Lake, and a full day and part of a night more before reinforcements could be here, still *Bi-aus-wah* wanted to be well away from here before then. He was a careful man who took no unnecessary risks. That was why he had been so successful as a war leader; followers had been easy to come by.

THE HEADWATERS WAR:
Conflict for the Mississippi Headwaters

Bi-aus-wah stood looking out at the lake with its many islands and tree-lined shore. Once the Sandy Lake area was clear of Dakota he would relocate some of his people here; not all, but enough to begin raids to the north and block the Dakota to the south. Perhaps he himself would move here as well. It was a rich, beautiful lake, away from the raging storms from the big lake near Fond du Lac.

Looking up, *Bi-aus-wah* was relieved to see Bitten-by-the-Loon approach looking tired and dirty, blood coating his right arm, but carrying a Dakota scalp. Bitten-by-the-Loon had a satisfied look, and *Bi-aus-wha* gave him a nod of approval before he returned to his discussion with Big Marten and Snake Skin. Bitten-by-the-Loon had proven himself; the ability to both fight and lead others.

Just before dark . . . .

White Water, Black Crane and several elders stood on the sandbar gazing at the village in the distance. The sun had touched the horizon, and soon full dark would fall. But the light was still enough to see the village, or what remained of it, while still burning was empty; the Ojibwe had left.

White Water said quietly to Black Crane: "As soon as it's full dark send scouts to make sure the Ojibwe are gone. Search for any survivors. Tonight we stay here."

"What then?" Black Crane asked.

Not saying anything for a moment, finally White Water answered: "Tomorrow, we return to the village to take care of our dead and collect anything of value we can find. Gather what we can from the fields. Then we hold council; my advice will be that we leave. If we do not heed the message the Ojibwe will return, and next time will not leave any alive."

THE HEADWATERS WAR:
Conflict for the Mississippi Headwaters

The next day . . . .

Otter and White Bird beached the canoe and waited while the two passengers jumped ashore. They were one of the last of the canoes to arrive and the beach was covered with the canoes of the earlier arrivals, while at the site of their former village dozens of people were trudging through the village ruins. It was a somber time for Otter; while his older brother Right Hand had made it safely to the islands, his father Rolling Thunder was unaccounted for and was presumed to have fallen early in the battle. Now they would find the body and prepare it for the next life.

Walks Tall, Otter's mother, would now join the family of Rolling Thunder's older brother, Shadow Walker, as Shadow Walker's second wife. That was the custom, and as soon as Rolling Thunder's body had been prepared she would make the move. Otter, for now, would move in with his older brother Right Hand and his new wife. There he would live until he himself became a full fledged warrior with a wife and a lodge of his own.

Otter, followed by White Bird, joined the others in their search for the dead, as one by one bodies were brought back to be laid out on the sand. It wasn't long before they saw Right Hand with another warrior carrying the scalped body of Rolling Thunder back toward the village to be placed with the others, their backs hunched with the weight.

Walks Tall and Shadow Walker, as well as Otter and Right Hand, joined in preparing the body. They couldn't dress the body in finery as was the custom, little remaining in the village, but they would do what they could; Otter contributing his blanket in which to wrap the body, with Walks Tall managing to beg a piece of red ochre with which to paint the body. Once preparation was complete, Right Hand and Otter lifted the body to carry it to the place of burial a distance away. There they dug a shallow grave and positioned the body of Rolling Thunder; accompanied by his medicine bag and those

THE HEADWATERS WAR:
Conflict for the Mississippi Headwaters

weapons they had been able to find.

Once the bodies had been buried, and everything of value collected, they would return to the island where the elders would meet in council and decide the future. White Water had said they should not stay here in the village; it was too close to the Ojibwe and too far from other Dakota villages, and it was believed his view would prevail, but where they should go was causing disruption. Some wanted to go to the southwest and either join the Dakota at Mille Lacs Lake or begin a new village there. Others wanted to go north to the lakes of the headwaters, although news of attacks from the Cree and Ojibwe to the north had been arriving at the village for a number of years. Others even wanted to go further south or west, some to the west to *Sissiton* or *Wapeton* country, or even further to than of the Yanktonaise.

Whatever the elders decided, in the following days they would salvage any crops that had survived and gather what food they could for an impending move. Within a week it was expected that they would leave, but the dissention racking the village would most likely mean the village would split; with most leaving for the big lake to the southwest, Mille Lacs. Otter and White Bird would go with whichever camp their remaining family members chose to join.

The daily routine continued until, about a week later, as the sun rose, all usable canoes pushed off from the island carrying the able-bodied planning to follow the well traveled trail to Mille Lacs; those unable to endure the long trek to travel by river; with the balance of the canoes allotted to the smaller group heading north for the headwaters.

Both Otter and White Bird smoldered with anger; someday, they vowed, they would come back and punish the Ojibwe. Someday they would reclaim the bones of their ancestors.

THE HEADWATERS WAR:
Conflict for the Mississippi Headwaters

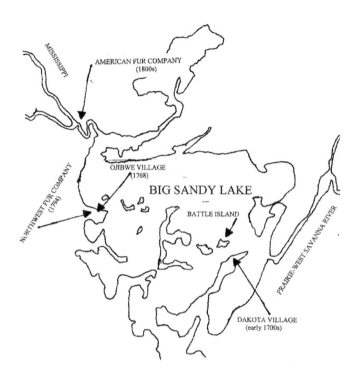

Figure 6: Big Sandy Lake (Lac du Sable)*

Estimated location of events described

THE HEADWATERS WAR:
Conflict for the Mississippi Headwaters

CHAPTER 3
BATTLE OF CUT FOOT SIOUX

Even before *Bi-aus-wah* opened the route through Sandy Lake the Ojibwe were free to follow the Pigeon River, Rainy River, Rainy Lake and Lake of the Woods route to the west. That area was largely occupied by the Cree, an Algic tribe who, while at war with the Dakota, were on friendly terms with the Ojibwe. Many of these new Ojibwe worked with the French, establishing villages near the string of French trading posts that extended as far west as the Red River and Lake Winnipeg. Following the breakdown of the truce between the Dakota and the Ojibwe in 1736 the Cree and Ojibwe from the north began raiding southward; Upper and Lower Red Lakes and the headwaters lakes the target. Once *Bi-aus-wah* established himself at Sandy Lake he joined the raids to the north; the headwaters lakes caught in between.

The primary lakes of the headwaters, all connected to the Mississippi (*or in some cases the Mississippi passed through*), were Leech, Cass, and Winnibigoshish, with other large lakes such as Bowstring, while not connected directly, only a short distance away. Heavily forested with white pine and the useful birch, it was rich in fish and wild rice, but not the preferred habitat of large game animals. Still, the less wooded areas near swamps and marshes were plentiful, and there the white tail deer and solitary moose could be found. Further west the prairie or prairie fringe, teaming with buffalo and elk, could easily be reached in a few days travel by hunting parties, even though that involved the danger of conflict with the western bands of the Dakota and the Nakota as well.

The conflict for these headwater lakes differed

THE HEADWATERS WAR:
Conflict for the Mississippi Headwaters

in many ways from that for Sandy Lake. This was largely a war of attrition, with the Ojibwe sending yearly war parties making life on those lakes difficult for the Dakota. In this the Cree and Ojibwe were aided by the Assiniboine, a Siouan tribe that Robinson, in his, *'History of the Dakota or Sioux Nation'*, states had broken off from the Yanktonais. But, while not by itself causing abandonment of the headwaters lakes by the Dakota, there is one battle reported by Warren that stands out; the battle of Cut Foot Sioux.

Sometime in the late 1740s, smarting from Ojibwe raids, the Dakota at Leech and the nearby lakes resolved to launch a major campaign to drive back the Ojibwe and their allies, and in approximately 1748, with support from some of the prairie Sioux to the west, a large force collected at Leech Lake. The attack was planned to be multifaceted, with the largest group moving down the Mississippi to assault Sandy Lake, a second headed north to drive back the northern Ojibwe and Cree at Rainy Lake, and a third northwest against the Ojibwe in the Red River and Pembina area.

All three of the Dakota assaults met with failure; that against Rainy Lake met an Ojibwe-Cree warparty and after a major battle was driven back, the second, directed at the Red River and Pembina areas, failed to encounter the enemy and broke up in disarray. The largest of the three warparties, that against Sandy Lake, encountered a large Ojibwe warparty from Sandy Lake headed north, culminating in the major battle of Cut Foot Sioux. Cut Foot Sioux is a small lake connected to Lake Winnibigoshish at its northeast corner.

The encounter of the two opposing warparties ended in a battle that lasted nearly all day. While neither side could claim full victory the Dakota abandoned the field first and returned home; the Ojibwe returning to Sandy Lake. Finding the Ojibwe threat intolerable, the Dakota later evacuated Leech and the other headwater lakes and moved west and southwest to the prairie

THE HEADWATERS WAR:
Conflict for the Mississippi Headwaters

country near the Red River, with the Ojibwe moving into the vacuum.

Even after northern Minnesota fell under Ojibwe control the Dakota fought back. The Dakota residing south of Sandy Lake were largely blocked from the headwaters by the Ojibwe presence there, with only more roundabout routes available. However, the Nakota (*Yankton and Yanktonais*) still occupied the prairie country on both sides of the Red River of the North in the Ottertail area and south, and the *Wahpeton* and *Sissiton* of the Dakota branch were present on the upper Minnesota River and its Pomme de Terre and Chippewa River tributaries, and all the Dakota branches still claimed the rich hunting grounds of the Crow Wing River basin. All were within a few days march of the Ojibwe at Leech Lake.

Of the major battles in this far northern region Warren records only one; the battle of Cut Foot Sioux. However, that battle was pivotal in that it led to realization by the Dakota of the headwaters lakes that they could not drive the Ojibwe back, leading to their eventual abandonment of those lakes. What led up to the battle of Cut Foot Sioux, and a fictional telling of the battle and its prelude, is the subject of this chapter.

Spring 1746 . . . .

Big Marten sat on the shoreline near the growing village watching the lake to the east for any sign of *Bi-aus-wah* and the new arrivals. While from the island the mouth of the combined East Savanna-Prairie River was not directly visible, within minutes of their entry into the lake the canoes of the newcomers would round the tip of the peninsula now blocking the view.

Three years earlier Big Marten had accompanied White Beaver, a Fond du Lac civil chief, and about 150 families to Sandy Lake to establish an initial settlement; temporarily located on the easternmost of the pair of offshore islands as protection against Dakota raids. But

71

THE HEADWATERS WAR:
Conflict for the Mississippi Headwaters

with new arrivals each year the village was bursting at the seams, and with *Bi-aus-wah* moving to Sandy Lake, accompanied by several dozen additional families, the island would be pushed beyond its limit. It would be up to *Bi-aus-wah* and the elders to decide where a new village would be established, whether on the peninsula south of the islands near where the former Dakota village had been located, or some other location.

There wouldn't be much time. In addition to the newcomers dozens of warriors were expected to arrive shortly from other villages to supplement those of Sandy Lake for the spring warparties against the Dakota to the north. The influx of Ojibwe from Lake Superior moving into the Fond du Lac and Sandy Lake areas was placing pressure on resources, and expansion to the large northern lakes was the best option. *Bi-aus-wah* was as yet unready to move against the powerful Dakota center of Kathio at Mille Lacs Lake, limiting his raids in that direction to the lands between to deprive the Dakota of their use.

Hearing shouts from some children on the shore Big Marten stood. Rounding the peninsula and less than half a mile distant the first canoes came into view, bringing the villagers to the shore shouting and waving welcome. From the flotilla of canoes came shouts and waving of paddles. Big Marten shook his head; there were far more than he had expected. It would be difficult to house them until the new village was established. But that was a problem for White Beaver and others.

Later that afternoon . . . .

The canoes, heavily loaded with both passengers and their possessions, had all been unloaded. Many of the new arrivals had erected temporary shelters in the open spaces near the resident's wigwams; others with relatives already here sheltered with them. It was crowded, but tomorrow *Bi-aus-wah* and the elders would tour the lake under Big Marten's guidance and decide the

THE HEADWATERS WAR:
Conflict for the Mississippi Headwaters

new village site; with over 300 families they had now grown to sufficient size that a mainland village could be made secure. But that was for tomorrow. Tonight the new arrivals would be welcomed with feasting and celebration.

Afternoon the following day . . . .

The tour of the lake had been completed by late afternoon, with the best locations for the new village examined in detail. Two locations were clearly the best; the peninsula less than one half mile to the south where the former Dakota village had been located, and a shallow peninsula on the western shore. Both had their advantages; the old Dakota village was already cleared of trees and brush and would be a short move. It would even be unnecessary to clear land for their crops; in fact, while the village had been left vacant some of the former Dakota fields had been planted because of the shortage of suitable land on the island. It was also near the trail and river route leading to Fond du Lac making evacuation easier than the other site in case of an emergency, and the offshore islands were always there to use as a refuge as the Dakota had used them a few years earlier. Still, the old trail to Mille Lacs Lake, while now mostly unused, provided an easy route for a Dakota attack.

The peninsula to the west would require much work, including clearing of trees; but it was a better overall location, much closer to the Mississippi portage. That danger of being too close to the Mississippi and the portage was what finally decided the question. They must constantly be on the guard against an attack from the Kathio Dakota at Mille Lacs Lake, only about 50 miles distant. The west shore location would be at risk from attack both by land and water. The Kathio Dakota, even without support from other Dakota to the south and west, could put together a warparty of several hundred warriors. It was thought that until the village had grown

THE HEADWATERS WAR:
Conflict for the Mississippi Headwaters

larger or the Dakota were finally driven from Mille Lacs the peninsula to the south would serve.

For now the village on the island would be maintained, with the overflow building the new village. While the mainland village would be of only moderate size, its closeness to the island afforded additional protection. Later they could consider eliminating the island base, and possibly the south-shore village as well, and move to the more desirable western shore location. There they would be near the portage to the Mississippi River; but first they must build their strength.

Spring 1748, at Leech Lake . . . .

Pale Horse walked the shore of the island in the magnificent lake, wondering at its size. He had grown up and lived all his life in the prairie country to the west, and his experience with large lakes was limited, although he had hunted near Ottertail Lake on occasion. It was difficult from this island village in the northwest bay to appreciate how big the lake really was, the view of the main body obstructed by the peninsula to the east. Still, accustomed to prairie country, to him it appeared staggering. Only the night before he had arrived from the Chippewa River tributary of the Minnesota River with his 200 *Sissiton* warriors and been transported to the island by their hosts.

Pale Horse found it difficult to understand how, with so many Dakota living here on Leech Lake, and with their secure positions on its islands, they could not keep the Ojibwe at bay; but he had been told the neighboring Cass and Winnibigoshish villages had already been evacuated and the Ojibwe raids were on the increase and coming nearer. Fearing attack by the Ojibwe the Dakota the previous fall had vacated the rest of their smaller villages on the mainland and retreated to several of the large islands dotting the lake. But that only partly solved the problem; most of their fields were still on the mainland, and often ruined by Ojibwe raids.

74

THE HEADWATERS WAR:
Conflict for the Mississippi Headwaters

Pale Horse had come with his *Sissiton* warriors in response to the call by the Leech Lake Dakota to assemble for a grand expedition to destroy the Ojibwe village at Sandy Lake. Now it was to end; they would put out the fires of their tormentors permanently and again reclaim those lands for the Dakota.

Pale Horse had not always lived with the *Sissiton*, the band of the Dakota furthest to the west, but had spent his early days among his mother's people, the Yanktonais. However, among the Yanktonais fame as a warrior was hard to achieve since they were on friendly terms with the Prairie Ojibwe and Assissiboine to the north, and while still in his early twenties he had gone to his father's people, the *Sissiton*. There he had gained the glory in battle he sought, and risen to become the war chief of his band.

His name, Pale Horse, was one he did not like, but could not shake. Of unusually pale complexion, his fellow tribesmen joked his mother must have encountered a white trader in the past; a jibe he did not like. But the name had stuck, and in time he had come to accept his difference.

Pale Horse had been told the village where they were being housed was the largest of the Leech Lake villages, but that there were some others nearly as large. Pale Horse estimated the number of lodges at over 300, and with the population now swelled by the visitors it was the largest gathering of Dakota he had ever experienced. Most of the western bands tended to be small since they were constantly on the move in search of the best hunting. Learning from the nearby Nakota how to live in their prairie country, most *Sissiton* villages were also small and used the tepee covered with buffalo hide, allowing frequent moves; even for their summer gatherings it was rare for more than a few hundred families to gather. Here the lodges gave the feeling of permanence.

Pale Horse thought to himself, these Leech Lake

THE HEADWATERS WAR:
Conflict for the Mississippi Headwaters

Dakota were powerful indeed. He didn't know exactly how many there were, but did know the bands driven from Winnibigoshish and Cass lakes formed their own villages. Now the numbers were being swelled by other Dakota arriving daily in response to the summons. He had been told as many as 1,500 warriors would be in the raiding party, even while leaving several hundred warriors behind to protect the villages.

Several days later . . . .

Pale Horse was not happy. The council had decided to split the force, sending a war party against the Cree and Ojibwe across the Red River of the North in the Pembina area, and another against those at Rainy Lake; reducing the size of the main group attacking Sandy Lake nearly in half. True, the party attacking Sandy Lake would be the largest, over 700 warriors; still he did not think dividing the available forces was wise. All Dakota knew of the power of the Ojibwe villages at Sandy Lake and nearby Fond du Lac, and even 700 warriors might not be enough. He had come with his *Sissiton* for the Sandy Lake assault, not to waste their effort on the small Ojibwe presence at Pembina and Rainy Lake.

But he had been at least partially mollified. Since his *Sissiton* were the largest of the arriving bands of warriors he was to lead the Sandy Lake assault, with the parties going north and northwest largely the northern bands from the area of Leech and Upper and Lower Red lakes. Still, he thought the decision to divide was a mistake that could well lead to disaster for all three groups.

Meanwhile, at Sandy Lake . . . .

The previous fall in meetings at Fond du Lac it had been decided to increase the pressure on the Dakota of the northern lake region, and this year their raid was

THE HEADWATERS WAR:
Conflict for the Mississippi Headwaters

larger than usual and timed to coincide with an assault south from Rainy Lake. With the aid of the northern Ojibwe and Cree they could finally go directly against the large villages on Leech Lake itself rather than the 'nibbling' around the edge as previous raids had done.

While they had already forced evacuation of Pokegama, a large lake about 30 miles downstream, and Winnibigoshish, raids on Cass and Leech up to now had been limited to rapid attacks by small war parties, followed by an equally rapid retreat. Still, it had been enough to force the most of the Dakota villages on the mainland to be abandoned, and to relocate to the large Leech Lake islands. Of the three only Leech Lake had large islands for the evacuees and now most of the Dakota population was located there.

The Sandy Lake Band had grown to where it was now larger than that at Fond du Lac, and, as the residence of *Bi-aus-wah* and Big Marten had become the major power base of the Ojibwe west of Lake Superior. The expected reinforcements had arrived, the warparty organized, and soon they would leave for the north with over 400 seasoned warriors. While not enough to dislodge the Dakota concentrations at Leech Lake, still once they combined with those from Rainy Lake, they could lay waste to the fields of the Dakota, and any villages scattered along its shore.

Bi-aus-wah had no illusion that even supplemented with the northern Ojibwe and Cree he could drive the Dakota from their island bases; but as the raids built in strength each year he was sure that soon the Dakota would tire of always being a target and take the easiest path; move west toward the prairies. Only then could the Ojibwe safely establish villages on Leech, Cass, or Winnibigoshish; although even now some adventurous Ojibwe families were starting to move into the areas vacated by the Dakota downstream.

Big Marten and his old friend and mentor, *Bi-aus-wah*, had spent the night before in discussion, and

77

THE HEADWATERS WAR:
Conflict for the Mississippi Headwaters

Bi-aus-wah had disclosed what was close to his heart. The war with the Dakota had been raging for over a decade and they were near one of his goals; clearing the northern lakes for Ojibwe villages. Pressure from the French for a truce was increasing, and he was growing old and had one more wish; not only clear the northern lakes of the Dakota, but drive them from their villages on Lake Mille Lacs as well, including their village at Kathio. Once that was done he would be content.

Kathio was less than a two day march from Sandy Lake for a warparty, and not only that, it connected by the Rum River to the Mississippi. While the Rum River route was long and roundabout, still it forced the Sandy Lake Ojibwe to prepare for a two-pronged attack and kept them from moving to the preferred site on the western shore. The Kathio Dakota, joined by its satellite villages, could easily supplement any land attack with one by water, and the combined population of those villages still greatly outnumbered the Sandy Lake Ojibwe. Allowing the Dakota presence at Mille Lacs posed a constant risk, forcing *Bi-aus-wah* to keep many of his warriors back during their yearly raids to the north, and depriving the Ojibwe of use the rich lands that lay between and north of that large lake. That was an intolerable situation he could not allow to continue; but first they must clear the northern lakes. Then they could take care of Kathio.

For some reason the Kathio Dakota had never attempted a major attack on Sandy Lake, limiting themselves to smaller warparties to the hunting and ricing lands between the two villages, but at any time that could change. *Bi-aus-wah* had also, up to now, been careful not to overly antagonize their powerful neighbors with raids against the lake itself. To attack Kathio now would require all their resources plus other Ojibwe from Lake Superior, and they could not weaken Sandy Lake while an attack from the north was a possibility. Kathio must wait.

THE HEADWATERS WAR:
Conflict for the Mississippi Headwaters

Nothing should be said, *Bi-aus-wah* instructed Big Marten, but learn from those who have seen the Mille Lacs villages; where the villages are, how many live there, and how they can best be approached. Send scouts to find out what others do not know. Find the paths and plan for next year or perhaps the year following. See how many of their lodges are of earth, and think of how they can be taken.

Then, he had said, "We will put out their fires."

This year, *Bi-aus-wah* had told Big Marten, do as much damage to the Dakota in the north as possible. If the Dakota remain too strong and do not leave, then next year they would try again with an even stronger force; maybe attack the island villages as well. Only after the headwaters lakes were abandoned would he risk an assault on Mille Lacs.

Big Marten walked down to the shore to inspect the massed canoes near the village. He would do a final inspection to ensure they were all in proper condition. He had made sure sap had been gathered and concentrated for any necessary repairs, all the warriors were well equipped with travel food and shot and powder, and any necessary repair of weapons completed. But now he and some of his most trusted, experienced warriors would do a double check. For such a major raid nothing could be left to chance.

Tonight the celebrations and war dances necessary to inflame the warriors would be held, lasting most of the night. By the time the sun rose tomorrow they would leave for their trip to the north.

Four days later . . . .

The lead canoe passed through the narrow passage where the Mississippi left Winnibigoshish at its northeastern corner. Ahead Big Marten could see the vast expanse of waters glittering in the setting sun. While Sandy Lake was large, this was much larger. Winnibigoshish was one of the most prized lakes in the

THE HEADWATERS WAR:
Conflict for the Mississippi Headwaters

northland in spite of the name the Ojibwe had given it, *Wiiniig*, 'filthy water'. That description did not really fit, although the water did have a clouded look. In size, of the headwaters lakes it was second to Leech, but differed by its lack of islands and peninsulas; miles away the distant shore could be seen as a mere haze.

As his canoe entered the lake Big Marten motioned to turn to the right and search for a suitable location for a camp; they would wait until the Cree-Ojibwe war party from the north was in position, which could mean staying hidden for several days. Finding a good camp site would be simple; the shallow tree dotted shoreline providing ample opportunities. Further out on the lake some of the scout canoes that had preceded the flotilla were returning for instructions.

After only a few minutes of paddling Big Marten signaled to pull into shore; here the would make their temporary camp. Ahead the bay they were in opened into the main body of the large lake where they could easily see anyone approaching from the west or south. The canoes immediately began to beach themselves at the selected site, those warriors first ashore heading inland to scout the nearby area for any hostile signs, the later arrivals moving inland to select and prepare the location for a camp away from the shore. It would be a camp without fire; even if the flames were concealed the smoke could be seen or smelled by others miles away.

Big Marten stood on the shore with Bitten-by-the-Loon, who over the years had grown in stature and was now one of Big Marten's lieutenants, and two other of his leading warriors, looking out on the lake that extended for several miles to the south and west. From here most of the main lake body could be watched, making the site safe from attack by water. The short length of the Mississippi connecting Winnibigoshish with Cass Lake to the southwest, about seven miles distant, was a route frequented by the Dakota, but was

THE HEADWATERS WAR:
Conflict for the Mississippi Headwaters

also the route their raiding party would follow. But before he went further runners must be sent to locate the warparty from Rainy Lake. Without their support it would be too risky to proceed to Cass Lake where they could be trapped.

While Leech Lake lay less than five miles to the south of Winnibigoshish, Big Marten had little concern of an attack by land, and any attack from the water would be easily seen. But still, he understood the risk he was now in. A Dakota warparty proceeding down the Leech River from Leech Lake would enter the Mississippi behind them, blocking their return downriver. When passing its outlet to the Mississippi earlier in the day scouts traveled upstream for several miles to examine its condition, and reported the low water at this time of year made it difficult for large war canoes, shallow and clogged with deadfalls. He hoped they were right.

Still, Big Marten was a cautious man; one reason for his success over the years. He had left several scouts and a body of about 100 warriors to block the mouth of the Leech River and give warning if necessary, leaving only 300 for his attack on Leech itself; however, supplemented by the 200 or more expected from Rainy Lake that should be sufficient.

Calling the scouts over, they were instructed to cross over to the outlet of the Mississippi from Cass Lake, then the next day scout all the way to Cass Lake, a distance of less than ten miles. After ensuring the passage was clear they were to take cover and post scouts to give warning of any significant body of Dakota observed. The main Ojibwe body would stay here at their camp, and if the way was clear and once they found the Rainy Lake warparty was in position, they would follow. Then he gave instructions to his warriors to pull the canoes into the tree line, cover them, remove all sign of their arrival from the beach, and post lookouts. They might have to camp here for several days.

THE HEADWATERS WAR:
Conflict for the Mississippi Headwaters

Early the next day, to the west . . . .

The party led by Pale Horse had broken camp just after dawn, having camped on Cass Lake at the outlet of the lake to the Mississippi River. It was still early morning and they were well down the short stretch of the Mississippi linking Cass to Winnibigoshish; the long string of canoes, strung out for over a mile, clogging the narrow passage.

Pale Horse, in the leading canoe, instructed the warriors paddling to stop. Ahead, paddling as fast as they could, came one of their scout canoes, the warrior in front pausing to frantically wave his paddle. In less than a minute he was beside Pale Horse's canoe with his message.

They had encountered Ojibwe, that upon seeing them had turned and paddled rapidly back toward Winnibigoshish. It could only mean the presence of an Ojibwe warparty. Signaling to pick up the pace, the Dakota party surged ahead in pursuit.

Little Man put all his strength into his paddle. In only some ways did the name fit; while short, his shoulders were broad, and he was enormously strong for his size. Behind White Dog, also short and powerfully built, exerted equal effort. While senior of the two, Little Man sat in the front of the canoe, the 'power' position, leaving White Dog to steer. They didn't have to look back; they knew the Dakota canoes were in pursuit, and could only hope the other Ojibwe scouts camped on the river's shore ahead would see them and take cover. But they also knew that, even though the pursuing war canoes had more warriors paddling, still their small, light scout canoe could maintain its lead.

Little Man and White Dog were used to the moves of each other; never in the races they sometimes engaged in had they been beaten, one reason they had been selected by Big Marten as advance scouts. It was the lake ahead they had to worry about; if a headwind

THE HEADWATERS WAR:
Conflict for the Mississippi Headwaters

slowed them on the long seven mile crossing they could be overtaken; a wind that would have more affect on their light birchbark canoe than on the dugouts used by many of the Dakota. They also had to think of where to head; the Ojibwe camp was near the entrance to the Mississippi, but should they go there, or try to lead the pursuing Dakota away? At least they knew they must go in that direction to allow themselves and the pursuers to be seen by the Ojibwe lookouts. They would decide what to do once on the lake and saw how numerous their pursuers were.

It was not long before the large lake loomed ahead, and they shot out from the mouth of the river and turned the canoe to point to the northeast. They were fortunate, the wind was light and from the south; it wouldn't impede their progress. Digging strongly into the water they surged ahead, not bothering to look back. After several minutes, however, Little Man turned his head in an attempt to count their pursuers who were still entering the open water of the lake. More and more Dakota canoes were streaming from the outlet to the lake; mostly the traditional Dakota dugouts, but many the lighter birchbark canoes copied from the Ojibwe. Turning the numbers over in his head he quickly estimated the number of warriors contained in the pursuing canoes. It was a very large party, perhaps twice that of their own, but not so large it couldn't be fought. That settled the question in his mind. He was sure they would be seen by Big Marten while crossing the lake, and if careful they could lead them into a trap.

Little Man thought carefully of their options, and immediately settled on one. He had been to Winnibigoshish with other war parties before, and on one occasion had explored the northern shore. There, less than a mile to the west of the Ojibwe camp, was a narrow outlet leading into a medium sized lake. They would lead the pursuing party there; while they themselves might be trapped, Big Marten would surely

THE HEADWATERS WAR:
Conflict for the Mississippi Headwaters

see what was happening and bring his warriors to box the Dakota in. Turning his head he shouted instructions to White Dog, and the canoe altered its direction slightly and headed for the northern shore.

Little Man blazed with the excitement that always flamed when in a race, but he had to hold himself back. Turning his head for a moment to gauge the pursuit, he slowed his pace slightly. While the smaller Dakota scout canoes were now far in the lead of the main body, still he had confidence in their ability to outpace them. He didn't want to get too far ahead, just stay beyond gun shot range. Little Man was intent upon leading the pursuing Dakota into the ambush.

It wasn't much later when one of the lookouts came running to Big Marten, pointing in excitement. "A Dakota warparty," he cried. "Crossing the lake headed this way."

Big Marten immediately jumped to his feet and ran after the lookout back to the shore, making sure to stay hidden in the tree line. Far out to the southwest he could see small figures on the surface of the water, but his eyes were growing poor. "Tell me," he said, jabbing the excited lookout in the side. "What do you see?"

The lookout covered his eyes, and his mouth worked as he counted to himself. "One canoe in the lead, followed by several small canoes; then maybe 100 large canoes, maybe even 150; several warriors in each."

After a pause. "Not headed here or to the river, headed for the north shore."

Big Marten shook his head in confusion, then smiled. "Yes," he said: "The little lake." Other warriors had been gathering around Big Marten, also watching the canoes far out on the lake. Big Marten gave his instructions: "Prepare for battle, go to your canoes. But stay hidden until my signal."

Soon all the warriors were assembled near their canoes, but Big Marten still gave no signal; he and the lookout still watching the lake where the canoe being

THE HEADWATERS WAR:
Conflict for the Mississippi Headwaters

pursued had now disappeared from view, the flotilla of canoes also beginning to disappear behind the point separating the small lake from Winnibigoshish. When most had entered, Big Marten gave the order to launch their canoes, which were soon in the water with their warriors paddling rapidly toward where the Dakota canoes were fast disappearing.

The distance was short, and in a little over ten minutes the Ojibwe arrived at the mouth of the inlet formed by a narrow point separating the two lakes. Big Marten ordered most of his warriors to beach the canoes on the point and take up positions. The rest he ordered to move into the inlet and wait.

Little Man and White Dog beached their canoe, and seizing their guns jumped ashore, the leading Dakota canoes no more than 200 yards behind. Without pausing they started running as fast as they could into the surrounding forest; but to his surprise Little Man soon discovered they weren't being pursued, the Dakota canoes had stopped offshore and were gathering together, turning to point their prows toward the south. Little Man shouted to White Dog to stop, and from the low hill on which they stood watched to see what would happen next.

Far in the distance, at the inlet to the lake, Little Man could see several canoes sitting still in the water; soon to be joined by more and more. He smiled delightedly and pushed White Dog's shoulder; the trap had been sprung.

Pale Horse sat in his canoe, the paddlers holding it in position as the rest of the warparty gathered nearby. To the south the canoes of the Ojibwe blocking the channel could be clearly seen, but also on the narrow point to the east of the inlet other Ojibwe could be seen moving behind the few trees or the low brush. He wasn't sure what to do; his experience in warfare was largely raiding on horseback or covert thefts of horses, not battles involving canoes, or in pitched land battles either.

85

THE HEADWATERS WAR:
Conflict for the Mississippi Headwaters

Swallowing his pride he called for some of the leaders of the Leech Lake band for their advice.

The two canoes with Makes Fire and Many Kills pulled up next to that of Pale Horse. What he heard was disconcerting. They were certainly trapped and had to fight their way out. Further, he was informed, while they may have numbers greater than did the Ojibwe, still the Ojibwe after seeing the size of the Dakota force had still issued a challenge; which meant it was a large warparty. Making the situation worse the Ojibwe would have guns, which few of them had. If they tried escape through the outlet to the larger lake the guns of the Ojibwe would be deadly. Such a gauntlet could not be attempted without losing most of their party.

Makes Fire and Many Kills advised they quickly head for the base of the point away from where the Ojibwe were gathered and land their warriors there, then attack the Ojibwe and at the same time drag their canoes across to the other side. If successful they could bypass the Ojibwe trap, and again be on the large lake; an additional advantage would be that would place them between the Ojibwe and any retreat back down the Mississippi; they might even be able to trap the Ojibwe if their numbers weren't too great. If the Ojibwe force was too strong, and it looked like they couldn't prevail, they could flee back to Leech Lake. It wouldn't be hard to drag the canoes across the point; at its base it was only about 150 yards across and they would have the protection of the scrub brush with which it was covered.

Pale Horse sat in thought. To flee from the Ojibwe party could not be considered until they discovered its strength. He gave the order to head for the base of the point. He and Many Kills would lead most of the warriors against the Ojibwe, while Makes Fire saw that the canoes were moved across to the big lake. If they found the Ojibwe force much smaller than their own Makes Fire's warriors would then man their canoes to block their escape.

THE HEADWATERS WAR:
Conflict for the Mississippi Headwaters

As soon as Big Martin had seen the Dakota canoes turn and head toward the base of the peninsula he understood their plan, and gave Bitten-by-the-Loon the assignment of stopping the Dakota from portaging across to the large lake. Reinforcements would follow as soon as they were organized.

It would not be easy. While Bitten-by the Loon had over 50 warriors assigned to him, most of the Dakota were headed toward the area he had to defend and he would be vastly outnumbered; it was clear the Dakota warparty was at least twice the size of their own. But even if they couldn't stop the crossing they could punish them badly.

Little Man and White Dog stood watching the unfolding events. Both were experienced enough to be able to predict what the trapped Dakota would do; they had few options. They watched as the Dakota canoes again got underway and paddled at full speed toward the base of point, away from where the Ojibwe were busy piling logs and brush for protection. As soon as they were within a few hundred feet the defending Ojibwe began to fire, but few of the Dakota were hit, the fast moving canoes making the warriors difficult targets. Soon the Dakota reached the sandy shoreline, leaped from their canoes, and ran to the nearest cover; in some cases finding it already occupied by Ojibwe, resulting in fierce hand-to-hand combat. But the Dakota were too numerous for the Ojibwe to withstand and the Ojibwe were gradually pushed back. Once they had cleared the area the Dakota began pulling canoes from the water and dragging them into the brush.

Little Man nodded to himself; as he thought, they would not immediately charge into the Ojibwe fire but first drag the canoes across and determine their strength. Glancing over at White Dog, Little Man smiled: "We should join them."

White Dog just nodded, and the two ran to their beached canoe and pushed off, then climbed in and

THE HEADWATERS WAR:
Conflict for the Mississippi Headwaters

dipped their paddles and drove the canoe toward the outlet.

By the time they reached the outlet the sound of battle further east was almost continuous; the firing of the Ojibwe mixed with the cries of warriors engaged in hand to hand battle. Little Man well understood what must be happening. While the Ojibwe would much rather fight from cover where their guns gave them an advantage, the Dakota could not allow that; they must force hand to hand combat where they would be on an equal footing. It would not be easy for the Ojibwe to withstand the Dakota attack. While their guns could keep the Dakota at bay for a time, once fired it took time to reload; time in which the Dakota could move forward. It would take all Big Marten's skill to keep from being overwhelmed. But then, perhaps the Dakota did not know of their own superiority.

Little Man and White Dog drove their canoe though the outlet into the big lake and then quickly turned toward the shore, covered with beached Ojibwe canoes. They were both wise enough to avoid the chance of being trapped in the little lake again. Leaping ashore they pulled their canoe a few feet up to keep it safe, seized their weapons, and headed at a run eastward toward where the sounds of battle were the greatest; elated by the exhilaration of battle.

Keeping low to avoid stray bullets, Little Man and White Dog soon reached the area where the battle was the fiercest. Warriors of both sides lay hidden behind trees or in the heavy brush, some having found cover behind the many dead logs littering the low peninsula, carried there by flooding of the lake by the spring snow runoff. The firing from the Ojibwe had slowed, the Dakota hidden behind whatever cover they could find making poor targets. In such a situation the bows and arrows of the Dakota were useless, and, except for the few among them who had guns there was little damage they could do to the Ojibwe, who were equally

88

THE HEADWATERS WAR:
Conflict for the Mississippi Headwaters

well hidden.

The lulls in the battle were broken whenever a group of warriors, or sometimes a single warrior, would vent their frustration by charging the enemy, or standing to dare hand to hand combat; a challenge usually accepted by the fired up warriors. On a few occasions others would join until more than a dozen were involved, with the others stopping their firing to watch.

Hours later . . . .

Pale Horse lay next to Many Kills and Makes Fire. Makes Fire had returned after paddling out onto the big lake to get a view of what they faced, and was able to count the beached Ojibwe canoes. While a strong party, the Dakota clearly had numbers on their side; perhaps as many as double. But Makes Fire had learned over the years that the guns of the Ojibwe often made numbers unimportant, and both Many Kills and Makes Fire stressed this in their advice to Pale Horse. Further, they had already learned there was little they could do to dislodge the Ojibwe, each attempt exposing them to Ojibwe fire and leading to unacceptable losses. The losses to the Ojibwe were also large, but still they stood their ground and managed to repel each charge.

When Pale Horse suggested they blockade the Ojibwe and keep them from leaving while they gathered more warriors, it was quickly pointed out most of the available warriors were already here. And even if they attempted such a trap the Ojibwe could slip through in the dark. If they did they might continue west to attack the lightly protected Dakota villages at Leech, or those villages depopulated of most of their warriors could be easy prey to any other Ojibwe or Cree warparty in the area. This was the season when raids from the north could also be expected. Perhaps it was best to break off the battle and return to their villages; they couldn't continue on with such a large war party in their rear, and they could not allow such a large Ojibwe warparty to

THE HEADWATERS WAR:
Conflict for the Mississippi Headwaters

advance to Leech.

Big Marten lay hidden in the underbrush watching the activity where the Dakota had lined up their canoes on the shore. The sun had passed from overhead and started its decline, and it was clear neither side could dislodge the other, and their time was running out; exposed as they were deep in Dakota country. It was also clear neither side could trap the other; all the Dakota canoes having been portaged across to the large lake. Not only that, it looked like the Dakota were beginning to ready their canoes for departure.

Big Martin issued orders not to fire on the departing Dakota. It was much better when the enemy were fewer or unprepared. If the Dakota left first he could claim a victory, although he well knew the purpose of his raid was now in shambles; they could not possibly advance further toward Leech Lake with such a large force in the region, and could never hope to force passage through the short link of the Mississippi to Cass Lake. And what if the Dakota had sent a messenger to Leech Lake telling of their presence? They almost certainly had, and to risk Dakota taking the Leech River to their rear could not be discounted.

As for the expected Cree-Ojibwe warparty from the north? He had still not received news of its whereabouts. He would have to send additional runners to inform them of the situation and that the combined raid was no longer possible.

It wasn't long before the Dakota warriors, after loading their wounded and those of their dead they had been able to retrieve, began to board their canoes and paddle beyond gunshot range, where they waited until all canoes had been launched. Then, both sides shouting taunts at the other, they paddled slowly to the southwest from where they had come.

Big Marten walked slowly along the line where the most intense fighting had taken place. Bodies of both Ojibwe and Dakota lay littered about, sometimes in each

THE HEADWATERS WAR:
Conflict for the Mississippi Headwaters

others arms as they died during their struggles; his warriors busily scalping and stripping of their valuables the dead Dakota, others inspecting the fallen Ojibwe searching for any alive. His own losses, while less that those of the Dakota, were large; perhaps the largest suffered by any of their war parties since the raid on Sandy Lake years earlier. But the size of the Dakota party had been larger than he had ever seen, and if they had succeeded in reaching Sandy Lake his village could have been overwhelmed. At least they had succeeded in stopping that.

A little ahead Big Marten noticed a number of Ojibwe warriors gathered around the body of a fallen Dakota, laughing and pointing. Approaching, the reason for their interest became clear; the warrior had only half his feet, as if sometime in the past much had been lost due to an accident or freezing. One of the Ojibwe warriors handed him one of the beautifully quilled moccasins he had removed from the fallen warrior, discovering the deformity. Big Marten carefully examined the moccasin and found it half filled with moss to make up for the missing part of the foot. As the Ojibwe warrior who had taken the moccasins kneeled to take the scalp of the fallen Dakota, Big Marten thought to himself as he walked away: "A brave man, to fight in such a condition."

A distance away one of the warriors searching for wounded Ojibwe called out, bringing a number of others to his side. After a moment one called out Big Marten's name, and he walked over to see the cause. There, locked in the arms of a dead Dakota, lay Bitten-by-the-Loon, a long gash across his throat. Big Marten shook his head; *Bi-aus-wah* would take this loss hard. Bitten-by-the-Loon had been his oldest son, destined to become chief someday. Well, he thought, he died bravely, motioning for two of the warriors to take Bitten-by-the-Loon's body to his own canoe.

The wounds of the living had been bound, and

THE HEADWATERS WAR:
Conflict for the Mississippi Headwaters

the bodies of the dead transported to the waiting canoes. When that was completed Big Marten and the rest of the Ojibwe boarded their canoes and started on the long trip back to Sandy Lake.

Comment

While other versions exist of how Cut Foot Sioux Lake got its name, all agree it was based on finding a Dakota (*Sioux*) warrior with damaged feet on the narrow peninsula separating Lake Winnibigoshish from what is now know as 'Cut Foot Sioux' Lake. While today, due to the dam at the outlet of Lake Winnibigoshish, parts of the peninsula are largely submerged, at the time the connection to the smaller lake must have been quite narrow.

The plan of the Sandy Lake warparty to meet up with one from Rainy Lake is fictional; or is it? Was the party of Ojibwe and Cree encountered near Big Falls on the Big Fork River, east of the Red Lakes, by the prong of the Dakota heading toward the border lakes intending to join that from Sandy Lake? If they had intended to attack the Leech Lake area that is the route they would have followed.

Also an assumption is that Big Marten led the Ojibwe at the battle. While Warren is silent on the subject of leadership, since at the time Big Marten was its most prominent war chief, it is very unlikely it would have been anyone else leading such a major warparty.

Finding the body after the battle with both feet cut half off by accident or freezing is from Warren, who states "*the lake where this fight took place is known to this day as 'Keesh-ke-sid-a-boin Sa-ga-e-gun, Lake of the cut-foot Dakota.*" While the Dakota left first, leaving the battlefield and many of their dead, it was essentially a draw; both sides returning to their villages.

Later, wearied by the constant harassment by the Ojibwe, the Dakota abandoned their final bastions on the islands of Leech Lake and retreated to the prairie fringe

THE HEADWATERS WAR:
Conflict for the Mississippi Headwaters

near the Red River. Warren states this abandonment was the year of the confrontation at Curt Foot Sioux Lake, and when the well documented Dakota expedition of 1768 (*nearly two decades later*) passed through all these lakes were in Ojibwe hands, and the area of contention in the north had shifted to the boundary between the forests and the prairie to the west, where the Dakota remained strong.

According to Warren the Ojibwe villages that developed on these northern lakes were populated by Ojibwe moving north from Sandy Lake, west from Lake Superior, and south from Rainy Lake. Today they are all contained in the 'Greater Leech Lake' Ojibwe reservation, which combined the contiguous Leech, Winnibigoshish, Cass, and White Oak Point reservations.

That does not say that the Ojibwe moving into the area were unmolested. Initially, even after Leech Lake was abandoned by the Dakota, the Ojibwe villages located there were under constant harassment. As with the Dakota before them, at first the villages were located largely on islands. Even in the late 1700s, when John Baptiste Cadotte led a large trapping and trading expedition from Fond du Lac through Sandy Lake, then up the Crow Wing River to Leech Lake, the Ojibwe villages were still located on islands for protection from marauding prairie Dakota or Nakota.

The war in the far north had become a stalemate, with the Ojibwe of the headwaters lakes harassed by Dakota war parties from the northern tributaries of the Minnesota River and prairie Sioux from and beyond the Red River, a situation that didn't change until the early 1800s with Ojibwe occupation of Ottertail Lake to the southwest and the area of the Long Prairie tributary of the Crow Wing River. Of necessity, the warriors of these villages, subject to frequent attacks from the Dakota and their allies, became some of most warlike of the Ojibwe.

THE HEADWATERS WAR:
Conflict for the Mississippi Headwaters

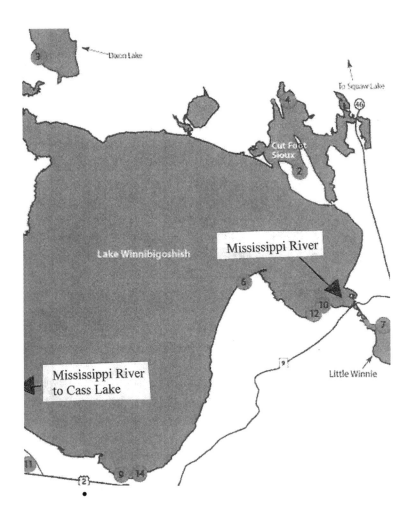

Figure 7: Lakes Winnibigoshish & Cut Foot Sioux*

* The small lake connected to the northeast corner of Lake Winnibigoshish is Cut Foot Sioux Lake.

THE HEADWATERS WAR:
Conflict for the Mississippi Headwaters

CHAPTER 4
CONQUEST OF MILLE LACS

While Warren includes a very 'fanciful' reason for the attack on the Dakota at Mille Lacs Lake, the true reason was more likely that the Ojibwe just wanted to remove a threat, as well as gain that desirable area for themselves. Mille Lacs Lake was exceptional both in size and its abundance of fish and wild rice. But its value to the Dakota was more than just its size and richness; it was *mde waken* (*spirit or mystic lake*), the source of the name of the *M'dewakanton* division of the Dakota, and to them a sacred lake.

While some claim the attack on Mille Lacs originated at the Ojibwe village of LaPointe on Madeline Island in Lake Superior, I have accepted Warren's view that, while warriors were summoned from many Ojibwa villages, including those along the shores of Lake Superior, they gathered at Fond du Lac prior to launching the attack. Since the date commonly assigned, 1750, places it after Big Sandy Lake had been occupied by the Ojibwe, and *Bi-aus-wah* was influential at both Fond du Lac and Sandy Lake, warriors from both those locations would have participated. It also appears to have been after the battle at Cut Foot Sioux Lake.

Kathio, the primary Dakota village on Mille Lacs, was located at the southwest corner of the lake near its Rum River exit, about 50 miles southwest of Big Sandy Lake. The Mississippi, after making a large loop, bypassed the lake about 20 miles to the west. As an 'inland' lake, Mille Lacs' only connection to the Mississippi was the long, twisting Rum River flowing south, entering the Mississippi north of present day Minneapolis. About 20 miles or so to the southeast of Mille Lacs was the Dakota village at Knife Lake, the

THE HEADWATERS WAR:
Conflict for the Mississippi Headwaters

lake from which the name Santee (*Isanyahti, 'people of the knife'; applied to all four Dakota bands*) was derived.

The Dakota villages at Mille Lacs and Knife lakes were dangerously close to Sandy Lake, and allowing such a powerful Dakota presence in the region was an intolerable situation; a warparty from Kathio could reach Sandy Lake in two days by land, with the longer water route of the Rum and Mississippi rivers also available. The key was Kathio; once it was removed the smaller nearby villages, and that at Knife Lake as well, would fall on their own.

November 1749, Fond du Lac . . . .

Earlier in the day *Bi-aus-wah* had arrived from Sandy Lake and gathered the elders and civil and war chiefs of Fond du Lac to discuss a proposal. The Dakota presence in the area near Sandy Lake was increasing, making hunting and dispersal to the smaller lakes in the area for the rice harvest more and more dangerous. At the same time, due to the continuing westward migration of the Ojibwe, population pressure was forcing them to impinge on areas the Dakota considered their territory, leading to increasing skirmishes between competing hunting parties. The situation was becoming intolerable.

Following the battle of Cut Foot Sioux the Dakota of the headwaters lakes of the far north had largely begun abandoning the area and moving west, but Ojibwe settlement that far north was still overly dangerous; although an Ojibwe village had been established at the lake near the rapids of the Pokegama about 20 miles west of Lake Winnibigoshish, and during the fall Ojibwe hunting parties had ranged as far west as Winnibigoshish. *Bi-aus-wah* suggested now was the time to drive the Dakota from Mille Lacs and light their own fires there. Driving the Dakota from their remaining villages on the northern lakes could wait; each year they were becoming fewer.

THE HEADWATERS WAR:
Conflict for the Mississippi Headwaters

Bi-aus-wah reported he had met with the elders at Sandy Lake, and his war chief, Big Marten, had returned after visiting the large La Pointe village to gauge its feelings, and reported many there appeared enthusiastic for such a major campaign. The Dakota of northern and central Wisconsin had been driven south and were now little threat to the La Pointe area, and their support was assured. With their participation the smaller Lake Superior villages would follow.

It was rare that the elders would deny *Bi-aus-wah's* wishes, and in this case they concurred in the wisdom of his proposal. Fond du Lac was becoming crowded with new arrivals, with many slated to move to Sandy Lake with the coming of summer. Additional lands safe for settlement must be obtained, and the area west and southwest of Sandy Lake was the obvious choice, with the large Dakota village at Kathio the key. The Mille Lacs Lake area was a prize they all agreed must become Ojibwe.

The elders unanimously endorsed *Bi-aus-wah's* plan to send his war club, tobacco, and wampum belt of war asking formally for the participation of other Ojibwe villages in the campaign. It would have to be a warparty larger than they had ever raised before, even larger than that for the Sandy Lake raid a decade earlier. The Dakota village of Kathio was exceptionally large, and there were two other smaller villages nearby; perhaps more. The Dakota would have many hundred warriors, and would be fighting to protect their homes and their sacred lake. Not only was the size of Kathio and its satellite villages a problem, they had seen for themselves what formidable fortresses the Dakota earth lodges were.

Early May, 1750 . . . .

It had been a late spring and ice had gone out of some of the smaller lakes only a couple of weeks before, although Lake Superior had been ice free for well over a month. As Big Marten stood watching the last of the

THE HEADWATERS WAR:
Conflict for the Mississippi Headwaters

arrivals the chilling breeze from the lake reached inland and caused him to pull his blanket around him. While the lake was a distance away, here at the higher level of the Fond du Lac village it still had its affect. Below, on the river bank, dozens of large lake canoes were pulled up, with an occasional late arrival still in the process of unloading. Even here the discordant sounds of the village, with its many visitors, made it difficult to concentrate.

Nearly all the warriors from LaPointe and the area of Chequamegon Bay in Wisconsin had arrived. Most were the veterans of many campaigns south into the Dakota regions of Wisconsin, which had been supported by war parties from both Fond du Lac and Sandy Lake. Now they would return the obligation and help cut the head from the snake at Mille Lacs. All day Big Marten had been meeting with the war chiefs of the various bands to ensure each understood exactly what the raid involved, and his plans for the assault. But now was the time for the gathered warriors to fire themselves up for the task ahead.

While in the Sandy Lake raid Big Marten had been a young war chief relegated to a secondary role, his prestige had grown to where even the proud warriors of La Pointe would accept his leadership. Even Long Walker, the primary war chief in the La Pointe area after the veteran Snake Skin had been killed, would accept Big Marten's leadership; news of what the Ojibwe hailed as a victory at Cut Foot Sioux two years before had spread far. Big Marten had finally reached his prime.

Tomorrow, in the hours before dawn, the warparty would start down the well traveled trail to the southern end of Sandy Lake, there to be joined by *Bi-aus-wah* and the Sandy Lake warriors and others from scattered Ojibwe encampments to the north. Days earlier scouts had had been dispatched from Fond du Lac and Sandy Lake to secure the trail and intercept any traffic, and a watch put over those Dakota women taken as

THE HEADWATERS WAR:
Conflict for the Mississippi Headwaters

wives by the Ojibwe whose loyalty might be tested. The trip to Sandy Lake for a warparty was two days, and then two more days from Sandy Lake to Mille Lacs, and during those last two days the risk of encountering Dakota using the trail was high. If they could reach Kathio undiscovered so much the better, but Big Marten was confident he had enough warriors to crush Kathio even if they were warned. It was the very size of Kathio that had caused *Bi-aus-wah* to change from the approach used for the earlier Sandy Lake raid, where the summer gathering time had been selected when its population swelled with visitors. Kathio was simply too large a target; even with its normal population it was a challenge. Something new was required.

Two weeks earlier Big Marten and *Bi-aus-wah* had held long discussions at Sandy Lake, and decided Big Marten was the one to organize the warriors of Fond du Lac and the new arrivals, while *Bi-aus-wah* and the rising young war chief, Bright Forehead, took charge of those at Sandy Lake. While Big Marten had his doubts, *Bi-aus-wah* had decided he himself would accompany this expedition, not wanting to miss such a major campaign even though he was growing old for a warparty. Still, his past fame would provide encouragement to the warriors.

Big Marten well understood the decision of *Bi-aus-wah*, but had his doubts. While still in his mid fifties, and many warriors continued at that age, it had been years since *Bi-aus-wah* himself had taken the war trail. Still, Big Marten did not underestimate the importance of *Bi-aus-wah* as a force in unifying the Ojibwe on this western frontier. He would see that he was well protected by assigning several of the most dependable warriors to watch over him. Watch over him but make sure their task was unknown to *Bi-aus-wah*; he was a proud man.

Long had Big Marten and *Bi-aus-wah* discussed the risks of this campaign, and the outcome was

THE HEADWATERS WAR:
Conflict for the Mississippi Headwaters

anything but certain. While the attacking Ojibwe would outnumber the Dakota, the many earth lodges at Kathio presented a formidable obstacle. Constructed from earth and sod, the lodges could not be burned, and dug into the ground, with holes punched into the walls for firing, they made formidable fortresses. While some similar lodges had been present at Sandy Lake they were few, and with the path to retreat left open only a few had been defended; with the few defended taken by dropping smoldering brush and firing through the smoke holes at the top while Ojibwe forced their way in. Still, that led to losses, and Kathio had many more earth lodges.

Bi-aus-wah was sure the Dakota would not abandon such a major center as Kathio and their sacred lake as they had their Sandy Lake village, and also knew attacking such fortified positions was not something the Ojibwe had experience with. In the face of major casualties some of the assembled bands of Ojibwe warriors might simply withdraw and decide to return home. A better way was needed, but neither *Bi-aus-wah* nor Big Marten had a solution, so the previous fall Big Marten was dispatched to consult with the French traders at Grand Portage, who also had an interest in the Ojibwe continuing their conquest of the fur-rich upper Mississippi. One suggested an approach that perhaps might work; an approach they would adopt.

Mid Morning, three days later . . . .

Big Marten had arrived with the Fond du Lac warriors at the junction where the little used branch to Mille Lacs Lake continued on, and the main trail turned north to Sandy Lake. While the trail to Mille Lacs was not as heavily used as it was when the Dakota controlled the area, still it was in good condition. At the junction Big Marten directed the column of warriors to wait and rest, while he turned up the trail to meet the Sandy Lake contingent. He didn't have far to go; within minutes he met *Bi-aus-wah* and Bright Forehead leading their

THE HEADWATERS WAR:
Conflict for the Mississippi Headwaters

column south, and joined its two leaders without pausing to slow the column. Once at the junction the Sandy Lake warriors halted while those from Fond du Lac reformed. After pausing to consult with a pair of scouts who had returned from the trail ahead, with Big Martin and *Bi-aus-wah* in the lead the combined column was again on the march west.

Late afternoon, two days later . . . .

None of the scouts carried guns; if Dakota were encountered they would have to rely on their bows and arrows or hand to hand combat. All wore Dakota style moccasins and hunting clothing without ornament, and if they met Dakota nothing would show they were Ojibwa until it was too late. Up to this point Lean Dog and Walking Bear had followed the trail while four other scouts traveled overland, two on each side several hundred feet ahead. The pace was set by those traveling on the sides, the underbrush sometimes slowing their advance. The main force lagged a mile or so behind, its speed limited by that of the advance scouts. So far they had been lucky; while they had encountered two Dakota hunters earlier that day, they had been disposed of without difficulty.

Both Lean Dog and Walking Bear, while still in their late twenties, were veterans with long years of experience in serving as advance scouts for war parties, and understood how important caution was. As they neared their destination the advance became slower, until finally Lean Dog stopped and signaled the flanking scouts to return and join him. They were nearing the northwest corner of the lake, and from the high ground where they stood the great sheet of water spread before them before disappearing in the distance; the far side only visible as a darker shade of blue.

This was as far as they dared go on the main trail, and after posting the other scouts by the trail to intercept any traffic, Lean Dog and Walking Bear left

THE HEADWATERS WAR:
Conflict for the Mississippi Headwaters

the path and headed west through the trees and brush to a lesser used route south to the Dakota villages on the southwest corner; a trail located in earlier scouting expeditions. Then a camp for the warparty for the night. With the Dakota villages so close it must be selected with care.

That night . . . .

Where they were camped, in a shallow area bounded by a low ridge on the east, and nearly half a mile west of the trail, silence reigned. The warriors had been organized for the attack planned for the next morning and firm orders given forbidding fires or any unnecessary noise. Additional warriors had also been posted near the trail to intercept any passing Dakota and dispose of them silently; firing guns was forbidden. The passage of so large a party would leave a clear sign, and no word of warning must reach the villages.

Earlier, after the moon had risen, Big Marten had climbed a large white pine on the ridge near where they camped nearly to the top, and in the distance could see not only the big lake itself, but the fires of the Dakota village at Cormorant Point as well. He knew the large village of Kathio lay south of and within sight of the smaller village, but it was beyond his view. Still, by observing the number of fires the size of the Cormorant Point village could be estimated; something to be verified by the scouts dispatched earlier.

First the Cormorant Point village must be overrun, and at the break of dawn Big Marten would lead about a third of the warriors in a surprise attack, while *Bi-aus-wah* and Bright Forehead took the larger group to block any Kathio warriors from coming to its defense. After seeing the size of the Cormorant Point village he didn't expect much opposition; it was doubtful whether, even if all the Dakota living there were present, it could field over a hundred or so warriors; few compared to the number of attacking Ojibwe.

THE HEADWATERS WAR:
Conflict for the Mississippi Headwaters

At first many wanted to make Kathio the first target, which would give them the advantage of surprise; but there were the earth lodges to consider. It was best to see just how effective their French inspired plan for their destruction would be before the attack on much larger Kathio was attempted; if it failed they still had the option of retreat. Cormorant Point would provide the test; if it worked there, it would make taking Kathio certain.

Lean Dog, Walking Bear, and the other scouts with the main party, were preparing for the coming battles. They had just learned they would be held back from the attack on Cormorant Point, and wouldn't fully participate until the assault on Kathio began the following day. At the meeting with Big Marten he had explained how the powder-bombs provided by the French were intended to be used, and that they, with a number of others, would be the ones to drop them on the unsuspecting Dakota when the time came. When they were alone Walking Bear had whispered his concern to Lean Dog; what Big Marten planned was strange and never trued before.

But first they had other things to do. Before they joined the group selected by Big Marten they and several of the other scouts had to scout the defenses of both Cormorant Point and Kathio and watch for any unusual activity, as well as estimating the number of warriors present. To ensure the Dakota wouldn't be warned of their presence by the many dogs in the village they had covered themselves with fresh deerskins to eliminate the man-smell, and rubbed their hands and face with them as well. While the dogs might detect the smell, they were unlikely to bark in response; deer in the area was a common occurrence.

Big Marten sat smiling. When, last fall, he had explained to the white traders at Grand Portage their intent to take Kathio in the spring, the French were delighted; the Dakota had always been difficult and dangerous to trade with, and now trade with them

THE HEADWATERS WAR:
Conflict for the Mississippi Headwaters

through the Ojibwe had stopped. But the French were familiar with the construction of Dakota lodges and well understood that, with the size of Kathio, it would not be easy. The earth lodges were impregnable to gunfire, with most Dakota villages laid out in a pattern allowing the lodges to offer protection to each other. Many thought it would be impossible.

But Big Marten was persistent; he knew the French knew ways of fighting they did not, and had many weapons at their disposal that the Ojibwe lacked. He stayed through the early winter and continued to explore with the French how it could be done. Finally one of the French traders suggested a possible way, a flaw that could be exploited. While the lodges could be a fortress, they could be a trap as well. The sides were easy to climb, and at the top was an opening to allow smoke to escape; but things could be dropped through that hole as well as had been proven with the 'smoky' brush during the Sandy Lake raid. But that had still led to Ojibwe losses, which, with the much larger number of lodges at Kathio would be unacceptable. The French trader suggested that perhaps an explosive could be dropped through the smoke hole that could kill all inside. But how to make such an explosive; loose gunpowder in a bag might just flare up, not explode. And if there was no fire inside? Anyway, once under attack the Dakota would likely extinguish any fire if for no other reason than their own comfort.

So they experimented, constructing a typical Dakota lodge for testing. As predicted loose powder in a bag dropped into the fire below would usually just flare, or if it did explode was likely to fail to kill all the occupants. The same was true if a fuse was used. Then clay pots filled with powder with a fuse was tried, which worked perfectly; in fact the explosion collapsed the lodge completely.

While they now knew clay pots would work, they were bulky and difficult to make and carry; so they

THE HEADWATERS WAR:
Conflict for the Mississippi Headwaters

rebuilt the lodge and continued the experiments. Finally they discovered that if gunpowder was tightly packed into a bark container covered with several layers of deerskin, made stiff by wetting and allowed to dry, and a length of fuse inserted and sealed with clay and pitch, it would explode most of the time. And when it did explode it was as effective as the clay pots, especially if a handful of pebbles was added. Finally a type was developed that almost always exploded. When it was clear it would work, Ojibwe women at Grand Portage were engaged to make enough for the task, with the French, always eager to push their trading and trapping range further west, supplying the gunpowder and lengths of fuse without charge.

With the breakup of the ice on Lake Superior the French had sent one of their large lake canoes manned by a number of half-breed voyageurs to transport the new weapons back to Fond du Lac. Now everything was ready. Each of the warriors in the selected group would hold back from the attack on Cormorant Point, and only enough of the new weapons would be used to gauge their effectiveness, and then only after the battle was almost won. They wanted to surprise the Dakota at Kathio the next day, but still make sure it would work.

The next morning . . . .

The attack on Cormorant Point took the Dakota by surprise, but fighting from the protection of their lodges lasted well into the late morning. Among the defenders was Strikes Many, formerly known as Otter, a proven warrior with a hatred of the Ojibwe that embittered him. Many Sandy Lake survivors had settled here, and now, enraged at this new assault, fought until overwhelmed by the Ojibwe. However, the battle finally ended as the holes made by the Dakota in the occupied lodges were blocked by dirt and sod, and the few remaining Dakota who had not taken refuge were forced to the shoreline, where they took what canoes remained

105

THE HEADWATERS WAR:
Conflict for the Mississippi Headwaters

and swam or paddled to Kathio to the south.

But not all Dakota had fled; some remained in the lodges, and Big Marten gave orders to identify which still contained Dakota and which did not; each containing Dakota to have any remaining holes from which they could fire packed with dirt and sod. Then the Ojibwe leaders gathered while two of the occupied lodges on the north side had powder bombs dropped into their smoke holes. It was even better than expected, the sides of the lodges were blown outward and the tops collapsed. When they dug through the debris they found no one inside had survived. Delighted with the result, Big Marten led his victorious warriors south to join *Bi-aus-wah* and Bright Forehead at Kathio. For now they would leave the occupied lodges undisturbed after placing guards near the entrances. After Kathio had fallen they could easily be eliminated without endangering themselves.

While Cormorant Point had fallen, the encircled village of Kathio dwarfed Cormorant Point in size, and even with their success Big Marten understood taking Kathio would be a much greater undertaking. The encircling Ojibwe had made no attempt to enter, and now, reinforced by Big Marten and the additional warriors, would wait until the next day before making the attempt. As dusk fell the Ojibwe lit their fires and prepared an evening meal, half on guard while the other half rested or celebrated the victory of the day before. There was no longer a need for stealth.

Big Marten, Bright Forehead, *Bi-aus-wah,* and the other leading war chiefs sat much of the evening comparing notes on what they had gleaned from the events of the day, and how best to approach the attack of the following day. Of concern were the number of guns they found the Dakota had, many more than expected, but all were delighted when Big Marten told of their success with powder bombs. Still, the number of earth lodges at Kathio was greater than the number of bombs

THE HEADWATERS WAR:
Conflict for the Mississippi Headwaters

provided by the French. Some might still have to be taken by assault if taken at all.

That evening, at Kathio . . . .

Strikes Many lay in the protection of the brush a distance from Kathio watching the Ojibwe celebrating their Cormorant Point victory. With the warriors arrived from there to reinforce those encircling the village it was clear the Ojibwe substantially outnumbered the Dakota defenders; even with the addition of those few Dakota who made it to Kathio from Cormorant Point. Still, the Dakota continued to be reinforced by Dakota away from the village for the hunt finding their way through the Ojibwe lines. But even with the reinforcements Strikes Many doubted it was enough to raise their numbers to match the Ojibwe.

When the Ojibwe presence was disclosed by the firing from the north the village civil and war chiefs had begun to implement the longstanding plan for defense of the village developed years before when relations with the Ojibwe had broken down. During the day the women and children were sent down the Rum River to the small village on the island in Lake Onamia or even further south. Strikes Many's wife, Evening Star, had not wanted to leave, but she and their year-old son must be protected. He had sent them with his mother Walks Tall, and her husband, his uncle Shadow Walker, to the Lake Onamia village. While Shadow Walker had now joined the elders, everyone must fight, and the former warriors and the youths still not warriors would have to protect the evacuees; at least until the Kathio battle was decided. However, if Kathio fell there was little hope that downriver village could be defended.

But Kathio fall to attackers? Few thought that could ever happen. Kathio had many of the old earthen lodges, arranged to provide mutual defense from attackers, and could field many hundred warriors when all were present; and even during the hunting season the

107

THE HEADWATERS WAR:
Conflict for the Mississippi Headwaters

number was substantial. While, during an attack many warriors would remain outside to fight the intruders, others would retreat to the lodges and fire through holes in the earth walls. Now, the sky was lightened as the village behind him blazed with the burning bark lodges which had been set afire to provide clear fields of fire and deny cover to any attackers. Also, now many Dakota possessed firearms. Yes, Kathio was impregnable, even to a superior force.

Strikes Many felt almost numb; first they had been driven from their Sandy Lake home, and now the enemy had driven them from Cormorant Point. Strikes Many could only shake his head at the complacency the former 'Sandy Lakers' had felt at Cormorant Point. They thought that with Kathio so close the Ojibwe would never dare attack them there, let alone attack Kathio itself. But they were wrong. When the attack on Cormorant Point started, Kathio had been blocked from sending aid by the encircling Ojibwe

Strikes Many was not the Otter of years before. Now a mature warrior in his late twenties he had been on numerous raiding parties against the Ojibwe, was known for fierce hatred of anything Ojibwe, and had the scalps of more than one to prove his prowess. He was gaining a reputation as one of the best of the Dakota warriors, one who would spare none; because of his success in battle he had been given the name 'Strikes Many', and in the struggle that he knew was coming the following day would fight to the last. He only wished Stone Hand, once known as White Bird, was here to fight with him as he had so many times in the past; but he was gone from the village on a hunting trip to the west. Strikes Many had made sure the wife and two small children of Stone Hand had also been sent to safety.

When younger, when both Strikes Many and Stone Hand had both lived at Sandy Lake, Stone Hand had been tall but thin, but suddenly he had begun to grow and fill out, and many said no one had told him to

THE HEADWATERS WAR:
Conflict for the Mississippi Headwaters

stop. Now one of the tallest and strongest warriors in the village it was said he had once killed an Ojibwe warrior with a single blow. That was how he got the name he now bore. Strikes Many was almost the opposite. While of average height, his reflexes and skill with weapons was often spoken of. But in battle the two were inseparable.

Well, Strikes Many had seen enough for now. Lame Bear, the war chief at Kathio, had directed him to select two dozen warriors equipped with guns to guard the canoe landing below the mouth of the Rum River. That was the escape route if needed, and had to be protected. For most of the way to Lake Onamia, where their other village was located, the wide fringe of reeds and swamp, flooded at this time of year, would keep the Ojibwe from coming within easy gunshot. In fact, only a narrow path through the swamp led to where the canoes were stored.

Morning, the next day . . . .

There was no longer a need for stealth. The Dakota knew of their presence, and had spent much of the previous day and night building barricades and preparing their defense. Now that so many of the Dakota had guns, obtained from their trade with the French who had established themselves south of St. Anthony falls or captured from the Ojibwe over the years, the lodges made even more formidable fortresses than before.

Lame Bear, the Kathio war chief, had planned carefully. As soon as the Ojibwe attack at Cormorant Point had begun, and it appeared any attack on Kathio itself would be delayed, a runner had been dispatched to Knife Lake. In addition, with every hour of delay more Dakota warriors returning from the hunt made it through the Ojibwe lines. While Knife Lake at best could field 200 or so warriors, they should be here by late the following day, or the morning the day after at the latest. With them at their back the Ojibwe would have cause to

THE HEADWATERS WAR:
Conflict for the Mississippi Headwaters

fear encirclement so deep in Dakota territory. Time was on their side, and Lame Bear was confident that if the Ojibwe could be held off for just one day they would be forced to withdraw.

Shortly after dawn the Ojibwe began to tighten the net. Foot by foot they worked their way closer until the outer ring of lodges was only a short distance away. Even then any Dakota exposing himself brought a rain of bullets; their friends the French had supplied extra powder and shot for their use, since their own supply would otherwise be soon drained. Much of the land near the village had been cleared for fields making it difficult to approach the well protected Dakota. Now, near the Dakota lodges, the Ojibwe could only advance on hands and knees using whatever cover they could find.

Gradually Ojibwe fire drove the Dakota back, forcing them to retreat to or behind their lodges or to prepared defensive barriers. Still the Ojibwe advanced, and by mid-morning had secured the outer ring of lodges, which were soon neutralized by packing dirt and sod in the firing holes. Now, thought Big Marten, it was time to use the powder bombs.

A short distance from the village the group of about 20 warriors waited in a wooded area. Each carried a sack over their shoulders carrying the gunpowder bombs, and each also carried a slow-burning match cord supplied by the French. Nearby a small fire was kept burning to allow lighting the matches when needed. The firing in the village that had been intense had slackened, and now Big Marten approached and gathered the waiting warriors for last minute instructions. It was time; time to see whether the new French supplied weapons would be as effective as Big Marten hoped..

Using whatever cover he could Lean Dog ran at a crouch toward the village, Walking Bear a short distance behind. Neither carried weapons to impede them except knifes and tomahawks. Reaching the outer ring of lodges, Lean Dog, making sure he wasn't

110

THE HEADWATERS WAR:
Conflict for the Mississippi Headwaters

exposed to fire from other lodges, scrambled to the top, removed a bomb from the sack, and lit it with his match cord; dropping it through the smoke hole before scrambling down.

Lean Dog was halfway up a second lodge before the powder dropped into the first exploded, immobilizing him with the shock. Looking back the sides of the lodge had been thrown to the ground and the top collapsed. Stunned, for several seconds he gazed at the damage, his eyes wide. He had not been among those who saw the experiment on the two lodges the day before, and was shocked at the completeness of the destruction. Similar explosions were occurring in other locations, and confusion reigned as he completed his climb to drop in his second bomb; almost forgetting to light the fuse.

Big Marten stood watching the carnage and the retreat of the confused and dazed Dakota as the Ojibwe swarmed into the village. Most of the Dakota, seeing what was happening to their lodges, abandoned their fortresses, and either retreated to the barriers erected in the center of the village or to the canoe landing and continued the fight; others using lodges as a barrier but afraid to enter. Even after the supply of powder bombs was exhausted the Dakota, having seen their affect, still feared to retreat to the protection the undamaged lodges provided.

The battle continued through the morning and into the afternoon, with the Ojibwe gradually pushing the defending Dakota back until they were forced to either flee along the shore or to the canoe landing. By late afternoon it was largely over, and by the time night fell the village was empty of Dakota except those few still sealed in their lodges, scalps of the fallen Dakota taken, and the village open to looting by the victorious Ojibwe.

For now the few still occupied lodges could be ignored. Big Marten assigned warriors to approach and

THE HEADWATERS WAR:
Conflict for the Mississippi Headwaters

pile sod and dirt over any holes remaining, and seal the entrances as well as possible, then assigned guards to block any attempts to escape. The rest of the warriors were recalled to prepare for the next day for an assault on the one remaining village; that on the island in Lake Onamia where they would find the women and children for the taking. The occupied lodges would be left until later; they weren't a threat.

While the third village was small, it would have been reinforced by those fleeing Kathio, and further its location on an island required access to canoes. The immediate task became to collect any repairable canoes left behind by the Dakota and make necessary repairs. All they needed anyway was to make them able to float a short distance. All night many of his warriors would be busy on that task.

That night . . . .

Bright Forehead had finally reported back on the success of his assignment, which was to block as many from reaching the village on Lake Onamia as possible and blockade the exit from the lake as well. The report hadn't been good; the Rum River, flooded at this time of year, passed through marshes and swamps all the way to Lake Onamia and was difficult to block; the reed-lined shoreline making approach impossible along much of its length. The exit from the lake wasn't much better. While, when they had found dry land near enough his warriors had made the retreating Dakota pay a heavy toll, still most had succeeded in making their way past. Still others, rather than run the gauntlet, had just retreated down the shore of Mille Lacs and waited for dark before making an overland attempt. The bright side was that the island was near the shore, and even with the river flooded was easy to reach with only a short swim. They didn't know how many managed to make it, but Bright Forehead thought it could be several hundred.

Tomorrow would not be easy, the flooded

112

THE HEADWATERS WAR:
Conflict for the Mississippi Headwaters

marshes and swamps along most of the shore of lake Onamia making an approach difficult. Yes, it would be more difficult than he had anticipated; they might even have to cut back the dense reed cover to prepare a place to assemble canoes for an assault. But still Big Marten was exhilarated with emotion, something unusual for him. He had found the way to drive the Dakota from their center of power, their sacred lake; now he would completely drive those remaining away or kill them. This would be a campaign talked of around the campfires of the *Anishnaabe* for generations.

Earlier he and Long Walker, the La Pointe war chief, had met with *Bi-aus-wah* for further instructions. *Bi-aus-wah* had made clear the Dakota still holding out in their lodges, both at Cormorant Point and Kathio, be left alone for now. The number was small, and they were no longer a problem; only those who continued to fire on the Ojibwe were to be rooted out. He did not want more Ojibwe casualties than necessary. Later they could decide what to do about the trapped Dakota.

Big Marten knew *Bi-aus-wah* well, and while he hadn't said so in the meeting just ended, he knew *Bi-aus-wah* was as likely as not to let the trapped Dakota leave unharmed. After the meeting he and Long Walker had stayed and talked for a long time about how to satisfy *Bi-aus-wah* and control their own warriors. Even if instructed not to molest the trapped Dakota, controlling their own warriors was not a simple problem and many might disobey their orders. In celebrating their victory some, to show their bravery in the face of taunting of fellow warriors, might enter the lodges to engage the trapped Dakota in hand-to-hand combat. And if the Dakota were allowed to leave the fired up warriors were still likely to kill many; if so, there was little they could do to stop them. While they couldn't completely stop such foolish acts, they would at least try to hold their warriors in check as much as possible.

THE HEADWATERS WAR:
Conflict for the Mississippi Headwaters

Early the next morning . . . .

Strikes Many had been one of the last to arrive at the Lake Onamia village, having found it necessary to cross the marshes from Mille Lacs on foot. There he found his wife and son in a lodge shared with Shadow Walker and his mother Walks Tall. Lame Bear, the Kathio war chief, had arrived earlier and taken charge of the defense of the village.

Strikes Many sat with Shadow Walker and Stone Hand, who had finally returned. All were apprehensive about the attack they knew was coming. At Kathio they thought they could depend on the protection of their earth lodges, but that hope had now disappeared. Here they could not even depend on that protection, the island's elevation too low for earth lodges; if dug into the ground they soon filled with water; and even if not could still be damaged by the frequent spring floods. They had only bark covered lodges that provided little protection. To make the matter worse much of their powder was exhausted, with much of what remained wet from swimming or crossing the marshes.

Already, along the shore, well within gunfire range, the Ojibwe gathered, and a distance away those canoes they had succeeded in repairing were bringing even more. While greatly outnumbered and lacking good cover all they could do was fortify the village to the extent possible. Before the Ojibwe prevailed they would pay a heavy price.

At the same time, on the shore . . . .

Bi-aus-wah stood observing the island a short distance away, at his side Big Marten, Bright Forehead, and Long Walker. During the dark of night scouts had tested the water depth and reported back that most of the way was over a man's head, meaning they could approach only by swimming or canoe. Both would expose the Ojibwe to casualties.

THE HEADWATERS WAR:
Conflict for the Mississippi Headwaters

Luckily the French traders had provided all the gunpowder and shot they needed, and except for the barriers the Dakota had erected the flat island gave little protection. The Ojibwe had also managed to repair enough canoes that they could land warriors on the island if they could keep the Dakota behind their barriers long enough; which they were sure they could do by subjecting the Dakota to heavy gunfire from shore. But one other thing *Bi-aus-wah* found of interest which he chose not to bring to the attention of Big Marten or Long Walker. The Dakota had dragged all their canoes to the center of the island and erected earth barriers for their protection. Why spend so much effort protecting their canoes, many of which were wooden dugouts that could better be used stacked near the shore for a defensive barrier? Unless they planned to abandon the island later.

Bi-aus-wah had thought long about this; but for now kept his thoughts to himself. When dark fell the Dakota would attempt to escape down the Rum, and with the high water there would be little they could do to block the escape; and *Bi-aus-wah* was not sure he even wanted to.

Bi-aus-wah had to think this through. He knew Big Marten and Long Walker, and most of the warriors as well, wanted to completely destroy the Dakota, leaving none to escape. But is that really what was best for his people? The Dakota were powerful, and *Bi-aus-wah* knew neither side could completely destroy the other; in the future they might want to again live side by side with them as neighbors. Further, he knew this lake was the sacred center of the largest branch of the Dakota, the *M'dewakanton*, and they would not give it up lightly. Was it best for the long term, when the Ojibwe and Dakota might again be at peace, that the Ojibwe showed a gesture the Dakota would understand?

Yes, he had to think this through. The number of Dakota facing them was large, and before they were subdued Ojibwe casualties would be high. He would

115

THE HEADWATERS WAR:
Conflict for the Mississippi Headwaters

wait and see how today's attack went before deciding. If he decided not to try to block the Dakota he knew he would have difficulty with Big Marten and Long Walker; Big Marten he could handle, but Long Walker was used to going his own way.

Dusk, on the island . . . .

Strikes Many and Stone Hand lay behind the low sand barrier watching the retreating Ojibwe. All day the battle had raged under constant gunfire from the shore which they were unable to return. The Ojibwe had managed to land over 200 warriors on the island's shore where they continued their attempt to advance to the lodges. But whenever they tried they were stopped, either by what few guns the Dakota could still provide powder for or with arrows; and finally hand-to-had combat. The casualties had been high, with Stone Hand badly wounded. Not that it stopped Stone Hand from continuing to fight. Now, with night approaching, the entrenched Ojibwe were evacuating by swimming back to the mainland.

The Dakota had no reason to expect a night attack. The Ojibwe would think they were trapped, and could renew their attack in the morning; but not if Lame Bear's plan was successful. Lame Bear had decided their only hope was to flee down the Rum, and in preparation had caused earth barriers to be erected to protect the canoes stacked in the center of the village. There were enough undamaged to hold the wounded, children, and those unable to make the journey by foot; but the healthy women, older children, and those warriors not needed to handle the canoes would have to swim to the south shore and escape cross county. The south shore was swampy, and few Ojibwe would be there to oppose them. Strikes Many and Stone Hand would be among the last to leave, both assigned to the rear guard.

THE HEADWATERS WAR:
Conflict for the Mississippi Headwaters

After dark, on the mainland . . . .

Bi-aus-wah's face was grim. Rarely had he been challenged as Long Walker had challenged him; and it was clear Big Marten also was not happy.

Bi-aus-wah had decided to withdraw the Ojibwe on guard near the Rum outlet and allow the Dakota to escape. Not that they could have stopped them all even if they wished; the swampy land near the outlet making it difficult to approach. Further, any Ojibwe approaching near enough to the river to be effective would be exposed and up their waist in water.

While *Bi-aus-wah* found it hard to contain his anger, he well understood the drive of younger warriors to take revenge on the enemy; in his younger days he had often felt the same blood lust in his wars upon the Fox. But now his responsibilities were broader; he must also think of the long term for those who had followed him to this new land.

From the counts of the dead at Cormorant Point and Kathio, and from his observation of today's battle, he was confident no more than half the Dakota warriors of the three villages remained. And among the Ojibwe? At least a quarter were dead or wounded, and killing more Dakota would not bring them back. *Bi-aus-wah* was also confident that if allowed to escape now the Dakota would understand the gesture. In the future, when there was again peace, the gesture would be remembered; just as allowing survivors to escape from Sandy Lake was remembered.

But Long Walker was still a problem. He had threatened to take his own La Pointe warriors to the Rum River outlet and block the retreat; something he had every right to do. *Bi-aus-wah* shook his head; Long Walker should value the lives of the warriors placed in his hands more highly. After the meeting he had met again with Big Marten and been given his assurance that, even though he agreed with Long Walker, he would try to hold his warriors back.

THE HEADWATERS WAR:
Conflict for the Mississippi Headwaters

Comment . . . .

In describing the battle for Mille Lacs I have taken many liberties; the first is that the attack originated at Sandy Lake and Fond du Lac, while some credit it to the Lake Superior or Saint Croix Ojibwe. Additionally, including French assistance to the Ojibwe is an assumption which I consider likely.

An example of where I have changed or modified the story Warren tells is the bags of powder dropped through the 'smoke holes' of the earth lodges. Warren says simply that bags of gunpowder were dropped into the smoke holes at the top of the lodges, which then exploded from the fire kept burning. This might work if the fire were indeed kept burning, but in milder weather and containing defending warriors there would be no reason to maintain a fire, and in fact it would be an inconvenience. It is also doubtful whether a bag of loose powder dropped into a fire would explode or just flare, although I chose not to experiment. Therefore I altered the approach to something I considered more feasible.

Equally a figment of my imagination is the decision of *Bi-aus-wah* to allow the Dakota to escape and his general attitude, although later some of the Dakota were allowed to stay in the area if they integrated into the Ojibwe bands; many of whom did.

The participants in the battle itself are also merely 'assumed', since the record lacks the names of the participants. However, *Bi-aus-wah*, Big Marten, and Bright Forehead were prominent at Sandy Lake at or near the time, and it is likely they participated.

The Dakota succeeded in their escape and later established a village on the Rum River near its confluence with the Mississippi, at about that time also abandoning their village at Knife Lake. Their Rum River village became the only major Dakota village remaining east of the Mississippi and north of St. Anthony Falls in

THE HEADWATERS WAR:
Conflict for the Mississippi Headwaters

present day Minneapolis. However, while for a time the Rum River village was a major powerbase of the *M'dewakanton* band of the Dakota, it was not to last. As to Mille Lacs Lake itself? With time the Ojibwe built villages near the site of Kathio, primarily on the south shore, but it never became the large 'center of power' for the Ojibwe that Kathio had been for the Dakota.

However, the Dakota never really left Mille Lacs Lake. To them the lake was sacred, and local legend says that at a peace council in 1750 or shortly thereafter at Mozomanie Point on the south shore the Ojibwe and many of the former *M'dewakanton* Dakota residents agreed to sharing of the lake. The *M'dewakanton* wanting to remain would be assimilated into the Ojibwe tribe, and in return the Ojibwe who wanted to live at Mille Lacs agreed to adopt many of the Dakota rituals concerning the lake.

The above is legend, but it, or something similar, almost certainly happened; a 'mixed' band did develop at Mille Lacs Lake, which later may have eased relations. It is a matter of record that Chief Shakopee II was the son of an Ojibwe Chief named Yellow Head adopted by Shakopee I, and also that there was a Chief Yellow Head at Mille Lacs at the time. While there were several Chief Yellow Heads among the Ojibwe, was Shakopee II the son of the Chief Yellow Head at Mille Lacs, and if so why this adoption? Shakopee I had many sons, or 'had' many; six from the first pregnancy of his first wife alone. Possibly all had died, but perhaps the adoption and naming the adopted son the heir was part of some agreement.

In recognition of these 'assimilated' Dakota, the Ojibwe added two totems to their clan system; the Wolf and Merman (*half fish, half man*). To this day the Mille Lacs Band is a 'mixed' band, serving as a link between the two nations; and the Wolf totem is one of the largest totems of the Mille Lacs Lake Ojibwe.

THE HEADWATERS WAR:
Conflict for the Mississippi Headwaters

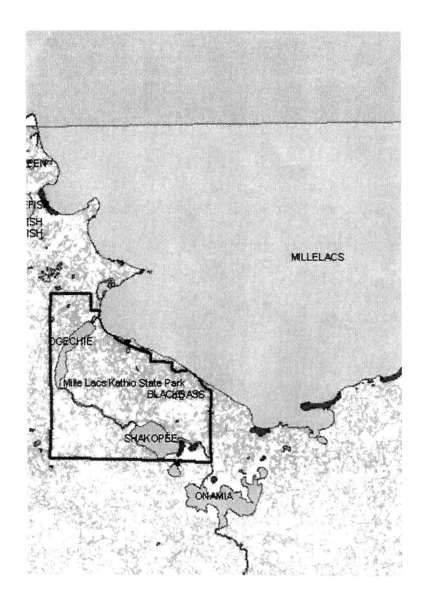

Figure 8: Kathio Area of Mille Lacs Lake

THE HEADWATERS WAR:
Conflict for the Mississippi Headwaters

CHAPTER 5
DAKOTA CAMPAIGN OF 1768

With their loss of Sandy Lake, the headwaters lakes of Leech, Cass and Winnibigoshish, and finally Mille Lacs, the Dakota sought revenge. Their counterattack launched from Leech Lake years earlier had failed, but undeterred a final major assault was planned for 1768; this time mounted from the Dakota villages on the Rum, Minnesota, and the Mississippi river below the mouth of the Minnesota. It would involve all the bands of the Dakota, with the goal of destroying the Ojibwe bastion at Sandy Lake and reclaiming that country for the Dakota.

Even following Ojibwe occupation of Mille Lacs and the northern lakes Sandy Lake retained its original significance, dominating trade routes to the east and controlling traffic on the Mississippi. It was from there that many of the Ojibwe campaigns against the Dakota had originated, and it became the prime target of reprisals. If the Dakota could regain control of Sandy Lake it could endanger the Ojibwe advances to both the Mille Lacs and headwaters areas.

The attack was planned for late August or September, the season for harvesting wild rice, when many of the Ojibwe would be dispersed into family groups for the harvest, making it difficult to gather a large enough force to stop a large, fast moving warparty. This was essential, because they planned a roundabout route that they hoped would find their target unprepared.

All four bands of the Dakota united for the purpose and promised their best warriors. As a result, in late August of 1768 one of the largest Dakota warparties in memory gathered near St Anthony Falls in present day Minneapolis, a day's paddle south of the

THE HEADWATERS WAR:
Conflict for the Mississippi Headwaters

Mississippi-Rum River junction. The express purpose was to destroy the Ojibwe at Sandy Lake and force an evacuation of that area, leaving it again open for Dakota occupation (*Warren says 400-500 Dakota warriors participated, Doan Robinson, in his 'History of the Dakota or Sioux Indians', says the Sioux claimed 2-3 times that number*).

When the Dakota had been forced to evacuate Sandy Lake nearly three decades earlier, in addition to being caught by surprise by the Ojibwe raid, they had few firearms to match those of the Ojibwe. However, in the intervening years most of that imbalance had been removed through trade with French traders near the Mississippi-Minnesota river junction or as war booty from the Ojibwe. Further, while the Ojibwe village at Sandy Lake was large, it could not match the number of Dakota in the war party, and would be further diminished by families already disbursed to the wild rice camps. Now the advantage lay with the Dakota.

The biggest problem was how to reach Sandy Lake undiscovered. The direct route up the Mississippi, the normal route to Sandy Lake, required passing through country heavily traveled by the Ojibwe, and if the expedition were discovered the Ojibwe could combine their forces from Sandy, Mille Lacs, and Knife lakes and put the entire expedition at risk. Even if not in time to help repel the attack, warriors from those other villages could block return down the Mississippi. Subterfuge was called for.

The Dakota warparty reached Sandy Lake and a major battle ensued, which, while the Ojibwe succeeded in repelling the attack, resulted in the Dakota taking a large number of Ojibwe women captives. But on their return the Dakota were ambushed by a much smaller Ojibwe warparty returning from raiding to the south, resulting in the decisive Battle of the Crow Wing River; a battle that resulted in a major Dakota defeat.

THE HEADWATERS WAR:
Conflict for the Mississippi Headwaters

Early September, 1768, St. Anthony Falls . . . .

Strikes Many, the war chief of the *M'dewakanton* Rum River village, sat with Falls Down, Many Bears, and Walker, primary war chiefs of the other bands of the Dakota, as well as those of the other *M'dewakanton* villages. Never before had the warriors of all four bands collected together in such numbers to strike a common target, and it had taken months of preparation by Strikes Many to convince the other war and civil chiefs, and the important elders as well, that the goal could be achieved. But he had succeeded. Now their hundreds of warriors sat around the fires, drums beating as ceremonial dancing continued, the warriors recounting their many achievements, and boasting of what they would now achieve on this raid as well. Supplies for the journey had been collected and stored near the canoes, which had all been portaged above the falls and pulled up on the shore, where other warriors were completing the loading and final preparations.

It had taken long discussions among the war chiefs before agreement was reached on the plan proposed by Strikes Many. In the past when they had launched their smaller strikes on the Sandy, Knife, or Mille Lacs lakes Ojibwe, they had usually gone overland from their Rum River village or stored their canoes in the contested territory somewhere below the mouth of the Elk River, about 50 miles south of Mille Lacs, and proceeded the rest of the way by land.

Now Strikes Many had proposed a daring plan that was a new thought the others had not considered. The war chiefs were intrigued by the plan of Strikes Many; he had proposed using the Crow Wing River and heading west, away from Sandy Lake, and then north through the string of lakes all the way to Leech Lake. Then, proceeding north to Cass lake and east through Winnibigoshish they would again find the Mississippi, which they could follow south and east to Sandy Lake. The Crow Wing and its tributaries lay west of the

THE HEADWATERS WAR:
Conflict for the Mississippi Headwaters

Mississippi, and while year round occupation of the eastern area near its entry into the Mississippi was too dangerous, it was still claimed by the Dakota as their hunting ground.

While the Crow Wing had been used for a few raids further to the northwest, using it as a circular route to create a deception was new. True, they might encounter Ojibwe on such a circular route, but even if the villages of the headwaters lakes were warned they would not think Sandy Lake was the target, but gather their warriors for their own defense. Besides, none of the northern villages were large enough to attack such a large party as it passed through, and once the passage was complete they would be blocked from sending warning downriver. All agreed the circular route Strikes Many had proposed was the best route; perhaps the only way to catch Sandy Lake unprepared.

The other assembled war chiefs grinned at each other at the ease with which they could pick off isolated groups they might encounter on the way. Killing Ojibwe, or capture of their women, was their interest; they lacked the smoldering rage against the Sandy Lake band that had embittered Strikes Many. For the western bands their grudge was against the Leech Lake Ojibwe not those at distant Sandy Lake. Still, his plan pleased all; easy pickings in the north, followed by Strikes Many's wish to extinguish the Sandy Lake Ojibwe band. Then the straight and fast return passage down the Mississippi, allowing them to bring their captives and loot without complicating portages. Sandy Lake would not even be able to send word to Mille Lacs or Knife lakes in time for them to arrange an ambush downriver. It was good.

The reason for Strikes Many's hatred of the Sandy Lake Ojibwe was well known. Driven from his Sandy Lake home, then driven from Mille Lacs, now the aggressive Sandy Lake Ojibwe had stepped up their raids near his new home on the Rum. Soon they would claim that area as well.

THE HEADWATERS WAR:
Conflict for the Mississippi Headwaters

The Next Morning . . . .

By sunup the beached canoes were pushing off from shore and organizing themselves into the four groups to be led by their respective primary war chiefs. First in line was Strikes Many with his *Mdewakanton,* then the warriors of the other three Dakota branches.

As the warparty began its long journey upriver a few canoes detached themselves from the advance group and paddled rapidly ahead, soon disappearing in the distance. These were the advance scouts, dressed in clothing typical of Ojibwe hunters, with light and fast birch bark canoes of the type favored by the Ojibwe. They would ensure the river was clear of Ojibwe, and even if sighted would only be thought to be a small Ojibwe hunting party. Once the scout canoes disappeared from sight the first section of the flotilla of canoes quickened its pace, the other sections following. Soon all had disappeared from the view of those gathered on the shore watching their departure.

Three Days Later . . . .

Dark was approaching as the last of the canoes beached themselves on the sandy shoreline opposite the mouth of the Crow Wing River, the advance scouts having arrived nearly two hours earlier. The country they were now in was mostly a buffer between the Ojibwe and the Dakota, but still hunting parties of both tribes were not unusual.

In previous days, as they had moved north, the advance scouts had met occasional small parties heading to the south, but they had all been parties of Dakota hunters; it wasn't until this morning that they had encountered a single canoe with several Ojibwe, who, thinking they were also Ojibwe had been easily disposed of. Once on the Crow Wing concern with discovery would be less; by tomorrow night they would have left

THE HEADWATERS WAR:
Conflict for the Mississippi Headwaters

the river and be across Gull Lake, and only then would they expect to encounter Ojibwe who, even if they managed to escape, would think they were moving against the villages on Leech, Cass, and Winnibigoshish.

Strikes Many watched from where he sat with Little Bear and several of his other warriors as the occupants of the final canoes found a place. As soon as the evening meal was ended, and any necessary repairs to the canoes made, it was time to sleep; it had been a long day, and tomorrow would start before sunup.

Later, after most of the warriors were already asleep, Strikes Many sat leaning against the trunk of a tree thinking. In all the years he had longed for revenge he often thought this day would never come; many of the Dakota becoming complacent in their homes on the Rum and further south. It was only by his constant nagging of the elders and chiefs of the other bands, as well as of his own *Mdewakanton,* that finally they had agreed to make one final effort to take back the Sandy Lake area, key to the trade routes to the north, south and east. Sandy Lake would again be his home, or he would die in the attempt.

Next day . . . .

Propelled by the powerful strokes of Beaver House and Prairie Dog the canoe glided quietly upstream, the only sound the 'dip' of the paddles and the 'shushing' sound of the parted waters. The string of canoes far behind could not be seen, but Beaver House knew it would appear as a never ending stream; only the canoes of the other scouts were visible. It was still early, and by mid-day they should reach Gull Lake; then the long journey up the lake to the first portage. They had to move fast if they expected to reach the portage before nightfall, but Falling Bear was a big help. He had traveled this route many times when his home had been on Leech Lake. He said it could be done, so it could.

As the most experienced, Prairie Dog kneeled in the rear, with the younger Beaver House in front. In the

THE HEADWATERS WAR:
Conflict for the Mississippi Headwaters

middle of the canoe, cradling a primed and ready rifle, the ever watchful Falling Bear sat scanning the shore for any sign of movement. Only minutes before they had turned from the Crow Wing and entered the Gull River, the small tributary entering from the north. The Gull was barely thirty feet in width and at this season shallow and cluttered with sandbars and deadheads, with the current slow and sluggish. Beaver House's attention was on the water ahead, looking for anything that could pierce the thin skin of the canoe.

Both Beaver House and Prairie Dog were young warriors, Beaver House only 19 and Prairie Dog in his early 20s, and the two had been selected for the lead canoe because of their strength and skill with a canoe. Falling Bear, an experienced warrior in his mid 40s and a veteran of many battles with the Ojibwe, knew what to look for along the route, and how to react if they encountered Ojibwe. Only Falling Bear was armed with a rifle, one he had taken from an Ojibwe years before.

The imbalance in weapons of years past had largely been remedied. Now most of the older warriors had managed to obtain rifles either from the enemy or from the traders, but powder and ball was always in short supply and had to be carefully conserved. The French traders had mostly left following the peace between the French and their British enemies, who they heard now claimed to own this country. But if they did, their traders had not as yet arrived.

Prairie Dog still felt the guilt he felt at the tears his young wife had shed as he left. He and Young Grass had been married less than a month, and she was fearful because of a dream he would never return; and for the Dakota the dream life was important. It was her dream, not his, but even if he had also dreamt the dream he could not stay behind. Sandy Lake had once been theirs and the other young warriors of his village were going. He would be shamed to stay behind with the women.

Falling Bear was well familiar with this area and

THE HEADWATERS WAR:
Conflict for the Mississippi Headwaters

the route they followed to the north, which is one reason he was in the lead canoe. This would not be the first time he had been part of a warparty targeting Sandy Lake. As a young warrior he had lived with his people on Leech Lake far to the north before being driven out by the attacking Ojibwe, and as a young warrior had been part of the Dakota force encountering the Ojibwe at Lake Winnibigoshish. Before that his family had lived at Sandy Lake where he had been a friend of Otter, now the Strikes Many who led the war party. His case was similar to that of most of the older warriors among the *Mdewakanton* in the force; they had been driven from their former homes and thirsted for revenge.

The sun had passed its zenith when they finally arrived at Gull Lake. Their instructions were to cross the lake to the northern end and secure the first portage. While a long day, according to Falling Bear they should easily be able to reach and scout the portage before the sun left the sky. The long string of canoes behind would have time to unload before dark, rest for the night, and complete the portage before sunrise.

Falling Bear was right; but then it seemed to Beaver House he was always right. The sun was still well over the horizon when the portage was sighted, with Prairie Dog altering direction toward the landing. Falling Bear had said this particular portage was about two miles, and after they unloaded the canoe Beaver House and Prairie Dog hoisted it to their shoulders and quickly started up the trail, Falling Bear in the lead his gun at the ready. Since the area around the landing was too small to hold all the canoes at once, or accommodate such a large party, it would have to spread out over the entire length of the portage for the night.

It was nearly dark before the last of the canoes of the main party arrived, many waiting offshore while the earlier arrivals hoisted their loads for the portage. It would be well after dark before the last could land and move to where they could spend the night. So far no

THE HEADWATERS WAR:
Conflict for the Mississippi Headwaters

Ojibwe had been sighted other than the single canoe encountered the day before, but after today they would have to be constantly cautious of encountering Ojibwe rice harvesting groups.

Two days later, just before sunset . . . .

Beaver House, Prairie Dog, and Falling Bear lay in the brush at the lake's edge gazing at the huge sheet of water spread out before them. Neither Beaver House nor Prairie Dog had ever seen a body of water so immense; they could hardly see the far shore, a mere hazy line. Where they crouched was east of the peninsula that separated the portage from the main body of water, but Falling Bear had wanted to again see the lake where he had spent his younger years, and both Beaver House and Prairie Dog were anxious to see the famous lake for themselves. On the western side of the peninsula the warparty was quietly preparing their canoes, isolated from view from the main body of water. As soon as night fell the canoes would be carried to the landing for the long night journey. This had been perhaps the most dangerous leg on their journey; so near the villages of Leech Lake they had encountered occasional Ojibwe parties heading for their ricing camps, but luckily, dressed as Ojibwe themselves, the advance scouts had been able to dispose of them before they could flee.

The two day trip from Gull Lake had been eventful. On the first day they encountered a family harvesting wild rice and had killed all except one small boy that Falling Bear kept for later adoption. Then, just yesterday they had encountered a second couple, which had paddled for shore and beached their canoe, escaping into the forest. They had, however, found their camp, and there discovered three small boys. When Strikes Many arrived later he was not pleased that captives had been kept, even small boys suitable for adoption. Not wishing to burden the warparty, he ordered all killed, including the young boy captured earlier.

THE HEADWATERS WAR:
Conflict for the Mississippi Headwaters

During the previous night Strikes Many had taken the scouts aside and explained what he expected over the next few days. Tonight, as they crossed the lake, they should be able to escape detection, but even if detected it would only be assumed they were headed for Cass Lake to raid villages there or on Winnibigoshish. Once across Leech they would start on the portage to Cass Lake, arriving late the next day. Then, if they remained undiscovered, time to repair damage to the canoes and a short rest. The following day they would start well before dawn and both Cass and Winnibigoshish would be crossed, and then without rest down the Mississippi to the mouth of the Leech River, which they should be able to reach before sunset.

Not that Strikes Many was concerned about danger from the Ojibwe of these northern lakes; even combined they wouldn't dare challenge so large a force directly, but still they could pose a problem along portages or on the narrow, winding river below Winnibigoshish. In any case, the Ojibwe would be intent on protecting their own villages, not in attacking the passing warparty. Only after they crossed Winnibigoshish would the Ojibwe realize their villages weren't the target, but by nightfall they would have blocked the river to the south, even the shortcut from Leech Lake by way of the Leech River; the last opportunity of the Ojibwe of the headwaters lakes to send a warning to Sandy Lake would be blocked.

Still, there was danger below Winnibigoshish, with the Mississippi narrow and winding, making passing canoes an easy target; even as far south as Sandy Lake the river was no more than 100 feet wide, usually much less. They could not allow themselves to be trapped here in the north, caught between the headwater's Ojibwe and those at Sandy Lake and Mille Lacs. After a night's rest at the mouth of the Leech River they would travel with only brief rests all the way to the portage around the Pokegama rapids; a short, easy

THE HEADWATERS WAR:
Conflict for the Mississippi Headwaters

portage, it was the last remaining portage other that the portage from the Mississippi to Sandy Lake itself. However, an Ojibwe village was located just to the south at Lake Pokegama, and from there a runner could reach Sandy Lake in a day and a night; so from there they would travel nonstop.

Two days later . . . .

The shore of the Mississippi was covered with canoes, some also beached up the Leech River beyond its mouth. Those not engaged in canoe repair were lying around trying to get some rest after the long day's travel all the way from the Leech-Cass portage. Many of the Ojibwe style birch bark canoes used by the scouts and adopted by a few of the other Dakota had small cuts or tears from obstacles encountered in the shallow lakes and streams they had navigated in previous days, and with the light remaining some of the temporary repairs made previously were being made permanent.

However, most of the Dakota canoes were undamaged. Birch trees were rare in the Dakota homelands in southern Minnesota, so most were the traditional wooden dugouts made from a hollowed-out tree trunk. Tonight would be only a short rest, only until the first-light of morning made travel down the narrow, twisting river possible. Traveling at night, especially at this time of low water combined with the new moon, was not an option.

Early-morning, two days later . . . .

Beaver House kept up the rapid pace. The entire flotilla was running late; as Falling Bear had predicted the confusing and twisting river below the mouth of the Leech River, with its many dead end channels, had led to some wrong turns. That first day they had travelled only half the distance they had hoped and been forced to make a night camp when cloud cover reduced visibility

THE HEADWATERS WAR:
Conflict for the Mississippi Headwaters

to nearly zero. Today they had been traveling from before dawn with only a brief rest, but with the river confined to a single channel after leaving the swampy country to the west were able to pick up the pace. Ahead the sound of the rapids of the Pokegama could be heard. The two other canoes that accompanied their own were only now again coming into view, having earlier gone after a family they had encountered and fallen behind.

Far ahead on the left bank Beaver House thought he detected movement, and looking carefully could make out, on the landing leading to the portage, a canoe being lifted by two persons about to cross. He called to Falling Bear and Prairie Dog and pointed; it could only be a pair of Ojibwe. Beaver House increased speed as Prairie Dog altered course toward the portage, Falling Bear checking the priming of his rifle. Since they were using Ojibwe style canoes, and wore normal Ojibwe hunting dress, hopefully those ahead would not recognize them as Dakota; but that was a risk they couldn't take. Within minutes they arrived at the portage, with Falling Bear running up the path ahead while Beaver House and Prairie Dog lifted the canoe and headed on as fast as they could trot. One of the two canoes behind had also picked up speed and headed for the portage, the other turning to take a warning to the fleet of canoes behind, still out of sight.

The portage was short and level, only a few hundred feet until the rapids were past, but before they reached the end they heard a gunshot; arriving they found Falling Bear reloading his gun, and in the distance the Ojibwe canoe rapidly paddling downriver. Beaver House and Prairie Dog quickly lowered the canoe, and while Prairie Dog and Falling Bear carried it to the water's edge Beaver House ran back to the top of the portage where he found the second canoe about to land. Upon hearing they had been discovered they reversed their canoe and paddled rapidly back upstream to warn the main party.

THE HEADWATERS WAR:
Conflict for the Mississippi Headwaters

Running back to the portage's lower end Beaver House found Prairie Dog and Falling Bear in the canoe, holding it to the bank. As soon as Beaver House had scrambled aboard they began paddling as fast as they could after the Ojibwe disappearing in the distance. Beaver House was confused; why had Falling Bear fired at the Ojibwe when they were already almost out of range? That was foolish. If he had not they would still have thought they were only another group of Ojibwe returning from the hunt, but now they would carry warning to Sandy Lake, destroying any hope of surprise. From here to the portage at Sandy Lake, if the river hadn't headed east before turning south, and twisted and turned as Falling Bear said it did, would only have been about forty miles; but the stretch below, according to Falling Bear, was so twisted and tangled that it was closer to eighty miles by river. They must try to catch the fleeing Ojibwe before dark; unlikely since the Ojibwe knew the twists and turns of the river and, while Falling Bear remembered much of it from years before, it was not well enough that they would be able to keep up their speed after dark, partially sunken logs that could sink the canoe a constant threat. To make it worse there would be no moonlight to guide them. Still, they were proud of their skill with the canoe; they at least had a chance to catch the Ojibwe before dark.

Hours later . . . .

It was a day and night that Beaver House would remember all his life. During the remaining daylight hours they had paddled at full speed without a rest, even once, and on a straight stretch of river the canoe they pursued was within view as it turned a bend. But when the sun set and darkness fell things changed and became a nightmare. The best they could do was cautiously work their way downstream guided only by light from the stars overhead, often partially obscured by clouds. More than once their canoe had scraped against floating

THE HEADWATERS WAR:
Conflict for the Mississippi Headwaters

deadheads or beached at a shallow bend, sometimes almost overturning. They had no doubt the Ojibwe they pursued, familiar with the twists and turns of the narrow river, had gained an insurmountable lead. It was nearly midnight when they finally reached the portage to Sandy Lake, Strikes Many with the lead canoes arriving about two hours later. More than a few had breached on the numerous deadheads anchored in the shallows, left to straggle in once they could make temporary repairs.

Exhausted or not, Strikes Many didn't allow even a brief rest before they began the short portage. There was no hope now the village would not have been warned; still even if warned the Ojibwe would probably assume they were a warparty returning from an attack on the northern lakes, without any indication of how large a party they were. If such was the case they might send most of their warriors for an ambush on the nearby Mississippi, leaving the village unprotected. Even though some of the warparty had not as yet reached the portage they would proceed with the attack with what they had; let the others join the battle when they arrived.

By the time the last of the party crossed Strikes Many had already left with about one-third of the warriors, leading them overland to block escape from the village. Many Bears had been placed in charge of the remainder of the force with instructions to assemble the late arrivals and, just before dawn, head straight for the village and attack from the water. With luck the Ojibwe would be trapped in spite of the warning they had undoubtedly received.

After dark, Sandy Lake portage . . . .
Holding Out and Kills Otter allowed the canoe to glide slowly to the landing, sure they were now far ahead of their pursuers. They had seen only one canoe but assumed more were coming behind; the Dakota would not be foolish enough to enter the heart of Ojibwe country without a sizable force. Upon first sighting the

approaching canoe they had just continued their portage crossing, assuming it was only another group of Ojibwe hunters; but when one had fired his gun at them they discovered their error. While out of range the shot had still ricocheted off the water and hit the rear of their canoe, but caused little damage.

No Ojibwe would have done that. If they were wrong in giving warning they would be shamed; but if they were right they would gain the glory of maybe trapping the party of Dakota before they could escape to the south. Now, after the day and part of the night of travel, they had arrived at the short portage. Once the portage was crossed the Sandy Lake village was only a short paddle south, leaving plenty of time to gather a force and block the river. Then they would see.

Both Holding Out and Kills Otter, in spite of their fatigue, were energized by excitement. Both had been too inexperienced to be included in the warparty to the south led by Bright Forehead, but this might be even better. What a triumph it would be if they could gather the remaining warriors and bring them to the river to ambush the Dakota. The story of how they had paddled a day and into the night to escape the Dakota and then gathered the village for an ambush would be remembered around the campfires of their people forever; maybe even other villages as well as their own. Their names would be remembered.

Later, Sandy Lake Village . . . .

Smiling Woman was hard at work quilling the deerskin jacket she was preparing for her husband, Black Dog. Nearby other women of the band were engaged either in similar or other activities. Around the fires the warriors were loud and boisterous, deep in the 'fire-water' brought back by those returning from their annual trip to Sault Ste. Marie and Mackinaw. Although when all were present the village boasted well over 300 warriors, now the number was much less; over 60 of the

THE HEADWATERS WAR:
Conflict for the Mississippi Headwaters

best and most experienced were with Bright Forehead on a warparty against the Dakota to the south, her husband Black Dog among them. Many of the others were with their families in camps around the shore or dispersed on the smaller nearby lakes preparing for harvest of the plentiful beds of wild rice that were just beginning to ripen. Her oldest son Holding Out, and his friend Kills Otter, had gone upriver to trade with some of the headwaters Ojibwe.

Smiling Woman's son, Holding Out, did not yet have a wife and still lived with them in their wigwam and relied on her for tasks such as she was doing now for her husband. He was a good hunter and should have found a wife by now, but although he had never said so she thought he was waiting until Dancing Fox was old enough to marry. Well, in spite of the extra work she was happy that Holding Out was still with them, although with her other children sometime it made the wigwam seem crowded.

Hearing the sound of excited voices near the shore, Smiling Woman looked up. While it was too dark to clearly see the cause, she stopped what she was doing and walked toward the shore to see what the excitement was. Soon she saw a small crowd gathering around a canoe that had just beached itself, and saw her son, Holding Out, and his friend, Kills Otter, running toward the center of the village where the warriors were sprawled in their drinking bout; shouting excitedly and shaking some to get their attention. At first she didn't know what could be causing the excitement, until she heard a voice call out "the Dakota are coming."

While attempts were being made to sober up and gather what warriors they could, Holding Out and Kills Otter met with some of the more sober warriors and explained what they had seen. Soon Noka arrived; with *Bi-aus-wah* and Big Marten away at Fond du Lac, and Bright Forehead leading the warparty in the south, he was the most experienced war leader still present, and he

136

THE HEADWATERS WAR:
Conflict for the Mississippi Headwaters

took charge.

There were differing opinions of what they should do since the number of Dakota was unknown. Some of the younger warriors wanted to rush to the river and ambush the Ojibwe as they passed, as did Holding Out and Kills Otter. However, wiser heads prevailed. With so many of their warriors gone to the south or off harvesting wild rice they could not take that risk. Noka decided they must gather what warriors they could and prepare to defend the village while they sent the women away into the forest to hide. Since the approaching Dakota had canoes the islands would not serve for refuge. Even without the warparty that had gone south they still had over 100 able bodied warriors to defend the village, even though some were too drunk to be effective. Plus, if the hunters scattered nearby could be gathered in time that number would be nearly doubled. Meanwhile they would build what fortifications they could near the shore from fallen trees, and also behind the village. Nearly all the warriors had guns and ample powder and shot; they could hold out against even a large warparty. And Noka was sure any Dakota warparty venturing as far north as the rapids of the Pokegama must be large.

There was still more than enough time to send the women and children away; during the night they could help in building defenses. Then, just before dawn, send them off berry picking in the bogs where they would be safe and could accomplish something useful. A dozen warriors could be sent to protect them on the way and at their destination, all Noka felt they could spare.

The sky was lightening before everything was ready. Neither Holding Out nor Kills Otter were happy as they saw their hopes for glory fade. They could not believe the Dakota would dare attack the village; they must be planning to pass and go downstream and both believed an opportunity was being lost.

Holding Out walked back to the family wigwam.

THE HEADWATERS WAR:
Conflict for the Mississippi Headwaters

All night had been spent in helping in sobering up the drunken warriors and making preparations. Canoes had been dispatched to circle the lake and gather the warriors at ricing camps, and runners sent to some of the nearby lakes; all warriors were to return to aid in the defense. A runner had also been sent to Mille Lacs, but it would be too late for them to provide any assistance. At best they might be able to block the Mississippi further south.

Entering the wigwam Holding Out began to set his things aside before he lay down to rest; Smiling Woman and her younger children already had left to join the other women gathering to be escorted from the village. But, feeling in his pouch Holding Out couldn't find his mirror, the most valuable thing he owned; something that had come at a high cost. It was neither in his pouch nor anywhere he looked; it must have been dropped when at the portage. He had used it only the day before so knew it had been there.

It was still just the light before dawn, and Holding Out did not think the Dakota would have reached the portage yet, and even if they had he expected them to continue on downstream; and the mirror was too valuable to lose. If he hurried he could get to the portage and be safely away before their arrival. Running down to the shore Holding Out pushed the smallest of the canoes into the water and, jumping in, started to paddle as rapidly as he could north toward the portage.

It was only minutes before Holding Out arrived at the sand bar, which at this season of low water connected the islands north of the village, and pulled his canoe across. The wind had died completely, and the lake ahead was disturbed by only small waves, allowing rapid progress. From the islands to the portage was only a short paddle, protected from what wind remained by the western shore. Paddling rapidly, Holding Out passed through the narrow passage in the northwest corner of the lake and the portage came in sight, teaming with Dakota either launching canoes or offshore waiting for

THE HEADWATERS WAR:
Conflict for the Mississippi Headwaters

the others. Holding Out quickly stopped and pivoted his canoe, paddling back in the direction he had come, but not before being noticed, a number of Dakota canoes breaking off in pursuit.

Even paddling with all his strength Holding Out could not outdistance the pursuing Dakota, who slowly gained. By the time he again reached the islands north of the village and pulled his canoe across the sandbar they were almost upon him. Several of the faster Dakota canoes had bypassed the island on its eastern side and were now less than 100 yards away; within gunshot range. Holding Out crouched as a bullet from one of the Dakota passed overhead, only to feel a jolt when struck by a second.

Within seconds one of the Dakota canoes reached that of the wounded Holding Out, shouting cries of victory as they took their first scalp of the day. On the shore, watching the chase underway but unable to intervene, the Ojibwe warriors gathered to repel the expected attack, and as more and more of the Dakota canoes rounded the island it became clear they were seriously outnumbered.

Meanwhile, to the west . . . .

It was well before dawn when Strikes Many arrived behind the Ojibwe village. In the distance he could hear the occasional dogs barking and the sounds of shouting and drums and gunshots signaling any nearby hunters to return. They had been warned; they knew the Dakota were near. Beaver House and Prairie Dog followed close behind Falling Bear, watching both the woods to the side and also what Falling Bear was doing. Maybe he had been foolish to fire at the fleeing Ojibwe the day before, but still he was one to learn from. The battle hadn't even started and already he had scalps taken from the Ojibwe encountered days before.

Strikes Many signaled for all to move quietly off the trail and spread out and block the entire width of the

139

THE HEADWATERS WAR:
Conflict for the Mississippi Headwaters

shallow peninsula, including the trail from the village. Within minutes all access to the village by land was blocked. Then all lay quietly waiting.

It was not long before the sky began to brighten, and in the distance Strikes Many heard the murmuring of quiet voices and the sound of many feet on the trail coming in their direction. Motioning his warriors to be ready, but to avoid use of their guns, they lay in wait.

Smiling Woman, carrying her baskets for gathering berries and her youngest child, was only one of the many Ojibwe women and children taking refuge away from the village. They made a long line guarded by the accompanying warriors. While they had instructions to be silent, there was still the low murmuring of voices and the sound of that many feet could not be subdued.

All the women, except some of the old ones, had gathered together in the darkness for their journey to the bogs to the southwest where they would spend their time until they received a message the village was again safe. They had left just minutes before, and while soon the sun would begin tipping over the horizon, here in the forest only a little of the pre-dawn light reached.

Strikes Many smiled to himself as the first of the Ojibwe warriors came into sight less than 50 feet away, then two more, then the long line of women and children walking in single file. The Ojibwe hadn't expected to find the Dakota here so early, and not only coming at them from the lake but from the land as well. They had delayed too long in sending their women and children to safety. His own warriors would know what to do as soon as he gave the signal; but he would wait until the line came to an end. The warriors would be killed first, then those women they didn't wish to keep and the children. Normally some children would be kept for adoption, but now they would pose a burden. Still, the number was so large than many would escape and run back to the village; no matter, soon the village would know of their presence in any case. This would be almost too easy.

THE HEADWATERS WAR:
Conflict for the Mississippi Headwaters

Strikes Many had little concern that the Ojibwe warriors at the village, hearing the tumult or being warned by the fleeing women, would come to the rescue. If Many Bears had left the portage when he was supposed to he would be near the village by now, if not there already. In fact, the gunfire from the village had changed from warning shots to a steady beat, which could only mean some of the attacker's canoes were arriving. He smiled with anticipation; it was going well.

Minutes later . . . .

Leaning over the dead Ojibwe to take his scalp, Strikes Many looked up to see the trail filled with his warriors struggling with the Ojibwe women. Many of the women and children had succeeded in fleeing into the brush, but still they had captured several dozen; killing some of the others who had attempted to fight back. Now what to do with them; with the attack from the lake beginning he had to move his warriors forward to assist the attack from the water. Calling to one of his warriors, he instructed him to have the children and unwanted women killed and the hands of those women they wished to keep bound, and then escort them back to the portage and wait.

Falling Bear was undecided; he had captured a fine woman, but to keep her he must leave the battle before it began. He kneeled down and looked carefully at the woman, who just stared at him in defiance; yes, she was older, but still had many good years ahead and looked as if she could still bear children. The child she was now holding, a little girl, could have been no more than three years old. While he already had two wives, one was old and bad tempered, and the other was young and needed instruction in many things; this one would make a fine third wife. No, he decided, I won't kill her, but keep her instead. Pulling her roughly to her feet he seized the child and slammed its head against a tree before taking its scalp. Then, seizing the rope that tied

141

THE HEADWATERS WAR:
Conflict for the Mississippi Headwaters

the woman's hands he dragged her along as he followed the other warriors and their captives back to the portage and the waiting canoes.

Once the Ojibwe women were gone, Strikes Many again started his warriors toward the village, spread out in a line stretching from the shore on each side. Ahead he could hear building gunfire from the village, and by the time they came near the battle was well underway. Many Bears had beached the canoes in two groups, one on each side of the village, and his warriors were fiercely attacking; but the Ojibwe, while fewer, were nearly all had firearms, and using stacked piles of logs for cover were successfully holding off the attack. However, within minutes Strikes Many and his force arrived to join the assault. The Ojibwe, finding themselves fired upon from three sides, retreated further into the village.

All morning the battle raged, with many killed and wounded on both sides, but the Dakota could not dislodge the Ojibwe; fighting from cover giving them a distinct advantage. By noon the gunfire had largely petered out, warriors on both sides staying under cover. It had become a stalemate, and Strikes Many sent word to Many Bears to disengage and return to the portage; he would hold his position until they were on the water to provide covering fire. Once Many Bears had succeeded in withdrawing Strikes Many gathered his remaining warriors and began the long retreat to the portage; the Ojibwe choosing not to follow.

Strikes Many wasn't satisfied. They had not succeeded in destroying the village and its occupants although they had taken many Ojibwe scalps and captured many of their women. With such limited results it would be hard to convince either his people, or the war chiefs of the other bands, to again try to regain the north. They had to find another way if they were ever to succeed. He would have to think about how that could be done. But that was for later.

142

THE HEADWATERS WAR:
Conflict for the Mississippi Headwaters

On the Mississippi near the mouth of the Crow Wing River . . . .

Was-uk-o-gub-ig (Bright Forehead) was not a happy man. Weeks had been wasted on this journey to the Rum River and south, and they had few scalps to show for it; and little plunder either. Rather than risk being discovered ascending the Mississippi they had discarded their canoes in Dakota country and traveled overland following the eastern shore of the Mississippi. Now, as they approached the mouth of the Crow Wing River, any danger of pursuit was minimal.

Bright Forehead stopped as a scout came running from ahead; all was not well. Signs of a large warparty stopping for the night on the beach opposite the Crow Wing River mouth. Bright Forehead knew that beach well, broad and sandy but exposed only during these seasons of low water. Motioning Turtle Shell to follow, the two followed the scout to examine what had been found.

Arriving on the sandy beach the signs of a large encampment was clear from the many tracks remaining, skid marks where canoes had been pulled ashore, and remnants of food. While attempts had been made to cover some of the signs, many remained. Whoever had been here had been sloppy; either that or they were not concerned with discovery. That suggested they were on the way home at the time, or so large a party it wasn't concerned with being discovered. Since it had been ten days since the last significant rain the signs could be that old. Further, many of the skid marks were clearly of wooden canoes, which meant a Dakota warparty.

Quickly Bright Forehead sent scouts to the explore both sides of the Crow Wing looking for signs of passage. Others he sent north along the shores of the Mississippi. It wasn't long before one of the scouts sent up the Crow Wing returned with a message; signs about

THE HEADWATERS WAR:
Conflict for the Mississippi Headwaters

half a mile upriver of a single canoe landing, clearly a Dakota dugout, but no signs of a camp. Later in the day the other scouts returned reporting no sign of passage up the Mississippi.

Bright Forehead was uncertain of what to do. The signs were not fresh, but still had been made after the rain ten days earlier. If the Dakota warparty had gone north up the Mississippi it was almost certainly to attack Sandy Lake, and in that case, from the age of the signs, the attack would have already taken place; but there had been no sign of the party returning downstream to their villages. But if it had traveled up the Crow Wing, as the signs indicated, it was likely it planned to attack the northern lakes; and in that case they might still be able to ambush them on their return.

Smiling, perhaps something could be salvaged from his so far unsuccessful expedition after all. He would set an ambush and wait for three days before continuing on. If they didn't come in that time it likely meant they had already passed.

Gathering his warriors Bright Forehead instructed them to return to the ridge about half a mile south of the mouth of the Crow Wing and dig pits. There the Mississippi narrowed and the current was strong, and any returning canoes would be forced near the eastern shore. Dug in as they would be their position would be strong and able to hold off ever a very large warparty. Others he sent upriver, both on the Crow Wing and the Mississippi, to give warning of any sightings. And just in case the target had been Sandy Lake, he sent his fastest warrior to Mille Lacs to find if it had heard of any attack by the Dakota.

Later that day Bright Forehead surveyed the preparations. He was gruff and ill tempered; while that was his nature, the current situation made it worse, causing the others to avoid him whenever possible. Even food was short, and as he surveyed the spot he had selected for the ambush he instructed some of his

144

warriors to scout up both rivers for deer coming down for their evening drink. Avoid using guns; while if a returning Dakota party heard gunfire they would likely think it was only a hunter, still he wouldn't take the risk. When Bright Forehead was ill tempered it was best not to approach him.

Walking to the side of the ridge Bright Forehead sat, accompanied by his childhood friend Turtle Shell; one of the few who could tolerate his presence when in such a mood. Searching his bag for a piece of jerky, he softened it in his mouth before chewing.

Turtle Shell commented: "Maybe many hundred warriors. They make little attempt to cover their sign, and going further they would certainly be discovered."

Bright Forehead didn't respond at first, as if he hadn't heard, and then looked at Turtle Shell. "Why did they pick such a camping site where signs could be found and use so little care? On either river they could easily have found other places where few signs would be left. As if they didn't care if they were discovered. And it was foolish to leave sign on the Crow Wing; foolish and unnecessary. Is their party so large they are not afraid of discovery?"

Turtle Shell looked up at Bright Forehead and frowned, but said nothing.

"I think they go up the Crow Wing, and are still there," Bright Forehead continued. "And I think they don't care if they are discovered. But why?"

After a pause: "Why would they have so many warriors for that? The villages on Leech and Winnibigoshish lakes are small, and this time of year many are away for the rice harvest."

Bright Forehead looked thoughtful for several moments, before saying. "Only the Sandy Lake village is large enough. This is too far north if they wanted the Mille Lacs villages; they could have just gone up the Rum or by land. I think they go to Sandy Lake, but are afraid of being seen on the Mississippi."

145

THE HEADWATERS WAR:
Conflict for the Mississippi Headwaters

After a moment he frowned: "If I were Dakota, and wanted to go against Sandy Lake, I would circle to the west and come at the village from the north. That is what I think they will do. So I think it is Sandy Lake."

"Maybe they have already returned," Turtle Shell responded. "Maybe they made this camp coming back."

Bright Forehead looked at Turtle Shell, and shook his head, "I think not."

Adding, "I hope not."

"We should send warriors to help the village," Turtle Shell answered,

Bright Forehead shrugged: "Our runner should be at Mille Lacs before dawn, and they will send a runner and warriors to Sandy Lake before we could arrive. We will not go; we will stay here and catch them when they come south. We still have more than 200 warriors at the village, almost all with guns, and warriors from Mille Lacs can be there sooner."

After a moment he added quietly, "If they are enough to risk an attack on our village, we can't risk meeting them on the river. We will stay here where the bank is high and the water is swift for an ambush. From here we can see where the rivers meet, and ambush them whichever river they descend."

Turtle shell looked thoughtfully at Bright Forehead. "We have only sixty warriors; I think the Dakota, from the sign, have many hundred."

"Yes", Bright Forehead responded with one of his rare smiles. "But we will be behind cover on the high banks of the river, and they will be in their canoes and cannot hide. Our sixty warriors are enough."

Smiling grimly at Turtle Shell, "We will get many scalps, and the Dakota will learn never to come north again."

Turtle Shell said nothing, just looked doubtful. When Bright Forehead made up his mind it was best to be quiet and just follow.

THE HEADWATERS WAR:
Conflict for the Mississippi Headwaters

The following day . . . .

The Dakota canoes swept downriver with little attempt at silence, with songs of victory and cries of triumph. Those warriors who had taken scalps waved them on makeshift lances, and all were loudly relating their achievements. In the center of many of the canoes sat the captured Ojibwe women. It hadn't even been thought necessary to send scout canoes ahead; their force was so large Strikes Many saw little reason to worry.

The day before, once away from the portage, and certain they weren't being pursued, they had stopped for the night on the western shore to care for their wounded. Now, as midday approached, they were nearing the mouth of the Crow Wing River where they had previously camped for the night; a good place to stop for a mid-day meal. There had been no sign of pursuit by the Ojibwe, and by nightfall they would again be in Dakota country.

Downstream the Ojibwe lookouts were signaling the presence of the approaching Dakota canoes to others further south, and within minutes the message reached Bright Forehead and his warriors. All quickly went to their prepared places, primed their weapons, and lay silently in wait.

In minutes the first of the Dakota canoes were visible upriver, but rather than continue past the mouth of the Crow Wing they turned toward the sandy shore opposite; soon dozens of canoes had beached themselves and the shore was covered by Dakota warriors, many first going into the bushes to relieve themselves. The captive Ojibwe women were dragged ashore and forced to collect wood and start fires, while the warriors were busy building a large fire and beginning a war dance, shaking the Ojibwe scalps in triumph as they danced.

Bright Forehead grimly watched the scene in the distance as he tried to count the canoes and estimate how many warriors there were; as well as how many scalps

THE HEADWATERS WAR:
Conflict for the Mississippi Headwaters

they displayed. The party was much larger than he had expected, and he had second thoughts. He had thought from the signs at the Crow Wing camping place there had been perhaps 200 warriors, or maybe as many as 300, but there were clearly more; many more. And the captured women and shaking scalps showed the raid had been a success. Never before had he seen a warparty this large, it might even be as large as the great warparty of *Bi-aus-wha* a generation before. He had been too young to be a part of that assault on Sandy Lake so many years ago, but he had watched from the island.

Perhaps this had been a mistake. Perhaps he should have gone to support of the Sandy Lake village and not stayed away in hopes of the glory of ambushing the Dakota. Well, it was too late to change his mind now; things had gone too far; and he clearly wouldn't have been in time anyway. Turtle Shell touched Bright Forehead's elbow and pointed, then said quietly. "They have many women and scalps. I think they are not afraid of pursuit. Maybe our village is no more."

Bright Forehead nodded, looking grim, "I see. They will pay."

Among the women dragged from the canoes was Smiling Woman, and her thoughts were on what best she could do now. Many of the other captive women were in tears, sometime crying out in their distress. But not Smiling Woman; she told herself she would keep her head and be ready for any eventually. She knew something the Dakota did not, and that the other women had forgotten. There had still been no sign of the Ojibwe warparty of which her husband Black Dog was a part. Yes, it was small compared to the size of that of the Dakota, but she understood the strength given the Ojibwe warriors by the firearms almost all of them carried. She hadn't given up hope. As she passed the other women she whispered a message to spread the word to be on their guard.

Still a handsome woman in her late thirties,

THE HEADWATERS WAR:
Conflict for the Mississippi Headwaters

Smiling Woman was one of the oldest of the captives. While most of the women had escaped into the brush when the Dakota attacked they still captured over 50; but most of the older ones had been killed as not worth bringing along, and some of the younger ones also when the captors did not want to remain behind when the main battle started; now only 30 remained. Even though many would consider her old, apparently the Dakota warrior who had captured her considered her worth keeping.

Falling Bear dragged Smiling Women roughly to a place on the beach, then sat and, fishing a piece of jerky and a handful of dried berries and nuts from his pack, started to chew. Smiling Women tried to ignore his presence, and furtively examined the river ahead. In the back of her mind was the fear the warparty with her husband, Black Dog, still somewhere to the south, would now be coming back upriver and unexpectedly encounter the Dakota party. If that happened they were far too few and would have to flee. But if they knew the Dakota were coming it could be a different story. If the Ojibwe warparty had discovered passage of the Dakota they could well have set an ambush. And where better than where the river ahead curved and forced passing canoes against the shore? It was the only hope she had; by the end of the day they would be in Dakota held territory.

Smiling Women knew little of what had happened at the village, only that after she was captured there had been much firing of guns and shouting that had lasted for hours. She didn't know if the village had been destroyed, but she didn't think so. If it had the Dakota would have many more scalps than she had seen. No, she thought, it is still there; but many must have been killed or they would have followed the Dakota downriver.

Motioning her captor that she had to go into the bushes, Falling Bear got up and roughly dragged Smiling Woman a short distance into the bushes, watching while she relieved herself. Falling Bear was

THE HEADWATERS WAR:
Conflict for the Mississippi Headwaters

pleased with his captive; he thought she was quite handsome, and looked strong, but was perhaps somewhat willful. Not as young as some of the others, she was still young enough to maybe have children, and once she accepted her new status she would make a good addition to the tribe. He himself would soon to be too old for the warpath, and even if the Ojibwe captive was older she was still much prettier than his present wives and also had more spirit, as the scratch across his face would attest. Well, the bruise that blackened her eye had been a first lesson; others would follow if she didn't learn proper behavior.

While many of the Dakota would have little to boast of when they returned to the Falls of Saint Anthony, to Falling Bear the raid was a complete success. At the portages north of the Crow Wing he had taken an Ojibwe scalp, followed by that of the captured child killed at Strikes Many's insistence. Then at Sandy Lake the scalp of an Ojibwe warrior and the child of the woman he now owned. He was well pleased.

The Dakota were in no hurry to leave. The middle of the day passed as the exuberant warriors continued their dancing and boasting of their achievements, occasionally stopping for some of the food being prepared. Others were busy preparing the scalps attached as decorations to the canoes. But eventually it was time to move on, and the Dakota started to again board their canoes, and Bright Forehead again felt it necessary to pass the word to his warriors to stay silent and hidden and not fire until he did. He could only hope the Dakota canoes would stay clustered together as they drifted past and not spread out into formation and start downriver prematurely. If they could catch the canoes while they were still massed together they would make better targets.

As the canoes prepared to leave, Prairie Dog and Beaver House jammed their paddles into the river bottom to allow Falling Bear and the captive Ojibwe woman to climb in; then pushed off and paddled out to where the lead contingent was assembling near Strikes Many's canoe.

Luck was with Bright Forehead and his hidden Ojibwe. Those canoes early off the shore didn't start downriver, but just drifted downstream while the rest of the party pushed off. Bright Forehead nodded in satisfaction; they were well led, they did not straggle or move on their own as sometimes happened with a less experienced or able leader. This must be led by a major war chief to show such discipline, but then that must be the case with this large a party. Also, to be this large more than one band of the Dakota must be present; which meant perhaps most of the leading Dakota war chiefs were here; perhaps the feared *M'dewakanton* war chief Strikes Many himself. His scalp would be a prize worth risking all for. Perhaps even Falls Down, Many Bears, or Walker of the *Wahpekute, Sisseton* and *Wahpeton* bands were also here. He could but smile; what if all could be killed? The story would spread to the fires of all the *Anishnaebe.*

Even after all the canoes had been pushed off, at first they just drifted downstream, staying clustered, some canoes held together as the warriors shared a smoke, beginning to spread out as the current increased near the ambush point. While well hidden, Bright Forehead could not help himself from crouching down in his firing pit; almost humming to himself with satisfaction. If they continued as they now were it would be a slaughter. As they passed many of the canoes would be little more than 150 feet or so away; too close to miss.

Black Dog wiped the sweat from his hands as he lay watching the canoes pushing off from the shore. When he had first noticed the presence of so many woman landing with the canoes he understood what had happened; the Dakota raid was on the Sandy Lake village, and had been at least a partial surprise, otherwise the women could have hidden. The beach was far, and it

THE HEADWATERS WAR:
Conflict for the Mississippi Headwaters

was hard to make out the features of the women, and beneath his seething anger the question remained; was Smiling Woman one of them? Probably not; even if captured usually only the youngest were kept alive.

As the canoes led by Strikes Many started downriver Smiling Woman studied the shoreline ahead as it changed to a high bluff, the current increasing as it approached. Soon the river narrowed and began to curve as the canoes, following the current, were swept near the eastern bank. The canoe she was in was less than a hundred yards behind the leader, the canoes still mostly bunched and not yet fully spread out, and she could not help but think if the Ojibwe warparty was near this would be the ideal place for an ambush; but the Dakota were not worried, laughing and joking and calling to each other between canoes.

It was only a matter of minutes before the canoes began passing below where the Ojibwe lay watching, training their rifles while waiting for Bright Forehead to begin by firing the first shot. Bright Forehead checked his priming one last time, and took careful aim at the warrior sitting in the middle of the lead canoe; that should be a war chief, and killing him would cause disorder. When he was sure of his aim he fired, followed almost immediately by the roar of the many other guns.

The shock of the sudden attack caused disorder among the bunched canoes, some coming to a stop, others frantically paddling downstream, others attempting to reach shore. Beaver House slumped over, hit in the first volley, and as Prairie Dog attempted to control the canoe by himself it brushed against another canoe. Taking advantage of the opportunity Smiling Woman threw herself to the side and into the water, keeping a firm grip on the side of the canoe and twisting her body underneath, using all her weight to pull the side down after her, resulting in throwing the occupants into the river. Then, ducking her head underwater she swam

152

THE HEADWATERS WAR:
Conflict for the Mississippi Headwaters

with all her strength toward the shore. The other women, while initially startled, saw what Smiling Woman had done, and soon were leaping from and attempting to upset their canoes as well.

Even though they greatly outnumbered the hidden Ojibwe all attempts to land and drive them from the bluffs above ended only in more dead Dakota; many of the canoes, without guidance, drifting downriver. Others, where one of the paddlers was dead or wounded, attempting frantically to get away.

Bright Forehead's instructions had been followed to the letter. His fear that some of the younger warriors would shoot too early had not happened; all had waited for Bright Forehead to signal the beginning of the barrage. The waiting Ojibwe had targeted those in the canoes who appeared to be the leaders, then shifted to the others. Few had missed as the current carried the canoes near the shore right below the bluff where the Ojibwe lay hidden, and even the poorer shots could hardly miss their targets. The canoe with Strikes Many lying in the bottom drifted slowly downstream. Walker lay dead, with Falls Down wounded.

But Many Bears, the only war chief remaining unwounded, took charge, and as they passed beyond the range of Ojibwe fire directed the remaining canoes to land on the shallow shore past the bluff. Casualties had been high, but hundreds of angered Dakota warriors remained, and in a short time Many Bears had them organized. Under his most reliable warriors he sent them to surround the bluff where the Ojibwe were dug in; a bluff about 50 feet high and 500 feet long. He easily had enough warriors remaining to block any escape.

As the last of the Dakota canoes passed beyond gunshot the Ojibwe warriors scrambled down the bank to the shore, yelling war cries as they searched for any Dakota yet living, and scalping what bodies they could find; even wading into the water to drag some to shore. Several Ojibwe women were helped ashore by the

153

THE HEADWATERS WAR:
Conflict for the Mississippi Headwaters

welcoming party, Smiling Woman among them. On the top of the bluff Black Dog looked with satisfaction as he saw Smiling Woman safely ashore, apparently unharmed. As he stood and watched, Smiling Woman looked in his direction and raised her hand. All was well; he would learn the full story later.

Bright Forehead could not suppress his shouts of glee as he ripped the scalp from a dead Dakota, running from place to place in his excitement. Many Dakota had died, and no one in his warparty had even been wounded. There were many dozen dead either floating or washed ashore; maybe as many as a hundred, maybe more. This was a victory that would never be forgotten, his only regret was the Dakota bodies floating downstream that remained unscalped; it was too dangerous to leave their place before they knew what the Dakota would do next. Some Ojibwe who attempted to use one of the Dakota canoes caught in the shoreline underbrush to go after floating bodies were ordered to halt and stay near.

But so far they had failed to find the body of a Dakota war chief. If they could find a war chief's body the victory would be complete. Still, many of the dead had floated downstream, and Bright Forehead was certain at least some of the war party's leaders were among those dead. Those appearing most prominent had been targeted.

Slowly Bright Forehead's excitement receded; he must gather the women together to discover the fate of the Sandy Lake village. If the village was lost all this could come to nothing. He walked over to where several of them sat on the shore squeezing some of the water from their soaked clothing and wet hair.

But the victory was not yet in hand. Before he could even speak to one of he women a warrior rushed up with the news the Dakota had landed on the shore further downriver and were coming back. Calling the scattered warriors together, all again climbed back up the

THE HEADWATERS WAR:
Conflict for the Mississippi Headwaters

bluff and prepared to withstand an assault. For their protection the women were gathered together, and accompanied by two warriors, sent to hide in the surrounding tree cover.

The several hundred approaching Dakota spread out and completely surrounded the ridge, but their attempts to climb the steep sides to where the Ojibwe were entrenched was disorganized, and many died in the attempt. The fight lasted until dusk, when most of the Dakota retreated to where they had landed and prepared to camp for the night.

The next morning . . . .

Strikes Many, his shattered arm tightly bound to his side to relieve the pain, sat with Many Bears in a circle with his primary warriors. Missing were the other two war chiefs, Falls Down and Walker; Walker killed during the ambush, and the wounded Falls Down killed during the attack on the Ojibwe positions yesterday afternoon. This was clearly not an Ojibwe hunting party they had encountered, but a large warparty. A party consisting of many experienced warriors under a wise war leader. It would not be easy, but their losses had been too heavy to allow them to return home without exacting revenge; their victory at Sandy Lake would be forgotten and they would be shamed. Nearly a third of their force was dead or wounded, and their captives had also been lost. Even many of the scalps they had taken had floated away.

The attack of yesterday afternoon on the entrenched Ojibwe led by Many Bears had ended in failure, with many warriors lost in the futile attempt to storm the heights. But the death of Walker was the biggest loss. Walker was the war chief of the *Wahpeton* band, and without their leader his warriors were threatening to leave. While the *Wahpekute* had also lost their war chief, Falls Down, Running Wolf had quickly stepped into his role, and the entire *Wahpekute*

155

THE HEADWATERS WAR:
Conflict for the Mississippi Headwaters

contingent was thirsting for revenge.

Now that he understood how strong the Ojibwe positions were, and exactly where they were dug in, his attacks today could not be allowed to fail. While he might be able to keep the *Wahpeton* here for one more assault a few had already left. If he failed today he was sure the rest would leave as well, and if they did the *Sisseton* under Many Bears might also leave. Both the *Wahpeton* and *Sisseton* bands had their homes on the upper Minnesota River, far to the west, and Strikes Many had little influence over the warriors or war chiefs of either band. Further, they could not stay in the area too long; the Ojibwe villages at Mille Lacs, while small, were only a long day's march away. Strikes Many decided they would make one more assault, and if they had not succeeded by the time the sun was overhead would leave.

During the night the hill had been kept surrounded, with several Dakota canoes filled with warriors offshore out of gunshot range. More of the scattered warriors had returned from further downriver, and even with their losses of yesterday they could assault the remaining Ojibwe with overwhelming force. But Strikes Many had learned from the failure of Falling Bear's assault of the day before; today the attack would not be as foolish. Today they would creep forward under cover of the brush and trees until close to the dug-in enemy. Rising, he gave his final instructions to begin moving his warriors forward.

At the crest of the ridge Bright Forehead watched as the Dakota began to work their way upward. Yesterday none of his warriors had been lost, although some had suffered wounds; but that would not keep them from the fight. But as he looked at the numbers below he thought that might not be enough. Their firearms were effective, but after each shot 20-30 seconds was needed to reload and prime; time in which the Dakota could be among them. And even if they

THE HEADWATERS WAR:
Conflict for the Mississippi Headwaters

could drive them off their supplies of powder and shot were growing low. Today was also different in that the angered Dakota were not wildly charging uphill, but slowly advancing, constructing or digging cover as they came. Sometimes even pushing logs ahead of them as they crawled forward. Well, there was no way out; they would sell their lives dearly, and if defeated at least teach the Dakota the cost of coming into Ojibwe country. Crouching down he took careful aim at one of the advancing Dakota who appeared to be a leader.

By noon the Dakota had made several attempts to reach the top of the ridge where the Ojibwe were dug in, but each attempt had been driven back, leading to additional Dakota losses. In the last attack some Dakota had made it all the way to the rifle pits, resulting in hand-to-hand fighting with tomahawks and war clubs, but had been driven off. Now things were again quiet.

Bright Forehead knew they were reaching the end; their powder was almost gone and he didn't think they could withstand another attack like the last one. While only one Ojibwe warrior had been killed many others bore wounds, although most of those were still capable of battle; the Dakota were just too many. Each must prepare for death in their own way, but Bright Forehead vowed the Dakota would pay heavily first.

But the afternoon passed and no further attacks came. About two hours before dusk Bright Forehead sent a pair of scouts to investigate, who reported back that the Dakota were no longer guarding the bluff, and while they had explored a mile downriver had found no Dakota. The Dakota had abandoned the fight and gone south. Bright Forehead stood and walked down the slope, his warriors following taking scalps from any fallen Dakota who still remained; most of the dead having been carried off. The lesson had been given.

Strikes Many sat in the canoe as it glided down stream, feeling the ache in his arm as well as that in his heart. The arm was one thing, and he suspected it would

THE HEADWATERS WAR:
Conflict for the Mississippi Headwaters

never be of use again even if he survived the fevers that he was sure would follow. Well, he was growing old for a warrior and perhaps it was time to take his place among the elders. It was the ache in his heart that would never heal; an ache caused by the knowledge any hope to regain his Sandy Lake home was now gone. Now that was at an end, he had failed, and in his heart he knew the final opportunity had ended with that failure. Never again would the bands of the Dakota unite for such a purpose. He was shamed by his defeat. Could they even defend their Rum River home? Strikes Many was not sure. The village was too near the Ojibwe villages of Mille Lacs, and even Sandy Lake was only two to three days away. The Ojibwe would surely seek revenge for the attack on their Sandy Lake village.

Maybe the time to leave the Rum had come; he would discuss this with the elders when he again reached his village. Yes, he was sure the Ojibwe would come, probably Big Marten himself, whose fame as a war chief was second to none. He would come if he had not died in the battle, but no one had reported sighting him there.

Several Days Later . . . .

Warren relates a Dakota legend obtained from a part-Dakota Ojibwe chief who had lived with the Dakota during his early years. According to that legend, while the Dakota warriors were gathering at the Falls of Saint Anthony prior to departure a newly married young warrior was planning to be a part of the raiding party; but his beautiful young bride begged him to stay behind. She had dreamed that, if he left, he would never return. But he could not stay behind; his friends from his village were going, and he would be shamed if he stayed behind with the women. To ease her mind he called upon the spirits to hear him as he promised that he would return.

About two weeks later all expectantly waited for the return of the raiding party, the time of its return having arrived and passed. One morning, in preparation

THE HEADWATERS WAR:
Conflict for the Mississippi Headwaters

for greeting her husband upon his return, the young woman went to the shore of the river where she sat combing and braiding her hair, using the still water by the shore as a mirror. Noticing a dark object floating beneath the surface she recognized a human figure. Reaching down, she pulled it ashore, and gazing down saw it was the body of her husband. He had kept his promise. The legend says this was the first news of the disaster upriver, with the remnants of the warparty returning later that afternoon. But the return of the warparty was an anticlimax; the debris, mixed with the floating bodies of their dead warriors, had already told the waiting women a story for all to read.

Whether the above legend reflects fact is unimportant, but in all legends there is usually the seed of truth. In any case, fearing reprisal the Dakota abandoned their village on the Rum River and left to find homes more secure from the avenging Ojibwe. With abandonment of their Rum River village no permanent Dakota villages remained east of the Mississippi and north of Saint Anthony Falls in present day Minneapolis. The land south of Mille Lacs and Sandy Lake, and that west of the Mississippi, became a no mans land frequented by hunters and war parties of both tribes. It was many years later, after the turn of the century, that the Ojibwe were able to absorb some of that no mans land into their own territory.

Comment . . . . .

Of all the battles between the Ojibwe and the Dakota, this sequence, both the attack on Sandy Lake and the ambush by Bright Forehead, is perhaps the best documented by Warren. The Dakota gathering at Saint Anthony falls in present day Minneapolis, the route used and killing the Ojibwe families discovered along the route, discovery near the Pokegama rapids, the race to the portage, the drunken state of most of the men in the Ojibwe village, the killing of one of the young Ojibwe

THE HEADWATERS WAR:
Conflict for the Mississippi Headwaters

the Dakota had been chasing when he returned to look for his mirror, capture of the women, the ambush below the mouth of the Crow Wing by the Ojibwe warparty under Bright Forehead, and the Ojibwe women overturning the canoes is as reported in Warren (*p.222 – 234*); as is the story of the young Dakota woman finding the body of her husband in the river. Beyond that it is fictional.

The exact location of the Ojibwe village attacked is subject to debate, but from the description in Warren it is unlikely it was on the south shore near the former Dakota village. In an article on the site of the 1794 Northwest Trading Post on Sandy Lake by Irving Hart, 'Minnesota History', Vol. 7, no.4 (*December 1926*), Hart concludes Brown's Point is the only location on the lake that fits Warren's description of the Dakota attack of 1768. He also states the point had been occupied by an Ojibwe village at or near that time. It is also only a short paddle from the Sandy River portage in the northwest corner of the lake, with some small islands in between.

Further, the topography of the surrounding area makes the placement of the Ojibwe village at Brown's point even more probable. Figure 6:, Sandy Lake Then & Now, illustrates the difficulty of land travel from the portage to the south shore. South and southwest of Brown's Point, at the southwest corner of the lake, an outlet opens to a smaller lake. While at the time the water level was as much as nine feet lower, still the river and surrounding wetlands would have posed a formidable obstacle. While the route could possible be used for an attack on a village on the southern shore (*such as the old Dakota site on the peninsula*), any retreat to the portage in the northwest corner could be dogged by angry Ojibwe, with the added danger of being cut off and trapped by Ojibwe closing the portage. The very fact the Dakota used the Mississippi portage to Sandy Lake for the attack pretty much limits the location of the Ojibwe village to Brown's Point.

THE HEADWATERS WAR:
Conflict for the Mississippi Headwaters

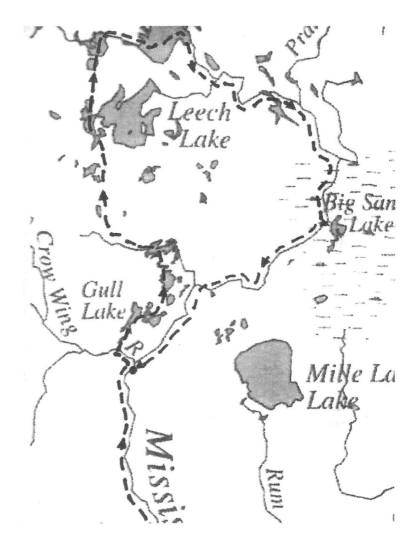

Figure 9: Route of Dakota Raid of 1768

THE HEADWATERS WAR:
Conflict for the Mississippi Headwaters

CHAPTER 6
BIG MARTEN'S WAR

The botched campaign of 1768 had cost the Dakota heavily and ignited a fire among the Ojibwe of Sandy Lake for revenge. The raid could not go unpunished. Between 1769 and 1773 Big Marten, along with a war chief named Noka, led a number of campaigns against the Dakota; the first by Noka in 1769, the later two by Big Marten. However, with the evacuation of the Rum River village Ojibwe war parties were forced to travel to unfamiliar country, the Minnesota River valley. The first raid, led by Noka, was a success, although only partial. The second raid, led by Big Marten himself, was a clear defeat for the Ojibwe. The final raid in 1773 at best was a draw, but ended in the death of Big Marten; a death that perhaps he sought, frightened at the thought of dying as an old man and not as a warrior should.

September, 1768 . . . .

Big Marten walked slowly through the village, stopping as he came to some of the warriors he had led on his past war parties, many nursing wounds; questioning, always questioning. How had it happened the Dakota had not been discovered earlier? How long before the attack had they been warned? Why were those who should have been guarding the village drunk with spirits? And how had their women been taken from them? How many Dakota had there been, who led them and why had not pursued them when they left? Had anything been heard of Bright Forehead and his warparty to the south, or were they dead as well?

It was only a little over 24 hours since word had reached Big Marten of the attack. He had been at Fond

THE HEADWATERS WAR:
Conflict for the Mississippi Headwaters

du Lac with *Bi-aus-wah* making plans for the following summer, and when things had been settled gone further up the south shore of Lake Superior to visit relatives. He had just returned to Fond du Lac when the runner from Sandy Lake arrived with the terrible news. Part of yesterday, all night and most of today, he had spent returning, and had arrived only shortly before.

The village was badly damaged and the losses had been larger than they had ever suffered from the Dakota. Over fifty warriors were dead or badly wounded, more than thirty of their women had been taken and dozens of women and children killed. All they had to show for it were a dozen Dakota scalps, and the knowledge that others had been killed and dragged away. It would be difficult to explain to *Bi-aus-wah* when he returned tomorrow.

But Big Marten had other worries as well; Bright Forehead and his sixty warriors had not returned and were overdo. If they had encountered the Dakota on their return it could be disastrous for the village; the loss of that many warriors, on top of their losses here, would greatly reduce their fighting force. Already, in recent years, many families had drifted off to the rich lands further up the Mississippi towards its headwaters, and only by an influx from the Lake Superior Ojibwe had Sandy Lake been able to maintain its position. Without the power of Sandy Lake the villages at Mille Lacs and Knife lakes, only a two day march away, might have to be abandoned.

Big Marten had been back at the village less than an hour when his attention was drawn to the shore where a number of people were shouting and pointing. Screening his eyes, rounding the island he could see a stream of canoes; Dakota canoes, but filled with Ojibwe warriors. Warriors singing and calling out, and raising high poles festooned with scalps; the sound of victory. As they rounded the island and approached, Big Marten could see several women seated in the canoes; it was

THE HEADWATERS WAR:
Conflict for the Mississippi Headwaters

clear where the scalps had come from. Big Marten could hardly counter his desire to run to the beach with the others; in his case a more dignified approach was called for. But his heart raced; he would be there to greet the returning party as it deserved.

Within minutes the canoes had reached the beach, and Big Marten was pleased to see nearly all the warriors had returned. In the bottom of the canoes sat or lay a number of wounded, but only one appeared to be unmoving. Quickly counting the women in the canoes he could see that most, but not all of those taken, had been freed. But his heart swelled at the sight of the Dakota scalps, well over 100, hanging from the poles. The story was written in the shouts and cries, the numerous scalps, and the homecoming of the captured women; Bright Forehead and his warparty had met and defeated the much larger group of Dakota attackers. They would have a story to tell.

Big Marten stood with the others as Bright Forehead's leading canoe was gleefully pulled ashore by the excited Ojibwe, his normally grim face loosened slightly; the Dakota had paid, but not enough. Not enough to cancel the affront his village had been given. But now was not the time for such thoughts; he walked over to Bright Forehead and nodded his approval. Tonight all must gather and hear of the things Bright Forehead and his warriors had done to avenge the insult; now was a time for rejoicing and the telling of what each of the returning warriors had done, and a time of mourning for the dead. Later they could consider what was to follow.

Early April, 1769 . . . .

It was several days after the council of elders of the band had completed their deliberations; the decision had been made, and *Bi-aus-wah* had endorsed that decision. They had learned the Dakota had left their Rum River village and gone south into country not

THE HEADWATERS WAR:
Conflict for the Mississippi Headwaters

familiar to the Ojibwe, and this year a scouting party would go into that new country and find where the Dakota had gone; a large party capable of defending itself from the Dakota if discovered. Next year they would gather an even larger warparty from all the villages of the Ojibwe and wipe those Dakota villages from the face of the earth.

But Big Marten wasn't happy; they had also decided that the party was to be led by Noka, an experienced war chief but still one lacking the prestige of Big Marten. The elders and *Bi-aus-wah* had found another mission they wanted Big Marten to undertake, a round of the Ojibwe villages of the north and those of Lake Superior to gather support for the campaign of the following year. He would carry the pipe and tobacco of *Bi-aus-wah* to the other villages signifying his intention of sending a party south the following year. With their own problems to contend with someone of importance must be sent to convince them to abandon their own plans and send their warriors. In his absence Bright Forehead, an older and more experienced war chief than Noka, would be left to defend the village.

While disappointed that he, himself, would not lead the mission to the south, Big Marten understood why. Who else could they send to the other bands? The most prestigious emissary, and the one most likely to garner their support, would be *Bi-aus-wah* himself; but his health was no longer good. He had grown too frail for such an extended, exhausting trip; and besides he was also often called to attend to problems at Fond-du-Lac. The next most honored name was that of Big Marten, unmatched as a war chief among all the Ojibwe. And convincing the northern tribes to join a campaign so far to the south would not be easy; they had not been hurt by the Dakota raid of the year before, and their anger was more against the Sissiton and Yankton to the west. The *M'dewakanton* villages far to the south were of little importance to them.

THE HEADWATERS WAR:
Conflict for the Mississippi Headwaters

The Ojibwe at La Plainte and on the Saint Croix could be hard to convince as well, although they were always eager to go against the Dakota to their south near the confluence of the Saint Croix and the Mississippi, having been hurt by them in the past. They also had knowledge of the area around the villages south of the mouth of the Minnesota River, and some on the Minnesota as well, which the Minnesota Ojibwe lacked. But, until this year's scouting mission was completed, it was difficult to tell where next years raid would be directed.

Now Big Marten would meet with his friend Noka and together they would plan the expedition. Never before had the Sandy Lake Ojibwe ventured so far south, and what they knew of the country below came only from travelers passing through and some of their own women captured from the Dakota in years past. True, they knew the general route of the rivers from those travelers, and had heard rumors of where some Dakota villages could be, but that was not enough, and much of that information was old. He and Noka would agree on the route and number of men to take, and work together to select the members. Only experienced warriors would go; the brash young braves who didn't listen well to what they were told would be left behind. This mission was for scouting, not the taking of scalps.

Several days later . . . .

Dawn was breaking as Big Marten and his friend and long-time companion, Good Thunder, stood on the shore watching the final boarding of the big war canoes; their two smaller canoes off to the side with the four warriors assigned to accompany them and do the paddling. The month of April was early in the year for a warparty, but for that reason it had been selected; they hoped to avoid encountering Dakota on the way.

Ever since the decision had been made to send the party south preparations had been underway, the war

THE HEADWATERS WAR:
Conflict for the Mississippi Headwaters

canoes dragged down to the beach from where they had been stored for the winter and carefully examined for damage incurred during their months of storage. Well into the evening repairs had been in progress, vats of heated pitch nearby for sealing any seams that had deteriorated, and now all stood ready.

The warparty consisted of nearly 200 warriors, large compared to most, and to obtain that number without leaving Sandy Lake undefended they had included some warriors from both the Mille Lacs and Knife lakes villages. It was large not because they planned to attack any specific village, but because they were going into unknown country, and unknown country meant unknown dangers. They would be in the middle of Dakota country, and if discovered needed enough size to defend themselves. The instructions to Noka were clear; north of Saint Anthony Falls they were free to attack any Dakota or Dakota villages they found, but to the south they were to limit themselves to scouting only.

Noka walked over to Big Marten and Good Thunder and stood facing them, waiting to see if there were further instructions, the pride at being assigned war chief for such an important expedition evident on his face. Big Marten took Noka's shoulder in his big hand, and looked him carefully in the face. "It is well. It is time things like this fell into younger hands."

Then, turning, he and Good Thunder walked down the shore to their waiting canoes. They would accompany the warparty until the portage was crossed, where they would part; Noka and his party heading downstream, while the two canoes with Big Marten and Good Thunder went upstream to the Ojibwe villages on the northern lakes.

In less than two hours the canoes had reached and crossed the portage; the canoes of the scouting party congesting the narrow Mississippi as they waited for the last to push off. With a nod to Big Marten, Noka climbed in, and soon the entire flotilla had disappeared

167

THE HEADWATERS WAR:
Conflict for the Mississippi Headwaters

around the bend in the distance.

Big Marten and Good Thunder watched quietly as the last of the canoes disappeared from sight. With a shrug, Big Marten climbed into the center of the canoe allotted to him while Good Thunder boarded the other, and soon both were propelled upstream by the strong strokes of those in front and back. He was growing old; nearly sixty winters, and his hair was streaked with white; by this time most warriors had retired from the warpath with some becoming honored elders. Where muscles had once bulged he was growing soft, and he knew he could not run with a warparty as he could when he was younger. Still, even now he was perhaps the strongest in the village, and the most skilled in war.

Big Marten glanced over at the canoe a short distance away where Good Thunder sat, seemingly dozing. While a year or two younger, of the friends of his youth only Good Thunder continued in the way of the warrior, and sometimes he thought that was only because of himself. Both should have joined the elders long ago and let younger leaders take their place. But he could not, and as long as he didn't neither would Good Thunder; even though the years weighed heavier on Good Thunder than they did on him. The two had grown up at Fond du Lac and were among the few warriors still active that had been with *Bi-aus-wah* on his great raid on Sandy Lake decades earlier. While a young man he had already gained renown as a war chief, and Good Thunder had always been there watching his back.

Glancing down at his middle, which bulged out as he sat in the canoe, he thought to himself. "I am becoming a big belly. But I will not die a big bellied elder, depending on the young to bring me tender meat for my toothless mouth. This one time I will do as the elders want; but when the next warparty goes south I will go also. I have lived as a warrior, and I will die as a warrior." That was a pledge he would keep.

THE HEADWATERS WAR:
Conflict for the Mississippi Headwaters

Later ....

The pace had been easy, the flood swollen Mississippi doing most of the work. By dusk they would reach the mouth of the Crow Wing River and make camp for the night, the last camp before entering country frequented by the Dakota; although during the fall and winter hunting seasons they ranged much further north. After today they would proceed with caution, scouts far in advance and with fireless camps at night. But tonight Noka would let his eager warriors let off steam; let them have their fires and dance their achievements. That had been what he had been taught by his mentor, Big Marten; when the enemy is far away allow the warriors to have their way, but when in enemy country use tight discipline and be ever on the watch. True, this was not really a warparty, but even if their purpose was only to scout the south, conflict was always a possibility; and in the contested area between they were free to attack any Dakota they encountered.

It was still at least an hour before sunset when they reached the Crow Wing and Noka ordered his canoe to the shore. While most of the sandy shore opposite the mouth was covered by the high water, still it was the only good camping spot for miles. As the canoe was beached Noka jumped out and surveyed the site. Yes, even with the high water this would do

Several of his senior warriors gathered around Noka as he gave his instructions for placing guards around the area and sending scouts downriver to make sure they were not surprised. He also directed canoes be sent up the Crow Wing to watch for any deer that might come to the shore for an evening drink; a supplement to the jerky they carried would be welcome. Then they were free to celebrate here in their final safe camp.

Later, his supper completed, Noka sat listening to the cries as he watched the nearly naked warriors dancing around the flames. He and some of the other warriors had just returned from the short walk

THE HEADWATERS WAR:
Conflict for the Mississippi Headwaters

downstream to where the ambush of the year before had taken place, and had carefully examined the pits and defenses built by the Ojibwe. Down the slope, washed up by the swift current, the remains of some Dakota canoes, not yet carried away by the spring floods, were still visible. Yes, Bright Forehead should be proud; that battle had perhaps been one of the most one sided battles against the Dakota in memory.

His assignment to lead this warparty had come as a surprise, Bright Forehead being the logical choice after Big Marten himself. While he had led a number of small warparties before, never a party this large. He could think of only one reason for his selection; Bright Forehead was approaching middle age, and before many more years passed would forsake the war path for the life of an elder. Younger leaders were required, and they must learn from experience. Smiling to himself, Noka stripped off all except his breechcloth and ran over to join the dance.

Two days later . . . .

Scarlet Leaf sat in the middle of the canoe carefully scanning the shoreline, the canoe in which he was seated staying to the right hand shore. Following the opposite shore was a similar canoe with Deer Killer and a pair of paddlers. Scarlet Leaf was the only warrior on the expedition familiar with these southern regions; at one time having lived for a winter among the Dakota at a village a half day paddle up the Minnesota River. Half Dakota himself, even with the animosity between the Dakota and Ojibwe he had welcomed when he brought his mother to her brothers upon the death of his Ojibwe father. While Deer Killer had never been south before, his mother had been a Dakota who stayed behind after their defeat at Kathio; many of the Dakota choosing to be incorporated into Ojibwe bands rather than leave. She had heard many tales of the Dakota villages in the valley of the Minnesota River that had been passed to

170

THE HEADWATERS WAR:
Conflict for the Mississippi Headwaters

her from old Dakota friends who had been there, and had related those stories to Deer Killer.

By mid-afternoon they reached the small river entering from the right, the Crow River (*south of the larger Crow Wing River*). This was their goal; further south the Mississippi bent and moved in an easterly direction until it neared the Falls of Saint Anthony, an area frequented by the Dakota. What Scarlet Leaf clearly remembered was that a trail existed starting a short distance up the Crow which led to one of the Dakota villages upstream of the mouth of the Minnesota, a trail he had taken on his return to his northern home. In his discussions with Noka it had been decided the overland route carried the least risk of discovery.

Motioning the warriors paddling the canoe to turn up the river, Scarlet Leaf signaled the canoe on the other bank to continue downstream a distance to act as lookouts; the warriors following on the shore stopping to move to concealment. In less than five minutes the canoes of the main flotilla came in sight, Noka in the leading canoe, and as they began to arrive, Scarlet Leaf motioned them to follow him upstream on the Crow for concealment. Scarlet Leaf took the lead and, after reaching a point where the view from the Mississippi was obscured, pointed his canoe to the southern shore, the other canoes following suite.

Where they had landed the dense reeds emerging from the water forced them to push themselves through before reaching dry land. But once past the reeds the sloping bank made landing and dragging the canoes into concealment simple, with Noka and some of his senior warriors supervising the operation. Once the canoes were ashore warriors waded into the water to straighten those reeds they could reach to partially conceal their presence. Then Noka called Scarlet Leaf to the side, and the two sat and discussed the next step.

Scarlet Leaf explained that, from where they had landed, the trail to the south started no more than a 300

171

THE HEADWATERS WAR:
Conflict for the Mississippi Headwaters

paces upstream in an area where the banks were higher and the reeds had ended. But here, concealed by the reeds along the shore, they could both camp for the night and ensure the canoes remained undiscovered. Noka nodded, and motioning one of his warriors instructed him to take two canoes back to the mouth of the Crow to stand guard, and also to send Deer Killer and the scouts hiding on the eastern shore and those that had proceeded down the Mississippi back; he wanted to consult with Deer Killer and review what he had been told of the location of the various villages. Then he selected several experienced warriors, instructing them to find the trail and follow it south until they were sure it was clear of roving Dakota.

Dawn, the following morning . . . .

Scarlet Leaf pulled the blanket around him as he joined Deer Killer. This early in the year the night without shelter or a fire had chilled him to the bone, and the dampness and light fog added to the discomfort. Both Scarlet Leaf and Deer Killer were assigned to the group of scouts that would precede the main body. As soon as they caught up with the warriors sent ahead the evening before, who had been instructed to go no further than they could cover in an hour, the advance scouts would spread out on each side of the trail with the main body following behind. It was their job to ensure any other travelers were caught and quietly killed to avoid discovery.

The job of the scouts in this type of country was difficult. While at first the trail passed through lightly wooded, rolling country, gradually it became largely treeless making it necessary to proceed slowly and with caution to avoid discovery, with the scouts, dressed as Dakota, far ahead. Scarlet Leaf remembered the trail well. A long day's journey to the south would bring them to the river across from the village where he had spent the winter, and another days march to the east would

THE HEADWATERS WAR:
Conflict for the Mississippi Headwaters

bring them to a village near the confluence of the Minnesota with the Mississippi. It would be a very long day at the cautious rate they would have to maintain. Even now the Dakota would be on the move, and some might even be returning from the spring sugar season. These southern Dakota had to travel far to the north to find suitable maple trees, but west of the Mississippi the land was still claimed by the Dakota and was largely free of Ojibwe except during the winter hunting season; there the maple trees could be found in abundance.

Only in this strip of relatively open country between the Crow and Minnesota rivers would they have to move so cautiously; once in the heavily wooded valley of the Minnesota River the main body could go into hiding, while scout parties explored along the river for Dakota encampments or villages.

Back with the main body of warriors Noka proceeded cautiously, those following moving in complete silence except for the sound of their light steps, stopping occasionally when signaled that they were getting too near the advance scouts. This day would tell the tale; if they remained undiscovered until they reached the wooded river boundary to the south.

The sun had set and dark was falling when the party reached the bluff overlooking the river valley, below the broad floodplain around the ribbon of the river broadened at this time of year by floodwaters, before rising to bluffs on the other side. The spring floods had begun to recede, but still the meadows of the floodplain were pooled with water in their low areas, and the hardy flood resistant trees were green with newly sprouted leaves. Here the trail branched to continue east and west along the top of the bluff, with a third trail winding its way to the tree-filled valley below. Noka could still make out in the failing light where that third branch went; across the river on some higher ground sat a sizable Dakota village partly obscured by trees; already some campfires marking its location That would be the

THE HEADWATERS WAR:
Conflict for the Mississippi Headwaters

village described by Scarlet Leaf.

Noka shielded his eyes as he tried to count the lodges visible among the scattered trees, attempting to estimate the number of warriors it might hold; but soon had to give up. That would have to wait until morning. Scarlet Leave had said that, when he had been there, the village contained only 100 or so warriors, but that may well have changed with an influx after abandonment of the Rum River village. In any case, the village must have grown in the years since Scarlet Leaf's stay.

Still, from what Noka could make out the village below definitely looked different from Dakota villages he had seen before. While nothing was growing as far as he could see, cleared areas that looked like fields for planting were much larger, and he even saw a number of horses near the bluffs. Even many of the hide covered tepees favored by the prairie tribes were present. Yes, these Dakota lived differently than those in the north.

Scarlet Leaf had told him that, a little south of the river, trails left the village below that led both to the east and west where additional Dakota villages were located. While Scarlet Leaf had never followed the trail west for any great distance, he said he had once gone with a party of Dakota to a village to the east below the junction with the Mississippi, but on the opposite shore; a large village of a powerful Dakota chief named Little Crow. On the way they had passed another village about the size of the one below.

Noka's mind was active with thoughts of what might transpire in the next few days. While it would be ideal if they found villages north of the river, he knew it was unlikely. All the villages they had heard of were located south of the river for their own protection, and while it was a simple matter for warriors to swim across, keeping powder dry meant preparation. The first requirement would be to find a safe crossing. In the meantime the main body would find a place where they could remain hidden.

THE HEADWATERS WAR:
Conflict for the Mississippi Headwaters

Several Days Later . . . .

For the last several days the scouts ranging the north bank had been reporting back. The village across the river had grown significantly since Scarlet Leaf's visit years before, and two other villages had been located; one downstream that Scarlet Leaf had at one time passed through, and the second a full day march upstream. However, both were on the southern shore of the river, and both about the size of the first or smaller. While they had observed signs of Dakota hunting and fishing camps on the northern side, all were small, and they had so far managed to avoid discovery.

For all three of the villages discovered scouts had crossed the river to carefully examine the surrounding terrain for approaches a warparty could best use. The pair of scouts sent far downriver to find the large village described by Scarlet Leaf as that of Little Crow had also just returned. Located east of the Mississippi, several miles below the mouth of the Minnesota, it had required crossing the Mississippi, grown broad this far south.

Noka had learned much, and it pointed to the first village near the Crow River trail as the best opportunity, although the village was larger than Scarlet Leaf had recalled, probably swollen by Rum River refugees. On one occasion Scarlet Leaf had, during the night, worked his way down to the river and lay hidden all the next day observing, and combined with his previous recollections there was little about that village they did not know. Scarlet Leaf reported several Dakota canoes stashed on the northern shore for use by travelers, and observed a large number on the southern shore. Much more was known of that village than of the one downstream, the second best option.

To attack either the village upstream or that downstream would take them far from their escape route; the trail to the Crow River. Still, the large village

THE HEADWATERS WAR:
Conflict for the Mississippi Headwaters

said to be that of Little Crow could not be completely ruled out; it was much larger, and traveling that far downstream with the Minnesota River villages at their back posed too much risk of their retreat being cut off. But if they could gather enough warriors an approach by land from the north was possible.

Noka knew the limit his instructions. He was to determine the location and size of the Dakota villages to prepare for next year's campaign, but not to attack any villages found south of the Falls of Saint Anthony on the Mississippi or on the Minnesota. Above all his presence was to remain undetected. Now was the time to return to Sandy Lake and report to Big Marten the information he had obtained, yet why not do even more? Rarely were 200 warriors gathered together, and neither of the nearby villages were likely to have more than 300 warriors, even if all were present; which was unlikely. Further, his scouts reported that, feeling secure so far from Ojibwe country, they didn't even post guards at night. They could catch the village below by surprise, and be gone before support could come from the other villages.

Noka had to think long and hard. He looked forward to the glory such an achievement would bring. True, when he had counseled with his senior warriors nearly all were cautious and advised against it; the risk of being stranded on the south bank without a way for rapid retreat or being caught by pursuing Dakota was high. Also, while they didn't completely know the orders given to Noka, still they knew their main purpose was to scout the Dakota villages, and were reluctant to incur *Bi-aus-wah's* or Big Marten's anger. But still, to miss such an opportunity?

It was clear to Noka that he would have to have a fully developed plan of both how to cross the river, and later how to escape the Dakota wrath, to convince his senior warriors to agree. True, they had the three canoes found by the scouts along the river, and could easily capture the five near the first village, but that couldn't

THE HEADWATERS WAR:
Conflict for the Mississippi Headwaters

hold all their warriors. The many canoes pulled up on shore by the village could be seized early in an attack, but were unlikely to have paddles. Still, the river channel was rarely more that 100 feet even in this period of high water, and if necessary most of the warriors could swim, using their few canoes to keep their powder dry.

Noka realized what he really needed was a hidden crossing place a distance from the village. After all, with 200 warriors, armed as they were, they could hold off the Dakota while they made the crossing again to the north bank using the Dakota canoes. Perhaps they could even make some makeshift paddles and bring them along in the three canoes they already had.

This would be going beyond his instructions, but still, if successful, it would accomplish what had been planned for the following year, and *Bi-aus-wah* and Big Marten would certainly approve of his initiative.

Several days later . . . .

The final decision had been made; it had been agreed the reward was worth the risk. The village they had gotten into the habit of calling 'Scarlet Leaf's' village would be the target. After crossing during the night several miles east they would camp away from the trail, then before dawn follow the trail upriver. The three canoes they already had would be brought to the main crossover point, and then would keep pace with the main body as it proceeded upstream. A few warriors would be left behind at the present location, their assignment to work their way toward the village from the bluff under the cover of darkness, seize the five canoes on the north shore, wait until they heard sounds of battle, then cross over and guard the many canoes on the southern shore for use for a later retreat. They should easily be able to be in position surrounding the village before sunup.

While a few of the older warriors, who well knew how Big Marten might view the scouting party exceeding its orders, had left to return north, the vast

THE HEADWATERS WAR:
Conflict for the Mississippi Headwaters

majority could not resist the opportunity of attacking the sleeping village.

Noka stood watching as the last of the warriors crossed to the southern shore. It had taken over an hour to complete the crossing, the tension of the danger of discovery filling the air. The warriors had been ferried across with the three canoes they possessed to ensure their powder remained dry, which slowed the process considerably. But luck had been with them; no Dakota had passed either by river or on the trail they would later follow. Now they could rest for several hours and still easily reach Scarlet Leaf's village well before dawn.

Before dawn, on the river . . . .

Scarlet Leaf and Deer Killer paddled slowly, making sure they made no splashing sounds; two warriors seated in the middle. Right behind followed the other two canoes, each also containing, in addition to the two paddlers, two warriors. In total that provided twelve warriors, deemed sufficient by Noka to hold the village's canoe landing area until the others could cross from the northern shore. While the new moon had set, the stars shed sufficient light to allow the nearby shorelines and deadheads stranded by the lowering of the recent high water to be clearly visible. Both listened carefully for sounds from the village ahead; if nothing else the occasional barking of dogs should provide that warning.

Noka's instructions were clear. Once near the village pull ashore on the southern bank and stay hidden until they heard firing; then head directly for the landing, secure the Dakota canoes, and wait for the warriors from the bluff to the north to cross with the stolen canoes and come to their support.

The path along the southern shore . . . .

Noka moved quietly at the head of the long train of warriors, careful not to approach too closely to the last

THE HEADWATERS WAR:
Conflict for the Mississippi Headwaters

of the scouts ahead. They had been on the trail for less than two hours and had encountered no other traffic when a scout returning from up the trail caused Noka to stop, motioning those behind him to also halt. The scout reported the sound of a barking dog had been heard, indicating the village was near. Noka instructed his train of warriors to remain where they were while he went ahead to where the other scouts were gathered listening. From ahead he could hear the occasional bark of a dog, normal for any village at rest, and Noka smiled with satisfaction; with the light wind from the southwest they should be able to almost encircle the village before the dogs sensed their presence and gave warning. Immediately Noka issued instructions to bring the column of warriors forward and move into position around the village, then wait until they heard his war cry; which, if they remained undetected by the village dogs, would come just as the sun tipped above the horizon. Then all were to charge the village.

If the dogs sensed their presence and gave the alarm? Just be prepared to begin earlier.

Just before dawn ....

Scarlet Leaf listened expectantly, the canoe pulled under the tree cover. No sign of excitement from the village indicating the main party led by Noka had been discovered; which also meant, unless some unknown difficulty had arisen, they should be in position. Now they awaited the sound of the first gunshots. Only minutes later the firing began, and Scarlet Leaf and Deer Killer pushed their canoe from its cover and paddled rapidly upstream toward the landing, followed by the others.

As the village neared the first few gunshots had turned into steady firing, and within minutes they arrived at the landing and, pulling their canoes ashore, rushed up the bank and searched for cover. Buffalo hide tepees were scattered among the bark lodges, and warriors, both

THE HEADWATERS WAR:
Conflict for the Mississippi Headwaters

Ojibwe and Dakota, could be seen breaking cover to seek a less exposed position.

Scarlet Leaf and Deer Killer took a position below the low bank cut by the river during high water and waited. A few of the Dakota rushed toward the landing, but retreated immediately upon being met by fire from Scarlet Leaf and the other waiting warriors. Soon the promised relief came and all was secure, allowing some to break off to inspect the row of canoes beached in front of the village. Those with paddles were brought to join the eight they had, and soon over twenty canoes were lined up on the shore behind the defending Ojibwe. That would be enough.

Noka huddled behind one of the bark lodges watching the progress of the attack. As he had feared the Dakota had been warned when the village dogs sensed their presence, but he was surprised by how fast the Dakota had responded. By the time the first wave of attackers reached the village Dakota warriors were emerging, weapons in hand, and the situation became chaotic with struggling combatants and fleeing women and children. While able to seize the outlying areas, soon the Ojibwe advance was slowed as the Dakota managed to organize their defense. Now, with the sun approaching its zenith, it had become a stalemate.

The steady firing had largely ceased with only occasional shots breaking the stillness. It was increasingly clear they could not overwhelm the defenders, and Noka knew they didn't dare stay much longer. If the Dakota had been able to send runners to the downstream village for support, as they almost certainly had, it would be night or early tomorrow before they could arrive; but that was not what concerned Noka. He could not forget the Dakota villages near the mouth of the Minnesota River were but a day or two paddle south of the Crow, perhaps only a day at full speed. If they were warned and sent a warparty upriver he could be trapped here in the south.

180

THE HEADWATERS WAR:
Conflict for the Mississippi Headwaters

They had taken many Dakota scalps, although losing a number of their own warriors, and it was time to pull back and retreat. First, though, was how best to disengage. Noka motioned to White Eagle, one of his leading warriors, and gave him instructions to take to the warriors guarding the landing to be ready for their evacuation. Then he sent several others to carry his instructions to his attacking warriors to slowly withdraw and work their way to the landing. The first of those across were to take positions to provide cover as the main party crossed. There would be little the Dakota could do to stop them, since the village they were defending was a distance from the landing.

Early Afternoon, the next day . . . .

The last of the canoes had been retrieved from their hiding places and pulled into the reed-filled shallows bordering the Crow River, and the warriors were embarking, protected by those already sitting offshore their guns at the ready. The warriors serving as the rearguard should soon arrive and then they could all be off.

The crossing of the Minnesota River had gone as planned, but the retreat to the Crow had been hurried, with the Dakota in pursuit. As soon as the advance group reached the bank of the Crow they were dispatched to block the Mississippi to the south; with each new group of arrivals sent as reinforcements. While in Noka's mind the mission was a success, all would come to nothing if the Dakota were able to block their retreat.

Noka was pleased with himself. He had found the location of the Dakota villages, scouted the approaches, and also succeeded in hitting the Dakota hard. He would be bringing back many scalps; a first step in revenge for the attack of the year before. But he had also lost a number of warriors and disobeyed his orders. Still, he thought Big Marten would be pleased.

THE HEADWATERS WAR:
Conflict for the Mississippi Headwaters

August, 1772 . . . .

Noka was not happy; while many hailed his raid on the Dakota village as a success, Big Marten had not been pleased. It had advertised the Ojibwe intent to raid far to the south in retaliation for their Sandy Lake attack; a plan that now had to be postponed. While the results of his raid increased his prestige among the warriors, with the Dakota aroused the expedition *Bi-aus-wah* and Big Marten had planned for the following year was abandoned, and in the years since raids had again been limited to attacks on isolated hunters and their families wandering north. But now, in council with the elders, *Bi-aus-wah* and Big Marten had decided the Dakota had forgotten the earlier raid and relaxed their guard. A warparty was being raised which Big Marten himself would lead, but Noka wasn't to be a part. This was a direct insult; since a young warrior Noka had been a trusted member of nearly all of Big Marten's prior raids.

Noka shook his head in frustration; he should not be surprised. By raiding the village he had exceeded his instructions to scout the area, and Big Marten was a proud and arrogant man, unwilling to share his fame with anyone. Maybe he should think about a move to one of the villages near the Mississippi headwaters, something he had thought of before. They were frequently at war with the western Dakota near the Crow Wing headwaters and the Red River, and they would welcome an experienced war leader. Here he would always come behind Bright Forehead and Big Marten, neither of whom showed a willingness to step aside.

Later the same day . . . .

Preparations were complete. The following morning they would begin their journey south.

Big Marten had spent hours with Scarlet Leaf and Deer Killer and the other scouts from the prior expedition, plying them with questions until he knew

THE HEADWATERS WAR:
Conflict for the Mississippi Headwaters

every detail of the country near the Dakota villages spread along the rivers to the south. White Eagle, Noka's lieutenant on that previous raid, as well as numerous other participants, had also been grilled. Big Marten had decided to bring White Eagle as one of his primary warriors on this new raid; he did not blame him for the premature attack years prior. He had not been the leader. Other warriors participating in that attack, and scouts such as Scarlet Leaf and Deer Killer, would also be welcome.

But this year things would be different. While they would follow the path pioneered by Noka three years earlier, he didn't plan to bring a group as large as the 200 warriors of the prior scouting mission; that number was too unwieldy. About 120 could be more easily handled, and with the information at hand should be sufficient for all except the large village of Chief Little Crow, located on the Mississippi between the mouths of the Minnesota and St. Croix rivers. The village targeted by Noka three years before was more suitable. Its exposed position made it a tempting target for a fast hit- and-run raid, even for his smaller warparty.

Meanwhile, the Dakota village on the Minnesota River. . . .

Shakopee sat with Beaver House discussing plans for the upcoming raid into the Mille Lacs area. Both young men were in their early 20s, and both also had reason to hate the Ojibwe. Shakopee had grown to hate the Ojibwe by living among them during his childhood, before moving from the Kathio area to the lower Rum River, Beaver House because he had lost friends and relatives at the ambush at the Crow Wing River four years before. True, that had been the Sandy Lake band, but they were also the ones largely responsible for driving the *M'dewakanton* from Kathio and the large lake it bordered.

THE HEADWATERS WAR:
Conflict for the Mississippi Headwaters

The name of the imposing young man sitting and talking with Beaver House had not always been Shakopee. Born and raised in one of those Dakota families that had integrated into the Ojibwe bands following the Battle of Kathio, he had lived among the Dakota here on the Minnesota River for less than four years. While at Mille Lacs his family had stayed clear of the frequent marriages between the two disparate groups, and had always been considered second-class members that lacked the kinship of the Ojibwe totems. It would take many years, perhaps generations, for full acceptance to be achieved.

While still in his early teens, Shakopee's family had abandoned the Mille Lacs area and moved to the Dakota village on the lower Rum River, where he had lived until the village was evacuated following the slaughter of their best warriors at the Crow Wing. After that his family had moved to this village on the Minnesota River, where relatives from the Mille Lacs expulsion had settled years earlier, only to again be attacked mere months later.

Shortly after arriving at this new village Shakopee had been given a first wife, named White Buffalo Woman. Then, just the year before in her first pregnancy, she had given birth to six boys. This astonished the Dakota; to have such a wife, and to be a man who could cause such a miracle, gave him instant fame. He must be aided by the spirits. In honor of his feat he was given the name *Shak'pi (Dakota for six)*; eventually with white settlement becoming Shakopee.

But it was fame as a warrior and revenge on the Ojibwe that Shakopee sought, a goal sought by many of the young men of the village. Like Beaver House, many had lost friends, fathers, or brothers when the Crow Wing disaster hit four years earlier. While Shakopee, prior to his arrival in his new village, had been unfamiliar with the horse, he was a fast learner and soon proved his courage in the hunt and games, becoming a

THE HEADWATERS WAR:
Conflict for the Mississippi Headwaters

leader of the young warriors through his single minded recklessness. In the evenings he and his new friends would sit by the campfires and plot their revenge on the Ojibwe; leading to an understanding that the following year they would gather like-minded young warriors in their bands and unite to make a raid of revenge on the Ojibwe. While a raid on Sandy Lake wasn't feasible, the Mille Lacs villages were smaller, exposed, and well known to Shakopee.

But such a raid was not necessary. Word had reached Shakopee and Beaver House that Little Crow, the leader of the large Dakota village of Kaposia, planned to lead a raid north that summer, and Shakopee, Beaver House, and the warriors they had collected agreed they should join Little Crow rather than mount an independent raid of their own. The plan of Little Crow told to them by his emissary was good. They would go by canoe as far as the mouth of the Crow River, and from there follow the trail that had, in earlier days, connected the Dakota villages on the Minnesota River with Kathio. The time selected was late August when many of the Ojibwe would be scattered harvesting the abundant wild berries or beginning the wild rice harvest, and if undiscovered the villages could be overwhelmed. Even if discovered, the size of the Little Crow warparty, supplemented by that of Shakopee and Beaver House, would be large enough to handle any opposition.

Both Shakopee and Beaver House were overjoyed; neither could hope to collect a warparty large enough for such an ambitious project. At most theirs would have been a hit and run raid. Many who planned to accompany their planned raid had already arrived, and others, hearing they were to join with Little Crow, were eager to volunteer. For both Shakopee and Beaver House, serving as leaders of such a large party, even while under the overall leadership of the famous Little Crow, would give them the recognition both wanted.

THE HEADWATERS WAR:
Conflict for the Mississippi Headwaters

Two days later . . . .

Shakopee, in spite of his youth and being new to his village, had been recognized as leader of his group. Not all the warriors committed to him had arrived as yet, some from further up the Minnesota River not expected until later in the day. Not willing to wait, early that morning Little Crow had left with a contingent of about 100 warriors collected from his own and nearby villages. Shakopee planned to wait until mid-afternoon when most of his missing warriors were expected, then follow with his party, leaving it to late arrivals to catch up.

Shakopee was pleased with himself; if the other warriors arrived as promised his group would be nearly as large as that of the veteran Little Crow. By mid-morning two days later Shakopee and his party would arrive opposite the mouth of the Crow River where Little Crow planned to land and stash his canoes, and should be able to rendezvous with Little Crow at the Elk River by nightfall. From there a day and a night march would bring them to the villages on Mille Lacs.

Mid-morning, two days later . . . .

The landing opposite the mouth of the Crow River was teaming with activity. Shakopee and his warriors were in the process of landing and concealing their canoes, as several of Little Crow's warriors, assigned to guard the canoes left behind stood nearby watching. He was informed that Little Crow had camped nearby the previous night and left shortly after daybreak; he was only a few hours ahead. Since Little Crow was moving more slowly, scouts in the lead to check for any wandering Ojibwe, Shakopee and his warriors should easily be able to catch up with them before sundown. After assigning some of his warriors to stay with those left by Little Crow, the long column headed up the trail at a ground-eating trot.

186

THE HEADWATERS WAR:
Conflict for the Mississippi Headwaters

Meanwhile, several miles north on the Mississippi, upstream of the Elk . . . .

The pace of the paddlers was slow, the current doing most of the work. Big Marten sat in the middle of the leading canoe, the others following in a steady stream. While he could not see them, he knew that ahead the scout canoes following the eastern and western banks would give warning of any danger. Not that he expected to encounter Dakota this far north. They rarely came north of the Crow River except during a fall or winter hunt, or during the spring sugar season.

By early afternoon Big Marten saw in the distance the familiar group of islands near the mouth of the small Elk River that branched off to the left, which were reached within minutes. Suddenly the paddlers slowed upon sight of their scout canoes paddling rapidly upstream waving, signaling to move to the eastern shore. Big Marten ordered the change of course after which his paddlers held the canoe in position. As the scout canoe arrived the excited scouts almost stumbled over each other with their report.

South of the mouth of the Elk they had heard the sounds of a group moving up the old trail on the eastern bank, and pulling into the shore had observed a large group of Dakota warriors marching north on the old Kathio trail. Soon the trail would bend away from the Mississippi to skirt the small lakes inland of the mouth of the Elk before again heading north to Kathio. While they hadn't waited long enough to determine the exact number of Dakota, they thought there were not too many; but perhaps 50 or more.

Big Marten immediately ordered his warriors to turn up the Elk and beach their canoes and prepare for an immediate attack, but to maintain complete silence. As the canoes began to land Big Marten, who knew the area well, called Good Thunder and White Eagle to his side for instructions. While the banks of both the Elk and the

THE HEADWATERS WAR:
Conflict for the Mississippi Headwaters

Mississippi were heavily wooded, a few hundred feet inland it changed to lightly wooded prairie. It was there the trail to Mille Lacs turned east to skirt the small lakes that fed the Elk. There, at the wooded edge of the Elk, they were to conceal themselves and wait for the Dakota to arrive.

Taking the lead, White Eagle started the warriors east following the south bank of the Elk. The meadow where the Mille Lacs trail passed was only a short distance inland, and if the ambush were to succeed they must be near the trail and hidden before the Dakota arrived. The band of trees along the Elk was narrow, and soon they arrived at its prairie edge only to see the approaching column of Dakota already emerging on the other side.

In spite of the planning that had come before, the excited Ojibwe, thinking they greatly outnumbered the Dakota, rushed in a disordered mob at the Dakota column. At first the Dakota attempted to make a stand, but seeing more and more Ojibwe emerging from the woods, soon dropped their blankets and most of their possessions and fled back along the trail by which they had come, the Ojibwe in pursuit. Once in the wooded valley of the Mississippi the Dakota made their stand against the oncoming Ojibwe.

But the battle was short, Shakopee and his warriors, hearing the firing, rushed ahead to join Little Crow, and the combined group charged the outnumbered Ojibwe, causing them to retreat. It was only when they again reached the open prairie area that the Ojibwe were able to find cover in a group of small trees. From there, given the cover of the trees, they succeeded in holding off the Dakota.

The battle raged all afternoon, the two groups closely matched. Finally, fearing the Ojibwe would escape in the dark, and with a wind from the south building, the Dakota tried one more tactic; they would fire the prairie. This they proceeded to do, and soon a

THE HEADWATERS WAR:
Conflict for the Mississippi Headwaters

fire raged toward and engulfed the grove of trees, causing the Ojibwe to flee in panic. Some were consumed in the flames, others fleeing to the east, while still others ran in disorder toward the Mississippi, not stopping until they reached the river's edge and either swam or ran across the submerged sandbar to the island offshore. There Big Marten organized a final defense.

A Short Time Later . . . .

Little Crow crouched with Shakopee in the cover of the bushes fringing the shore, peering at the island across the shallow sandbar. Although only sparsely wooded, logs and branches brought by the spring floods made the island a maze of obstacles. Little Crow shook his head doubtfully. "The water is shallow, and their powder will not even be wet; many will die," he said.

Adding, "but they cannot escape."

"Unless they swim away when dark comes," Shakopee commented. "We can guard the shores."

Little Crow nodded, then glanced over at Shakopee. "You are young," he said. "For the young nothing is enough or too much. I think it is enough; let them escape. We have our victory, and the lesson has been learned. They are still strong, and we have lost many. If we attack more of our warriors killed will make the victory hollow. And warriors from Mille Lacs may hear of this and come also."

After a moment Little Crow added. "Remember, my young friend, an animal fights hardest when trapped; sometimes it is better to let it run away."

Shakopee smiled, and nodded to the old warrior. "I will learn," he said. "Let them carry their story home, but let them go in disgrace. First we break up and burn their canoes and make them walk."

Little Crow glanced over at Shakopee as Shakopee gave orders to his warriors to search for and destroy all the Ojibwe canoes they could find. "Yes," he

189

thought to himself. "He is a fast learner."

After spending the night on the island, and finding the Dakota had left and their canoes destroyed, the remaining Ojibwe gathered their wounded and what dead they could carry and began the journey back to Sandy Lake. Their losses had been heavy, and no glory would come from this campaign. The Dakota could boast of their victory, the flight of the Ojibwe, and those they had killed.

Aftermath . . . .

The Ojibwe force had been shattered, and many of the warriors who had left a week before never retuned. Big Marten was in disgrace; never had a warparty he led failed so badly. It was said he was too old to be a war leader anymore, and should join the 'big bellies' where his wisdom would be of use. They said he should let go and let younger warriors like the proven Bright Forehead, or even the younger Noka, now lead. But Big Marten knew he could not.

The Dakota losses had been light compared to those of the Ojibwe, and there was rejoicing in their villages. Little Crow had added to the prestige he had long held, but the one covered in glory was the newcomer Shakopee. Without his assistance many said Little Crow and his warriors would have been all killed; unlikely, but a story Shakopee chose not to dispel. Some were even beginning to call the village on the Minnesota River where he lived 'the village of Shakopee'.

July 1773, the Dakota villages . . . .

The Dakota of the Minnesota and lower Mississippi rivers gloried in their defeat of the Ojibwe the prior summer. It had removed much of the sting of their defeat at the Crow Wing five years before, and they began to believe they could once again reclaim Mille Lacs. While the year before only Little Crow and

THE HEADWATERS WAR:
Conflict for the Mississippi Headwaters

Shakopee, with about 100 warriors each, were involved, this year there were calls for another major attack like the one of 1768, forgetting the disaster with which it ended. In response to the growing sentiment, Little Crow sent his pipe and tobacco to the other bands, and many agreed to join in a major expedition, including those of Redwing and Wapasha (*aka Wabasha*) further down the Mississippi. Both agreed to gather their warriors and join them with those of Little Crow and Shakopee. With such a force they believed they could drive the Ojibwe from the small Ojibwe villages scattered along the south shore of Mille Lacs, and use that as a foothold to expand further north. If just those *M'dewakanton* bands that still resided on or near the lower Minnesota united, perhaps with some help from the nearby *Wapekute*, they could easily field 400-500 warriors without stripping their villages of enough to be safe.

That was enough; they could do without the *Sissiton* and *Wapeton* of the upper Minnesota River and its tributaries who had little interest in the problems of their downstream neighbors; it was the *M'dewakanton* who had lost the lakes of Mille Lacs, Knife, and Big Sandy, not them, and it was the *M'dewakanton* who longed for their return. The *Sissiton* and *Wapeton* were more interested in the prairies with their teeming herds of buffalo, and besides, both well remembered how they had been burned when they joined in the raid of 1768, and still smarted from their losses.

At Big Sandy Lake . . . .

Big Marten felt old, and he had not fulfilled the pledge he had made five years earlier. He had pledged to himself he would exact revenge for the Dakota raid on his village, and would die as a warrior should; not an elder 'gumming' the soft meats provided by others. He would have that revenge, and die in battle; nothing else was acceptable. Last year he had been everywhere in the battle, but death had eluded him. When they had

THE HEADWATERS WAR:
Conflict for the Mississippi Headwaters

retreated to the island in the Mississippi, expecting to be overrun, he had made all his final preparations. He had painted himself the color of death, and sung his death songs. But it was not to be; the Dakota had left without attacking.

This year Big Marten tried hard to raise another warparty, but it was difficult. Over the winter *Bi-aus-wah* had died, and the prestige of Noka and Bright Forehead as war chiefs had risen and they were favored by the newer leaders and younger warriors. All remembered Big Marten's defeat of the previous year and the success of both Noka and Bright Forehead several years earlier. The losses last year had been heavy; the depletion of the number of Sandy Lake warriors was beginning to be a concern, and with *Bi-aus-wah* gone and his lost prestige Big Marten had little chance of attracting many from Mille Lacs, Lake Superior, or the northern lakes.

Few wanted to follow such an old man except some of the older warriors who themselves were beyond their prime. Yes, some of the young men would join, eager to say in the future they had once fought with Big Marten, but not many. Finally he managed to put together a party of about 60 warriors.

Well, that would have to do; it was as many as Bright Forehead had during his victory at the Crow Wing five years earlier. Much could be done with such a warparty; they could attack a group double their size without fear. Most would be seasoned veterans of many campaigns who would not run if outnumbered, and could be depended on to follow instructions. Big Marten recognized his mistake of the year before of including less experienced warriors on such a campaign.

While this year his goal would be the same, the village Noka had attacked four years earlier, he would use a different approach. Rather than face the risk of discovery on the Mississippi they would go overland to Mille Lacs, then take the trail south to the mouth of the

THE HEADWATERS WAR:
Conflict for the Mississippi Headwaters

Elk River, the scene to the battle of the year before. There they could easily cross the Mississippi using the islands in the river and travel overland to the Crow River. Crossing the small Crow River further south would be simple; it was narrow and shallow at this time of year. Then, once across the Crow, they could take the trail Noka had taken. Only after they crossed the Crow would they be in country completely controlled by the Dakota, north of the Crow the land was either unoccupied except for seasonal hunting camps or contested by the Ojibwe.

Sixty experienced warriors should be enough for a quick hit-and-run raid, even that deep in Dakota territory; unencumbered by canoes they could rapidly again retreat to the north. And all the warriors selected were deep in experience; he had rejected the wild young warriors who could not be depended on to follow orders.

Big Marten gazed pensively at the glowing coals, his two companions Good Thunder and White Eagle quietly watching. Since his youth Good Thunder had been an inseparable companion, and both had grown old, and knew war was for young men; this would be the last campaign for both.

Glancing over at White Eagle, Big Marten was pleased with his presence in the raiding party. White Eagle had been on the raid several years before with Noka, and on that of the previous year as well, and had proven himself. Big Marten had questioned all who were on the Noka expedition, and most agreed that White Eagle would become a leading war chief someday. While still in his early years, and lacking the experience of many, he was steady and could be depended on to carry out the purpose of the raid and bring the party home. True, he had not been able to control the hot-blooded younger warriors last year when they broke away and charged the Dakota column, but Big Marten felt he had learned from that mistake. Also, this year all the warriors were experienced veterans.

193

THE HEADWATERS WAR:
Conflict for the Mississippi Headwaters

Big Marten was depending on White Eagle to bring the warparty home, although he had not told him this. He himself did not expect to again see Sandy Lake, and he expected Good Thunder would follow him at the end. Big Martin also felt the other warriors in the party, while experienced, also lacked qualities of leadership, but would willingly follow the increasingly respected White Eagle.

Meanwhile, the village of Little Crow . . . .

The village was teaming with warriors with more still arriving. The excitement attending the nearly continuous war dances was intensified by the throbbing of war drums, and the cries and shrieks of the dancing warriors hitting the pole and boasting of their exploits and the exploits to come. The warriors of Little Crow, Wapasha, Red Wing, and the newcomer Shakopee were gathering to make one of the largest warparties in memory, nearly as large as the well remembered 1768 expedition of Strikes Many; among the dancers many veterans of that disastrous expedition.

While the failure of several years before was etched in the memory of the warriors, the success of Little Crow and Shakopee the previous year had reignited hopes of the Dakota. They would not repeat the risky Strikes Many raid that had circled around to the north before attacking the Sandy Lake village, or again allow the threat of an ambush on the river. To avoid discovery they would do as Little Crow and Shakopee had done the year before; stash their canoes at the Crow, and go overland. And they would not again attempt the ambitious goal of destroying the large and distant Sandy Lake village; now it would be the series of smaller villages strung along the south and western shores of Mille Lacs. If the Ojibwe could be driven from Mille Lacs their Knife Lake village would be threatened, and the Dakota could again consider reestablishing their Rum River village; maybe even again occupy Kathio

194

THE HEADWATERS WAR:
Conflict for the Mississippi Headwaters

itself. Then, and only then, would they be ready for the more distant Sandy Lake.

While among the leaders Shakopee was junior, still he was the center of attention and the contingent of warriors he led was among the largest; many attracted by his rising fame. He was an imposing and charismatic man, and all had heard of his six sons. He was a bearer of good medicine. Now Shakopee sat with Little Crow, Wapasha, Red Wing, and their primary war chiefs developing the final plans for the upcoming expedition that was scheduled to begin at sunrise the following day. Shakopee was not only seen as an equal, here he was listened to as the only one of the leaders intimately familiar with the area around Mille Lacs, the country of his birth and youth.

Officially Little Crow was the overall leader of the expedition, but in many ways he deferred to the younger Shakopee. Shakopee's contingent would be given the honor of being first in line on the trip north.

Near Mille Lacs Lake. . . .

Big Marten and Good Thunder led the long column of warriors at a leisurely pace, no effort made to maintain silence. There was little danger of encountering Dakota this far north. Further, with the long march ahead there was no need to tire the warriors without cause.

Tonight they would spend at the largest of the Ojibwe villages on Mille Lacs Lake, and perhaps augment their party. But Big Marten didn't expect much from the Mille Lacs Ojibwe, who he mockingly referred to as 'pretend' Ojibwe. With the integration of numerous Dakota into their band two decades before he felt they had lost their spirit, with some of the Ojibwe customs diluted by addition of customs copied from the Dakota. The newcomers fell outside the accepted Ojibwe totem system, which he felt was weakened by their presence. Some of these 'new' Ojibwe were even sitting in the councils limited to the totem elders, having established

195

THE HEADWATERS WAR:
Conflict for the Mississippi Headwaters

new totems reflecting their mixed heritage.

Still, if their villages were added together the Mille Lacs Ojibwe numbered nearly as many as those at Sandy Lake, and they were gaining more and more influence. With *Bi-aus-wah* now dead, Big Marten could see the day when they would even council peace with the hated Dakota. Well, Big Marten swore to himself, "I will never see that day."

The sun was still above the horizon when they entered the largest of the villages accompanied by crowds of children and dogs, and preceded to the area set aside for visitors. Tonight he would talk to the village elders and seek their advice. Perhaps some of the warriors would join the expedition; but he would be selective. None who had not proven themselves would be taken. He did not want many, perhaps five or six.

The next day, opposite the mouth of the Crow River . . . .

Shakopee stood on the bluff watching as the flotilla of canoes filling the river beached themselves, some waiting offshore while those already ashore were pulled further inland. He was confident no Ojibwe they encountered could withstand such a force. Shakopee smiled to himself; he would wipe the Mille Lacs villages from the earth if he could, sparing none. Even those traitor Dakota who had joined the Ojibwe.

At least, that is what he would like to do. Little Crow, Wapasha, and Red Wing didn't share his hatred, and neither did many of the warriors he led from his own new village. True, they disliked all Ojibwe and considered them their enemy, but an honored enemy. Shakopee well knew the older leaders would prevail.

Leaving the bluff, Shakopee began to gather his warriors together. They had been the first at the landing, and it was becoming crowded; best to start now for the Elk to relieve the congestion and let the others follow

THE HEADWATERS WAR:
Conflict for the Mississippi Headwaters

when they could. It was still early morning, and if they moved at a fast pace could reach the designated camping area by early evening and prepare the camp for the others. Tomorrow they planned to rest part of the day before beginning the long day and a night march north.

Meanwhile, to the north . . . .

It had been as Big Marten expected. He had received little support from the Mille Lacs elders. Many of the younger warriors had wanted to join his party, but those he had rejected. He had, however, selected five experienced warriors from the Marten totem who he felt he could trust completely. There would be no repeat of the disarray of the expedition of the year before.

They had left the village at midmorning after spending much of the night dancing and celebrating, and planned to make camp for the night on the trail. Tomorrow they would complete this leg and cross the Mississippi near the mouth of the Elk River and camp on the western side. Then a long day's march, or perhaps two, should take them to the Crow.

Evening of the same day . . . .

About a mile south of the mouth of the Elk the trail began to curve gradually to the northeast away from the Mississippi to allow a circuit of the lakes through which the Elk passed. While following the Mississippi the trail had passed through largely wooded areas which provided cover, but as they moved further from its edge the fringe of trees thinned, and the country gradually became more open; changing to prairie bordered in the distance by the wooded fringes of the two small, shallow lakes feeding the Elk. Shakopee half-smiled with satisfaction; here was where they had overwhelmed the Ojibwe warparty the year before; a warparty led by the legendary Big Marten himself. While in the increasing darkness it was difficult to see the damage the fire of the

THE HEADWATERS WAR:
Conflict for the Mississippi Headwaters

year before had caused, it appeared that it had largely repaired itself, and many of the trees on the far side remained leafless and dead. At the tree-edge Shakopee gave orders to halt and prepare a camp to be ready for the warriors of Little Crow, Wapasha, and Red Wing, spread for miles along the trail behind, when they arrived.

Later that night, after all had arrived, Shakopee met in council with Little Crow, Wapasha, Red Wing and their chief warriors to coordinate final planning. A count of all warriors present was made and came to a total of 420, some having been left behind to guard the canoes. Tomorrow they would rest most of the day and, traveling at night, make camp off the trail several hours south of Mille Lacs, dispatching scouts north to the villages. On the march north the group led by Shakopee would take the lead, a place of honor. Then, the next night, once the scouts had reported back, they would start for Mille Lacs, allowing time to divide into groups and make simultaneous attacks on all the villages when the sun first breached the horizon.

With their numbers they were confident they could sweep through the villages before they could be defended. If successful they could destroy all the villages and drive the Ojibwe from Mille Lacs. Their biggest risk was being discovered while camped waiting for their scouts to return.

Total destruction; Shakopee had argued hard for a plan to send warriors to seize the Ojibwe canoes and trap the Ojibwe, blocking escape. But his view had not prevailed. The senior chiefs were afraid that, not only would that lead to excessive Dakota casualties in the fighting needed to root out the defenders, it would also lead to uniting the Ojibwe villages further north leading to their own destruction. Their view was that most Ojibwe wouldn't unit to avenge an attack on the mixed villages of Mille Lacs unless they themselves felt threatened; be satisfied with scalps and destruction of the

THE HEADWATERS WAR:
Conflict for the Mississippi Headwaters

villages and fields. Attack from the forest side and leave the shoreline alone so flight was possible. The message would be sufficient to show they were not safe at Mille Lacs. If that message were not enough, they would do the same the following year.

Little Crow, Wapasha and Red Wing expressed the same view. If angered by total destruction of the Mille Lacs bands the Sandy Lake and Leech Lake Ojibwe, united with those of Lake Superior and central Wisconsin, could sweep down both the Mississippi and Saint Croix rivers and threaten the Dakota villages on the Mississippi, and perhaps those of the Minnesota River valley as well. The senior chiefs well understood the Ojibwe could not be driven completely from the lands they occupied, and the balance must be maintained. They would understand the gesture, and while they would seek revenge that was to be expected.

Late the following afternoon . . . .

While the Dakota rested and prepared their weapons before their departure, from the north the Ojibwe under Big Marten were finally approaching the clearing, Big Marten leading his warriors in single file preceded by several scouts. Suddenly one of the scouts was sighted running back along the trail, stopping when he reached the column.

"Dakota," were the first words of the scout. "Perhaps many hundreds; but not yet on the march."

Big Marten raised his hand to halt the file of warriors, and motioning for Good Thunder and White Eagle to come, said quietly, "I would see these Dakota." Following the scout to the edge of the forest where the other scouts were laying hidden, Big Marten and his companions lowered themselves to the ground and crawled to the edge of the tree cover where the activity of the Dakota across the field could be observed. Finally Big Marten turned his head and whispered to Good Thunder. "Bring the warriors; we will camp here where

THE HEADWATERS WAR:
Conflict for the Mississippi Headwaters

we can be seen. Build fires and cook our evening meal."

Adding: "And send our fastest runner to the villages of Mille Lacs to give warning and ask their warriors to come."

Smiling to himself: "And a runner to the village at the lake of the knife as well, asking that they send their warriors to the Crow."

When Good Thunder looked at him in surprise, Big Marten added, his normally somber face nearly breaking into a grin. "They follow the trail, leaving their canoes behind. I would take them from them and then see how many can escape."

It was only a matter of minutes before, at the other side of the meadow, the resting warriors of the Dakota began to rise, pointing in agitation at the Ojibwe emerging from the wooded area. Their first thought was to gather their weapons and prepare for battle, but something strange was happening. The Ojibwe, although appearing far fewer in number, were not retreating upon discovering the size of the Dakota camp, but had stopped and begun to build cooking fires as if nothing was amiss. The massed Dakota warriors stood in confusion, not sure what to do.

Shakopee and the other Dakota leaders gathered to the side, watching the strange activity across the field. Shakopee looked in wonder at Wapasha standing next to him. "I think they are making their camp for the night. What causes this strange action?"

Wapasha didn't respond as Little Crow moved over to join them, then, turning to Little Crow. "There must be many more we don't see, or they are mad. I count no more than 50 or 60 warriors."

Little Crow nodded: "They are not mad. See the large man watching? That is Big Marten; these are not from Mille Lacs, but from Sandy Lake. Those of last year; I think they come to avenge their defeat. But yes, the warriors from Mille Lacs, and more warriors from Sandy Lake as well, may be hidden behind waiting."

THE HEADWATERS WAR:
Conflict for the Mississippi Headwaters

Shakopee responded: "We should attack now."

Little Crow merely chuckled. "No. If they are few they will just run back to Mille Lacs. If they are many it could be a trap. We should light fires and make camp for the night. Clearly we do not march north this night, but must see what these fools will do. Tonight send scouts to see what lies beyond, whether others lay in wait. Tomorrow, if they do not all come out against us, we can fight then. For now," he said grinning, "I think I will lay down and sleep."

Shakopee glanced over at Little Crow. "When it is full dark I will cross the meadow to where they camp and listen." Spitting on the ground, "I well understand their mongrel language. It is like the barking of dogs."

As darkness fell, at the north end of the meadow Big Marten gathered his leading men. "Now all must work, but silently. They will send scouts to see if we are more than we seem; send our own to keep them away from here. Dig holes for cover. Now the Dakota wonder, but tomorrow they will attack and we will be ready. They will pay."

Good Thunder quickly left, but White Eagle remained, clearly with something to say. "I count over 400 warriors, we are little more than 60. We will all die."

Big Marten nodded. "Perhaps, but 60 warriors, well protected and well armed, can do much. Would you attack such a force, even with 400 warriors? When you did, how many would die?"

"Yes," he said thoughtfully: "They will come in the morning, but we can punish them so they will always remember what comes to them when they leave the safety of their villages and come into our lands. Now the dead grass is gone and they cannot burn us out. And when we think we cannot hold longer? Why," he said, "The trail to Mille Lacs is open behind us. And if they block the trail? Those who wish can flee into the woods. They will not follow far for fear the Mille Lacs warriors are on the way or hidden nearby."

THE HEADWATERS WAR:
Conflict for the Mississippi Headwaters

"But," he added, "We must hold until nightfall; then warriors from Mille Lacs can be here before the following morning. And if they stay here too long the warriors from the lake of the knife will be behind them; then we will see."

Glancing over at White Eagle, Big Marten added. "Remember what Bright Forehead did with 60 warriors; he destroyed a warparty perhaps larger than that we see now."

"Yes," Big Marten said, glancing at White Eagle: "We will make this a fight to be spoken of, and the names of those here today will be remembered. But we must keep them here long enough to set the trap."

After White Eagle left to join the others in their preparations, Big Marten said to himself: "But for me, I will not flee."

Before dawn the following day, village at Mille Lacs. . . .

The village was only beginning to stir, a few of the early risers occasionally leaving a lodge to go to the forest to relieve themselves, some others raising the fires of the night before from their beds of ash-covered coals. Soon fires would be burning and the activities of the day beginning, such as checking the nets placed in the lake behind for the nights catch, or perhaps leaving for the days hunt. The sprawling village spread along the southwestern shore of Mille Lacs Lake was at rest; its attention disturbed by shouts as an Ojibwe warrior entered the village from the south at a slow run, his exhaustion obvious to the few onlookers.

Bear Killer was exhausted. Starting late afternoon yesterday, and without any but short rest stops and long enough to refresh himself at a stream or with a strip of dried jerky, he had covered over 60 miles in his long run. Rather than stop when he reached the village outskirts he continued on to the lodge of the village chief

THE HEADWATERS WAR:
Conflict for the Mississippi Headwaters

at the center, where he called loudly that he carried an important message.

Immediately people began to emerge from the lodges to gather around the exhausted Bear Killer, but he stood stoically staring ahead, regaining his breath. Soon the village chief emerged and walked slowly over to Bear Killer, other senior warriors and elders also appearing.

Once the important men were present Bear Killer gave the message he had memorized the day before. A Dakota warparty of several hundred warriors was headed for Mille Lacs, and were now either at the Elk River or on the trail behind him. Only Big Marten and his outnumbered warparty were there to oppose them, and he asked the warriors of Mille Lacs to come. Big Marten had told him to say that, if the warriors could arrive before he was overrun the Dakota could be trapped; they had no canoes nearby, and would have to flee down the trail to the Crow or wherever their canoes were hidden.

The result was immediate. The village became a beehive of activity, and soon dozens of warriors were gathering being organized under the overall war chief, Broken Foot. Runners were immediately sent to the other nearby villages and to Sandy and Knife lakes as well. Over the years the Mille Lacs Ojibwe had largely stood aside from conflicts with the Dakota, their own mixed Dakota-Ojibwe families holding them back. But in the summer when the people gathered after their dispersed winter camps, and when aroused, they could field well over 300 warriors.

But Broken Foot was experienced in war and had learned the value of caution and careful planning. He stopped the gathering warriors from immediately starting pell-mell down the trail to the south; he knew that is what they would do if not held back by a tight hand. Selecting a group of 60 of the younger warriors, those best able to run all day without rest, he assigned

THE HEADWATERS WAR:
Conflict for the Mississippi Headwaters

them to Bloody Club, one of his younger, more dependable war chiefs, with instructions to leave immediately and proceed as fast as they could. While the trip would be exhausting, they should be able to cover the distance and reach the Elk by early morning and provide the support Big Marten asked; if only Big Marten could hold the Dakota that long. If not, they could at least block the trail and stop them from reaching the villages. The older more seasoned warriors would move slower, but still should reach the Elk by mid-day tomorrow. They would leave immediately, with those from the other Mille Lacs villages coming behind.

But Broken Foot was not finished; the messenger had also told him of the message Big Marten had sent to the Knife Lake village in an attempt to trap the Dakota north of the Crow. He selected 40 of his best warriors, instructing them to go as fast as they could down the Rum River and get behind the Dakota. They were to then go up the Mississippi, locate the Dakota canoes, and destroy them. They could arrive before the warriors from Knife Lake, and later when the two groups combined they would be enough to block a Dakota retreat. Without a way to escape they could destroy these invading Dakota, as Bright Forehead had destroyed them several years earlier at the Crow Wing River.

Motioning to a young warrior noted as one of their fastest runners, he instructed him to go south and tell Big Marten of what he had done, and when help would arrive.

Broken Foot knew both the Elk River area and Big Marten well, and knew what he would do. When here a few days earlier he had studied Big Martin's warparty, and knew it contained only experienced, dependable warriors. He was sure Big Marten would dig pits in the trees to repel a Dakota assault, and would not retreat. If the Dakota fled south he would follow at their heels like a village dog. Yes, he smiled to himself, this can be a day that is remembered.

THE HEADWATERS WAR:
Conflict for the Mississippi Headwaters

Before dawn at the Elk River meadow . . . .

Little Crow, Wapasha, and Red Wing sat considering the report given by Shakopee. During the night Shakopee, with several scouts, crept across the meadow, and while Shakopee crawled to where he could hear the talk of the Ojibwe, the others circled their camp to examine the trail behind. There were no more Ojibwe warriors hidden on the trail, but from the sound of digging and low voices overheard by Shakopee it appeared the Ojibwe were there to stay; at least they were digging pits in which to conceal themselves. They had also talked of the messenger sent back to Mille Lacs for support and their belief he would reach the village before morning.

If the Mille Lacs villages were warned and warriors started south their time here was limited; while an advance party might be here sometime after nightfall, a large warparty would take well over 24 hours to cover the 60 miles.

It was not the Ojibwe they faced, or those that would come from Mille Lacs tomorrow, that worried Little Crow. He was confident the 400 Dakota warriors could withstand any attack. But if they sent warriors down the Rum to get behind them they could well be trapped. Walking aside to talk privately to Wapasha he told of his concern, and the two experienced chiefs considered how much time they would have. To travel down the Rum and up the Mississippi to the Crow River would take well over a day, even travelling after nightfall. Either they start back now, or send enough warriors to add to those now watching the canoes. They had until tomorrow morning to destroy the Ojibwe, then they must withdraw; because of the warning there was no hope of catching the villages unprepared.

It was decided; they would send 50 of their best warriors to the Crow, leaving more than enough to deal with the entrenched Ojibwe. With the two dozen already

THE HEADWATERS WAR:
Conflict for the Mississippi Headwaters

there that would be enough to deal with the limited number Mille Lacs would be able to send. Yes, they had to assume the Ojibwe at Knife Lake would also be warned, but they could not arrive either here or at the Crow until at least nightfall the following day.

Little Crow called to Red Wing and Shakopee to join them, and told them of the plan. They must kill the Ojibwe party or drive them away either today or by early morning tomorrow, and be back at their canoes before the following morning. Tomorrow, at two hours after the sun was fully above the horizon, they must be prepared to leave. The warriors for supplementing the two dozen warriors left behind to guard the stashed canoes were selected, and began heading south, the remaining warriors preparing for the attack.

None of the experienced leaders among the Dakota relished the task they faced. Attacking such an entrenched foe could be expensive, even though the Ojibwe were greatly outnumbered. They well remembered what a similar sized group of Ojibwe had done to the raiding party of Strikes Many at the Crow Wing five years earlier; and the warparty of Strikes Many had been even larger than the one they now led. They could not depend on simply overwhelming the Ojibwe; the pits they had dug for concealment would make charging warriors easy targets crossing the open meadow.

They had to find a way to make the Ojibwe task of defending themselves more difficult. The scouting party reported that, to get within shooting range of the entrenched Ojibwe, they could find cover in the grove of trees near the other side of the meadow, in easy gunshot of the Ojibwe. While the grove was small with many of the trees leafless and dead from the fire the year before, the brush was heavy and could conceal many warriors. Concealment in the meadow itself was also possible; while the dead grass had been burned off the year before, the new meadow grass was tall enough for concealment,

THE HEADWATERS WAR:
Conflict for the Mississippi Headwaters

but it also kept them from returning fire without exposing themselves. For the protection of those advancing directly on the Ojibwe positions they first must seize the grove of trees.

It was agreed; that is what they would do. Wabasha's warriors would charge across the field and take the grove, while those of Little Crow, Red Wing, and Shakopee spread out and carefully approached from the front and sides. It was early decided they would not attempt to block the path behind the dug-in Ojibwe, but would try to drive them back north. The losses resulting from trying to overwhelm a trapped foe would be high. Still they could not retreat from such an inferior force without a battle, and leaving them at their backs on their return to the Crow would also be unacceptable. Best just drive them north; this campaign was at an end in any case. When the Dakota again headed south they didn't want Big Marten and his Ojibwe dogging their heels.

When everything was decided, Wapasha left to meet with his assembled warriors, picking 50 of the most experienced and sending them to position themselves as close as possible to the wooded area he wanted to seize. Meanwhile the other warriors spread out opposite the dug-in Ojibwe. Within minutes all was ready, the signal given, and the long line of Dakota warriors began a slow advance, while at the same time Wapasha's assigned warriors charged the grove of trees.

Across the field . . . .

Big Marten lay concealed, Good Thunder next to him. Across the field he could see the growing activity in the Dakota camp, most of the warriors spread out in a long line, but with one concentrated group at the side. He well knew what the intention of that group of warriors was; they wanted the grove of trees on his left, and there was nothing he could do about it; with his sixty warriors he simply didn't have enough to occupy the grove himself.

THE HEADWATERS WAR:
Conflict for the Mississippi Headwaters

During the night he had held council with his chief warriors, and the discussion had been long. Few thought his decision to stand and fight was wise; most wanting to withdraw during the night to Mille Lacs. Perhaps along the trail they could fight delaying actions to allow the warriors from Mille Lacs to arrive, but outnumbered as they were they thought they had little chance of holding off the determined Dakota in a direct confrontation.

Big Marten thought differently. He had fought in many battles and been wounded countless times. He knew what a small, determined group of warriors could do if well armed and well protected. He was confident the Dakota would not attempt to storm their position, the losses would be unacceptably large. Instead they would fire from a distance, and perhaps make some limited direct attacks. He was confident he could not be dislodged, and time was on their side. The longer they could hold them here the better the chance of trapping them north of the Crow.

Once Big Marten had made up his mind few would oppose him; he angered easily and legends were built around him. Any who wished were free to leave and return to Mille Lacs, but none did; none dared the shame abandoning the fight would bring. The stand would be made here.

It was as Big Marten had predicted. The Dakota seized the grove of trees without opposition, and once within range the advancing line of warriors went to ground and concealed themselves in the meadow grass, the ripple in the grass showing their continued crawling advance. Any of his warriors who raised their head or moved was subject to fire from the Dakota in the grove of trees. Any Dakota advancing across the meadow had to stand or kneel to fire, making them easy targets. Also if they came too close the grass near their positions thinned and they could be seen. Thicker patches had been cut or trampled by his warriors during the night.

THE HEADWATERS WAR:
Conflict for the Mississippi Headwaters

The work of the night before paid off; concealed in their pits, and with the meadow in front providing poor cover, there were few casualties among the Ojibwe, and their return fire was taking a toll on any Dakota who exposed himself. Soon gunfire diminished, limited to only when a clear target was exposed.

The day dragged on, and Big Marten smiled to himself; every hour they could hold the Dakota was an hour longer for the Mille Lacs warriors to prepare and come to their support; and an hour longer for other Ojibwe to get to the Crow. But as evening approached the warriors on both sides were beginning to lose their caution; an Ojibwe occasionally jumping from tree to tree to expose himself, or one or more Dakota in the meadow jumping to their feet to taunt the hidden Ojibwe, before again dropping to the ground. There was little Big Marten could do to stop them; he felt the growing desire to do the same.

As sunset approached, which would signal the end of today's battle, the warriors on both sides grew bolder. Occasionally Dakota warriors, leaving their guns behind, would charge toward the dug-in Ojibwe, then stop and taunt and dare them to come out and fight, causing more and more to respond. On those occasions firing halted and bloody hand to hand combat resulted, with casualties increasing. Sometimes, when warriors from one side or the other would rush out to retrieve the bodies of their comrades or join the fight, the number of casualties rose even higher. While knowing the risk, Big Marten could not hold even such veteran warriors back, and found it hard to resist the pull of such combat; it lit a fire in his blood.

Just as the sun began its descent below the tree line, a larger than normal group of Dakota made their taunting advance, and Big Marten joined the responding Ojibwe, followed immediately by Good Thunder. While it had been customary for the watching Ojibwe and Dakota to hold their fire during such individual combat,

THE HEADWATERS WAR:
Conflict for the Mississippi Headwaters

the sight of Big Marten proved irresistible to some of the Dakota, and the fighting warriors soon became the target of firing from both sides. The warriors began to fall, some continuing to fight, while some broke off the combat and retreated to their own lines.

In defiance Big Marten did not turn back. He had vowed to die fighting and never join the elders; and there was no better time. As long as a Dakota remained he continued to wield his war club. Finally, pierced by multiple wounds, he staggered toward the nearest Dakota before finally falling to the war club of another Dakota charging from the side.

Silence settled over the battlefield as firing from both sides stopped. Big Marten had been a legend among both the Ojibwe and the Dakota, and suddenly he had fallen. Night was approaching and both sides withdrew to their positions.

The next morning . . . .

The Dakota warriors were again getting into position in anticipation of battle. This attack would be the last; then they must begin their retreat or face the threat of the warriors from Mille Lacs arriving, or even the worse threat of Ojibwe blocking access to their canoes at the Crow. While yesterday had been largely fought from cover, today would be different. Now they would assault the depleted Ojibwe positions and wipe them out, or at least remove the threat of being followed as they headed south. With the Ojibwe losses of yesterday, and especially with the loss of their leader, the Dakota leaders were sure they could end it.

Wapasha stood at the edge of the meadow intently watching for activity across the meadow, but saw none. Glancing over at one of his waiting warriors he instructed him to find Little Crow and Shakopee and bring them to him. In a matter of minutes both arrived.

"I see no movement," Wapasha said. "Yesterday some could be seen. I think they are gone."

210

THE HEADWATERS WAR:
Conflict for the Mississippi Headwaters

Shakopee walked out into the meadow a distance and stopped, gazing at the tree-line on the other side. Walking slowly toward the Ojibwe positions of the day before nothing happened, still no Ojibwe visible. Some of the other warriors followed.

The meadow was only about 200 yards across, and Shakopee soon neared the tree-line followed by an increasing number of Dakota, including Little Crow and Wapasha. There they fanned out, but found no sign of the Ojibwe of yesterday.

Immediately warriors were sent to search the woods and scouts dispatched to check the trail to Mille Lacs, while Little Crow and the other chiefs walked over to the bodies still scattered around yesterday's 'killing field'. The scalped bodies of several Dakota lay were they had fallen, but the dead Ojibwe had been removed. After a moment Little Crow raised his voice and looked at the gathered crowd.

"Who struck the fatal blow to Big Marten? Did any claim his scalp?"

There was murmuring among the bystanders before a young warrior named Yellow Jacket stepped forward and pointed to one of the Dakota bodies. "Broken Rib", he said. "But the Ojibwe struck him down before he could take the scalp."

Little Crow nodded and thought for a moment, then instructed some of the warriors to pick up the body of Broken Rib before walking away. His body must be given special honors.

The battle had ended, and the scattered Dakota warriors began gathering for the march south. During the night stretchers had been constructed for the few wounded and the many dead, so little time was wasted. It would be a long trek to where the canoes were hidden, and soon the Ojibwe from Mille Lacs would be on their heels. The long procession was soon in motion headed south. Their mission a failure, but the killing of Big Marten could be spoken of.

THE HEADWATERS WAR:
Conflict for the Mississippi Headwaters

Comment

While *Bi-aus-wah* is mentioned by Warren related to all the events of the previous chapters, Big Marten only appears in his recounting of these events following the 1768 Dakota raid on Sandy Lake. However, in other sources Big Marten is identified as the primary war chief of *Bi-aus-wah*, and with *Bi-aus-wah* as early as the Chapter 2 raid on Sandy Lake. As such he would likely have been involved in all major campaigns that *Bi-aus-wah* instigated or that involved the Sandy Lake band. At Fond du Lac the Marten Totem was one of the most powerful of the Ojibwe totems, and, since Fond du Lac initiated the occupation of Sandy Lake, it was most likely powerful there also, and that Big Marten was a prominent member. While Warren fails to note whether either *Bi-aus-wah* or Big Marten were present during the 1768 raid on Sandy Lake, the very lack of mention suggests they weren't. If such was the case, upon their return their anger can only be imagined.

As to Bright Forehead, he is identified as the leader of the war party that ambushed the Dakota at the Battle of the Crow Wing in 1768. Noka is more a mystery, at least to me. The name 'Noka' means 'Bear', and since one of the Ojibwe totems was the Bear totem, was probably fairly common. Warren identifies Noka as the leader of the first revenge raid to the south, but he, or someone with the same name, figures in the history of the Leech Lake Ojibwe as well. Further, a 'Noka' or 'Nokay' later formed a village where the Nokasippi River enters the Mississippi a little south of the Crow Wing; a river named after him.

With abandonment of their Rum River village following their disaster at the Crow Wing the center of Dakota power became their villages on the Mississippi below the mouth of the Minnesota River (*Mini-sota, River of the cloudy sky*) and on the Minnesota River itself. When the Ojibwe, upon first arrival in early May

THE HEADWATERS WAR:
Conflict for the Mississippi Headwaters

of 1769, noticed leaves already on the trees they named it *Osh-ke-bug-e-sebe* (*New-Leaf River*). The first whites called it St. Peter's River, and it didn't become the Minnesota River until the Territory of Minnesota was organized in 1849.

The village attacked by Noka was most likely that located near present day Shakopee. While Warren states Noka's war party returned with many scalps, he also says the story as told to him by White Fisher (*not the famous White Fisher from La Pointe*), the grandson of Noka, was so obscure and filled with the unnatural he chose not to repeat it. However, Robinson (*25*) says it was a draw, with few scalps taken on either side.

Shakopee I, who was involved in the campaigns in this chapter, was reportedly born in 1750 either near Kathio or near the Minnesota River. However, since he led Dakota warriors at Elk River in both 1772 & 1773 that date is doubtful; he would have been only 22-23 at the time, although he did live until 1827 suggesting he was quite young at the time. Because of the lack of information my description of his origin and rise to prominence is purely fictional, except for how he obtained his name.

By the late 1770s the driving force behind the Ojibwe move into the Mississippi headwaters, *Bi-aus-wah,* and his war chief, Big Marten, were dead, and their long-time allies and patrons the French were gone, having ceded their lands in northern North America to the British in the early 1760s. Then, for four years the rebellion of Pontiac that followed the French withdrawal isolated the area. Only beginning in the late 1760s were the British able to exercise any significant influence over the Ojibwe of Lake Superior and further west, largely gained by moving their traders into the area. Acceptance of the British by the Ojibwe was sometimes slow and troubled; they missed the French and the close relationship they had developed.

THE HEADWATERS WAR:
Conflict for the Mississippi Headwaters

Figure 10: Minnesota River

THE HEADWATERS WAR:
Conflict for the Mississippi Headwaters

CHAPTER 7
THE SAINT CROIX RIVER

Chapters 2-6, while based on historical records, were of necessity reduced to 'historical fiction'. From this point on fiction is abandoned, and the following chapters are historical in nature; although at times what really happened could be debatable.

Additionally, up to this point the story has largely ignored the contests between the Ojibwe and Dakota occurring in Wisconsin and stayed strictly with the contest within the borders of present day Minnesota. However, a brief coverage of some of the key events occurring on the Saint Croix River, which forms much of the boundary between Minnesota and Wisconsin, and which drains a part of Minnesota as well, is a fitting, perhaps essential, addition to the story of the war for the Mississippi headwaters.

Three large tributaries drain the state of Wisconsin and feed the Mississippi; two, the Saint Croix and Chippewa rivers, enter above the present border between Minnesota and Iowa, and one, the Wisconsin River, below. The headwaters of all those tributaries were a smaller version of those of the Mississippi; rich in lakes, game, fish, and with abundant fields of wild rice. When the Ojibwe appeared on the scene Wisconsin was occupied largely by the Dakota and the Fox, and as they pushed south and west conflicts for those headwaters raged there as well; at times even bloodier than those for the Mississippi. However, these battles were fought largely by the Ojibwe of La Pointe and other Ojibwe villages along the southern shore of Lake Superior, and, except for that for the Saint Croix, were largely independent of the struggle for the Mississippi headwaters to the west.

THE HEADWATERS WAR:
Conflict for the Mississippi Headwaters

The Saint Croix River rises largely in north-central and north western Wisconsin, and for much of its length defines the border between Wisconsin and Minnesota, entering the Mississippi just below the cities of Minneapolis-St. Paul. However, two of the Saint Croix's western tributaries, the Snake and Kettle rivers, extend beyond the border of Wisconsin into Minnesota; making them accessible to both Big Sandy Lake and Fond du Lac. As a result the Saint Croix became a convenient route to the Mississippi below Saint Anthony Falls for both those villages, and both often supported the Lake Superior bands in their attacks on the Dakota villages located near the Saint Croix's mouth.

The area near the junction of the Saint Croix with the Mississippi was an important bastion of the Dakota in the late 1700s. French traders had established themselves there as early as the last decade of the 1600s, and following their expulsion from Sandy and Mille Lacs lakes, and later their Rum River village, the nearby Dakota villages formed their power-base. The Saint Croix not only provided access to the wild rice of the north, to the west and south the prairie began, rich in buffalo.

While the conflict for the St. Croix is peripheral to the main story of The Headwaters War, it is interesting in that, more than any of the other tales Warren relates, it illustrates the complex relationship that developed between the two powerful, competing tribes; the Ojibwe and the Dakota. It also was the scene of two major battles, one with the Dakota and the other the Fox and their Dakota allies. That second battle, in about 1770, was the final effort of the Fox for revenge against the Ojibwe for their earlier ejection from Wisconsin.

The early Europeans knew little of the tribes south and west of Lake Superior. Peter Espirit Radisson, in recounting his expedition to the Lake Superior area in 1654, refers to the fierce ongoing conflict then underway

THE HEADWATERS WAR:
Conflict for the Mississippi Headwaters

between the Ojibwe, who he refers to as '*Christinos*', and the '*Nadoneseronons*', his name for the Dakota. Warren states that, sometime after 1695, the Lake Superior Ojibwe had begun moving south to the wild rice rich lakes of the upper St. Croix, coming into conflict with both the Dakota and the Fox; a conflict that continued until French traders among the Lake Superior Ojibwe, in concert with the French traders near the confluence of the St. Croix with the Mississippi, managed to arrange a truce. However, that truce was between the Ojibwe and Dakota only, the recalcitrant Fox continued to inhibit the fur trade; only eliminated as a threat in the early 1700s when the French organized an alliance of Algic tribes that drove them from the current boundaries of Wisconsin.

During the long period of peace that resulted the Ojibwe and Dakota co-existed and often intermarried, with by common custom the man taking up residence in the village of the parents of the woman. In time, as with the mixed bands of Mille Lacs Lake, this led to the creation by the Ojibwe of new totems, the Wolf and Merman (*part fish, part man*), denoting that mixed heritage. At the time Warren was recording events, the early 1850s, he states the Wolf Totem was common among both the St. Croix and Mille Lacs bands of Ojibwe, and concludes these new totems, by creating a 'blood kin' relationship between the two tribes, was a key to why the Ojibwe and Dakota of the St. Croix remained at peace while in other areas war raged.

During this period of peace the Ojibwe continued to move south, and established their first permanent village in the St. Croix headwaters at Rice Lake at the source of the Shell River feeding into the St. Croix. There the Ojibwe lived peacefully in an area otherwise dominated by the Dakota. But the peace ended eventually, as conflicts caused by the Ojibwe southward pressure reemerged.

THE HEADWATERS WAR:
Conflict for the Mississippi Headwaters

Battle of Point Prescott

Warren states that about four generations before (*he was writing between 1850-53*), sometime after the battle of Kathio and the turnover of the French forts on the Great Lakes to the British (*1760s*), an event occurred that shattered the peace of the Saint Croix. If the 40 year intervals between generations used at the time by the Ojibwe were used it would result in an improbably early date, about 1690, far earlier than the battle of Kathio or the British takeover. However, the length of a generation today in the less developed countries is in the low 20s; probably typical of the early Ojibwe as well, and even in developed countries it rarely reaches 30. Using 25 years/generation would place it sometime after 1750, which is the commonly accepted date for the battle of Kathio.

The description provided by Warren of the event causing the breakdown appears rather fanciful and precise, but in any case something shattered the peace that had endured for decades, leading to what Warren refers to as the Battle of Point Prescott. Point Prescott was located near the confluence of the St. Croix with the Mississippi at present day Prescott, Wisconsin. However, calling it a battle illustrates Warren's natural bias toward his people, the Ojibwe. It was actually the massacre of several hundred Dakota by the Ojibwe at what was supposed to be a peace ceremony. The story leading up to the massacre as told by Warren is as follows;

Sometime in the mid 1700s, at a Dakota village on Lake St. Croix (*widening of the St. Croix River near its junction with the Mississippi*), in preparation for the Dakota going on the war trail against enemies to the south, an Ojibwe warrior who lived in the village with his Dakota wife joined the dance, intending to accompany them on their raid. However, a distinguished

THE HEADWATERS WAR:
Conflict for the Mississippi Headwaters

Dakota warrior, in the frenzy of the dance, fired an arrow wounding the Ojibwe, crying out *"he wished to let out the hated Ojibway blood which flowed in his veins."*

The wounded Ojibwe recovered, but continued to brood over the injury, and later left the Dakota village to visit his Ojibwe relatives on Lake Superior. However, he had more in mind. While there he convinced the Lake Superior Ojibwe to gather a warparty to avenge the insult he had received, and march against the Dakota at Lake St. Croix.

The offended warrior had a cunning plan. First he returned to the Dakota village and told the Dakota a large party of Ojibwe from his relative's village would soon arrive to smoke the peace pipe. The delighted Dakota called in their hunters and others away at other villages for the ceremony, and the entire group gathered, most making camp on the south shore of Lake St. Croix at Point Prescott, others on the opposite shore at Point Douglas, waiting for the Ojibwe to arrive. The Dakota, believing the story of the Ojibwe warrior who had long lived in their midst, didn't bother to set a watch or send out scouts. The Ojibwe party arrived undiscovered near Point Prescott and hid a distance away, sending five young men fluent in Dakota to the camp to spy out the layout and number of the enemy. To ensure they remained undiscovered the scouts entered after dark and at different times and walked around without suspicion.

Upon their return the scouts reported they counted 300 leather lodges (*Tepees*), but then became confused and could count no more. They also reported that both Sissiton and Yankton were present, although they normally resided in far western Minnesota.

That was all the information the hiding Ojibwe needed. At dawn the Ojibwe approached the Dakota encampment through a deep ravine, and once out of the ravine surrounded the village. Gradually they approached, tightening the ring, until the camp dogs

THE HEADWATERS WAR:
Conflict for the Mississippi Headwaters

began barking; at which time they sounded the war whistle and the war whoop and attacked, firing bullets and arrows at and into the frail tepees. While the men gathered in defense many of the women and children attempted to escape by canoe, but the wind and waves were high, and many filled with water and were upset with many drowning.

While the unprepared Dakota attempted to defend themselves they were eventually overwhelmed. How many were killed in the attack is unclear, since many drowned attempting to escape, but the Ojibwe claim they counted 335 scalps. How many were of Dakota warriors, and how many women or children, is unclear; all would be counted. In such warlike times women and children usually greatly outnumbered men.

Following the Point Prescott massacre total war again broke out between the Lake Superior Ojibwe and the Saint Croix Dakota, but the ties developed over the long years of peace proved too strong. Eventually peace was again restored and the two tribes began to again co-exist on the St. Croix and its headwaters. Co-exist, but with feuds and hatred still causing occasional conflicts, both big and small. With time both tribes became mixed, with the Ojibwe largely absorbing the remaining Dakota. Today there are no Dakota reservations remaining in Wisconsin; the last eliminated following the Minnesota Dakota uprising of 1862.

Battle of Saint Croix Falls

While the Saint Croix Dakota and Ojibwe managed to 'usually' live in peace, the Ojibwe continued to be in conflict with the Dakota villages on the Mississippi and Minnesota rivers, which includes the villages of Little Crow, Wapasha, and Red Wing; all located on the Mississippi within a few hours paddle of the mouth of the Saint Croix.

THE HEADWATERS WAR:
Conflict for the Mississippi Headwaters

Warren tells the story of a battle between the Ojibwe and the Fox, assisted by their Dakota allies, that occurred in the 1780s or early 1790s at the Saint Croix falls portage, a few miles above the junction of the Saint Croix with the Mississippi. While Warren provides no date, the Ojibwe forces were led by the Lake Superior chief *Waub-o-jeeg* (White Fisher), one of the most prominent chiefs of the time, who lived from 1748-1793. A daughter of *Waub-o-jeeg* married John Johnson, a prominent trader, and his granddaughter became the wife of Henry Schoolcraft, discoverer of the source of the Mississippi.

Warren also states the father of *Waub-o-jeeg*, also a famous chief, was the half brother of the Dakota chief Wapasha, the chief of one of those Dakota villages on the Mississippi against which the attack was planned.

According to Warren, the Fox, who had fled to Iowa following their retreat from Wisconsin several decades earlier, thirsted for revenge and persuaded the Dakota of the Mississippi and Minnesota rivers to accompany them on a major raid up the Saint Croix River. These were not the Dakota of the Saint Croix discussed earlier, who usually lived in peace with the Ojibwe.

At about the same time chief White Fisher from La Pointe had decided to call the Ojibwe together for an attack down the Saint Croix on the Dakota villages near its mouth, and had headed downstream with 300 warriors. While White Fisher expected to be reinforced by Sandy Lake warriors at the Saint Croix-Snake River junction, they did not appear, and rather than wait he continued downstream to the falls of the Saint Croix. Even without the added warriors he felt he still had plenty for the task; 300 was an exceptionally large warparty. At the falls it was necessary to land the canoes and take the portage to the lower river.

As chance would have it, the Fox-Dakota party started across the portage at the same time and met the

THE HEADWATERS WAR:
Conflict for the Mississippi Headwaters

Ojibwe at the midpoint.

An interesting aspect of this battle is the formality, and perhaps chivalry, displayed by the two opposing sides. The Fox-Dakota party was the larger, so the Fox, thirsting for revenge, asked the Dakota to stand aside and allow them to take the scalps of the Ojibwe by themselves, and the Dakota agreed. However, before the battle was joined, both sides temporarily withdrew to apply war paint and prepare themselves. When that was completed, and the battle between the Ojibwe and Fox finally began, the Dakota moved to a height of land to smoke their pipes and watch as interested bystanders.

The battle was fiercely fought, with the terrain making retreat for either side difficult. About mid-day the Ojibwe gained the upper hand and the Fox began to give way, and, to avoid defeat the Dakota joined the battle. With the odds against them the Ojibwe would have been annihilated had it not been for the timely arrival of sixty warriors from Sandy Lake, the party they had expected to meet at the Snake River junction.

With the Ojibwe reinforcements the Fox and Dakota were pushed back and were finally forced to flee, but the terrain left few paths of retreat, and the slaughter was great. Some of the Fox and Dakota were driven off the bank into the raging waters and drowned, others were lost when their 'tippy' wooden canoes overturned. Warren says of the battle;

> *"Every crevice in the cliffs where the battle had been fought contained a dead or wounded enemy. The Ojibwe suffered a sever loss in the death of their bravest warriors. . . But few of the Odugamies (i.e., Fox) escaped . . . "*

In honor of this battle, White Fisher, the Ojibwe chief from La Pointe, created the following poem titled 'Waub-o-jeeg's Battle Song', translated to English by his son-in-law, John Johnson (*22, pp.27-28*).

THE HEADWATERS WAR:
Conflict for the Mississippi Headwaters

"On that day when our heroes lay low, lay low,
On that day when our heroes lay low
I fought by their side, and thought, ere I died,
Just vengeance to take on the foe,
Just vengeance to take on the foe.

On that day, when our chieftains lay dead, lay
dead,
On that day, when our chieftains lay dead,
fought hand to hand at the head of my band,
And here on my breast have I bled, have I bled,
And here on my breast have I bled.

Our chiefs shall return no more, no more,
Our chiefs shall return no more
And their brothers in war, who can't show scar
for scar,
Like women their fates shall deplore, deplore,
Like women their fates shall deplore.

Five winters in hunting we'll spend, we'll spend,
Five winters in hunting we'll spend,
Till our youth, grown to men, we'll to the war
lead again,
And our days like our fathers' will end, will end,
And our days like our fathers' will end.

In the story of his life, *Life, History, and Travels of Kah-JGe-Ga-Gah-Bowh, (4, p.37-38),* first published in 1847, George Copway quotes this song as a standard war song sung by 'pagan' Ojibwe during their war dance prior to leaving on the war path; with at the end of each stanza a recitation by the warrior of former victories. Above is his version, although some translations vary slightly. I find the third stanza an interesting view of the warrior culture; if a warrior fails to match the others in valor (*can't show scar for scar when compared to the*

223

THE HEADWATERS WAR:
Conflict for the Mississippi Headwaters

leaders who were killed) they were like women.

Neither the Dakota nor the Fox ever again attempted to challenge Ojibwe control of the Saint Croix. The Fox losses were so great they asked to be assimilated into the Sac tribe, a request that was granted. Interestingly, the final stanza, referring to the five winters they would have to forego the warpath and engage in hunting; until their teenage youths would be able to take the warpath. That simply reflects the culture of never ending warfare of these warlike tribes, but it also indicates how high the Ojibwe losses were.

Eventually white settlement forced the mixed Saint Croix bands onto reservations, but during the Dakota uprising of 1862 some provided support, probably influenced by their Dakota and mixed Ojibwe-Dakota members. Following the uprising all were removed from Wisconsin, first to the Leech Lake reservation, and later to White Earth. Later some moved to the Mille Lacs reservation, with some eventually settling near Sandy Lake. Only by the 1934 Indian Reorganization Act were some small reservations near the Saint Croix restored and these 'mixed' bands given federal recognition. There are no purely Dakota reservations in Wisconsin at this time.

The Ojibwe takeover of the Saint Croix is but a part of the conflict in Wisconsin; that over the Chippewa and Wisconsin tributaries to the east were probably both bloodier and more significant. However, that is beyond the scope of this book.

THE HEADWATERS WAR:
Conflict for the Mississippi Headwaters

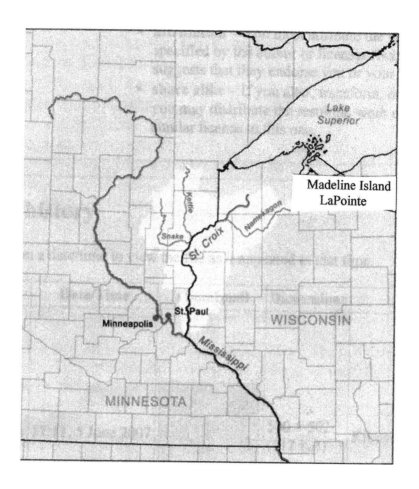

Figure 11: St Croix River Watershed

THE HEADWATERS WAR:
Conflict for the Mississippi Headwaters

CHAPTER 8
UK-KE-WAUS AND BATTLE LAKE

In some ways the events described in both this chapter and the one that follows may lack the importance of those events described in the earlier chapters, but form a necessary addition to the story of the war for the headwaters of the Mississippi. Both help show the mood of the times, the often 'blundering' nature and lack of planning in Indian warfare, and why achieving peace between the Ojibwe and the Dakota was so difficult. Both chapters also feature events in the early life of one of the most prominent and long lived Ojibwe chiefs of the time; Flat Mouth the elder.

The following story is told by Warren in describing the legendary bravery of the Leech Lake Pillager Band, honed over their years of conflict with the Dakota and Nakota to the west. Warren states he heard it from Flat Mouth himself, the venerable Pillager chief, who as a young man was a participant in a revenge raid that closely followed the battle itself.

In the fall of the year, sometime in the early 1790s, a group of Ojibwe at Leech Lake decided they should raid the Dakota to the west, even though it was not the normal season for warfare; fall and winter were usually reserved for hunting. Additionally they were short on ammunition; but still, it seemed like a good idea at the time. Luckily the trader, John Baptiste Cadotte (*brother of William Warren's maternal grandfather*), had just arrived at nearby Cass Lake and established his winter camp. The warriors immediately rushed off to obtain the needed ammunition.

When Cadotte learned the purpose of their need for ammunition he tried to dissuade them, knowing it would interfere with his ability to trade for furs. He tried

226

THE HEADWATERS WAR:
Conflict for the Mississippi Headwaters

to convince them to wait for spring or summer, the normal time for war, and promised that then he would provide all the ammunition they needed. For a final convincer he gave them a quantity of whiskey to take back to Leech Lake with them. The Ojibwe agreed, and told Cadotte they would wait until spring.

Upon return to their village all got properly drunk, and the following day when they had sobered up, an elderly warrior named *Uk-ke-waus* left his wigwam and made a round of the others, stating he still planned to go on a warparty, and dared the others to come along. Soon a group of about fifty warriors, including the four sons of *Uk-ke-waus*, assembled, gathered their weapons, and began the march toward Dakota country to the west.

It wasn't long before the warparty left the heavy tree cover near the headwaters lakes and arrived in the area where the terrain changed to groves of trees mixed with prairie. After four days marching to the southwest, late one afternoon they reached a small lake named Leaf Lake and discovered sign of Dakota. Then, in the distance, they heard gunfire, so they made camp for the night, and early next morning headed toward the source of the gunfire of the day before. On the way they crossed a well beaten trail that led them to a large lake, and again they heard guns in the distance. Strangely, they seemed to be hearing guns in all directions, and some of the warriors thought they were being surrounded and wanted to retreat, but *Uk-ke-waus* insisted on continuing.

Following the beaten trail they soon arrived at a deserted encampment with fires still burning, from which, as they neared, three Dakota warriors who had been sitting smoking jumped up and fled toward the lake shore, the Pillagers in hot pursuit. Once at the shore the Pillagers could see a moving camp of Dakota families winding along the beach to their right, of which apparently the three pursued Dakota had been the rear guard.

The Dakota, seeing the Ojibwe emerge on the

THE HEADWATERS WAR:
Conflict for the Mississippi Headwaters

lake shore and the three Dakota throwing up their blankets in warning, dropped their loads and fled in panic, pursued by the Ojibwe led by their three fastest runners.

The three Ojibwe pursued the Dakota into a wooded area, only to emerge on the prairie on the other side and see a Dakota village of about 300 lodges; perhaps housing over 400 warriors. Further, the village was filled with running warriors preparing for battle.

Upon being warned of what lay ahead, *Uk-ke-waus* realized they could not escape and must fight. He selected the best position they could find, near a small creek flowing into the lake, bounded on both sides by tall grass, and prepared for battle. There, hidden in the tall grass, he posted his warriors.

Battle was not long in coming. Soon long lines of Dakota warriors were marshaling on the lake shore, led by an imposing man holding a spear who wore a blue military coat with a large silver metal denoting his rank as chief. Once the Dakota had assembled in overwhelming force the chief led the warriors at a run toward the outnumbered Ojibwe, dodging from side to side to avoid the expected gunfire.

While the Dakota charged, led by their chief, *Uk-ke-waus* ordered his warriors to hold their fire. Only when the Dakota were well within range did the hidden Ojibwe fire, with the first shots bringing down the leader, causing the enraged Dakota to charge blindly at the partially concealed Ojibwe. But the Dakota had few guns, and were driven back with heavy losses.

The battle continued, and the Ojibwe retreated to a grove of trees for their final defense. *Uk-ke-waus*, informed one of his four sons was already dead, and knowing he was the one who had led them into this disaster, called out to the others, "*Let those who wish to live, escape by retreating, while singly I will stand in the path of our enemies.*"

All the surviving Pillagers, except the three

228

THE HEADWATERS WAR:
Conflict for the Mississippi Headwaters

remaining sons of *Uk-ke-waus*, took him at his word and fled. When the Dakota finally again attacked, *Uk-ke-waus* and his three sons managed to hold the Dakota off until the other Pillagers were safely away; only about one third of the party returning to Leech Lake.

After that the lake where the battle occurred was called 'Battle Lake', the name it still bears. Battle Lake is southwest of Leech Lake, about five miles south of Ottertail Lake, which places it in the Red River drainage basin just beyond the furthest west extension of the Crow Wing River. While Warren refers to the tribe that was attacked as Dakota, if so it was probably *Sissiton* or *Wapeton* who made their home on the Chippewa or Pomme de Terre tributaries of the Minnesota River (*Figures 10, 12*) to the south and southwest of Battle Lake. It could, however, as likely been Yankton or Yanktonais who occupied the area to the west. Their shortage of firearms as late as the 1790s points to one of the prairie Sioux branches.

However, that did not end the story. Flat Mouth, a young warrior at the time but already a chief, was returning from Red Lake when he heard of the death of *Uk-ke-waus*. Although it was midwinter a warparty of 130 warriors, Flat Mouth among them, left Red Lake and traveled west by snowshoe to the Dakota hunting grounds. There they found a large hunting camp of 50 lodges and made a night attack, firing into the defenseless lodges, killing many before they withdrew.

After the attack Flat Mouth and two others stayed near the lodges listening. Creeping closer, they again fired into the lodges before fleeing.

THE HEADWATERS WAR:
Conflict for the Mississippi Headwaters

CHAPTER 9
OVATURES OF PEACE

By the early 1800s the Ojibwe occupied the Red River valley of far-north western Minnesota, but the Dakota still held the area from Ottertail Lake and to the south. Further to the west and southwest lay the land of the Yankton and Yanktonaise. Warren states that sometime before the war of 1812 the Yankton, pressed by the Ojibwe from both Red and Leech lakes as well as Pembina on the Red River, attempted to arrange a general peace with the Ojibwe. Robinson (*23*), based on information from Joseph Renville, who was present in the area at the time, places it about 1817. As a first step the Yankton head chief, Shappa, took his favorite wife, an Ojibwe woman captured years before, and sent her carrying his peace pipe to Pembina, which had originally been her home, to express his friendly intentions and inform the Ojibwe that Shappa would like to come to Pembina and smoke the pipe of peace with them.

The offer was accepted, and on the appointed day Shappa met with the Red River (*Pembina*) Ojibwe and smoked the peace pipe as the Yankton representative. On the same day, near the Platte River (*small river in Minnesota, not the Platte tributary in Nebraska*) junction with the Mississippi, about 30 miles south of the Crow Wing, a group of Dakota met with Mississippi Band Ojibwe (*Crow Wing area, Mille Lacs, and Sandy Lake*) to also smoke the pipe of peace.

After the above ceremonies, the Dakota and Ojibwe at the Platte River meeting decided to play a game of ball. However, a Dakota survivor of a previous Ojibwe attack could not resist striking one of the Ojibwe with his ball-stick; a blow that was promptly returned. To keep the game from degenerating into a general

230

THE HEADWATERS WAR:
Conflict for the Mississippi Headwaters

brawl, *Wah-na-tah*, a son of Shappa, rushed out to separate the combatants. Years later *Wah-na-tah* became a very influential chief among the Yankton.

Missing from the above meetings was Flat Mouth, the Pillager chief, who continued to have doubts as to Shappa's sincerity and suspected him of treachery. Shortly thereafter, while hunting near Otter Tail Lake, Flat Mouth ran across a large trail heading south toward Battle Lake. Noticing the sign of a beaver carved in a tree, the sign of Shappa, he concluded it was Shappa himself who was the leader; but knowing there were no Ojibwe near Battle Lake he returned to his Otter Tail camp. The next day, seeing smoke in the distance, he found two of his cousins murdered, and also the bodies of some dead Dakota/Nakota (*Warren tends to identify all Sioux as Dakota*).

To avenge his cousins Flat Mouth sent out his pipe to notify other Ojibwe camps of his intent to gather a war party, and invited their warriors to join him. However, before the war party gathered a runner arrived from Col. Dickson, a British trader on the Red River, with a message from Shappa that he had no hand in the affair, and asking him to meet at Dickson's trading post for the purpose of smoking the pipe of peace. Flat Mouth complied, and headed for the trading post with 30 warriors. A day after his arrival Shappa arrived with only two warriors.

When Shappa offered his pipe to Flat Mouth it was refused; at which time Shappa knew he was to be killed. However, when Flat Mouth's warriors asked permission to kill the Yankton chief they were told they could not spill blood on the white man's property; they must wait. The next day, after they left the trading post, the Yankton chief and his two warriors were followed and killed. Dickson, when he discovered what had happened, was enraged; he was a friend of Shappa and also his brother-in-law. He threatened to withdraw Ojibwe rights to trade at the trading posts, which failed

THE HEADWATERS WAR:
Conflict for the Mississippi Headwaters

to impress Flat Mouth.

The following year, when another attempt was made at a meeting on the Platte to establish a peace, Ojibwe and Dakota war parties accidently encountered each other. Smoking the pipe of peace together, both then returned home. Shortly thereafter Broken Tooth from Sandy Lake (*son of Bi-aus-wah*) proceeded down to the Minnesota River with a small party to pay a visit of peace to a Dakota village. The Ojibwe encountered the Dakota in a large camp at the junction of the Mississippi and Minnesota rivers, near where Fort Snelling was later located. Startled by the appearance of the Ojibwe canoes, the Dakota were about to fire on the Ojibwe when Joseph Renville, an influential half-breed (*mother a Dakota*) trader, took them under his protection. Broken Tooth and his party, under the protection of Renville, made only a short stay before again heading north escorted by the trader; a Dakota war party following all the way to Sandy Lake, near where they killed one lone hunter. Chief Curly Head, who divided his time between Sandy Lake and the Gull Lake-Crow Wing area, quickly put together a war party from those hunting near Gull Lake and went in pursuit.

Curly Head and his party followed the Dakota all the way to their village and, while the Dakota were engaged in a dance of victory over the scalp they had taken, took cover and watched. Shortly a canoe with five young women coming to join the celebration came near, and the Ojibwe fired on them, running out to take their scalps. Following this successful attack Curly Head and his warriors returned home without incident.

Thus ended attempts of the Dakota and Nakota to arrange a peace with the Ojibwe; war again flared along the entire length of their frontier with the Ojibwe. It would be years before the white government would succeed in suppressing the warfare.

THE HEADWATERS WAR:
Conflict for the Mississippi Headwaters

CHAPTER 10
CROSSING THE MISSISSIPPI

Following the disastrous 1768 Dakota raid on Sandy Lake, and Big Marten's 1772-1773 failed attempts at revenge, the lines of settlement between the two tribes became static. *Bi-aus-wah* and Big Marten were gone, and the conflict in eastern Minnesota spiraled down to occasional raids by one party or the other. A good example are the small raids and conflicts described in the previous two chapters. While in the early 1780s the British had arranged a truce between the two tribes it was limited and short lived. However, both sides were exhausted by their four decades of warfare, and new chiefs capable of replacing *Bi-aus-wah* had yet to prove themselves.

Everything east and north of the Mississippi River from Mille Lacs Lake north to the Canadian border was firmly in the hands of the Ojibwe. The Dakota, who had resided east of the Mississippi at Sandy, Mille Lacs, and Knife lakes, and later on the Rum River, had fled south. Largely *M'dewakanton*, their strength was now concentrated on the lower Minnesota River and the Mississippi below the mouth of the Minnesota. The smaller *Wahpekute* band also maintained villages on the Mississippi below the Minnesota. There was not a single Dakota village east of the Mississippi and north of St. Anthony Falls.

The upper reaches of the Minnesota River, and its Chippewa and Pomme de Terre tributaries, as well as the area surrounding the Red River from the Ottertail area and south, were still controlled by the Dakota, primarily the *Wahpeton* and *Sissiton* bands.

Between the Dakota and Ojibwe dominated lands lay a no-mans land still claimed by the Dakota, but

233

THE HEADWATERS WAR:
Conflict for the Mississippi Headwaters

frequented by both tribes during the hunting seasons, sometimes under a temporary peace agreement arranged for the season. The richest of the contested lands lay west of the Mississippi, the area drained by the Crow Wing River and its tributaries.

The Crow Wing River basin includes the present day Brainerd lake area, containing numerous large lakes such as Gull and Cross Lake, along with dozens of others. Also included was the area drained by the Long Prairie tributary of the Crow Wing, borderlands where the forests met the prairie, rich in game including deer, elk, and buffalo. Few Dakota dared live year round in this contested area, but the *Sissiton* and *Wahpeton* considered that territory near the Long Prairie River their own, and they were often joined by western bands such as the Yankton or Yanktonais in their fall-winter hunts. The Ojibwe also hunted throughout the Crow Wing watershed; something they dare do only when large numbers came together.

It was this land west of the Mississippi upon which the Ojibwe now cast their eyes. Claimed by the French from 1699 to 1782, when it was transferred to Spain, in 1800 in the midst of the Napoleonic wars it was reclaimed by France. When in the early 1800s the Americans began negotiations for the city of New Orleans, in need of funds Napoleon threw in all the Mississippi drainage basin west of the Mississippi for an additional $5 million (*total $15 million*), resulting in what is now known as the Louisiana Purchase. For the first time the United States had a claim to country west of the Mississippi to add to its claim to the Northwest Territory east of the Mississippi resulting from settlement of the Revolutionary War.

However, having a claim is not control. East of the Mississippi the 'Northwest Territory' remained under the control of the British, who refused to evacuate their forts and trading posts in spite of the settlement with the American Colonies, and west of the Mississippi the

THE HEADWATERS WAR:
Conflict for the Mississippi Headwaters

Americans were still a non-factor. It wasn't until after the war of 1812 that the British evacuated their Northwest Territory forts and trading posts allowing the Americans to move in and establish a presence in Minnesota, and it was only after the construction of Fort Snelling in 1819, located west of the Mississippi at the mouth of the Minnesota River, that even a semblance of control over the two tribes was achieved.

Two additional factors in addition to a loss of their leaders contributed to delay the Ojibwe advance. First, in 1782 a smallpox epidemic swept the area, with the Ojibwe at Sandy Lake particularly hard hit. Some sources say the Sandy Lake village was reduced to seven wigwams. It took several years before an influx of new migrants, primarily from Lake Superior, allowed the band to again regain its strength, only to be again decimated by the Cross Lake massacre near the turn of the century, and again in 1820 by a measles epidemic. Second, the Ojibwe had much of what they wanted; the headwaters of both the Mississippi and the St. Croix and the country that lay between. It took time to fully occupy those areas with immigrants from the north and east and pressure to build for more land.

During the period of stalemate blood still flowed. Attacks of one party on the other still occurred, many small attacks of opportunity, others well planned raids or massacres involving as many as 400 warriors on a side. The difference was that both sides seemed to realize they lacked the power to dislodge the other from the territory they then occupied, and the contests were primarily for the purpose of revenge or attacks of opportunity; not the land conquests of earlier years. Anyone entering the large no-mans land between did so at their own peril, and it became the staging ground for raids deep into the territory of the opposing tribe.

Fortunately, the fall and winter hunting season was not normally the season for war, and neither side wanted the constant risk of attack during such a critical

THE HEADWATERS WAR:
Conflict for the Mississippi Headwaters

time. During such a time it became customary for a party of Ojibwe, when venturing west of the Mississippi, to approach a Dakota hunting camp and formally request a truce for the season, usually granted with smoking of the pipe of peace. For that season the Dakota and Ojibwe would hunt side by side and share friendly visits. It even became common for warriors of the two tribes to adopt each other as brothers. At season's end both camps would go their own way, knowing that with the coming of spring their warriors might again face each other in battle.

As the above practice became entrenched it became customary for the Leech Lake and Sandy Lake bands to meet at Gull Lake and join forces before proceeding into the heart of the Crow Wing country for the fall hunt. Upon encountering a Dakota camp they would then negotiate a truce for the season. Complete families would be present, moving from area to area, at each location constructing temporary camps of light birch bark covered wigwams. This they would continue until the end of the hunting season, often ending only in February. Then was the time to move to their maple syrup camps, and when that season came to an end to their primary villages for the late spring and summer. That was the time for raiding and war.

While all the country near the Crow Wing was frequented by hunting parties of both tribes, the Long Prairie River tributary, where the forests merged with the prairie, was especially desirable. The *Wahpeton* and *Sissiton* bands of the Dakota from the southwest commonly established their hunting camps in that area, and it often attracted hunters of the Nakota or Lakota as well. Because of the abundance of large game the Ojibwe were also attracted to that area, and without a temporary truce blood was sure to flow.

But even with a truce incidents and misunderstandings could lead to bloodshed. Warren describes what followed a truce negotiated by Yellow

236

THE HEADWATERS WAR:
Conflict for the Mississippi Headwaters

Hair, the prominent chief at Leech Lake and father of Flat Mouth. The story he relates describes both the relationships developed during these temporary truces, and illustrates the ease with which one could be broken. To a large extent it also shows the brutality of Indian warfare.

According to Warren, one winter the allied camps of the Pillager (*Leech Lake*) and Sandy Lake bands met a group of Dakota near the Long Prairie River, and a temporary truce was arranged. During the truce Yellow Hair and a *Wahpeton* warrior agreed to become brothers, and during the balance of the season treated each other as such. The friendship between the two became so close that a lasting peace was discussed, with an understanding to meet during the summer on the Mississippi River. Robinson reports these events as occurring in 1785-86. When it was time to travel to the sugar making camps the two tribes parted, and both moved slowly back toward their villages; only Yellow Hair and a few others remaining for a few more days of hunting.

One day, while Yellow Hair was away on the hunt, his wife heard moaning at the door of the lodge, and rushing forth saw the form of her oldest boy painfully crawling homewards through the snow, bleeding and scalpless. The mother and those from the other lodges followed the track her son had made, and found three more children lying dead. Upon his return Yellow Hair said little, but early the next morning all headed back to Leech Lake to bury the four children. However, when that was done Yellow Hair gathered five warriors and headed back to the Crow Wing to seek revenge.

When Yellow Hair reached the Crow Wing area he found the Sandy Lake Ojibwe still present, and when told of what had happened and his intention to seek revenge, recognizing the value of the friendship with the *Wahpeton* they had entered into, the Sandy Lake Ojibwe

THE HEADWATERS WAR:
Conflict for the Mississippi Headwaters

attempted to pacify him with gifts; an example of 'covering the body'.

While the killing demanded revenge, which could consist of killing the culprits or any innocent Dakota encountered, an alternative was to 'atone' for the killing by 'covering the body'. 'Covering the body' could be done two ways. First, gifts could be given to the aggrieved party, either by the culprit or a third party, to atone for the killing. Alternatively, a member of the offending tribe, usually a child, could be adopted to replace the one lost. When an adoption took place the adoptee became fully integrated into the adopting tribe, and rarely was there a betrayal. An example is the adoption by the Dakota chief Shakopee I of a son of Ojibwe Chief Yellow Head; who later went on to succeed his adoptive father as Shakopee II, chief of the Shakopee band.

In the present case, Yellow Hair accepted the gifts from the Ojibwe intended to cover the dead, but once away from camp circled and continued to follow the trail of the departed *Wahpeton*. At Sauk Lake, near the Long Prairie River, the trail of a small band broke off from the larger, which he determined to follow.

The Ojibwe finally caught up with the Dakota, consisting of only two tepees, near the headwaters of the Crow River far to the west. Surrounding the tepees Yellow Hair waited until dawn, then he and his men began firing. The *Wahpeton* returned fire, but they were outnumbered and at a disadvantage. During an interval in the firing one of the Dakota called out, asking why they were being attacked; a voice Yellow Hair recognized as that of his adopted brother.

Yellow Hair answered that it was revenge for the killing of his son, his adopted brother denying any involvement by his people; claiming it must have been the work of 'the wolves of the prairie', *i.e.*, the Lakota or Yankton. Unsure of how to respond, Yellow Hair paused to smoke a pipe and think. Then he called out and asked

THE HEADWATERS WAR:
Conflict for the Mississippi Headwaters

if the *Wahpeton* had a child present who could replace his dead son. Warren then states;

> *"The Dakotas, thinking he wished for a captive to adopt instead of his deceased child, took one of the surviving children, a little girl, and decking her out with such finery and ornaments as they possessed, they sent her out to the covert of the Ojibwe warrior. The innocent little girl came forward, but no sooner was she within the grasp of the avenger that he grasped her by the hair of the head and loudly exclaiming, "I sent for thee that I behold thee as I once beheld him," he deliberately scalped her alive, and sent her back to her agonized parents; not a being in the Dakota lodge survived."*

In time two new chiefs established ascendancy; Broken Tooth, the son of *Bi-aus-wah*, at Sandy Lake, and Flat Mouth, the son of the Yellow Hair of the above story, at and near Leech Lake. The Crow Wing would have to wait.

1797 - Cross Lake Massacre

In the fall of the year, sometime between 1797 and 1800, a major part of the Ojibwe village at Sandy Lake traveled down the Mississippi and joined the Pillager band from Leech Lake at a camp near the Crow Wing River. While Warren makes no mention, the Leech Lake chief was probably either Yellow Hair, the star of the previous tale, or his more famous son, Flat Mouth, while the Sandy Lake chief was probably Broken Tooth. If Flat Mouth, he would have been in his early 20s at the time. From there the combined group traveled to the Long Prairie River area about 50 miles to the southwest for the annual winter hunt.

239

THE HEADWATERS WAR:
Conflict for the Mississippi Headwaters

As discussed earlier, the custom was that, when both tribes were in the area a truce would be arranged, but this year the Dakota avoided the Ojibwe, and no truce was formed. Instead the Dakota gathered together a group of about 400 warriors and waited. As spring approached, and the combined Pillager-Sandy Lake bands returned to their camp in the eastern Crow Wing area, the Dakota followed. There the Dakota waited until the two groups split for their return to their villages, Leech Lake to the north, and Sandy Lake to the northeast. Once they started the Dakota followed the smaller of the two groups, that from Sandy Lake.

The Sandy Lake group moved leisurely toward home, moving their camp from place to place, and about 30 miles northeast of their Crow Wing camp decided to spend the night on a point projecting into Cross Lake. Considering themselves safe they neither bothered to place lookouts, nor erected a barricade of trees or logs around their wigwams. Early the next morning the Dakota were discovered by some hunters leaving the camp, and under the impression the Dakota were peaceful two Ojibwe went out on the ice to meet them; but the Dakota fired on them. Both the Dakota and the Ojibwe warriors were immediately joined by others, and a general battle began on the ice near the shore.

But the outnumbered Ojibwe were no match for the Dakota and were forced to retreat and find what limited protection they could behind their wigwams, where they continued the fight, but greatly outnumbered, were soon overwhelmed and killed. Once the Ojibwe warriors were disposed of, the Dakota entered the wigwams and killed the women and children, with a few children spared to be later adopted into the Dakota tribe.

One of the children adopted was reportedly a grandson of *Bi-aus-wah.* Edward O'Neil, in his *History of the Ojibways,* places the massacre at February 19, 1798, and says 40 Ojibwe were killed. However, O'Neil, in providing counts, normally includes only heads of

THE HEADWATERS WAR:
Conflict for the Mississippi Headwaters

families (*warriors*). O'Neil also states both Sauk and Menomonee's accompanied the Sioux in the attack.

The Sandy Lake band had still not fully recovered from the smallpox epidemic of 1782, and their number was further reduced by the above attack; but, as with that earlier occurrence, in time it was again restored by immigrants from other villages. Sandy Lake was just too desirable and important to abandon.

Seizure of Crow Wing by the Ojibwe

While the smallpox epidemic of 1782 decimated the Sandy Lake village, it also resulted in new immigration into the area. One of those new immigrants was Curly Head, a dynamic new chieftain from Lake Superior. However, at Sandy Lake Curly Head was just one chieftain among many; Broken Tooth, the son of *Bi-aus-wah*, had precedence.

Following the Cross Lake massacre Curly Head decided to directly challenge the Dakota claim to the eastern Crow Wing River basin by establishing permanent or semi-permanent camps at Gull Lake, on the west side of the Mississippi south of where the Cross Lake massacre had occurred. His act attracted many other adventurous warriors who the Dakota repeatedly tried to dislodge, without success. It is arguable during how much of the year these villages established by Curly Head were occupied; some sources say they were permanent, but Warren and others imply they were not.

In any case, Curly Head continued to consider Sandy Lake his home, and as late as the Treaty of 1825, the year of his death, signed as a representative of Sandy Lake. However, in time his ascendancy over the Crow Wing and Gull Lake areas established him as a principal chief of those bands spending much of the year in the Gull Lake area in parallel with Broken Tooth at Sandy Lake.

THE HEADWATERS WAR:
Conflict for the Mississippi Headwaters

While the above move by Curly Head gave the Ojibwe dominance near Gull Lake and much of the lower Crow Wing River basin, the areas further west remained frequented by the Dakota, including the rich hunting grounds near the Crow Wing's Long Prairie River tributary. As long as that area remained dominated by the Dakota any settlement in the eastern part of the Crow Wing basin was at risk of attack. Eventually, however, the Ojibwe found justification, and the will, to drive the Dakota from that area as well.

Sometime in the early 1800s a pair of distinguished Ojibwe warriors and their families, while camped near Mille Lacs Lake, were attacked and killed by a Dakota warparty; an incident taken personally by Curly Head. Flat Mouth, the Pillager chief and son of Yellow Hair, also had a grudge against the Dakota to settle, and the two prominent chiefs agreed to meet at the Crow Wing for a warparty. From there they led the combined force of 160 warriors into Dakota country, proceeding first to the Long Prairie River region about 50 miles to the west. Near the Long Prairie the Ojibwe party discovered a trail often used by the Dakota, which they began to follow, eventually discovering a group of about 40 Dakota lodges on the banks of the river.

During the night the Ojibwe surrounded the Dakota lodges, and early in the morning, before the Dakota rose for the day, began firing at the lodges. Finally about 60 Dakota warriors emerged to oppose them, and a bloody fight ensued which lasted until nightfall, by which time all the Dakota warriors except seven had been killed. Retreating to the lodges the seven remaining Dakota could not be dislodged, and the Ojibwe finally abandoned the effort and retreated from the area, claiming they had suffered only five killed in the battle.

The Ojibwe considered this action a fitting revenge for the killing near Mille Lacs and the Cross Lake attack years before. Shortly thereafter the Dakota

THE HEADWATERS WAR:
Conflict for the Mississippi Headwaters

evacuated the Long Prairie River area, and never again located a village so far north.

It should be noted that Warren refers to the village as Dakota, in which case it would have been *Wahpeton* or *Sissiton*. However, because of the large number of horses reportedly present it suggests a band adapted to prairie life, and could well have been Nakota (*Yankton or Yanktonnai*).

Even after evacuation of the Long Prairie area by the Dakota it continued to be too dangerous for establishment of villages by the Ojibwe and remained a shared hunting ground. Attempts by the Dakota to hunt in that area led to frequent conflict until Curly Head's heirs and successors, Hole-in-the-Day and his elder brother Strong Ground, aided by Flat Mouth of the Pillagers, finally forced the Dakota to give up all claim to the area.

When, upon Curly Head's death in 1825, Hole-in-the-Day the elder and his brother Strong Ground, both adopted by Curly Head, gained civil chieftainships at Sandy Lake, it didn't mean they were in charge of anything beyond Curly Head's original band. Curly Head's real influence had been in the Gull Lake-Crow Wing area even though he continued to consider Sandy Lake his home. While the two brothers remained at Sandy Lake they, like Curly Head before them, were only two among the five or more bands residing in the area at the time, each with their own chiefs. However, of those chiefs Broken Tooth still had precedence inherited from his father, *Bi-aus-wah*, and when he died in 1832 his Sandy Lake chieftainship passed to his son Big Mouth (*Bad Boy*), who because of his lineage also had precedence. However, like Curly Head before them, Hole-in-the-Day and Strong Ground were dominant in the Gull Lake area.

Even while Hole-in-the-Day and Strong Ground were solidifying their control of the eastern Crow Wing basin, to the west the Pillagers under Flat Mouth were

THE HEADWATERS WAR:
Conflict for the Mississippi Headwaters

pressuring the Dakota and Nakota further west. By 1830 Flat Mouth had established a permanent village at Otter Tail Lake, forcing the Dakota further south and west, and removing some of the pressure on the western Crow Wing watershed. Otter Tail Lake was west of the Mississippi headwaters, a part of the Red River watershed flowing north into Hudson Bay.

Sometime around 1836 Hole-in-the-Day and Strong Ground finally decided it was time to leave Sandy Lake and move permanently west of the Mississippi. Hole-in-the-Day established a village at Swan River, near Gull Lake, and Strong Ground established his village a distance to the north. However, since the village of Hole-in-the-Day was only about 30 miles north of the treaty line established by the Treaty of Prairie du Chien and under constant threat by the Dakota, subsequently it was moved to Gull Lake. Soon the area near where the brothers settled attracted other chiefs and other villages, until in a few years the area around Gull Lake surpassed Sandy Lake as the center of power of the Ojibwe, with Hole-in-the-Day the unchallenged overall chief.

While Hole-in-the-Day gained more fame and influence than his older brother Strong Ground, the two brothers were a team sharing much of the credit for the conquest. However, as Hole-in-the-Day rose to principal chief of the Mississippi band Strong Ground was forced to sit in his shadow. While both were noted for their bravery, Strong Ground claimed thirty six eagle feathers, each denoting a Dakota scalp.

Even during the mid 1830s, when the above takeover of the area west of the Mississippi was underway, relative peace between the Ojibwe and Dakota reigned, with the two tribes again often joining to share hunting grounds; on occasion the Ojibwe even hunting on the prairies west of the Red River in present day North and South Dakota. However, following a conference between Hole-in-the-Day the elder and the

244

THE HEADWATERS WAR:
Conflict for the Mississippi Headwaters

Dakota Chief Rattling Cloud an incident occurred leading to a flare up of hostilities. The two chiefs had met in a conference, and Rattling Cloud had requested Hole-in-the-Day's support in stemming white migration into Dakota lands, a request declined by Hole-in-the-Day. This angered Rattling Cloud, and when a stepson, nephew, and cousin of Hole-in-the Day were ambushed and murdered while he was returning from the conference, it was blamed on Rattling Cloud.

When Hole-in-the-Day heard the report of the killing of his relatives, he traveled to the area and met with the Dakota, where he agreed not to seek revenge in exchange for hunting rights on Dakota land to the west (*i.e., an example of 'covering the dead'*). During the spring of 1838 Hole-in-the-Day led a party west and was feasted at a Dakota encampment, but during the night he roused his warriors and slaughtered the Dakota. This led to the events of 1838-39 at Fort Snelling, discussed in Chapter 11.

However, tensions eventually cooled, and by the mid 1840s the period of conflict again eroded into a period of co-existence, marked by occasional killings of opportunity. More and more the two tribes found their common enemy to be the growing white influence. Knowing direct confrontations with the Dakota would alienate the increasingly powerful white presence at Fort Snelling, Hole-in-the-Day thereafter adopted a new policy; to gradually press the Dakota south by establishing villages in what had previously been joint or contested hunting grounds. By 1842 Ojibwe villages had been established at Rabbit and Rice lakes between Sandy Lake and Mille Lacs, and southward on the Mississippi at the mouths of the Crow Wing and Nokassipi rivers, with one short-lived attempt at the Little Elk River right on the 1825 Prairie du Chien treaty line near Little Falls. Other additions were on the Snake River, south of Sandy Lake, and further down the Rum and Snake rivers.

The new village of Crow Wing on the eastern

THE HEADWATERS WAR:
Conflict for the Mississippi Headwaters

shore of the Mississippi opposite the mouth of the Crow Wing River soon became a dominant center and attracted white traders and settlers as well as Ojibwe, by the late 1840s rivaling St Paul in size.

As the Crow Wing-Gull Lake area gained in influence it attracted additional bands, even the Sandy Lake hereditary chief, Big Mouth (*Bad Boy*), moved to Gull Lake. Sandy Lake had been reduced to two bands from the five or more in just the few years following the brothers' departure. To be fair, much of this was due to the attractiveness of the Crow Wing-Gull Lake area, not necessarily a shortcoming of Big Mouth. Once safe from Dakota attack the Crow Wing had advantages Sandy Lake lacked. Not only did the Crow Wing area exceed Sandy Lake in the number and richness of its lakes, it was also much nearer the rich hunting lands near the Long Prairie River transition zone.

As additional villages were added west of the Mississippi, Hole-in-the-Day, recognized as principal chief over the entire newly acquired area, gained influence, even claiming authority over the mixed white-Ojibwe settlement at Crow Wing. He continued to acquire territory, pushing the Ojibwe area further south into territory claimed by the Dakota. Hole-in-the-Day was once heard to boast that, but for the interference of the whites, someday he would make his home at Saint Peter. While there is a city of Saint Peter north of Mankato on the Minnesota River, it was not established until 1853, well after the death of Hole-in-the-Day the elder. He must have meant the Saint Peter agency near Fort Snelling. At the time the Minnesota River was called the Saint Peter River.

The conquest of the Crow Wing and its tributaries was a truly joint effort. Initiated by Curly Head aided by Flat Mouth, later solidified by Hole-in-the-Day the elder and Strong Ground, who also worked closely with Flat Mouth, It took the combined forces of both groups to force the final Dakota evacuation.

THE HEADWATERS WAR:
Conflict for the Mississippi Headwaters

Figure 12: West of the Mississippi*

*The first 'unnamed' river west of the Mississippi branching off to the south from the Crow Wing River is the Long Prairie River

THE HEADWATERS WAR:
Conflict for the Mississippi Headwaters

CHAPTER 11
FORT SNELLING AND AFTERMATH

In the 1700s and early 1800s the new United States had little if any influence in the Mississippi headwaters, or in any part of the current state of Minnesota. East of the Mississippi was the Northwest Territory where the English continued to be influential, largely ignoring the rights granted the United States by the 1783 Treaty of Paris ending the revolutionary war. It wasn't until after the December 1814 Treaty of Ghent, formally ending the War of 1812, that the United States was finally able to exercise control over that part of Minnesota.

West of the Mississippi had been French, then Spanish, then again French territory, with their presence in the area limited to a few fur traders. However, with the Louisiana Purchase in 1803 the United States took title to that area as well. But the newly purchased territory was far from the nearest American fort or settlement, and claiming title without a physical presence was meaningless.

In 1805, following purchase of the Louisiana Territory, a party led by Lieutenant Zebulon Pike was sent by the Governor of those newly acquired lands on a mission to search for the source of the Mississippi; a mission not authorized by the federal government. Later that same year, while in what would later become Minnesota, Lieutenant Pike arranged purchase from two Dakota chiefs of a nine square mile parcel near the junction of the Mississippi and Minnesota rivers, and a second parcel at the junction of the Mississippi and Saint Croix rivers, for the purpose of building future military posts. That the two chiefs had little if any greater claim to ownership of the land than many others was a minor

248

THE HEADWATERS WAR:
Conflict for the Mississippi Headwaters

item that seemed to bother no one.

While the federal government had never authorized this purchase, nonetheless it ratified the treaty in 1808. However, it was never 'proclaimed' by the President, a required step, and it's questionable whether the Dakota involved considered it a land cession; but more as their permission to build a trading post on land they used jointly with other bands.

The Dakota didn't realize the direction their lives would take as a result the brief stay of Lieutenant Pike and the sale of those two small parcels. It seemed like a good thing for the Dakota to have traders nearby, and in addition they were promised they would be given presents in exchange for the land. The Dakota didn't understand that this was but the first step in a series of land concessions that would lead to the 1862 expulsion of all Dakota from the State of Minnesota.

Following signing of the treaty, Pike continued up the Mississippi, but the oncoming winter and freeze-up of the Mississippi caused him to stop about 30 miles below the mouth of the Crow Wing River for a winter camp. Rather than spend the full winter idle, Pike proceeded by foot upriver, making a temporary stop at the British Northwest Fur Company post at Big Sandy Lake, where he met both Broken Tooth and Curly Head. Recognizing both as chiefs, he gave each an American flag and a metal, explaining the Americans had replaced the British in the area, and they should have no more relations with the latter.

From Sandy Lake Pike continued on to Leech Lake, where the British Northwest Fur Company also had a post, and then on to Cass Lake, which he thought was the source of the Mississippi. At Leech Lake he provided the Pillager Chief Flat Mouth with an American flag and metal; Flat Mouth in return giving Pike the British flag he had been given previously. Flat Mouth then pledged to forego his relationship with the British and replace it with that of 'the Long Knives', as

249

THE HEADWATERS WAR:
Conflict for the Mississippi Headwaters

he referred to the Americans. This served the Americans well, in that Flat Mouth was instrumental in keeping the Minnesota Ojibwe from joining other Ojibwe in supporting the British during the War of 1812.

During this trip Pike made an estimate of the Minnesota Ojibwe population as:

	Men	Women	Children	Total
Sandy Lake	45	79	224	348
Leech Lake	150	280	690	1,120
Red Lake	150	260	610	1,020

Pike lists the chiefs of the three villages as:

1) Sandy Lake: Broken Tooth,
2) Leech Lake with 3 chiefs: Flat Mouth, Of the Land, and Burnt, and
3) Red Lake: Sweet.

Of the many Ojibwe villages at that time only the above three locations are counted, and there is reason to question their accuracy. Pike lists one chief at Big Sandy Lake, Broken Tooth; but still he gave a medal to Curly Head in recognition that he was also a chief. While bands were typically small, often less than 100 families, still multiple bands under multiple chiefs often resided at any significant location. In the mid 1830s Sandy Lake had at least five bands, and in the summer of 1839 Hole-in-the-Day the elder, based at Gull Lake at the time, was able to bring 500 Ojibwe, including women and children, to Fort Snelling, finding an additional 300 already there.

The numbers could also be depressed by when made. Pike didn't sign the 1805 Treaty with the Dakota until September 23, 1805, and made slow progress upriver, using a 70 foot keelboat. Freeze-up occurred before he reached either Sandy or Leech lakes, and he then proceeded on foot to Sandy Lake, then by dogsled

THE HEADWATERS WAR:
Conflict for the Mississippi Headwaters

to Leech Lake. Pikes stay at Sandy Lake was brief, and the count there would have been made in the winter when many were away for the fall-winter hunt, and it was only a few years after the Sandy Lake band had been decimated by the Cross Lake Massacre. Since Pike wintered at Leech Lake, the Leech and Red Lake counts could have been in the spring; but even during the spring many could have gone directly from their hunting camps to their sugar-making camps and not counted.

However, whether low or not, the above numbers do show the impact of the ongoing conflict between the Ojibwe and the Dakota; nearly double the number of women and 4-5 times the number of children as men at all three locations.

In spite of the doubtful legality of the 1805 land purchase, in 1819 construction of Fort Saint Anthony (*later changed to Fort Snelling after first commander*) began on the western parcel (*i.e., mouth of Minnesota River*) of 'Pikes Purchase', and continued until 1824. The fort had two primary roles; first, to mediate between the Dakota and the Ojibwa to halt tribal conflicts, and second, protect United States interests in the area, including the influx of new settlers. This influx was difficult to stop; soon settlers were arriving and squatting on both purchase land and Indian land as well.

Located at the mouth of the Minnesota River, Fort Snelling was ideally located for the above roles, at least for establishing control over the Dakota of the Minnesota and nearby Mississippi rivers, and the mixed Dakota-Ojibwe bands of the lower St Croix as well. However, most of the Ojibwe lands in Minnesota lay to the north beyond Fort Snelling's effective range, and it would be decades after the building of Fort Snelling before a fort was established in Ojibwe country near the Crow Wing River.

One of the first steps taken after the construction of Fort Snelling was establishing treaties with the tribes in an attempt to halt tribal warfare. Between 1825 and

251

THE HEADWATERS WAR:
Conflict for the Mississippi Headwaters

1830 four treaties were negotiated and signed at Prairie du Chien on the Mississippi River in present day Wisconsin, primarily for establishing tribal boundaries, but some land cessions.

The first of those treaties, signed August 19, 1825, set boundaries between the Ojibwe and the Dakota (*see Figure 13*), plus Dakota boundaries with several other tribes. Therefore, the first major treaty affecting Minnesota was not a land cession treaty, but was intended only to halt tribal conflicts. Two other treaties, one in 1829 and one in 1830, involved the Dakota and several other tribes, but not the Ojibwe. The treaties of 1829 included land cessions not involving any Minnesota land, but the 1830 treaty ceded some Minnesota land along the upper Des Moines River in southwestern Minnesota claimed by the Dakota.

Interestingly, the 1825 treaty, with both Broken Tooth and Curly Head listed as Sandy Lake chiefs, gave back to the Dakota the area of the lower Rum River and other areas they had fled from over 50 years before. It did, however, confirm Ojibwe ownership of the Crow Wing/Gull Lake/Brainerd area.

Following the 1825 Treaty of Prairie du Chien violations of the peace between the Ojibwa and Dakota continued. Breaches of the agreement by the government led to the Ojibwe contesting the dividing line, and the enmity of the two tribes developed over their nearly ninety years of almost constant conflict was impossible to eliminate, resulting in sporadic conflict. The main difference was that now the United States attempted to serve as an intermediary, often seeing that justice (*sometimes 'strange' justice by current standards*) was carried out. While the fort and surrounding area was supposedly neutral ground, with free, unmolested passage, the volatile nature and many grievances of both tribes led to almost yearly violations; both of the treaty line and the neutrality of the area near the fort.

Some examples of violations after the

THE HEADWATERS WAR:
Conflict for the Mississippi Headwaters

construction of Fort Snelling, and the 'frontier justice' meted out, or lack thereof, are summarized below. These incidents are reported, among other sources, by Rev. Neill in *History of the Ojibways and Their Connection With Fur Traders,* which can be found as parts of both bibliography items (20) and (37).

1827

Flat Mouth, the Leech Lake Ojibwe chief, with seven warriors and about sixteen women and children, arrived at Fort Snelling, and was granted permission to camp near the walls of the fort for protection. During the day a group of Dakota arrived and were feasted by and smoked the pipe of peace with Flat Mouth and his group. Upon leaving some of the Dakota fired on the Ojibwa, killing two and wounding several others.

When the incident was reported to the fort commander, he sent a party of soldiers after the offending Dakota, which brought back thirty-two prisoners, who were displayed in front of the Ojibwe who were asked to pick out the culprits. Two were recognized by the Ojibwe and turned over to them to decide their punishment. The Ojibwe took the offenders to a nearby field and gave them a thirty yards head start. All were shot and killed and then scalped. The following day a group of Dakota arrived and delivered two more culprits to Flat Mouth. The two were promptly killed.

Some modern sources claim Shakopee I (*Chapter 6, Big Marten's War*) was one of the Dakota killed when released in the field, and almost succeeded in eluding the Ojibwe bullets. However, while he is reported to have died in 1827, he would have been near or over 80 at the time and, if true, the presence of so prominent a chief among those sacrificed to the Ojibwe would certainly have been noted by Neill.

THE HEADWATERS WAR:
Conflict for the Mississippi Headwaters

1838

Nine Ojibwe under Hole-in-the-Day the elder, who had inherited half the band of Curly Head upon his death in 1825, encountered a group of Dakota, mostly women and children, camped on the Chippewa River in western Minnesota. Claiming to be peaceful, the Ojibwe were feasted by the Dakota and spent the night in their lodges. During the night the Ojibwa rose and killed all the Dakota except three, two women and one boy. This incident was discussed earlier in the chapter involving the takeover of the Crow Wing area.

Sometime later Hole-in-the-Day, with a small party, visited Fort Snelling. The Dakota discovered him and his group and attacked, but succeeded in killing only one of the party; Hole-in-the-Day escaping. No punishment was meted out to Hole-in-the-Day for his massacre of the party of Dakota earlier that year, but the Dakota who did the shooting were required to undergo public humiliation for a violation of the sacred ground near the fort.

For clarification, Hole-in-the-Day became the dynastic name of a long line of chiefs, and the above was Hole-in-the-Day the elder, the first of the line. Later more will be said both of him and his son Hole-in-the-Day the younger, both of whom became prominent leaders of the Ojibwe; especially the Mississippi Band.

Summer 1839

Hole-in the-Day, discussed in the previous 1838 set of events, was not mollified by his escape from punishment the prior year, and in the summer of 1839 again went down to Fort Snelling, this time with a group of about 500 Ojibwe, making the total number of Ojibwe present at the fort over 800. At the same time about 1,200 Dakota were present. Three days after his arrival

THE HEADWATERS WAR:
Conflict for the Mississippi Headwaters

Hole-in-the Day, after smoking the pipe of peace with the Dakota, departed to return to Gull Lake. However, two Ojibwe remained behind and killed one of the Dakota. The enraged Dakota gathered warriors from their villages on Lake Calhoun and the Mississippi and Minnesota rivers and started in pursuit. In early July the pursuing Dakota caught up with the Mille Lacs band of Ojibwe, who were innocent of the above killing, in the valley of the Rum River below Lake Mille Lacs and attacked them, killing or wounding about 90. Most of the casualties were woman and children, since the Ojibwe warriors had left them behind as they ranged ahead searching for game.

At the same time another Dakota warparty pursued a group of Ojibwe from the Saint Croix band and found them camped with the white trader named Aitkin (*probably William Aitkin, the father-in-law of William Warren*) near Stillwater on the Saint Croix River. Unfortunately the Ojibwe were largely drunk on whiskey provided by the trader, and 21 were killed and 29 more wounded.

Hole-in-the-Day, who had caused the problem in the first place, was in neither of the above groups and escaped punishment again.

At the time Hole-in-the-Day the elder was recognized as principal chief of the Crow Wing-Gull Lake area, and also the new villages established east of the Mississippi by incursion into the Dakota hunting grounds south and east of Mille Lacs. But he was also influential at Sandy Lake, where he had resided until 1836. However, he was never able to gain significant influence over the Mille Lacs bands, who steadfastly denied his principal chief claims.

As an example of how stories can change as they are passed on, on August 24, 1839, Henry Schoolcraft entered in his journals(1) a story of a purported massacre of the Ojibwe on their return from the St. Peter Indian Agency at Fort Snelling, which is undoubtedly a twisted

THE HEADWATERS WAR:
Conflict for the Mississippi Headwaters

version of the above events. At the time Schoolcraft was the Indian Agent at Michilimackinac on the northern straights of Lake Michigan, with sub-agencies at Sault Ste. Marie and La Pointe on Madeline Island, with responsibility for the Ojibwe of Michigan, Wisconsin, and Minnesota; therefore he should have been aware of the July incident. I find the Schoolcraft version reported no where else in this form, and Schoolcraft admits he acquired the story third hand. Why he should include it in his journal without verification is strange. That he was at odds with Lawrence Taliaferro, the Indian Agent of the St. Peter Agency at Fort Snelling, could partially explain the confusion.

Schoolcraft and Taliaferro had long been at odds; Taliaferro, angered at the transfer of the Ojibwe of the upper Mississippi from his agency to that of Schoolcraft, freely voiced the opinion that Nicollet, not Schoolcraft, should have been credited with discovery of the source of the Mississippi. As Indian Agent at St. Peter (*at the time the Minnesota River was still called the Saint Peter River*) Taliaferro had responsibility for the Dakota, but he had already submitted his resignation and left in October 1839.

Schoolcraft, ever since his transfer from Prairie du Chien, also seems to have become detached from direct dealings with the Indians; his journals related more to personal or academic pursuits. Toward the end of his tenure he rarely traveled to the western posts from his primary base on Lake Michigan.

In any case, the story Schoolcraft reports is as follows. A peace conference had been held between the Ojibwe and the Dakota at the St. Peter Agency in August (*partly true, in July Hole-in-the-Day and some Dakota smoked a pipe of peace*), and upon leaving the larger part of the Ojibwe party camped at the St. Anthony Falls, about ten miles from Fort Snelling, while a smaller party camped on the St. Croix. The report says the Dakota attacked both camps during the night, killing about 150

THE HEADWATERS WAR:
Conflict for the Mississippi Headwaters

Ojibwe at Saint Anthony Falls and 20 more at the St. Croix camp; with a loss of less than 50 Dakota.

The attack at the St. Croix fits with the previous version, but the part about the attack at St. Anthony Falls is clearly erroneous; a somewhat less deadly attack occurred upstream on the Rum River near Mille Lacs, and it appears to have been during the day, not a secretive attack at night.

The story of Hole-in-the-Day's return to Fort Snelling that summer, and the subsequent events at Mille Lacs and Stillwater, were well documented. While Schoolcraft is usually meticulous in his reporting, if nothing more this story illustrates how rumors can soon become reported as fact; Schoolcraft's rendition appears to be a 'garbled' version of the incident of earlier that summer.

1841 - Dakota Attack on Lake Pokegama

In 1841 the Dakota attacked the Ojibwe village at Lake Pokegama, 30 or so miles SE of Mille Lacs Lake. This isn't the larger, better known Lake Pokegama near Grand Rapids that connects to the Mississippi, but the smaller lake of the same name several miles west of Pine City, that connects via the Snake River to the Saint Croix River about 20 miles distant.

The Lake Pokegama village was established in 1837, and was one of the southernmost villages of the Ojibwe, precariously close to land frequented by the Dakota. To make matters worse it was also easily accessible to the Dakota, since its Snake River outlet was a tributary of the Saint Croix. However, a mission and school were present at the village, which perhaps provided a false sense of security. Luckily, many of the Ojibwe residents had abandoned their bark wigwams for log structures, providing added protection from the attacking Dakota.

This battle is different from most in that there

257

THE HEADWATERS WAR:
Conflict for the Mississippi Headwaters

were two reports of this battle, both by eyewitnesses, which differ somewhat in detail;

Mrs. Elizabeth Ayer, widow of the Rev. Fredric Ayer: (*original version by W. H. Folsom, '50 Years in the Northwest', pp. 262-266, 1888*)

According to Mrs. Ayer, who was present at the time, the attack was in revenge for the killing of two sons of Little Crow, the M'dewakanton chief, whose village of Kaposia was on the Mississippi River southeast of Fort Snelling.

The Dakota arrived at night, and hid, planning to attack the Ojibwe when they arrived to tend their gardens in the morning. However, most of the Ojibwe women and children were away from the village, having slept on an island in the lake for fear of Dakota attacks. Apparently some of the men also slept on the island, since the story refers to some coming from there and killing at least one Dakota.

However, the Dakota presence was discovered when several Dakota guarding the far shore fired prematurely on a passing canoe, and after the canoe overturned, pursued and killed two young Ojibwe girls.

In the ensuing fight near the Ojibwe cabins no Ojibwe were killed, although several were wounded. An unreported number of Dakota were killed, with the bodies removed; but, perhaps fearing pursuit, the bodies were left leaning against some trees a distance away, dressed in finery and with their weapons beside them,.

Upon discovering the bodies the Ojibwe took them and cut them in pieces for distribution among those who had in the past suffered from losses to the Dakota; with some pieces cooked and eaten.

Rev. E. D. Neill (*Collections of the Minnesota Historical Society, Vol.1 (20); a version also included as section contributed to the History of the Ojibway by William Warren (37), @ pp. 491-493*)

THE HEADWATERS WAR:
Conflict for the Mississippi Headwaters

This version was given Rev. Neill by a teacher at the mission at the Ojibwe village, E. F. Ely, an eye witness. While a more 'sanitized' version that doesn't include some of the 'pagan' Ojibwe eating the body parts of the dead Dakota, it includes more information in some areas, including that the party of Dakota numbered over 100, and there were two Dakota dead. It places the attack on May 24, 1841, and differs in some of the details surrounding the attack itself.

A significant addition is provided by Reverend Neill on events leading up to the battle; apparently two sons of Little Crow had been killed by the Ojibwe sometime earlier, which was likely the reason for the attack. Also, much added detail relates to the movements of the attacking Dakota, of which it is unlikely Mr. Ely would have direct knowledge. Both of the above suggest Rev. O'Neill also had other unnamed sources.

Following the attack the Ojibwe abandoned the village at Lake Pokegama and retreated to the Fond du Lac area where, the following year (1842), they returned the complement by attacking Little Crow's village at Kaposia on the Mississippi, killing about ten warriors and one woman. Luckily for the Dakota, Kaposia had been moved three years earlier from its original exposed location on the east bank of the river to a more secure location on the west bank several miles further south. At the new location the Mississippi, quite broad so far south, provided a barrier that made direct attacks difficult without canoes to cross the river, and any Ojibwe attack so far south in Dakota controlled country would have been overland.

1858 - Battle of Shakopee

The battle at Shakopee was the last major battle between the Ojibwe and the Dakota, and occurred after both tribes were supposedly confined to reservations.

THE HEADWATERS WAR:
Conflict for the Mississippi Headwaters

Shakopee is a mere 15 miles or so upstream on the Minnesota River from Fort Snelling.

Angered by the killing of an Ojibwe family near the Crow Wing, the Ojibwe put together a warparty of 150-200 warriors and marched south to the Minnesota River. Near Shakopee they saw an encampment of Dakota on the south shore, so they concealed themselves on the north shore. At this point the valley is wide, separated from the higher land both north and south by bluffs; with the Dakota village of Shakopee below the southern bluff.

Before sunrise the Ojibwe saw a young Dakota fishing from a canoe near the north shore and fired upon and killed him. Immediately the Dakota, numbering about 70, were aroused and began firing from the southern shore; but the distance was too great to be effective. Taking advantage of the ferry the nearby white settlement at Shakopee had established, the Dakota crossed to the northern bank of the river and engaged the Ojibwe.

The battle was intense, and the sounds could be heard in the white settlement on the southern bluff, bringing the white population out to watch. About 10:00 AM the Ojibwe disengaged and retreated northwest to Lake Minnetonka, the Dakota picking up their dead and returning to their camp on the south side. The number of Dakota dead was three, with no estimate for the Ojibwe. On hearing of the conflict the only action taken by Governor Sibley was to order the Dakota to return to their reservation.

This was at the time Hole-in-the-Day the younger, who previously had led attacks on the Shakopee Dakota, was principal chief. Some report the war party was from the Mille Lacs/Rum River area. If so, Hole-in-the-Day may not have been involved; his relationship with the Mille Lacs Ojibwe was poor.

There were many other incidents of violence besides those mentioned above, rarely punished unless

THE HEADWATERS WAR:
Conflict for the Mississippi Headwaters

they occurred at Fort Snelling itself. While the justice meted out by the white authorities in the above cases may seem primitive and uneven by the standards of today, it reflects the standards of the time, and the fact the whites in the area were still outnumbered by the indigenous population.

But events were underway that would greatly affect the Ojibwe-Dakota relationship. While some white settlers had begun to reach the area even before Fort Snelling was built, establishing themselves on Dakota land, after 1819, with the protection provided by Fort Snelling, white immigration increased, and formal land cession treaties became necessary. North of Fort Snelling settlement in the area of present day Minneapolis began on the western bank of the Mississippi near the falls of Saint Anthony, and on the eastern bank the village of Saint Anthony began to take form, years later to combine into the single city of Minneapolis. Further to the east, several miles downstream from Fort Snelling, the city that is now Saint Paul also began to emerge around the area of Pigs Eye's tavern.

The problem of the influx of new white settlers had to be solved, treaty lands were inadequate and 'squatting' on Indian lands led to friction. In addition the burgeoning demand for timber to support the cities of the middle and lower Mississippi caused covetous eyes to be turned to Minnesota's vast northern forests.

In 1837 the first major land cession by either the Dakota or Ojibwe occurred when treaties were entered into with both tribes. The Dakota agreed to give up their claims to all Dakota lands between the Mississippi and Saint Croix rivers to provide land for white settlement. Also, that same year the Ojibwe signed the White Pine Treaty, giving up their claims to a large parcel south of Mille Lacs Lake, extending to the line established by the 1825 treaty of Prairie du Chien, including the territory in Wisconsin south of that line. This land cession by the

THE HEADWATERS WAR:
Conflict for the Mississippi Headwaters

Ojibwe provided access to the timber of central Minnesota, but also served to further separate the Ojibwe from the Dakota.

But the really rich farmland in Minnesota was west of the Mississippi and immigration was increasing. In 1851 the Dakota ceded all their land in Minnesota except a 20 by 150 mile strip along the Minnesota River extending from Lake Traverse at the boundary between Minnesota and South Dakota and southeast to the area of New Ulm; seven years later reduced to the 10 mile strip south of the Minnesota River only.

However, following the events of Chapter 13: Uprisings of 1862, all treaties with the Dakota were abrogated and their reservations confiscated, with all Dakota who couldn't 'prove' they had aided the settlers during the uprising expelled from Minnesota. It was over two decades before the 'banned' Dakota were given some small reservations and allowed to return.

The path of the Ojibwe to the reservation system of today was long and convoluted. The major land cession treaties of the Ojibwe, with subsequent modifications, took place later, and are described in the next chapter, Chapter 12, The Sandy Lake Tragedy, and Chapter 16: The End Game.

THE HEADWATERS WAR:
Conflict for the Mississippi Headwaters

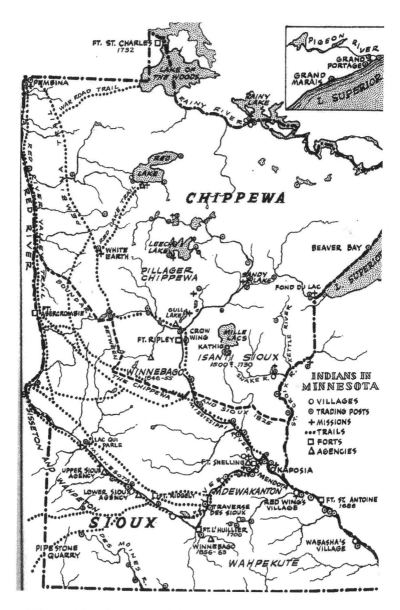

Figure 13: The Line of the 1825 Treaty of Prairie du Chien

THE HEADWATERS WAR:
Conflict for the Mississippi Headwaters

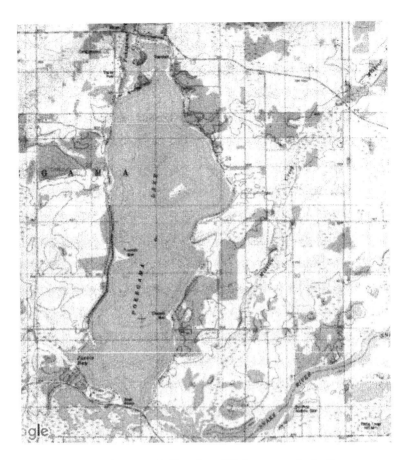

Figure 14: Battle of Pokegama Lake*

* *Snake River connects to St. Croix River. This Pokegama Lake, located Near Pine City, is sometimes confused with the larger, better known Lake Pokegama near Grand Rapids; one of the four 'reservoir' lakes that control water levels on the Mississippi.*

THE HEADWATERS WAR:
Conflict for the Mississippi Headwaters

CHAPTER 12
THE SANDY LAKE TRAGEDY

When we look at the early days of our country it is easy to overlook the failings of our forefathers, or for late arrivals those we have adopted; failings which, as is frequent with the powerful, are many. Often, when those failings come to the surface, they are simply left out of the history books, or pushed into an obscure corner where they can easily be overlooked. For the events described in this chapter, failings at both the federal and territorial levels intersect, and lead to betrayal of long-time friends for private and political gain.

Today, as one drives north through Minnesota on HY 65, one might be tempted to stop at the rest stop overlooking Big Sandy Lake. If they do, and should they choose to read the memorial sign located there, they would find the following story told; a story of what has been come to be known as 'the Sandy Lake Tragedy.

"In late 1850, some 400 Ojibwe Indians perished because of the government's attempt to relocate them from their homes in Wisconsin and Upper Michigan to Minnesota west of the Mississippi River. The tragedy unfolded at Sandy Lake where thousands of Ojibwe suffered from illness, hunger and exposure. It continued as the Lake Superior Ojibwe made a difficult journey home.

In the 1840s Minnesota's politicians began pressuring the U.S. government to remove Ojibwe people from lands the government claimed they had ceded, or given up, in 1837 and 1842 treaties. Territorial governor

265

THE HEADWATERS WAR:
Conflict for the Mississippi Headwaters

Alexander Ramsey and others claimed they were acting to "ensure the security and tranquility of the white settlements." But their true motivation was economic. If Indians were moved from Wisconsin and Upper Michigan onto unceded lands in Minnesota, local traders could supply the annuity goods the Government had promised to provide the Ojibwe under the treaties, and they could also trade with the Ojibwe themselves. Minnesotans could also build Indian agencies and schools in return for government funding and jobs.

From the outset, the Lake Superior Ojibwe vigorously opposed removal. They pointed to promises made at the treaty negotiations that they could remain on ceded lands. Knowing that the Ojibwe would not consent to the removal, government officials devised a plan to entice the Ojibwe to Sandy Lake, hoping that they would simply remain here and abandon their homelands in Wisconsin and Michigan.

In 1850, the Ojibwe were told to arrive at Sandy Lake no later than October 25th where their treaty annuities – cash, food, and other goods promised in exchange for the land cessions would be waiting for them. In prior years, these annuities had been distributed at La Pointe on Madeline Island in Lake Superior.

By November 10th, some 4,000 Ojibwe had arrived. They were ill prepared for what they faced at Sandy Lake. The promised annuities were not waiting for them, and the last of the limited provisions that were provided were not distributed until December 2nd after harsh winter conditions had set in. While they waited for

THE HEADWATERS WAR:
Conflict for the Mississippi Headwaters

nearly six weeks, they lacked adequate food and shelter. Over 150 died of dysentery caused by spoiled government provisions and from measles. Demonstrating their steadfast desire to remain in their homelands, the Ojibwe began an arduous winter journey home on December 3rd. As many as 250 others died on the way. On the same day Aish-ke-bo-go-zhe, the Ojibwe leader also known as Flat Mouth, sent word to Ramsey that he held him personally at fault for the broken promises that resulted in suffering and death.

As word of the Sandy Lake disaster spread, so did opposition to the government removal policy Non-Indian settlers-including missionaries, newspaper editors, legislators, and local citizens-voiced their support for the Ojibwe. Ojibwe leaders traveled to Washington to secure guarantees that annuities would be distributed at La Pointe and that the Ojibwe could remain in their homelands. In 1852, the U.S. government abandoned the efforts to remove the Ojibwe. And in 1854, Congress passed a law authorizing that future Ojibwe treaties would instead provide for permanent reservations in areas the Ojibwe traditionally occupied."

In this story of 'The Sandy Lake Tragedy' use of fictional embellishments seems out of place; the bare historical facts require no modification or elaboration. Therefore, I will only summarize the tragedy, and what led up to it, and include it here for one reason only. While a tragedy for those concerned, it was the one event that halted the plan to move all Ojibwe east of the Mississippi to the western states, and convinced the government to negotiate treaties for establishment of permanent Ojibwe reservations in northern Minnesota.

THE HEADWATERS WAR:
Conflict for the Mississippi Headwaters

How had this all come about? Following the Ojibwe takeover of the headwaters a third power entered the scene, a power the Ojibwe had welcomed as a friend; the white man. Yes, prior to the 1800s the white man exercised influence over the tribes, but that was largely through the power of trade. Beginning with the French through the time they were succeeded by the English, and later by the newly independent United States, the Ojibwe and the whites had coexisted in peace. While on occasion they engaged in warfare, such as in the French-Indian war with England and Pontiac's rebellion, normally Ojibwe interactions with the whites, particularly those in Minnesota, were friendly.

When the French and English were in control their footprint in Minnesota and the surrounding areas was light, and except for the traders in their midst or passing through few demands were made. However, with the population pressure following the War of Independence that began to change. In the area of the Mississippi headwaters, or Minnesota in general, it began with the 1805 purchase by Zebulon Pike of nine square mile parcels at the junction of the Mississippi with the Minnesota and Saint Croix rivers; land that lay fallow until construction began on Fort Saint Anthony (*name later changed to Fort Snelling*) in 1819.

With construction of Fort Snelling white influence increased, and use of the new military presence to quiet the incessant quarrels between the tribes began. The treaty of Prairie du Chien in 1825, which drew a line between Ojibwe and Dakota areas of occupation, was a part of the effort to force that peace, but was only partially successful.

In the 1800s white settlement surged. Political turmoil in Europe resulted in a large influx of immigrants, many from Germany and the Scandinavian countries. The many independent states in Germany were being united for the first time, followed by a long war with the French. In Sweden farmers were being

THE HEADWATERS WAR:
Conflict for the Mississippi Headwaters

forced to move from their isolated farms to villages, many of the young men were being claimed by the army, and there was general turmoil. For immigrants from those northern European regions Minnesota, Michigan, and Wisconsin were much like their homelands, and immigration soon placed increasing pressure on the native Indian population.

In Minnesota, for those from areas like Germany, the fertile lands west of the Mississippi ceded by the Dakota in 1851 were ideal, and for those from the Scandinavian countries northern Minnesota was much like their homeland. But, in addition to immigrants from Scandinavia, other interests had their eyes on northern Minnesota as well; one of the most powerful the lumber industry. While in 1837 the Ojibwe had been pressured to give up claims to land south of Mille Lacs Lake, that was only a temporary solution; the vast forests of white pine lay further north.

When the story in this chapter unfolds, the Ojibwe still held those coveted lands of the north, and Fort Snelling was far away. Only when construction of Fort Ripley, near the mouth of the Crow Wing River, began in 1849 was a threat of force, in addition to the 'power of trade', available to influence the Ojibwe.

The situation was similar for the Ojibwe who still held lands in northern Wisconsin and Upper Michigan; the land was similar to the homelands of many of the immigrants, and held rich forests. In the late 1840s this led to building pressure on the Ojibwe to give up all their land east of the Mississippi River, including Upper Michigan and Wisconsin, and accept land further west. When the Ojibwe of Michigan and Wisconsin were approached with the idea of moving it was rejected.

The Sandy Lake Tragedy was actually an unintended result of two independent actions, the first brought about by the Ojibwe Chief Hole-in-the-Day the younger. As principal chief of the Mississippi Band that included the Crow Wing/Gull Lake, Mille Lacs, and

THE HEADWATERS WAR:
Conflict for the Mississippi Headwaters

Sandy Lake areas, he had pressured the government to move annuity payments for the Minnesota Ojibwe from La Pointe on Madeline Island to somewhere closer. He was successful, and in 1850 annuities were to be paid at Sandy Lake.

The second cause of the tragedy was due to manipulations of white officials and their attempt to apply the Indian Removal Act of 1830 to the Ojibwe of Wisconsin and Northern Michigan to force their removal to the western states; essentially the story on the commemorative sign quoted earlier.

In 1830 Congress had passed the Indian Removal Act empowering the government to negotiate treaties with the Indians of the southeast, primarily Georgia, providing for them to give up their eastern lands in exchange for new reservations in the west. While in theory the removal from the east was only by agreement of the tribes, in fact there was both deception and coercion. When the native tribes, such as the Cherokee, Shawnee, and Choctaw, were removed and sent to reservations west of the Mississippi disaster resulted; disasters well documented in books and films such as The Trail of Tears.

In 1849 Minnesota was first organized as a 'territory' (*see Figure 15*) that included most of present-day Minnesota, and parts of present-day North and South Dakota, with a government appointed governor, and remained a territory until it gained statehood in 1858. Alexander Ramsey, a Pennsylvania politician, was appointed the first territorial governor, a position he held until early 1853. He later served as governor of Minnesota from 1860 to 1863, and is perhaps one of Minnesota's most honored early leaders. But he had his dark side; while governor he became notorious for his demands for revenge on, even the death, of all Dakota after the Dakota uprising of 1862. His pressure was an important factor in the 1863 removal of nearly all Dakota from Minnesota to reservations in the west.

THE HEADWATERS WAR:
Conflict for the Mississippi Headwaters

In 1850 officials of the federal government of Zachary Taylor, in complicity with officials of the Minnesota Territorial Government and officials in Michigan and Wisconsin, sought to apply the Indian Removal Act of 1830 to those Ojibwe living east of the Mississippi and move them as well. While this had never been the intent of the original Act, which was narrowly written to apply to the southeastern tribes only, still the mood of the country was that Indians were both a nuisance and a danger standing in the way of further settlement and access to needed resources.

To apply pressure on the Michigan and Wisconsin bands, the officials decided to take advantage of the agreement entered into with Hole-in-the-Day for payment of annuities to the Minnesota Ojibwe at Sandy Lake, and also change the location of fall annuity payments for the Wisconsin and Michigan bands from La Pointe, on Madeline Island, where it was customarily held, to Sandy Lake, far to the west. The idea was that, if brought to Sandy Lake in late fall, the Wisconsin and Michigan Ojibwe would be forced to stay during the winter as well, and be more amenable to signing over their lands. Whether President Taylor or Territorial Governor Ramsey were complicit in the action has never been established, but President Taylor signed the order, and it is unlikely that it was without the cooperation of Territorial Governor Ramsey.

Nineteen bands of the Ojibwe were affected by the order to collect their fall annuities at Sandy Lake, and included those in Michigan and Wisconsin as well as most if not all of those in Minnesota. While for the Minnesota Ojibwe the annuity journey was shortened, the bands to the east didn't fare so well. LaPointe, on Madeline Island in Lake Superior, had been centrally located, but Sandy Lake was far to the west for the Ojibwe of Upper Michigan and eastern Wisconsin. In some cases travel of up to 430 miles each way was required.

THE HEADWATERS WAR:
Conflict for the Mississippi Headwaters

That the distribution involved the fall annuity payment made the situation even worse. The payment was to be in October, and in 1850 the Little Ice Age was in its last stage, winter coming earlier than we see today. If the annuities had come in time Lake Superior would still have been open, simplifying return of the Wisconsin and Michigan Ojibwe to their homes. But if delayed, or the winter storms came early, the trip back could be challenging for the eastern bands. Not only could much of the lake freeze over, storms on Lake Superior are notoriously savage even today, as the fated freighter Edmund Fitzgerald is but an example.

However, the Ojibwe had no choice but to come to the new distribution point; they had become dependent on the annuity payments. Over 4,000 Ojibwe gathered at Sandy Lake for the payment. There they waited; but whether by plan or accident the annuity payments were late, much of the food was moldy or spoiled, causing many to die of food poisoning and dysentery. Measles also swept through the area, a disease to which the Native American population was especially susceptible.

But, even though late in the season and much of Lake Superior was frozen, the Ojibwe from Wisconsin and Upper Michigan did not stay and spend the rest of the winter at Sandy Lake as the officials had hoped. When given what was available of their annuity payments they embarked by land on the long trail back to their home villages; but it was December and January, mid-winter, many were sick from the bad food, and the result was another Trail of Tears. During their sojourn at Sandy Lake over 150 Ojibwe had died of starvation or disease, and by the time they reached their homes that had risen to more than 400, ten percent of the total that had begun the journey months before.

The result turned the stomach of even the hardened public of the day, resulting in a public uproar. Hole-in-the-Day the younger held meetings in Saint Paul

THE HEADWATERS WAR:
Conflict for the Mississippi Headwaters

that gained national attention by his condemnation of Governor Ramsey, and the defense of Ramsey by William Warren caused a breach in their close relations that lasted almost until Warren's death in 1853.

In any major action there may be unintended consequences. Had the action not been taken leading to the Sandy Lake Tragedy, in time the Government would likely have succeeded in obtaining agreement from the Ojibwe to vacate Michigan, Wisconsin, and eastern Minnesota, and possibly western Minnesota as well; they had always been successful in obtaining treaties in the past, often with trickery, and subject to 'unilateral' changes later. But when their plot was put in motion there 'were' unintended consequences, in that the public uproar that followed required a change in plans; a change in plans that altered the trajectory of the Ojibwe presence in Minnesota. As a result of that public uproar the plan for moving the Ojibwe to the west was dropped, and in 1854 and 1855 treaties a number of Ojibwe reservations were established, many east of the Mississippi River.

Today the Sandy Lake Tragedy is a largely forgotten event, commemorated only with memorial signs at Big Sandy Lake; one, near the dam separating the lake from the Mississippi, and the second at the HW 65 rest stop on the western shore overlooking the lake. While it is difficult to find anything positive about the 'tragedy', it did do one thing for the future generations of Ojibwe. Had it not been for that event, and the public outrage that followed, the Ojibwe would likely have been banished from Minnesota and Wisconsin and relocated to the arid regions of the west, as were the Dakota following the Dakota Uprising of 1862.

Ojibwe leaders cannot be held blameless in the unfolding drama. At the time of the Sandy Lake Tragedy, Hole-in-the-Day the younger had only three years previously assumed the mantle of his father, Hole-in-the-Day the elder. Nonetheless, he had been

273

THE HEADWATERS WAR:
Conflict for the Mississippi Headwaters

instrumental in convincing the government to move the annuity location for the Mississippi Band from La Pointe to a location in Minnesota. An 'unintended' consequence of that agreement was the government decision to also move the location for the Ojibwe of Wisconsin and Upper Michigan there, leading to the death of so many.

There can be little doubt the Sandy Lake Tragedy ended any lingering trust between the Ojibwe and the government. The heading on the memorial sign quotes Flat Mouth, the prominent Pillager chief from Leech Lake, following the annuity distribution on December 2nd, in which he registered the blame he placed on the Territorial governor, Alexander Ramsey:

"Tell him I blame him for the children we have lost"

Up to that time Flat Mouth, one of the most influential Ojibwe chiefs, had been loyal to the government; often credited with being a major factor keeping the Minnesota Ojibwe from joining the British in the war of 1812.

THE HEADWATERS WAR:
Conflict for the Mississippi Headwaters

Figure 15: Minnesota Territory 1849

THE HEADWATERS WAR:
Conflict for the Mississippi Headwaters

Figure 16: Sign commemorating Sandy Lake Tragedy of 1850

THE HEADWATERS WAR:
Conflict for the Mississippi Headwaters

CHAPTER 13
UPRISINGS OF 1862

By 1862, with the exception of at Red Lake, the Dakota and the Ojibwe of Minnesota had been confined to reservations, with the balance of the state opened to white settlement and lumbering interests. The Ojibwe reservations were larger than those of the Dakota, more remotely located, and since the land near their reservations was still largely unsettled, they could at least supplement annuities from the government with local food supplies. The food staple, wild rice, was plentiful in the areas occupied by the Ojibwe.

However, the Dakota were in more dire straights. By 1851 they had ceded all their land in Minnesota except a 10 mile wide strip along each side of the Minnesota River, stretching from the Minnesota-South Dakota border to near present-day New Ulm. Then, one month after Minnesota became a state in 1858, the Dakota leaders were taken to Washington D.C., where they were coerced into signing away the 10 mile strip bordering the northern bank of the river under the argument white settlers had already begun to move into that area and could not be removed.

With the loss of their hunting lands the Dakota, particularly the *M'dewakanton* and *Wahpekute* bands on the lower Minnesota River, were in dire straights. It became increasingly difficult to leave their reservations for hunting to supplement their annuity food supplies without coming into conflict with settlers. If they ventured further north they encountered the Ojibwe who, while the conflict between the Ojibwe and Dakota had become largely quiescent, still harbored age old grudges. The last major battle between the two tribes had been at Shakopee as recently as 1858.

THE HEADWATERS WAR:
Conflict for the Mississippi Headwaters

When the War Between the States began in 1861 conditions began to worsen, and by the summer of 1862 the situation along the lower Minnesota River had become dire for the Dakota. The attention of the government was on the war in the east, with increasing neglect of its treaty obligations. The promised annuity payments and supplies had not arrived, and to make the situation even more flammable, many of the soldiers normally stationed at Fort Snelling and Fort Ridgely, further up the Minnesota River, had been moved east to support the Union. Even many of the able bodied men among the settlers had left to join Minnesota regiments.

The inevitable happened; on August 17, 1862, a small Dakota hunting party near Mankato on the Minnesota River killed five settlers. News spread rapidly, and when it reached the *M'dewakanton* chief, Little Crow, in spite of his previous hesitancy he agreed to lead an uprising.

What few know is that, on the same day as the initial incident, August 17, the Ojibwe at Leech and Ottertail lakes, and those near Crow Wing, also rose in rebellion. This was at a time when Indians in the state outnumbered whites, and had all the Dakota and Ojibwe joined together they quite possibly could have, temporarily at least, driven the white man from the state.

In this section these two uprisings will be only briefly covered, since the Dakota uprising at least is the subject of many books, and that of the Ojibwe amply covered by Treuer and Lund in the sources listed in the bibliography. However, the Dakota uprising also heralded the final end of the Headwaters War, with the government imposing a final solution by removing most Dakota from the current boundaries of the State of Minnesota, and moving the Ojibwe reservations to more remote areas of the state. But it also heralded the beginning of the Sioux wars of the plains, culminating only following Custer's battle at the Little Big Horn.

THE HEADWATERS WAR:
Conflict for the Mississippi Headwaters

Dakota Uprising

In August of 1862, as the War Between the States was ramping up, the Dakota of the Minnesota River rose in rebellion. While the initial spark may have been unplanned, the situation was ripe for a wildfire; and that is what happened.

Having given up nearly all their land in Minnesota the Dakota were unable to provide for themselves, and had become dependant on supplies provided by the government. But delivery of supplies was sporadic and often late. While an August 17, 1862, killing of five white settlers is usually referred to as the start of the conflict, the burning fuse was actually lit in early August. The annuities required by treaty had not arrived, crops had failed, and the Dakota were starving. Even though sufficient food was available in the storehouses of the local traders, they refused to allow its release until the 'cash' annuity arrived. Repeated meetings with the Indian Agents and other prominent white officials gained no relief. In a meeting on August 5th with Indian Agency leaders, the head trader at the Lower Agency, Andrew Myrick, was reported to have said, *"let them eat grass."* Little Crow and the other chiefs stormed out, many never to return.

As it so happened, on August 17, when the killing of the five settlers occurred, Little Crow, Shakopee, Wapasha, Big Eagle, and a number of other chiefs were camped about two miles south of the Lower Sioux Agency which served the *M'dewakanton* and *Wahpekute* bands. When the deaths were reported to Little Crow he is reported to have said, *"so the time has come"*, and immediately called a conference. Wapasha, the senior chief of the *M'dewakanton*, and many other chiefs, including Little Crow, argued for peace, but others, such as Shakopee, and the Warrior's Lodge, organized earlier, argued for war. In the end it was

THE HEADWATERS WAR:
Conflict for the Mississippi Headwaters

decided; it would be war. Little Crow, designated as the leader, ordered an attack on the Agency at sunrise.

Since the names 'Shakopee' and 'Little Crow' refer to dynasties of Dakota chiefs, and they appear in several chapters, more explanation is necessary. The Little Crow of this chapter is Little Crow IV, the eldest son of Little Crow the III, who died of an accidental gunshot wound in 1846. Little Crow III appeared in Chapter 11 related to the attack on Pokegama Lake, and Little Crow I in Chapter 6, Big Marten's War.

The Shakopee featured in 'Big Marten's War', Chapter 6, was Shakopee I, who lived from 1750 to 1827. Shakopee II, chief of the Shakopee band from 1827 until 1857, was actually an Ojibwe, one of the twin sons of Yellow Head, an Ojibwe chief, who was given to Shakopee I for adoption to forge an alliance. This was probably the Chief Yellow Head located at Mille Lacs Lake at the time. Since both the Mille Lacs and Shakopee villages were particularly vulnerable to attack, a peace agreement between them would benefit both. Further, Shakopee I was believed to have been born and lived some of his early years in the Mille Lacs area as one of the Dakota who assimilated with the Ojibwe following the battle of Kathio in 1750.

Shakopee III, the son of Shakopee II, was the Shakopee involved in the uprising of 1862, and became chief of the Shakopee band following his father's death five years earlier. He was in his fifties at the time of the uprising, but he proved to be one of the most barbarous of the Dakota chiefs; largely staying away from the main force of Little Crow and concentrating on attacking civilians.

While the rebellion is often called 'Little Crow's rebellion', Little Crow was a reluctant participant, and in many ways is a sad figure. He was one of the Dakota who had begun to adapt to the white man's way of life, living in a frame house and operating a successful farm. But when Wapasha, the most senior of the Dakota

THE HEADWATERS WAR:
Conflict for the Mississippi Headwaters

chiefs, refused to become involved, Little Crow had only a limited choice; lead the uprising himself, or let it fall under the leadership of some of the violent less influential chiefs, such as Shakopee. Even when Little Crow finally agreed to lead the uprising, he attempted to concentrate on attacking soldiers, government facilities and forts, or significant towns such as New Ulm. He even sheltered some of the settlers in his own home. However, he was swept along by events beyond his control. In the end, when the uprising had failed, he was reduced to scrounging the woods for food, accompanied only by his son, only to be killed by a farmer who had no idea who he was, or had once been.

On August 18, 1862, just before dawn and in full war paint, the Dakota left their camp to attack the Agency. A number of whites were killed, including "*let them eat grass*" Myrick, after which they stuffed grass in Myrick's mouth. About 50 others from the Agency managed to escape, most making it to Fort Ridgley to the southeast.

At about the same time a second group of Dakota killed the operator of the ferry at nearby Redwood and then set a trap. First they managed to kill a number of settlers approaching by wagon. Later troops sent from Fort Ridgley were also successfully ambushed, resulting in the Battle of Redwood Ferry, in which the militia lost 24 of their number. On August 19 they attacked New Ulm, about 16 miles downstream from Fort Ridgley, but were repulsed, and on August 20 killed 15 settlers and took several women and children captive at Lake Shetek about 50 miles to the southwest. From there things swept completely out of control; parts of the *Wahpeton* and *Sissiton* bands of the upper Minnesota River becoming involved, with isolated raids extending as far as the Red River and southern Canada.

On August 20 and 22 the Dakota besieged Fort Ridgley on the Minnesota River southeast of the Lower Agency with as many as 800 warriors, but the

281

THE HEADWATERS WAR:
Conflict for the Mississippi Headwaters

undermanned fort had been reinforced by militia units and the attacks were repulsed. On August 23, repulsed at the fort, the Dakota again turned their attention to the town of New Ulm. While they were finally repulsed, the battle was so fierce it involved house to house fighting.

The last major victory of the Dakota was on September 2nd at the Battle of Birch Coulee, where they attacked a detachment of 150 soldiers sent from Fort Ridgley to search for survivors. The detachment had 13 killed and 47 wounded, with a loss of two for the Dakota.

However, even with their early successes Little Crow and his allies recognized their strength was inadequate in the face of the overwhelming power of the government, even with their numbers depleted by the demands of the war with the south. The incident causing the uprising had come as a surprise to Little Crow, but he recognized the die was cast. Upon deciding to join and becoming its overall leader he sent emissaries to the *Sissiton* and *Wahpeton* of the Dakota, and to the Lakota and Nakota of the west as well, asking for aid in the uprising. He even sent emissaries to their neighbors the Ojibwe asking them to join in the uprising.

But support was limited, even from inside the Dakota branch. The uprising remained primarily a *M'dewakanton* and *Wahpekute* effort, while the *Sisseton* and *Wahpeton* bands further west stood largely aside; and in some cases actively opposed the uprising. Some exceptions were the *Wahpeton* chief Sleepy Eyes and the *Sissiton* chiefs White Lodge and Lean Grizzly Bear, the primary actors in the Lake Shetek massacre. Even many, if not most, of the *M'dewakanton* and *Wahpekute* refused to become involved, such as the band of Wapasha.

The Lakota and Nakota also declined to give support; the links between the branches of the Western Sioux Nation had become weak. In general, except for the Ogallala band of the Teton far to the west, who were disturbed by emigrants passing through their lands and

THE HEADWATERS WAR:
Conflict for the Mississippi Headwaters

forts being built for their protection, most were under little pressure from the whites and saw no reason to interrupt their peaceful relations with the white traders.

Little Crow's appeal to the Ojibwe was also largely rejected, although he gained some limited support, especially from the mixed Saint Croix bands. The Ojibwe had up to that time had few problems with the white settlers, and they could still obtain adequate food supplies both on and off their reservations. However, prior to the arrival of the Dakota emissaries, whether by accident or planning, on the same day as the incident of the killing of five settlers by the Dakota, August 17, the Mississippi band Ojibwe under Hole-in-the-Day the younger, and the Pillagers under Buffalo and Flat Mouth the younger, also staged an uprising. This uprising, however, was too limited and short lived to provide any support to the Dakota.

This does not mean than individual warriors of all the above groups, eager for fame in war and booty, didn't join in the uprising on an individual basis; the Ojibwe, and all the branches of the Sioux Nation, were attuned to war, and young warriors were difficult to control. In fact, many of the worst atrocities were committed by small bands of warriors away from the main forces of Little Crow.

The Dakota uprising itself had been an act of desperation, and when pressed by the white soldiers Little Crow and his supporters fled westward, only to be followed by the white soldiers. By November of 1862 the bulk of Little Crow's supporters had been captured or killed, with only a few, in addition to Little Crow himself, evading capture. Among other prominent chiefs still evading capture were Shakopee, White Lodge, and Sleepyeyes. Many of the captured Dakota were sentenced to death for their actions, but President Lincoln intervened; eventually the number reduced to 38 who were hanged at Mankato on December 26, 1862.

But punishment for the uprising did not end in

283

THE HEADWATERS WAR:
Conflict for the Mississippi Headwaters

1862 with the hanging of the 38 Dakota. Little Crow, while escaping capture, was killed by a settler in southwestern Minnesota in early July of 1863, his identity only discovered later upon capture of his son. Shakopee fled to and gained sanctuary in Canada; perhaps eased by his Ojibwe blood (*his father was Ojibwe*). However, his sanctuary was fleeting; in 1865 Shakopee was kidnapped from Canada, brought back to Fort Snelling, and hanged.

In the summer of 1863 General Sibley led an expedition west into Dakota Territory in pursuit of the remaining Dakota, resulting in three major battles. The following year two expeditions were sent west, one commanded by General Sibley and the second commanded by General Sully. The force under General Sully ended when it defeated a large force of Dakota, Lakota, and Nakota; forecasting the war on the plains that would later erupt. However, many of the Dakota succeeded in escaping beyond the Missouri River.

While the Dakota uprising of 1862 was the largest and most destructive Indian war in American history, few even know it occurred, hidden behind the War Between the States. It was also one of the few incidents of either forts or towns actually being attacked. Nearly 100 soldiers and 400-500 civilians were killed, and probably less than 200 Dakota, including those hung in Mankato and elsewhere; although many others died in captivity.

The end of the Dakota uprising signaled the closing chapter of the conflict between the Ojibwe and the Dakota. In 1863, by Acts of Congress, all treaties with the Dakota were abrogated with annuities forfeit, their reservations were seized, and their right of 'occupancy' in Minnesota was ended. Shortly thereafter they were removed from Minnesota and resettled in the west, mostly in the Nebraska and Dakota Territories. The only exceptions were those who could 'prove' they had aided the whites during the uprising.

284

THE HEADWATERS WAR:
Conflict for the Mississippi Headwaters

But the conflict between the Government and the Sioux Nation had just begun; only the scene shifted from the Dakota of Minnesota to the Lakota of the prairie states to the west. Beginning with the rebellion of Red Cloud in 1866, and culminating with the destruction of the 7th Cavalry under Custer in June of 1876, it was a long and drawn out struggle. Some would say it only ended at Wounded Knee in December of 1890.

The above is only a summary of some of the events of the uprising, with much more detail on the subject available. Both Robinson's *History of the Dakota or Sioux Nation* and Volume II of Folwell's *History of Minnesota* are excellent sources.

Ojibwe Uprising

The year 1862 was a critical time for the Ojibwe as well as the Dakota, but for different reasons. The Ojibwe had larger reservations, and also had access to the surrounding country to supplement their annuity supplies. It was a different set of events that led to the Ojibwe uprising, and only 'chance' it coincided with that of the Dakota.

For years Little Crow and Hole-in-the-Day the younger, as well as Hole-in-the-Day the elder before him, had been discussing a joint uprising to drive out the white settlers. Over two decades earlier the refusal of Hole-in-the-Day the elder and his brother, Strong Ground, to join the Dakota in an uprising led to the 1838-39 violence described in Chapter 10. However, there is no evidence this resulted in any concrete plan. For the Ojibwe their anger initially arose over thefts of annuity supplies and embezzlement of annuity funds by the Indian Agent at Crow Wing. Hole-in-the-Day had complained to officials in Saint Paul of the thefts, and had made one trip to Washington, but the government failed to take action.

THE HEADWATERS WAR:
Conflict for the Mississippi Headwaters

That, however, was not the spark; the spark was when, in August of 1862, the army began enlisting young Ojibwe men to fight for the north, often plying them with liquor to obtain their enlistment. The enraged Hole-in-the-Day sent runners to Leech Lake informing them of the practice and asking for their support in an uprising.

The Pillagers immediately reacted; on August 17, the same day as the incident leading to the Dakota uprising, mission schools and trading posts were burned and captives taken at Leech and Ottertail lakes. In the Crow Wing area mission churches were burned at Gull and Lower Mission lakes, and a number of whites, some of whom later escaped, were captured. Cattle were killed, and other property destroyed as well.

By August 19 up to 200 settlers had taken shelter at undermanned Fort Ripley near the town of Crow Wing, and the Fort commander's unsuccessful attempts to arrest Hole-in-the-Day had failed. Hole-in-the-Day reacted by sending additional runners to the Pillagers at Leech Lake and to as far away as Lake Superior, informing them he planned to destroy Fort Ripley, kill the settlers sheltering there, and asking for their support. He also called for his Crow Wing and Gull Lake warriors to gather for an assault.

However, Hole-in-the-Day had strong opposition within the Mississippi band. Chief Bad Boy at Gull Lake was no friend of Hole-in-the-Day, and he had always been opposed by the Mille Lacs Band as well. Further, the Pillagers were having second thoughts, and their distrust of Hole-in-the-Day was growing. The venerable chief Flat Mouth, a close friend of Hole-in-the-Day, had died two years before, and now chiefs Buffalo and Flat Mouth the younger were the leading chiefs at Leech Lake, and caution led them to order that no whites be killed. Chief Buffalo, who had been a co-signer of the Treaty of 1855 with Flat Mouth the elder, was senior of the two chiefs, and decided to go to Crow

THE HEADWATERS WAR:
Conflict for the Mississippi Headwaters

Wing to investigate the situation for himself and determine whether the Pillagers should join the Fort Ripley attack. Upon his arrival, seeing no activity, Chief Buffalo had an angry conference with Hole-in-the-Day, and as a result the Pillagers abandoned the uprising.

However, the final straw was the attitude taken by the Mille Lacs Ojibwe. When they heard of the intent to attack Fort Ripley, Chief Eagle and the head warrior, First Seated Feather, gathered over 100 warriors and went to the fort's defense. Unwilling to fight brother Ojibwe, the local forces Hole-in-the-Day had gathered for the assault melted away. In the end the uprising fizzled out, with not a single white person killed.

Hole-in-the-Day was never punished for the above actions, but managed to outfox soldiers sent to capture him, and succeeded in forcing negotiations with the government on the Ojibwe complaints, ending with payment of the annuities and personal payments to himself. While his actions angered many and may have weakened his influence among the Ojibwe, it may well have raised his status with the government. As long as the Civil War raged peace in Indian country was essential, and the government was willing to pacify Hole-in-the-Day and other strong minded leaders.

But the government had a long memory. Once the Civil War ended the influx of settlers and associated business interests resumed. By a series of treaties between 1863-67 the Mississippi Ojibwe were coerced into signing away the reservations they then held for an expanded reservation on the headwaters lakes of Leech, Cass, and Winnibigoshish, which they would share with the Pillagers, and a large two million acre reservation far to the northwest at White Earth.

THE HEADWATERS WAR:
Conflict for the Mississippi Headwaters

Figure 17: Chief Hole-in-the-Day the younger

THE HEADWATERS WAR:
Conflict for the Mississippi Headwaters

Figure 18: Chief Little Crow IV

THE HEADWATERS WAR:
Conflict for the Mississippi Headwaters

Figure 19: Chief Shakopee III

THE HEADWATERS WAR:
Conflict for the Mississippi Headwaters

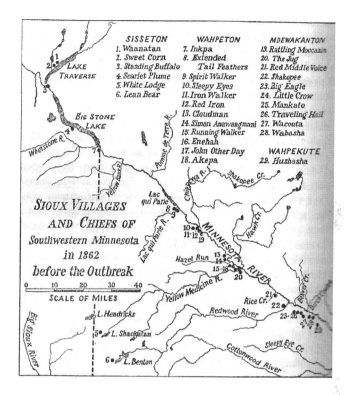

Figure 20: Dakota Chiefs & Villages 1862

THE HEADWATERS WAR:
Conflict for the Mississippi Headwaters

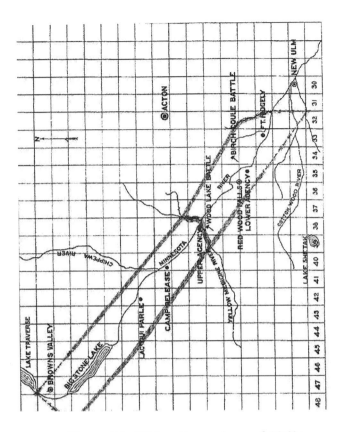

Figure 21: Sibley Campaigns of 1862

THE HEADWATERS WAR:
Conflict for the Mississippi Headwaters

Figure 22: Fort Ridgely, 1862

THE HEADWATERS WAR:
Conflict for the Mississippi Headwaters

Figure 23: Dakota Attack on New Ulm, 1862

THE HEADWATERS WAR:
Conflict for the Mississippi Headwaters

Figure 24: The Hanging of 38 Dakota
Mankato, 26 December, 1862

THE HEADWATERS WAR:
Conflict for the Mississippi Headwaters

CHAPTER 14
THE OJIBWE CHIEFS

The term 'principal chief' is in itself a misnomer when applied to the Ojibwe of the time, since no such position existed. By custom each band had its own chiefs, and while when several bands lived together in a single village or area one might have precedence, in general the chiefs either made decisions in council or acted independently. Yet, beginning in the early 1700s, and continuing through the late 1860s, a series of Ojibwe chiefs gained such influence that they became recognized as the principal chief over a broad area containing multiple bands; only the size of the area and the scope of their authority is in dispute. Five of these 'principal' chiefs were associated with what was later defined by the government as the Mississippi Band; *Bi-aus-wah*, his son Broken Tooth, Curly Head, Curly Head's adopted son Hole-in-the-Day the elder, and Hole-in-the-Day the younger.

While not usually referred as a 'principal chief', at least one chief of the Pillager Band also attained preeminence far beyond his local band, Flat Mouth the elder. In fact, his bust is one of the very few busts of Native American leaders on display at the Capitol Building in Washington. Perhaps there were others as well, but they lacked a 'press agent' such as William Warren, who resided at Crow Wing (*bastion of the Mississippi Band*), and being further from contact with the white settlements near Fort Snelling had less contact with the government.

To understand why 'principal chiefs' were so unusual one must first know something of the method of governance of the Ojibwe nation. Three types of chiefs existed, sometimes several in a village representing

296

THE HEADWATERS WAR:
Conflict for the Mississippi Headwaters

different groups or bands, with decisions affecting more than a single band usually made in council. These chiefs were;

1) Civil: usually hereditary from the Loon or Crane totems
2) Religious: not necessarily hereditary, and could be of either sex, and
3) War: often hereditary and from the Marten or Bear totems, but open to others who showed outstanding merit in war

While all chiefs of a type in a village were considered equal, that did not preclude recognition of one as dominant. For example, at Sandy Lake at its peak there were at least five bands, with precedence given the chief of the band passed down by *Bi-aus-wah*. Also, the 'bands' led by a civil chief varied in size, with individual families joining or leaving as they chose, depending of the popularity of the chief.

But to rise to the status of 'principal' chief recognized over a broad area required much more than inheritance. It usually arose based on a special situation of the time; often the impetus being acquisition of new territory. But that alone was not enough; much of their authority came from their ability to dominate conclaves of chiefs through oratory and personal magnetism. Later, during the period of treaties and land cessions, it also usually included recognition by the white authorities of a chief's special status.

When a principal chief died their heirs sometimes attempted to claim the position by right of inheritance, as with any civil chieftainship; sometimes successfully, sometimes not. Examples of successful claims are Hole-in-the-Day the younger, who through sheer audacity and force of personality seized that status following his father's death, then managed to solidify the position by adding to Ojibwe territory and gaining

THE HEADWATERS WAR:
Conflict for the Mississippi Headwaters

recognition as treaty negotiator for the Ojibwe. Another was Broken Tooth, who rapidly gained acceptance as the successor to his father, *Bi-aus-wah*.

This did not, however, always hold; Broken Tooth's sons never achieved that status. It is also possible that in his later years much of Broken Tooth's authority passed to Curley Head, a newcomer to Sandy Lake, who, while based at Sandy Lake, succeeded in extending Ojibwe influence west of the Mississippi to the Gull Lake area. In any case, both are sometimes referred to in the early documents as more than just common chiefs.

The supremacy of the principal chiefs varied with the area and with outside pressures, and even within the area of supposed control was not necessarily recognized by all bands. For example, while generally accepted as principal chiefs of the Mississippi Band, neither Hole-in-the-Day the elder nor the younger controlled all those grouped by the government under the title 'Mississippi Band'. The government considered the Mississippi Band to begin at the outlet of the Leech River to the Mississippi, several miles downstream of Leech Lake, and to continue downstream until it encountered Dakota territory. However, the Hole-in-the-Days' authority was never recognized by the Mille Lacs Band, and much of the area west of and around the Long Prairie River and upper Crow Wing was under the influence of Flat Mouth of the Pillagers. Also much of the northern part of the designated area was nearer to, and subject to, influence by the powerful Pillager chief, Flat Mouth the elder.

In effect, the Hole-in-the-Days' were principal chiefs over the eastern Crow Wing and Gull Lake areas, the new villages they formed outside those boundaries, and perhaps Sandy Lake at the most; which did not stop them from attempting, often successfully, to interject himself into the affairs of bands outside that area.

THE HEADWATERS WAR:
Conflict for the Mississippi Headwaters

Bi-aus-wah . . . .

Little is known of the later life of *Bi-aus-wah*, the first to achieve principal chief status, since he both lived and died before the white man entered the area in force and began to keep records. However, legends say he was born at La Pointe on Madeleine Island where his father, also named *Bi-aus-wah*, was a war chief. According to legend (*see final pages of Chapter 1, subtitled 'The Legend of Bi-aus-wah)*), when still a youth he was captured by the Fox, who were about to burn him when the elder *Bi-aus-wah* entered the village alone and offered to trade his life for that of his son; an offer that was accepted.

Eventually the younger *Bi-aus-wah* became a great warrior and war chief at Fond-du-Lac, where he waged a relentless war against the Fox of upper Wisconsin. By the early 1730s the Fox had been driven from the area by an alliance put together by the French, and *Bi-aus-wah* became civil chief; as a member of the Loon totem, coupled with the reputation gained as a war chief, he had the necessary credentials.

With relinquishment of his war chief role to the able warrior Big Marten, and his elevation to civil chief, *Bi-aus-wah* had to broaden his vision. To the west of the Fond du Lac Ojibwe enclave all was Dakota; and for all of his life the Ojibwe and Dakota had been at peace, sharing the rich hunting and fishing grounds and rice beds of the upper Mississippi. The ties between the Fond du Lac Ojibwe and the Dakota had grown strong, strengthened by intermarriage and sharing of customs.

Fond du Lac and the large Dakota center at Sandy Lake were separated by only about fifty miles, and passage of the Ojibwe through that lake to reach the shared headwaters must have been common. But that peace had been shattered by the Dakota in 1736 by their massacre of a group of Frenchmen at Lake of the Woods on the present-day Minnesota-Canada border.

THE HEADWATERS WAR:
Conflict for the Mississippi Headwaters

While the Ojibwe had been friends of the Dakota for nearly six decades, they had been friends and allies of the French for even longer. It was to their benefit to side with the French over the Dakota; it was from the French that their trade goods came. The Ojibwe and the Dakota were now at war.

Few records mention *Bi-aus-wah*, and Warren is silent on his life following the raid on Sandy Lake described in Chapter 2. However, since his son Broken Tooth, who inherited his chieftainship upon his death, wasn't born until 1753, he likely lived well into the 1770s. It was during *Bi-aus-wah's* life that first Sandy Lake, then the large northern lakes of Leech, Cass, and Winnibigoshish, and later Mille Lacs Lake in central Minnesota, fell under Ojibwe control; the villages established in these new territories only adding to his prestige. In effect he became the first 'principal chief' of the newly conquered areas, with the possible exception of the large headwaters lakes, where many of the migrating population came from the border lakes with Canada as well as from Lake Superior.

Broken Tooth
(*Katawabeda*, aka *Breshieu*)

Following the death of *Bi-aus-wah*, his son Broken Tooth inherited his civil chieftainship, and initially at least was considered principal chief over the lands of his father. The date of *Bi-aus-wah's* death is unclear, but was probably sometime in the mid 1770s; a time when the footprint of the white man was still light.

Broken Tooth is believed to have been born in 1753 when *Bi-aus-wah* was well into late middle age. If so, he became chief at a relatively early age. There are conflicting views on how far the authority of Broken Tooth extended. Some say he was recognized as principal chief of the Ojibwe as far away as the southern

THE HEADWATERS WAR:
Conflict for the Mississippi Headwaters

shores of Lake Superior, but there is little to back that up. In any case, for a time at least he was recognized as principle chief over most of central and possibly northern Minnesota, but it appears that he may have been matched or surpassed in importance by the 1820s by Curly Head, a newcomer who had migrated to Sandy Lake from Lake Superior.

In his history of the Ojibwe, written in the early 1850s, Warren refers to Broken Tooth only as the Sandy Lake chief, and when Schoolcraft met Broken Tooth at Sault Ste. Marie in 1822 he also referred to him only as Sandy Lake chief. Three years later five chiefs signed the 1825 Treaty of Prairie du Chien for Sandy Lake; Broken Tooth, Curly Head, Grosse Gruelle, and two other chiefs, without an indication of any special status.

However, when Schoolcraft met with Broken Tooth at Sault Ste. Marie in July of 1828, after the death of Curly Head, Schoolcraft identified him as 'patriarch of the area around Sandy Lake', recognizing him as the most important of the Sandy Lake chiefs. But what exactly did Schoolcraft mean by 'patriarch of the area around Sandy Lake'? By that time Hole-in-the-Day the elder and his brother Strong Ground had divided the band of Curly Head between them, and while they also held influence over the Crow Wing/Gull Lake area they continued to reside at Sandy Lake. Naming Broken Tooth as the 'patriarch' may have referred only to his age; about 75 at the time. Or it may indeed have reflected his preeminent status.

Broken Tooth died during the winter of 1831-32 at the age of 79. At his death his civil chieftainship passed to his son or sons, Bad Boy, *aka* Big Mouth, and Le Brochuix (*Berry Hunter*); both of whom signed the Treaty of 1837 as chiefs for Sandy Lake. However, neither gained the prestige of their father, and by the time of the Treaty of 1847 Bad Boy was missing from the Sandy Lake signers, having moved his band to Gull Lake, and sometime after 1862 to Mille Lacs.

THE HEADWATERS WAR:
Conflict for the Mississippi Headwaters

While the death of Broken Tooth ended the *Bi-aus-wah* dynasty of principal chiefs, other descendants gained fame in their own right. Hole-in-the-Day the younger claimed descent through his mother, who he claimed was the daughter of Broken Tooth, although that is questionable. His father had other wives besides the daughter of Broken Tooth, including a daughter of Flat Mouth the elder. Roger Jordain, a prominent 20th century leader of the Red Lake Ojibwe who dominated the Red Lake Band for over four decades in the late 1900s *(34, pp. 241-303)*, also claimed descent from Broken Tooth.

Curly Head
(*Babejigaundibeg*)

Sometime in the late 1700s a new leader, Curly Head, purportedly a chieftain of the Crane totem, came from Lake Superior to Sandy Lake, where his prestige soon challenged the leadership of Broken Tooth. It is unclear whether he brought his band with him, or whether his following developed after he became resident. In any case, sometime around 1800, after the massacre at Cross Lake, he decided to establish himself in the Crow Wing area, west of the Mississippi and south of where the Cross Lake massacre had occurred, and challenge the Dakota for control of the area. Soon he was joined by other adventurous Ojibwe. The Dakota tried repeatedly to dislodge the alien enclave, but finally gave up and conceded the area to Ojibwe control.

Lund, in his book, *The Lives and Times of Three Powerful Ojibwe Chiefs: Curly Head, Hole-in-the-Day the elder, and Hole-in-the-Day the younger (14)*, claims the settlements were permanent. Anton Treuer, in his book, *The Assassination of Hole-in-the-Day (32)* says that by the early 1820s Curly Head had become the principal chief of the Sandy Lake Ojibwe. Warren *(37,*

THE HEADWATERS WAR:
Conflict for the Mississippi Headwaters

p.349), says Curly Head became principal chief of the *"men of the river" (Mississippi band?)*, Broken Tooth chief at Sandy Lake, and Flat Mouth the overall chief of the Leech Lake area. Clearly exactly what status Curly Head actually had is subject to debate; as is whether the villages he formed in the Gull Lake area were permanent or seasonal settlements.

Whichever the case, Curly Head continued to make Sandy Lake his home at the same time he was recognized as principal chief of the *"men of the river"*. As late as 1825, the year of his death, when he signed the Treaty of Prairie du Chien he signed as a Sandy Lake representative, with no signers for the newly acquired Crow Wing area. The first incidence of a treaty signing with the Crow Wing-Gull Lake area separately identified is that of 1837 by Hole-in-the-Day the elder. That strongly suggests the settlements west of the Mississippi established by Curly Head were not occupied year round.

But Curly Head's reach was not limited to the Sandy Lake and the eastern Crow Wing area near the Mississippi. Later, in revenge for the Dakota killing of some prominent Ojibwe, Curly Head teamed with Flat Mouth the elder, the Pillager chief from Leech Lake, and drove the Dakota from the Long Prairie River area to the west as well. With that the bulk of the Crow Wing watershed, except the far western portion, was free of permanent Dakota villages and claimed by, or at least contested by, the Ojibwe.

When William Warren first arrived in the Crow Wing area in 1845 Broken Tooth and Curly Head were both dead, but Hole-in-the-Day the elder was still alive, although he died two years later. Warren became not only a friend and confidant of Hole-in-the-Day the younger, but also a friend and frequent visitor with Flat Mouth, a contemporary of Broken Tooth, Curly Head, and both Hole-in-the-Day the elder and younger. Flat Mouth often referred to Hole-in-the-Day the younger as

THE HEADWATERS WAR:
Conflict for the Mississippi Headwaters

grandson, which he may have been. Hole-in-the-Day the elder is reported to have married daughters of both Broken Tooth and Flat Mouth, and it is unclear as to which, if either, was the mother of Hole-in-the-Day the younger; although when first asserting his claim as principal chief following his father's death Hole-in-the-Day the younger claimed descent through Broken Tooth. However, that may have been political expediency.

While Curly Head is included among the principal chiefs, his relationship to Broken Tooth (*who outlived him*) remains unclear. However, it was Curly Head, working in conjunction with Flat Mouth of the Pillagers, who was instrumental in placing the rich Crow Wing and Long Prairie River areas under Ojibwe control, and he was at least recognized as principal chief of the newly added Gull-Lake and eastern Crow Wing territory.

At Curly Head's premature death from food poisoning while returning from the 1825 Treaty of Prairie du Chien his chieftainship passed to two 'commoners', Hole-in-the-Day the elder and his brother Strong Ground, who divided Curly Head's band between them. Both continued to make their home at Sandy Lake, although making frequent visits to the Crow Wing area for seasonal hunts; finally making the move permanent sometime around 1836. With that move Sandy Lake began its long decline in importance.

Hole-in-the-Day the elder
(*Bagone-gizig*)

Both Hole-in-the-Day the elder and his older brother, *Zoongakamig*, Strong Ground, as young men were immigrants to Sandy Lake from Lake Superior. Early they drew the attention of Curly Head, who, without a son began to treat the two as if they were his own. Both were commoners of the Bear Clan, not a

THE HEADWATERS WAR:
Conflict for the Mississippi Headwaters

normal path to civil chieftainship, but Curly Head began to groom them by making them his official pipe bearers, a prestigious position in which they attended Curly Head to official functions, such as meetings with other chiefs or treaty negotiations.

After his arrival at Sandy Lake, Hole- in-the-Day acquired two unrelated claims to chieftainship, and in addition had the added prestige of becoming a son-in-law of Flat Mouth, the Pillager chief at Leech Lake, and also of Broken Tooth, the paramount chief at Sandy Lake and claimant to principal chieftainship.

The first claim to a chieftainship came in 1820 when he was appointed a civil chief by Governor Cass of Michigan Territory, of which Minnesota was a part, as a reward for intervening with warriors of the Sandy Lake band in a confrontation with the British and their Ojibwe allies at Sault Ste. Marie, and possibly saving the American delegation's life. While elevated to chief by the Americans that did not give him a band to lead, or acceptance as chief by the Ojibwe; that came later. But it did bring him to the attention of the white government and Governor Cass, something that would later serve him well.

The second claim came in 1825 when Hole-in-the-Day and his brother Strong Ground accompanied Curly Head to the council for the first Treaty of Prairie du Chien. At that conference he gained added status in defending Broken Tooth's demand for inclusion of much of the Crow Wing area in the territory designated as Ojibwe, his argument accepted by his old acquaintance, Governor Cass. Then, when Curly Head died on the trip back, he passed his hereditary chieftainship at Sandy Lake to Hole-in-the-Day and his brother Strong Ground, who each took half of the band. While unconventional, this was eventually accepted. It does, however, suggest their adoption as sons by Curly Head may have been officially recognized earlier.

None of the above, however, was sufficient to

THE HEADWATERS WAR:
Conflict for the Mississippi Headwaters

explain Hole-in-the-Day's ascendance to the role he eventually attained of principal chief of the Mississippi Band and primary treaty negotiator with the white government.

Following the death of Curly Head in 1825 both Hole-in-the-Day and his brother Strong Ground maintained their home at Sandy Lake, but following the death of Broken Tooth in 1832 their relationship with Broken Tooth's successors soured. Ever since Curly Head seized control of the eastern Crow Wing-Gull Lake area in the early 1800s it had been used by the Sandy Lake bands for much of the year, but was deemed too close to the Prairie du Chien treaty line to be safe for permanent habitation. However, in about 1836 Hole-in-the-Day moved his band west of the Mississippi to the Swan River near Gull Lake and established a permanent village, soon to be followed by his brother Strong Ground. The move by Hole-in-the-Day and his brother started a general migration from Sandy Lake and elsewhere. By the mid 1840s only two bands remained at Sandy Lake, those of Berry Hunter and Cause of Day, while the Crow Wing-Gull Lake area had grown to at least five bands; replacing Sandy Lake as the center of Ojibwe power, with Hole-in-the-Day recognized as its principal chief.

Even Bad Boy, the son of Broken Tooth, moved his band to Gull Lake, although he continued to be at odds with Hole-in-the-Day. While Chief Bad Boy signed the Treaty of 1837 for Sandy Lake, he signed the important Treaty of 1855 for Gull Lake right after Hole-in-the-Day the younger. After the 1862 Ojibwe uprising led by Hole-in-the-Day the younger, which he opposed, Bad Boy moved to Mille Lacs.

The first treaty signed by Hole-in-the-Day and Strong Ground as chiefs from the Crow Wing-Gull Lake area was the Ojibwe land cession treaty of 1837. While influential at the negotiations, there is no indication Hole-in-the-Day's status at that time was higher than that

THE HEADWATERS WAR:
Conflict for the Mississippi Headwaters

of the many other Ojibwe chiefs present. However, as his influence grew he was eventually recognized as the most powerful and influential of the Ojibwe chiefs, and as Curly Head had before him became recognized by the government as principal chief of the Mississippi Band. Gaining that stature was a gradual process, and even then certain Ojibwe centers, such as that at Mille Lacs Lake, refused to recognize his authority.

While easy to anger, Hole-in-the-Day was also a pragmatist. Even as he applied pressure on the Dakota he continued to work with them; although sometimes with something else in mind. An example is the winter of 1837-1838 in which, following a conference with the Dakota, some Dakota attacked and killed his stepson, nephew and cousin. At first infuriated, Hole-in-the-Day raised a warparty to obtain revenge, but in the end reached a settlement in which the Dakota offered reparations; the right for the Ojibwe to hunt buffalo on the prairies to the west. This was a significant enough offer that Hole-in-the-Day agreed to forgo revenge for the killings, and in the spring, along with a number of other prominent Ojibwe, met the Dakota at Lac qui Parle in western Minnesota preparatory to the hunt.

However, Hole-in-the-Day's memory was long; he hadn't forgotten the murder of his nephew and cousin. After being feasted in the Dakota lodges and all had retired to the lodges for the night, Hole-in-the-Day arose and led an attack on the Dakota. Eleven Dakota were killed (*the majority women and children*), and a woman taken captive; later released as a peace offering. Hole-in-the-Day's eleven year old son, 'Boy', was forced by his father to participate in the killing.

While Taliaferro, the Indian Agent, attempted to restore peaceful relations, he failed and for several years tensions ran high. This massacre at Lac qui Parle led to the confrontations at Fort Snelling several months later in 1838, and also that of 1839, discussed earlier in Chapter 11: Fort Snelling and Aftermath. It also

THE HEADWATERS WAR:
Conflict for the Mississippi Headwaters

demonstrates a typical approach to revenge by both the Dakota and the Ojibwe; use deceit and surprise where possible to minimize your own losses.

While often Hole-in-the-Day was a man of peace, negotiating directly with the Dakota and the government, much of the reason for his advancement was based on his extensive war record, and his often reckless bravery. He dared almost anything, even near Fort Snelling. Treuer reports that he was reported to have killed at least 40 Dakota with his own hands. Due to his personality and volatile nature he soon became one of the most influential and famous figures of the day. By 1842 he was firmly established as the primary negotiator with the white government and its agent for the Mississippi Band, and often attended and spoke at treaty negotiations for other bands as well.

Some examples of Hole-in-the-Day's bravery, bordering on foolishness, are his actions in 1841 when, angered by the 1839 killing of nearly 90 Ojibwe by the Dakota on the Rum River, he attempted revenge on Little Crow, the prominent Dakota chief based at the major village of Kaposia. In 1841 he raised a warparty of 200 for the purpose of attacking the village of Little Crow a few miles southeast of Fort Snelling.

Once those committed to the warparty learned of the risky nature of what Hole-in-the-Day planned he was deserted by all but two. Undeterred, with his two warriors Hole-in-the-Day continued on. When he reached Little Crow's village he crept close enough to fire into one of the lodges. The enraged Dakota chased him all the way to the Saint Croix River before he escaped.

In the spring of 1842 Hole-in-the-Day again attempted revenge, his anger increased by an attempted Dakota attack on the Ojibwe village at Pokegama Lake, just west of present day Pine City. Again he tried to attack Little Crow's village at Kaposia, this time with a war party of 160. He succeeded in setting an ambush and

THE HEADWATERS WAR:
Conflict for the Mississippi Headwaters

killing a dozen Dakota and wounding a number more at the cost of five Ojibwe.

Adding to the challenge of the above two raids, was that in 1839 Little Crow had wisely moved his village south several miles and to the opposite bank of the Mississippi; placing the Mississippi River between the country occupied by the Ojibwe and Kaposia. Attempting to approach by river that deep in Dakota territory would not go undiscovered.

In was in 1847, the year of his untimely death at the age of 47, that Hole-in-the-Day reached his zenith both in prestige and as a peacemaker. He eagerly supported the government's plan to move the Ho-Chunk (*Winnebago*) and the Menominee from their home in Wisconsin to create a buffer between the Ojibwe and the Dakota. He not only convinced his own Mississippi Band to cede their land south of the Crow Wing River for that purpose, but was also instrumental in gaining agreement of the Pillager and Lake Superior bands to give up their claims also. The Ho-Chunk were to be given the land west of the Long Prairie River as far west as Ottertail Lake, and the Menominee the land east of the Long Prairie River to the Mississippi. It was on his return from a visit to the Winnebago and Menominee at their homes in Wisconsin to determine their willingness to accept the new land that he was fatally injured.

There were a wide range of views on Hole-in-the-Day the elder. Stories of his nature in the eyes of white men diametrically oppose each other. Following are some quotes:

> Reverend Brunson, later U.S. Agent for the Ojibwe, provides a description at the time of the events of 1838. He described him as "*the dirtiest, most scowling, and savage looking*'" of the group of about fifty he was sitting with. But elsewhere Mr Brunson also said he was the most influential chief of the Ojibwe nation.*(20,p.496)*

THE HEADWATERS WAR:
Conflict for the Mississippi Headwaters

Henry Schoolcraft, while misidentifying him as a Pillager war chief, perhaps because he was in the company of Flat Mouth the Pillager chief, in 1838 describes Hole-in-the-Day as "*one of the most hardened, bloodthirsty wretches of whom I have ever heard. Mr. Aitkin, the elder told me that having once surprised and killed a Sioux family, the fellow picked up a little girl, who had fled from the lodge, and pitched her into the Mississippi. The current bore her against a point of land. Seeing it, the hardened wretch ran down and again pushed her in.*" (27, Chapter LXIV).

The above view wasn't shared by all, as shown by the following quotes: *(5, preview page)*

Ezekiel Gear (1843): "*Hole-in-the-Sky is admitted by all that know him, to be no common man. By his energy and intellectual superiority, he has acquired a most extensive influence among all the bands of his nation, and is anxious to be instructed in the Christian religion, and to enjoy the blessings of civilization. He has long been the terror and scourge of his enemies, and has sought and obtained peace for this very purpose.*"

L.H. Wheeler (1843): "*Hole-in-the-Sky, at once an orator and a warrior, is evidently the greatest and most intelligent man in the nation, as fine a form of body, head, and face, as perhaps could be found in any country. He is said to have killed some forty Sioux with his own hand.*"

Hole-in-the-Day the elder was able to invoke strong emotions in the onlookers. He was complex and

310

THE HEADWATERS WAR:
Conflict for the Mississippi Headwaters

ambitious, and if not the most was at least one of the most influential Ojibwe leaders of the day. However, while recognized as principal chief of the Mississippi Band his attempts to exercise broader authority were often rebuked, as when he attempted to exercise authority over the Pillager and Lake Superior bands.

When Hole-in-the-Day died in 1847 as a result of a fall from a cart while drunk, his nineteen year old son inherited his civil chieftainship. His dying instructions to *Gwiiwizens (Boy)* were to take care of his people. His brother, Strong Ground, also a very well regarded chief, had died the previous year due to mixing a native drug with alcohol.

Hole-in-the-Day the younger
(*Gwiiwizens,* Boy)

Before the death of Hole-in-the-Day the elder his son, who succeeded him, carried the name *Gwiiwizens*, or Boy. Boy began his training early, accompanying his father on nearly all his missions, and by the age of eleven became his constant attendant. Also, by the age of eleven he had taken his first Dakota scalp; that of a young Dakota girl on orders from his father.

When people refer to Hole-in-the-Day today it is usually 'the younger', partly because he presided during the time of the major land cession treaties and his actions were often reported in newspapers. In 1827, two years after Hole-in-the-Day the elder had assumed his chieftainship from Curly Head, he had a son. The son went by the name of 'Boy', and was 19 at the time of his father's death. There are conflicting reports on whether the mother was the daughter of Broken Tooth, the son of *Bi-aus-wah*, or Flat Mouth, but on at least one occasion, perhaps for political reasons, he claimed descent from *Bi-aus-wah*.

As a commoner Hole-in-the-Day the elder had to

THE HEADWATERS WAR:
Conflict for the Mississippi Headwaters

achieve preeminence the 'old fashioned way'; by hard work and being at the right place at the right time. The path to leadership of 'Boy' was completely different; he had been schooled in Ojibwe politics at his father's knee, and claimed the mantel of his father as principal chief by pure audacity.

Following the death of Hole-in-the-Day the elder, and as soon as the period of morning ended, Boy traveled to Fort Snelling and informed the fort commander he was assuming his father's name of Hole-in-the-Day and his position as principal chief. This claim was pure audacity; while the civil chieftainship of his father's local band was typically inherited, any claim to principal chieftainship was another matter.

After returning from Fort Snelling, the newly renamed 'Hole-in-the-Day' learned of a meeting at Fond du Lac for the purpose of signing by the Mississippi and Lake Superior bands the treaty his father had promoted related to the plan to give up the land south of the Crow Wing River for Menominee (*Ho-Chunk*) and Winnebago reservations with the intention of creating a buffer between the Dakota and the Ojibwe. This was a policy Hole-in-the-Day the elder had supported, and it was upon his returning from meeting with the Menominee and Winnebago in Wisconsin to obtain their willingness that he had the accident leading to his death.

Hole-in-the-Day the younger immediately traveled to Fond du Lac, and when the conference started preempted the more senior chiefs and rose to speak. He immediately claimed the overall chieftainship his father had held, and questioned why the other chiefs were even there, claiming the land to be conveyed was his by inheritance from his father. He also claimed that on his mother's side he was descended from the *'hereditary head chief of the nation'*, which could only mean Broken Tooth, the son of *Bi-aus-wah,* and therefore *Bi-aus-wah* himself. This was clearly bluster to impress the white treaty signers, since even *if* his mother

THE HEADWATERS WAR:
Conflict for the Mississippi Headwaters

had been Broken Tooth's daughter it wouldn't provide a claim; chieftainships descended through the male line, and a principal chief gained his position by merit. However the claim of descent from *Bi-aus-wah* would certainly add to his pedigree.

The above claim, and what followed, illustrate Hole-in-the-Day the younger's arrogance and nerve. While only 19, he apparently cowed the other chiefs present since none chose to dispute his claim, even though some were senior chiefs in their 70s and 80s; which may have been merely an example of politeness on their part. There was not even an objection from the Lake Superior Band chiefs present.

In his speech he is reported to have told the government negotiators present that all negotiations were to be with him, not involving the other chiefs. The government negotiators were sufficiently impressed that they agreed, and he alone negotiated for the Ojibwe, with all the chiefs present signing the agreement he had negotiated. He even insisted his signature not appear with that of the 'common' chiefs, and it was included on a separate sheet.

To some extent Hole-in-the-Day's question as to why the other chiefs were there was valid. The area in question adjoined and was south of the Crow Wing-Gull Lake area over which his father was undisputed principal chief. The land had been cleared of the Dakota by his father and Flat Mouth of the Pillagers, who was not present at that meeting; the Pillagers were scheduled to sign later at a separate conference. Why, indeed, were the other Mississippi and the Lake Superior chiefs there? Under the western concept of 'ownership by force of arms', also a concept with the Ojibwe, only Hole-in-the-Day and Flat Mouth should have been involved.

Following the conference Hole-in-the-Day the younger managed to gain acceptance of his supremacy over the Mississippi Band, but not by all. He never gained full recognition at Sandy Lake, and was strongly

313

THE HEADWATERS WAR:
Conflict for the Mississippi Headwaters

opposed by the Mille Lacs leadership. Even some of the Gull Lake area chiefs never fully accepted his authority, such as Bad Boy, the son of Broken Tooth, and White Fisher, the grandson of the well known Nokay, after whom the Nokassipi tributary of the Mississippi was named. After the treaty was signed and the conference ended the Mille Lacs band even objected in a letter to Washington, but that was after the fact. To the end the Mille Lacs band denied Hole-in-the-Day the younger's claim as principal chief.

Much can be said of Hole-in-the-Day the younger. He was clearly the ideal man for the times; a time when the Dakota nation to the south was being dismantled by coerced land treaties and it was clear to all that the Ojibwe would be next. The times required a man of outstanding personality and ability, backed by an impeccable pedigree. Hole-in-the-Day the younger had all those things, plus the audacity to oppose the government when he thought it necessary.

While Hole-in-the-Day's protests in the wake of the Sandy Lake Tragedy raised his profile, especially among the whites of the area, and probably among the Ojibwe as well, much of his prestige among the Ojibwe would be lost by his actions involving the treaties of 1855 and later; including his actions in the aborted Ojibwe uprising of 1862. In those treaties he ensured he personally profited in land and money, and moved from Gull Lake, leaving Bad Boy as its senior chief, to a new residence opposite the village of Crow Wing. There he built a large house and developed a successful farm on the 660 acres he had been granted by the treaty of 1855, but continued to claim overall leadership of the Mississippi Ojibwe.

Who the above Chief Bad Boy was is subject to debate; Bad Boy is a common name among the Ojibwe. A Chief Bad Boy was among the signatories of a treaty between the government and the Saint Croix Ojibwe some years earlier. Additionally, a Chief Bad Boy (*or*

THE HEADWATERS WAR:
Conflict for the Mississippi Headwaters

Big Mouth), the son of Broken Tooth at Sandy Lake, had inherited his civil chieftainship, and was purported to have later moved his band to Gull Lake when Sandy Lake fell into decline. This later case could explain the antipathy between Bad Boy and both Hole-in-the-Day the elder and the younger; considering Hole-in-the-day the elder a commoner who had only gained a civil chieftainship through adoption by Curly Head. In this book when I refer to Chief Bad Boy, it is with the assumption he was the son of Broken Tooth.

In any case, the opposition of Chief Bad Boy only added to that exerted from Mille Lacs. While among the Ojibwe the influence of Hole-in-the-Day the younger waned, he remained as the key negotiator with the white government, who recognized in him a leader with whom they could work.

In some ways Hole-in-the-Day the younger was like his father, a warrior of exceptional, often foolish bravery. When his brother was killed by the Mdewakanton Dakota in 1848 he raised a 300 man war party at Crow Wing to attack the offenders at Shakopee on the Minnesota River. However, like his father's planned attack on the village of Little Crow earlier, most of his warriors deserted him, leaving him with 28. Still he carried on, but succeeded in killing only one Dakota. The Dakota later retaliated by attacking Sandy Lake. This was one of many similar cases showing his disregard for danger.

Where Hole-in-the-Day the younger gained much of his fame in the white world was as intermediary between the Ojibwe and the government; not only for the Mississippi band but for the Pillager and Lake Superior bands as well. However, his attempts to become involved with treaties for the Red Lake band failed, and those treaties lack his signature; the Red Lake Ojibwe even refusing his request to speak at their treaty negations.

The year after Hole-in-the-Day the younger's

THE HEADWATERS WAR:
Conflict for the Mississippi Headwaters

ascendancy construction of Fort Ripley began near the mouth of the Nokassipi, a short distance below the Crow Wing junction, bringing white power to his doorstep. Hole-in-the-Day immediately began a campaign to have the location for annuity payments for the Mississippi Band moved from Sault Ste. Marie or Madeline Island in Lake Superior to Fort Ripley. In that he failed, but he did succeed in getting it moved to Sandy Lake, an easy trip for Mississippi band members. It was that move that resulted in the infamous Sandy Lake Tragedy.

Hole-in-the-Day the younger strictly interpreted treaties and attempted to hold the government to account; sometimes succeeding, sometimes not. As part of his interaction with the government, he made six trips to Washington, meeting with President's Pierce, Lincoln; and Johnson. While he attempted to gain full citizenship for Indians, he failed; that didn't come until the Indian Citizenship Act was passed over 75 years later, in 1924. However, he did succeed in achieving full citizenship for himself through a special act of the Minnesota legislature.

In his treaty negotiations Hole-in-the-Day the younger was also careful to see that he benefited personally from the terms; in the Treaty of 1855 he acquired 660 acres on the Mississippi near Gull Lake, which he developed into a successful farm. There he built a large home where he lived until it was later burned by some of his opponents; but in a later treaty he had a clause inserted for the cost of rebuilding that burned home. In the Treaty of 1867, which established the White Earth Reservation, he saw that he and his family were granted an annual stipend of $1,000. This self serving only added to the discontent.

In 1862 the rising star of Hole-in-the-Day began its decline, ending in his assassination six years later. That was the year of the Dakota uprising, but at the same time a little-known uprising by some of the Ojibwe led by Hole-in-the-Day had taken place. While the Ojibwe

THE HEADWATERS WAR:
Conflict for the Mississippi Headwaters

uprising was short lived and without casualties on either side, the government understood the danger of antagonizing Hole-in-the-Day, and also the danger of allowing Ojibwe reservations and white settlement to exist adjacent to each other. It solidified the view of many in the government that the Ojibwe had to be moved 'out of the way'.

The Ojibwe uprising had another affect that was just as important; Hole-in-the-Day had antagonized not only the government, but the Pillager band had withdrawn its support following what they considered Hole-in-the-Day's duplicity. Further, he had antagonized many of his Mississippi Band allies as well. He was opposed by the powerful chief Bad Boy at Gull Lake, and the Mille Lacs band went so far as to send warriors to oppose his attempt to take Fort Ripley, an action that led to the end of the uprising. Near the end of the War Between the States, when the government made its move to remove all Ojibwe to the new White Earth reservation, Hole-in-the-Day lacked the support to successfully block the transfer, leading to the conspiracy to have him assassinated.

During the same month Lee surrendered at Appomattox, Hole-in-the-Day signed the 1865 treaty, which was largely a repeat of an 1864 treaty, in which the Mississippi band ceded the Gull, Mille Lacs, Sandy, Rabbit, Pokegama, and Rice lake reservations in exchange for a reservation adjoining those of the Pillager, Winnibigoshish, and Cass Lake bands. In both treaties property owned by Hole-in-the-Day and the Mille Lacs chief were exempted. Many refused to move, and the treaties were only partially effective.

In the spring of 1867 a new treaty to supplement those earlier treaties was signed by Hole-in-the-Day in which it was agreed the Mississippi Band Ojibwe would give up all land in Minnesota in exchange for a reduced reservation in the Leech Lake area (*see Figure 28*) and a large new reservation at White Earth, estimated at 2

THE HEADWATERS WAR:
Conflict for the Mississippi Headwaters

million acres, for those who had not already moved to the Leech-Winnibigoshish set of reservations. As before, many opposed the new treaty and refused to move to White Earth. By Executive Order in 1873 the deal was sweetened by addition of the small White Oak Point reservation *(see Figure 29)* adjacent to the headwaters lakes reservations around Leech and Winnibigoshish. Eventually the government yielded, and allowed a few other small reservations, such as at Mille Lacs.

It was not only that they were required to leave their homes that angered many of the Ojibwe, particularly the half-bloods at Crow Wing. In addition to providing a $1,000/yr stipend to Hole-in-the-Day and his heirs, plus retention of their half-section of land in the Gull Lake area, Hole-in-the-Day had insisted on inserting an Article IV in the treaty of 1867 that said;

> *"No part of the annuities provided for in this or any former treaty with the Chippewas of the Mississippi band shall be paid to any half-breed or mixed-blood, except those that actually live with their people upon one of the reservations belonging to the Chippewa Indians."*

That clause was like sticking a finger in the eye of the large band of mixed-bloods at Crow Wing, many of whom had integrated into white society and become important traders and businessmen. It was those mixed-bloods who would later engineer Hole-in-the-Day's downfall.

While Hole-in-the-Day had previously agreed to the Treaty of 1867, he held a well-earned distrust of whether the government would keep its word. Recognizing the past deficiencies in the government's adherence to treaty obligations, when the government attempted to enforce the treaty he refused to allow Ojibwe to move until agreed-to facilities had been constructed. While partially successful, his influence had

THE HEADWATERS WAR:
Conflict for the Mississippi Headwaters

dropped to the point that he was unable to stop bands from moving, even from the Crow Wing area.

In addition to problems caused by the 1862 uprising and the 1867 Treaty, there were other reasons for dislike as well. Hole-in-the-Day's attempt to claim supremacy extending beyond the Mississippi band to include the Pillager and Lake Superior bands had angered many. He had even attempted to be appointed to negotiate for the government for the Red Lake band treaties; a request denied by President Lincoln, and when he tried to speak at Red Lake treaty negotiations his request was denied by the Red Lake chiefs. His use of the treaties for personal gain also angered many, as did his taking Ellen McCarty, a white woman, as his third wife. To many it must have appeared that he was adopting the white man's way in both dress and his style of living, and abandoning his Ojibwe heritage.

Hole-in-the-Day the younger was assassinated in 1868 at the age of 43 by dissident Ojibwe, which removed the one Ojibwe chief capable of standing in the government's way. Since the murder occurred on Indian land white officials failed to fully investigate, and the murder was never officially solved. However, it was common knowledge that it was the act of a group of Pillager men hired by half-blood and white businessmen from Crow Wing, angered by Hole-in-the-Day's attempts to limit their influence and disagreements as to the White Earth move. Anton Treuer, in his book *The Assassination of Hole-in-the-Day,* identifies each of the murderers by name, and also the instigators; none of whom were ever punished. In fact, some of the businessmen who instigated and paid for the killing managed to gain appointments to controlling positions at White Earth.

Outside the reservation Hole-in-the Day's fame remained, and his murder was national news. This is what observers of the time, and those at a later date, had to say: *(5, preview page)*

THE HEADWATERS WAR:
Conflict for the Mississippi Headwaters

Minneapolis Daily Tribune (1868): *"Hole-in-the-Day was in some respects one of the most extraordinary characters in Indian history. He was the Chippewa Cid, or Coeur de Lion, from the gleam of whose battle axe whole armies of Saracen Sioux fled as before an irresistible fate...We might fill columns with narratives of the exploits in which Hole-in-the-Day has figured as the hero. "*

Bernard Coleman (1967): *"Adjectives pale in the description of so dynamic a personality. Only deeper study of Hole-in-the-Day's life and actions can create a proper perspective concerning his remarkable spirit and character, compelling and even romantic in his day. His death, no matter how described, was a real tragedy, greatness cut down at its height."*

There are many other quotes, but the above serve to show the high regard given the man.

During his lifetime Hole-in-the-Day the younger lived in the Crow Wing-Gull Lake area, and like his father strove to mold the Ojibwe into a western model. He operated a large farm in the area, and lived in a large western-style house. In an attempt to westernize, in addition to taking a white wife, he even gave all his children European names. However, his attempts to persuade his people to take up farming was largely unsuccessful. One of his goals in treaty negotiations was to gain full citizenship for the Ojibwe; something he never achieved. It took until well into the 1900s before that finally came to pass.

While becoming quite westernized himself, still Hole-in-the-Day the younger led numerous war parties against the Dakota, right up to a few years before his death. He also was involved in numerous confrontations

THE HEADWATERS WAR:
Conflict for the Mississippi Headwaters

with other Ojibwe, especially the half-breed Ojibwe at Crow Wing.

With his assassination Hole-in-the-Day's fear was realized; when coerced and enticed into moving the Ojibwe found White Earth lacked the promised facilities, and other promises had also not been fulfilled. Many resisted the move in spite of acts of congress in the 1870s and 1880s, many preferring to stay where they were even if their reservations had been dissolved. The last Ojibwe leader capable of withstanding government pressure was gone.

While he was personally self-serving, Hole-in-the-Day the younger was the only Ojibwe leader with the strength and craftiness to delay the inevitable and gain better terms for his people, and that very strength contributed to his assassination; he stood in the way of the traders who made their living picking the bones of the Indians.

Following Hole-in-the-Day's death his two Ojibwe wives and seven children moved to the White Earth reservation. Included among the seven children was Ignatius, who claimed the name Hole-in-the-Day, and later attempted to step into the Hole-in-the-Day's role. His white wife, and the son born shortly before his death, Joseph, moved to Minneapolis, where Joseph was adopted by a white family named Woodbury. Upon the death of Ignatius, Joseph Woodbury moved to White Earth and attempted to assume the hereditary chieftainship, also assuming the name Hole-in-the-Day. Neither Joseph nor Ignatius succeeded in gaining the supremacy their father possessed.

A claimed descendant of Hole-in-the-Day also gained fame at Leech Lake in 1898 when the government attempted to apprehend Chief *Bugonayshig* (*also known as Hole-in-the-Day*), resulting in the last battle between the army and the American Indians; the Battle of Sugar Point. Until recently at least, the head of the Sandy Lake band made claims to that title. However,

THE HEADWATERS WAR:
Conflict for the Mississippi Headwaters

laying claim to the name is one thing, but achieving recognition as principal chief is a different matter; it is a matter of prestige and acceptance more than heredity. All the claimants to Hole-in-the-Day the younger's mantel as principal chief lacked that acceptance.

Flat Mouth the elder

Born about 1774, Chief Flat Mouth the elder inherited the chieftainship of his father, Yellow Hair, at Leech Lake sometime around the turn of the century, and influenced history in northern and central Minnesota until his death in 1860. Flat Mouth, while a fierce warrior and deadly enemy of the Sioux, was a statesman, almost the opposite of his father Yellow Hair, who gained a chieftainship more by coercion than merit (*15, pp.18-20*).

In 1806, when Pike visited Leech Lake and confronted the British traders still active in the region, Flat Mouth, who had already succeeded his father as chief, pledged loyalty to the new American government, and was steadfast in his support until his death.

While during its peak five separate bands and villages made their home on Leech Lake, Flat Mouth soon gained ascendancy, recognized as the most important chief of the Pillager Band. His chieftainship covered the period from before Pike's visit in 1806 through the key treaties of the 1850s, making him a contemporary of Broken Tooth, Curly Head, and both Hole-in-the-Day the elder and younger. Exactly how far Flat Mouth's influence reached is open to question. While clearly the leading Pillager chief at Leech Lake, and influential in both the Ottertail and western Crow Wing areas, when the Treaty of 1855 first established reservations for the Ojibwe the Winnibigoshish Band was given a separate reservation, although later, when the government officially assigned names to the bands, they were grouped with the Pillagers.

THE HEADWATERS WAR:
Conflict for the Mississippi Headwaters

Flat Mouth worked closely with Curly Head and both Hole-in-the-Days to drive the Dakota from the Crow Wing-Gull Lake and Long Prairie River areas; one of his daughters becoming a wife of Hole-in-the-Day the elder. While much older than Hole-in-the Day the younger, the two maintained a close relationship during his lifetime, and he also became close to William Warren, the chronicler of the Ojibwe move into Minnesota.

While not normally identified as a principal chief, Flat Mouth clearly had influence extending beyond the Leech and Winnibigoshish lakes to Ottertail Lake and southwest into the western Crow Wing watershed. Through his partnership with the Mississippi Band principle chiefs he was also instrumental in freeing the Gull Lake and Crow Wing River and its tributaries of the Dakota, and may have exceeded the influence of either of the Hole-in-the-Day's in the area of and to the west of the Long Prairie River. Separated as he was from the *M'dewakanton* and *Wahpekute* Dakota on the Minnesota River, his primary adversaries were the *Wahpeton* and *Sissiton* bands of the upper Minnesota River and its Chippewa and other tributaries in western Minnesota, and the Yanktonais bands claiming the prairie on both sides of the Red River. Raids back and fourth between those western bands and Leech Lake and the other headwaters lakes were common.

In the 1850s Flat Mouth made two trips to Washington, and died in 1860 when in his eighties. During those years some considered him the most influential Ojibwe chief in the headwaters area, but living further from Fort Snelling and the white officials at the nearby community of Saint Paul, Hole-in-the-Day (*both elder and younger*) tended to have a higher profile. However, his influence was a moderating force on the more volatile Ojibwe elements, such as the two Hole-in-the-Days, and as a peacemaker he garnered less attention since he rarely challenged the government.

THE HEADWATERS WAR:
Conflict for the Mississippi Headwaters

Flat Mouth certainly exerted strong influence on events outside his home at Leech Lake. He signed treaties and traveled to Washington in behalf of the broader Pillager band (*as later defined by the government, which folded in the Pembina and Red River bands, as well as those at Cass and Winnibigoshish*), and his bust is still on exhibit to this day in the Capitol Building in Washington; only three other Indians share that honor.

Much more of a statesman than his father Yellow Hair, Flat Mouth pledged loyalty to the fledgling newly independent colonies, and was instrumental in keeping the Ojibwe of the Minnesota area from supporting the British in the war of 1812. When he died he was succeeded by his son, Flat Mouth the younger, who lived into the 1900s. Flat Mouth the younger never gained the prestige of his father, but shared leadership at Leech Lake with the older Chief Buffalo.

Flat Mouth has to a large extent been ignored by modern writers, one of the few books on his life that of Dr. Duane Lund who lives not far from Leech Lake, *Minnesota's Chief Flat Mouth of Leech Lake.* However, the timeline and sequence of events he presents varies greatly from most other sources. He also assigns an unusually expansive definition to the term 'Pillager'; including bands of the Gull Lake-Crow Wing complex, and sometime even Sandy Lake. Originally the name 'Pillager' had applied only to the band(s) occupying the islands of Leech Lake.

Since Flat Mouth is the only Pillager chief grouped here with the principal chiefs, I will diverge slightly from the main storyline to clarify how the name 'Pillager' arose, and how its use expanded with time to include bands not covered initially. Originally the name was assigned to a group of Indians from Leech Lake who robbed some traders in the Crow Wing area. Later it began to be applied to all from Leech Lake, then all from neighboring lakes as well. In assigning reservations in

THE HEADWATERS WAR:
Conflict for the Mississippi Headwaters

the treaty of 1855 the government officially designated all Indians west of the Mississippi River and north of the Leech River junction with the Mississippi as the Pillager Band. They also included those at Ottertail, and as far west as the Red River and Pembina.

Others, as well as Lund, also sometimes assign the name 'Pillager' to Indians far from Leech Lake. As an example, in his journals Schoolcraft refers to Hole-in-the-Day the elder as a Pillager war chief; perhaps because at the time he was in the company of Flat Mouth. It is true the frequent movement of Ojibwe bands between villages and areas serves to cloud the question.

By the definition of boundaries in the Treaty of 1855, everything downstream of the entry of the Leech River into the Mississippi is part of the Mississippi Band, not the Pillagers. However, since the presence of any significant villages of the Mississippi Band were far to the south and east, it is likely the influence of the Pillagers and Flat Mouth extended far downstream, with assimilation of groups that might have been originally part of the Mississippi Band. After all, the designations 'Pillager' and 'Mississippi' when assigned to the Ojibwe was that of the white man; Ojibwe groups and families moved freely from location to location.

Other Prominent Ojibwe Chiefs

Since this book primarily addresses the area of the Mississippi headwaters little is said of the personalities and occurrences outside those headwaters. However there were other chiefs of note outside those boundaries that gained influence over wide areas, and their actions directly influenced the history of the Mississippi basin.

White Fisher (*Waub-o-jeeg*) from La Pointe on Lake Superior is an example. While not directly associated with the Mississippi headwaters, it would be a disservice not to include him in the list of great chiefs,

THE HEADWATERS WAR:
Conflict for the Mississippi Headwaters

even though his base was in Wisconsin. He is really the star of the events on the St. Croix tributary of the Mississippi covered in an earlier chapter.

Other examples, this time from Red Lake, are Chief Moose Dung (*Moo-ze-mo*) and 'He-Who-is-Spoken To', who were instrumental in the Red Lake Ojibwe expansion to the west, and also in opposing government attempts to coerce the Red Lake Ojibwe to give up their land and independence. To this day the memory of Moose Dung is preserved in the name of the Mosomo Campgrounds near Cut Foot Sioux Lake, the scene of the battle between the Dakota and Ojibwe in the mid 1700s.

Summary

In some ways the Hole-in-the-Days, both father and son, exceeded even the primacy of the earlier *Bi-aus-wah,* Broken Tooth, and Curly Head. By their connections they became recognized by the government as overall chiefs for purposes of negotiating treaties for the Mississippi Band, but often succeeded in injecting themselves into treaty negotiations of the Pillager and Lake Superior bands as well. While this may have added to their prestige with the white government, it also resulted in their gaining many enemies.

The time of the two Hole-in-the-Days and Flat Mouth the elder were a particularly critical time for the Ojibwe. It was their sad duty to preside over the end of the Ojibwe empire and restriction of their people to reservations. Fort Snelling, and later Fort Ripley and Fort Ridgely, were present to further whatever goals the government chose to establish; and in Minnesota during this period that goal was to remove the Indians from the path of white settlement and provide space for the lumber industry.

While the War Between the States provided a short interlude during which the government, occupied

THE HEADWATERS WAR:
Conflict for the Mississippi Headwaters

elsewhere, placed a priority on peace on the frontier, that was short lived. Toward the end of that war the policies of removal escalated, and by the late 1860s the removal of all Mississippi Band Ojibwe to a new reservation at White Earth was attempted. The Dakota had already been banished from the state after the Dakota uprising of 1862, with many removed as far away as Nebraska.

After the end of the War Between the States in 1865, only Hole-in-the-Day the younger stood in the way of removal of the rest of the Ojibwe to White Earth; insisting the government first keep its commitments for facilities to serve its new residents. However, at least partly due to his devious manipulations during the Ojibwe uprising of 1862, and his use of treaties to obtain personal gain, he had managed to alienate many of his supporters, including the Leech Lake chiefs, and much of his support evaporated. Even at Crow Wing, his center of power, he was unable to stop defections to White Earth. Further, with the death of his friend and close associate (*and 'possibly' grandfather*) Flat Mouth the elder several years before, the support of the Pillager bands could no longer be guaranteed. His end came when he was assassinated in 1868 by Ojibwe from Leech Lake at the instigation of white and half-blood traders at Crow Wing.

For those who would like a more detailed review of the two Hole-in-the-Days and their lives I recommend *The Assassination of Hole-in-the-Day*, by Anton Treuer (*32*). Based on a wealth of research and interviews with Ojibwe elders, it also contains a good record of the treaties and subsequent executive orders and Acts of Congress affecting the Ojibwe. He goes beyond just those topics and includes detail on the functions and customs of leadership, as well as how chiefs of the 19th century changed that model.

THE HEADWATERS WAR:
Conflict for the Mississippi Headwaters

CHAPTER 15
BIG SANDY: THEN AND NOW

As to Big Sandy Lake and the Sandy Lake Band, there is little doubt that in the 1700s it was perhaps the most powerful force in Minnesota. It was a primary target when the Leech Lake Dakota launched their grand campaign against their tormentors in the mid-1700s, resulting in the battle of Cut Foot Sioux, and the target of the 1768 campaign that ended in the Dakota disaster at the mouth of the Crow Wing River.

After the 1770s the Big Sandy Band was plagued by bad luck. About 1782 the band was decimated by smallpox, and it took years for the population to recover. Then, sometime between 1797 and 1800, the band was hit hard by the massacre at Cross Lake. Both times they recovered, only to again be decimated by a measles epidemic in 1820.

But in spite of its setbacks Big Sandy Lake and the Big Sandy Lake Band retained their prominence well into the 1800s. Supplemented by migration from Lake Superior it remained key to the fur trade and access to the Mississippi River basin, with the British Northwest Trading Company establishing a combination fort-trading post at Brown's Point on the western shore in 1794. That post was the first stockaded fort west of Lake Superior, and became the standard stopover for traffic west from Lake Superior and up and down the Mississippi. The post was described by Bousquet, the trader located there from 1794-1797, and Zebulon Pike on his 1804 stopover, as a 100 foot square, 13 foot high stockade with blockhouses at two corners, containing four major buildings. From the description it appears to have been located on the northern shore of Brown's Point facing the portage to the Mississippi about two

THE HEADWATERS WAR:
Conflict for the Mississippi Headwaters

miles to the north.

When the Northwest Trading Company's Sandy Lake post was constructed the British still disputed ownership with the new United States of the Northwest Territory, which included Big Sandy Lake. However, following the 1814 treaty ending the War of 1812 the British, and the Northwest Fur Company as well, withdrew from the Northwest Territory. Congress had prohibited foreign ownership of fur trading posts, and the Sandy Lake fort and post were turned over to the American Fur Company organized by John Jacob six years earlier. Later that post was abandoned and a new American Fur Company post erected on the north shore near the Sandy River outlet to the Mississippi.

When about 1836 Hole-in-the-Day the elder and his brother Strong Ground permanently moved their bands from Sandy Lake to the Crow Wing-Gull Lake area Sandy Lake began to decline in importance. While before their move at least five bands called Sandy Lake their home, in less than a decade that had been reduced to two. The Crow Wing-Gull Lake area had replaced Sandy Lake in importance. Later, as the location for annuity payments beginning in 1850, the first year marred by the infamous 'Sandy Lake Tragedy', it gained back some of its prominence.

In 1838 Frederick Ayer, at the request of the Scotch trader in charge of the American Fur Company at Sandy Lake, William Alexander Aitkin, opened a school at Sandy Lake for the 'voyageurs' children. It was here that Ayer completed an Ojibway dictionary and spelling book. This was the Frederick Ayer whose widow's eyewitness account of the 1841 Dakota attack on the Ojibwe Pokegama Lake village (*near Pine City*) is related in Chapter 11.

When the Treaty of 1855 forced the Ojibwe onto reservations the Sandy Lake Reservation consisted of over 27 square miles and encompassed the entire lake. However, the Treaties of 1863-65 extinguished that

329

THE HEADWATERS WAR:
Conflict for the Mississippi Headwaters

reservation along with other Mississippi Band reservations, in exchange for a single reservation at and near the headwaters lakes of Leech, Cass, and Winnibigoshish. In the Treaty of 1867 the Mississippi band agreed to boundary changes for the Leech/Cass/Winnibigoshish reservation, with the result shown in Figure 28, and a newly formed White Earth reservation near Minnesota's western border.

Some of the Sandy Lake Band refused to move following the above treaties, and remained at Big Sandy, retaining their federal recognition but without a reservation. In 1873, to encourage more to move, White Oak Point reservation was established for the Sandy Lake Band by Executive Order adjacent to the larger reservation at the headwaters lakes, (*see Figure 29*). This was also of only limited success.

Big Sandy Lake today is much changed from what it was in the 18th and 19th centuries. In 1895 a wooden dam was put in service at the Sandy River outlet to the Mississippi, and a set of locks in 1896; replaced with a concrete dam and lock in 1909 and 1912. A negative of dam construction was that the higher water level changed the contour and characteristics of the lake, and covered the sites of many of the original Dakota and Ojibwe villages. Some ponds and lowlands adjacent to the lake became bays and some peninsulas separated into islands, while many existing islands were reduced in size or disappeared. Battle Island, featured in Chapter 2, was reduced in size by as much as two-thirds.

With construction of the locks in 1896 steamboat access from the Mississippi to Big Sandy Lake began, with the steamboat 'Oriole' maintaining regular service from 1908-1910. The steamboats largely serviced the lumber camps that dominated the area during the early 1900s, with the Weyerhaeuser Pine Tree Lumber Co. the dominant player. With discontinuance of steamboat service the U. S. Army Corp of Engineers acquired the Oriole and used it for dredging and channel

THE HEADWATERS WAR:
Conflict for the Mississippi Headwaters

maintenance until the end of 1918.

In 1915 a small 32 acre reservation was established a short distance northeast of the lake for the Sandy Lake Band; the band later purchasing some additional land on the north shore. Then, under the Indian Reorganization Act of 1934 (*Wheeler-Howard Act*), the Sandy Lake band lost its federal recognition and was placed under the jurisdiction of the Mille Lacs Lake Band. While the reservation remained, those remaining at Sandy Lake, to this day, dispute their assignment to the Mille Lacs Band.

Now, over 270 years after the Ojibwe raid on Big Sandy Lake, the only mark left of earlier Indian presence is the small Ojibwe reservation, two memorial plaques commemorating the Big Sandy Lake Tragedy, and a sign at the location of one of the old trading posts. Even the old sign at Battle Island is gone, and the location of the original Dakota and Ojibwe villages are uncertain. Few who live on or near the lake today even know it once had an importance beyond that of any other of Minnesota's many northern lakes.

But once upon a time it was different. As early as the 1660s, beginning with Radisson and Groseilliers, nearly all early European explorers, adventurers, and traders headed into central Minnesota or the Mississippi headwaters crossed the waters of Big Sandy Lake or used it as a stopover, and from the 1740s until it fell into decline in the late 1830s the influence of the Sandy Lake Band of Ojibwe spread throughout Minnesota and beyond. While a quiet backwater today, Big Sandy is arguably the most historically significant lake in Minnesota, an important center dating to before Minneapolis, St Paul, or the settlements that preceded them, were even a dream; the 'Lac du Sable' or 'Lac des Sables (*lake of the sands*) of the early French, known in European capitals over a century before the colonies gained their independence.

THE HEADWATERS WAR:
Conflict for the Mississippi Headwaters

Figure 25: Wooden Sandy River Dam, 1895

THE HEADWATERS WAR:
Conflict for the Mississippi Headwaters

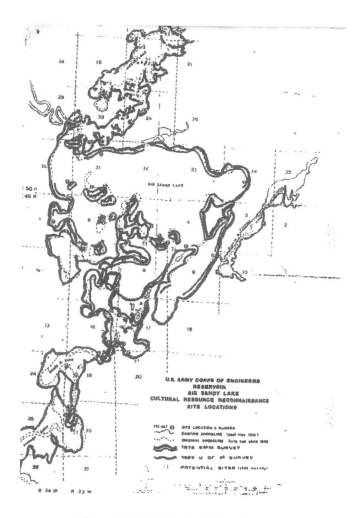

Figure 26: Big Sandy: Then & Now*

* *'Dotted line shows approximate shoreline prior to dam erection in 1894, solid line(s) the range of the water level after the dam was in place. As a reservoir lake, Big Sandy is subject to considerable water level variation due to periodic drawdowns or holdbacks to manage water levels on the Mississippi.*

THE HEADWATERS WAR:
Conflict for the Mississippi Headwaters

CHAPTER 16
THE END GAME

The Headwaters War never came to a formal end, but petered out as the white man took control of the destinies of both tribes. The last major advance of the Ojibwe was their take-over in the early 1800s of the Long Prairie River country west of the Mississippi River, and the area around Ottertail Lake in western Minnesota. By the early-mid 1800s the Ojibwe were in firm control of the northern two-thirds of the state, with the Dakota entrenched on the Minnesota River and its tributaries. While sporadic conflict continued, neither tribe had the strength to dislodge the other from the land they then held, and in addition they were held back by the white presence at Fort Snelling, and later Forts Ridgely and Ripley.

With the construction of Fort Snelling in the center of the Dakota controlled country in 1819, and the influx of settlers that followed, the Dakota faced an additional threat; of the soldiers at Fort Snelling. The purpose of Fort Snelling was two fold; first to stop the ongoing Dakota-Ojibwe conflict, but also to protect the settlers flooding into the area. Since the land purchased by Pike in the early 1800s that allowed the building of Fort Snelling was small (*9 square miles*), most of the new arrivals just moved past and settled on tribal lands, confident the soldiers at the fort would provide protection. Conflict between the Dakota and the plague of settlers would have been inevitable without the presence of the soldiers at Fort Snelling.

Initially this influx of settlers had little impact on the Ojibwe. The Ojibwe homeland was far away, and it lacked the attractiveness of the rich lands ideal for farming held by the Dakota. Something had to break,

334

THE HEADWATERS WAR:
Conflict for the Mississippi Headwaters

and in 1851 the Dakota ceded all their Minnesota lands for a reservation 20 miles wide, starting about 50 miles upstream on the Minnesota River and extending to the border of what is now South Dakota. Since settlers continued to flow into the lands reserved for the Dakota, seven years later that was later reduced to a 10 mile wide strip bordering the south shore.

While isolation of the Dakota to their reservation south of the Minnesota River caused a decline in the conflict, it did not stop. Only after the Dakota uprising of 1862, when the Dakota either fled or were evicted from the state, did the conflict finally come to an end.

Following the end of the Dakota uprising, the Abrogation Act of 1863 was passed by Congress, which provided for abrogation of all treaties between the U.S. Government and the Dakota, and forfeiture of all annuities, reservations, and their right of occupancy in Minnesota. Two weeks later the Dakota Removal Act of 1863 was passed providing for forceful removal of the Dakota from the state. However, any Dakota who could show they had aided the whites during the 1862 uprising were exempt from the removal order, and given an allotment of 80 acres.

Still, the bond of the Dakota with their long-time homes in Minnesota remained strong, and many continued to drift back to the state, where they remained homeless. In 1886, the same year as the Treaty of Fort Laramie ending Red Cloud's War and establishment of the 'Great Sioux Reservation *(all of present-day South Dakota west of the Missouri River)*, by Act of Congress the following four small reservations were established in Minnesota for the 'homeless' Dakota still in the state, or that had returned to the state:

      a - Prairie Island Dakota
      b – Shakopee M'dewakanton
      c – Lower Sioux
      d – Upper Sioux

THE HEADWATERS WAR:
Conflict for the Mississippi Headwaters

The total area of the four reservations is only a few thousand acres, with an estimated 1,500 residents. While the location of some of these reservations leads to a sparse existence, some near population centers have grown prosperous due to the Minnesota casino gambling monopoly held by Native Americans.

While the Dakota have returned, and presently have their four small reservations, the Abrogation Act of 1863 has never been repealed, resulting in an important difference between the above Dakota reservations and those of the Ojibwe discussed later. Since the original treaties with the Dakota had been abrogated in 1863, and the reservation land seized, they exist only through an Act of Congress, and lack the 'sovereignty' implied by a treaty; even the limited sovereignty assigned by the Supreme Court to treaties with the tribes.

The story for the Ojibwe is different. While by the late 1860s all except those at and near Red Lake had ceded all their land and, except for a few hold-outs, been moved to isolated reservations, the process took time and involved multiple treaties, Acts of Congress, and executive orders.

While the treaties refer to Lake Superior, Pillager, and Mississippi bands, it was only by an Act of Congress in 1871 that the names became official. The first treaty, in 1854, related to the Lake Superior Band, which gave up all lands except for reservations at Fond du Lac, Grand Portage, and Bois Forte (*Nett Lake*). While not a member of the Lake Superior Band, Hole-in-the-Day the younger still signed as 'head chief'. This is a hint at how his influence with both the Ojibwe and the white government had increased.

In the second treaty, that of 1855, the Mississippi, Pillager, and Winnibigoshish bands ceded their Minnesota lands for reservations. Initially, to convince the Ojibwe to accept the treaty, many small reservations were established located where the bands

336

THE HEADWATERS WAR:
Conflict for the Mississippi Headwaters

lived at the time. The initial reservations established by the 1855 treaty were:

1. The Northern bands (*Red River, Ottertail, etc*) and Pillager and Winnibigoshish Ojibwe were given reservations at Leech, Cass, and Winnibigoshish lakes. This excluded the Red Lake Ojibwe.

2. The Mississippi Band (*Mississippi River from the Leech River to the Crow Wing River and surrounding areas*) were given reservations at Sandy, Mille Lacs, Gull, Rice, Rabbit, and Pokegama lakes (*near Pine City*).

Figure 27 shows the boundaries of these initial reservations, including those of the Dakota, at the start of the War Between the States; after that everything changed. Through a number of new treaties in the mid to late 1860s some reservations were eliminated or reduced in size, some expanded, and new ones added to pressure the Ojibwe to move further and further from the growing white population.

While the Lake Superior, Pillager and Winnibigoshish bands' reservations remained largely unchanged from those provided in the 1854 and 1855 treaties, it took years before the final set of Mississippi Band reservations was settled. In treaties in 1863, 1865, and 1867, the Sandy Lake, Mille Lacs, Gull, Rice, Rabbit, and Pokegama Lake reservations were extinguished in exchange for a new reservation for the Mississippi Band adjacent to those of the Leech, Cass Winnibigoshish lakes set of reservations of the Pillager and Winnibigoshish bands (*Figure 28*), and the large White Earth reservation.

But still many members of the Mississippi Band refused to move, and, even without a reservation stayed where they were. In an attempt to encourage more of the

THE HEADWATERS WAR:
Conflict for the Mississippi Headwaters

Sandy Lake Band to move, an executive order in 1873 added the small White Oak Point reservation at the southeast corner of the existing Leech, Cass, and Winnibigoshish lakes complex, see Figure 29. The Indian Reorganization Act of 1934 combined all those reservations into one, the Greater Leech Lake reservation, which continues to this day. To appease some Mississippi Band members who still refused to leave, eventually an additional reservation was established at Mille Lacs Lake.

A comparison of Figure 27, reservations in Minnesota as they existed in 1858, prior to the War Between the States, and Figure 30, the reservations as they exist today, shows the affect of the changes after the war's conclusion. The Ojibwe reservations are primarily isolated in the north and west, and for the Dakota only the four small reservations formed upon their return from their banishment remain.

Also notice, in the middle of Figure 27, the large area marked as 'unceded' west of and across the Mississippi from the Mille Lacs Lake reservation. That is the land allocated to the Menominee and the Winnebago by the Treaty of 1848, intended to act as a buffer between the Ojibwe and the Dakota. However, some Winnebago and Menominee joined the Dakota uprising of 1862, and as a result both tribes were also banned from Minnesota and their land confiscated. Perhaps the number joining was small, but still, that land in the middle of the state was just too desirable for farming to allow it to remain in tribal hands.

Red Lake is a special case. Since the land had never been ceded to the United States it operates under its own set of rules. The land is owned by the tribe, which has the right to restrict visitors and residents. While originally only tribal and federal laws and courts applied on reservation land, in recent years the state was awarded jurisdiction in some criminal cases.

Today the Ojibwe population in the state is

THE HEADWATERS WAR:
Conflict for the Mississippi Headwaters

estimated at over 55,000; perhaps higher than at any time in history. Of those about 40% live on their approximately 4,000 square miles of reservation, about 40% in the cities of Minneapolis and Saint Paul, with the balance scattered in other towns and cities across the state. The numbers are fluid, with movement on and off the reservations common. As with the Dakota, some of these bands, especially that at Mille Lacs Lake, have grown prosperous due to the casino monopoly.

The above forms the backbone of the Native American presence in Minnesota. But it is impossible to estimate how many others identify as Ojibwe or Dakota but lack the 'blood quantum' or other tribal enrollment requirements, or the number with Native American heritage who have fully assimilated into American life.

Who qualifies as Ojibwe in Minnesota, and therefore can gain tribal membership, is an issue that has caused dissention within the various bands to this day. Not only is listing on the tribal roles necessary to gain federal benefits, in these days of Indian casinos it can also determine how casino profits are divided.

Before 1961 each band decided who was a member, one-eighth, or even one-sixteenth of Ojibwe blood was sometimes enough, and sometimes Ojibwe blood credited to tribes from other states or Canada was counted. Such small percentages were often, however, not recognized by the federal government. The Indian Reorganization Act in 1934 used the following guidelines for voting on whether or not a tribe agreed to the conditions of that Act.

> a - be a member of a federally recognized tribe
> b - be a descendant of such a member
> c - have one-half Indian blood

Following enactment of the Indian Reorganization Act, the Minnesota Chippewa Tribe was formed to represent all Ojibwe in the state except those

339

THE HEADWATERS WAR:
Conflict for the Mississippi Headwaters

at Red Lake, and since 1961 its constitution has required that, to be recognized for Ojibwe tribal membership, an applicant must have at least one-quarter 'Minnesota' Ojibwe blood; but those on the roles at the time with less were 'grandfathered' in.

This one-quarter 'Minnesota' blood requirement applies even to the children of currently enrolled members before their names can be added to the tribal roles, which clearly causes a serious issue; children of a parent recognized as a tribal member sometimes cannot qualify for tribal membership even if they have lived all their life on the reservation. This requirement is opposed by many, and is expected to be relaxed; either by counting 'non-Minnesota' Ojibwe blood, or reducing the percentage.

With restriction of the Ojibwe to reservations by the treaties of 1854 through 1867 the die was cast. The Treaty of 1867 marked the end of the pretence of treaties with the Ojibwe of Minnesota as if they were a sovereign nation, to be replaced by Acts of Congress. In fact, the government didn't feel fully bound by those treaties as they would a treaty with a government outside United States borders, and in some cases Congress failed to even bother to ratify them, making them legally unenforceable.

Why this cavalier attitude toward treaties with the tribes; especially the later treaties? In 1832 the Supreme Court refused to hear the case of *Cherokee Nation vs Georgia*, Justice Marshall arguing that, since the tribes were within the national boundaries of the United States, their treaties were not equivalent to those between two independent countries, and the tribes were classed as 'domestic dependents'. He argued the government relationship under the treaties was more like the relationship of a trustee to its ward. The implication of that decision was that, as the trustee, the government had the power, and also the obligation, to do what it thought best for its wards; and the ward's agreement was

THE HEADWATERS WAR:
Conflict for the Mississippi Headwaters

not required.

Shortly thereafter, in *Worchester v. Georgia*, the Court found that the individual states lacked jurisdiction over the reservations within their borders, and found treaties necessary, up to a point. It found that a tribe retained all the attributes of sovereignty that they had not voluntarily surrendered to the federal government. This confused the issue, but didn't stop using Acts of Congress or Executive Orders to establish new rules or conditions that didn't directly contradict treaty terms; as long as it could be argued it was 'good for the tribe'.

Even after *Cherokee Nation vs Georgia* opened the door for later Acts of Congress, the federal government, warned by *Worchester v. Georgia,* continued to follow the path the British had pursued before them; treaties with the tribes 'almost' as if they were sovereign nations. While the more sophisticated tribes like the Cherokee probably understood the affect of the interpretation of treaties contained in *Cherokee Nation vs Georgia*, it is unlikely the tribes of the frontier did; and they continued to sign treaties with the government as if they were between nations.

That doesn't mean Acts of Congress affecting the tribes weren't used. They were, but whenever a land cession and restriction to a reservation was involved a treaty was used instead. Only when the tribes had ceded their lands in exchange for reservations, and the location and borders of those reservations were deemed acceptable, did the government shift to Acts of Congress having a direct affect on the reservations themselves.

When the tribes agreed to the restriction of reservations it is doubtful they understood the role the reservation Indian Agent would assume. Once on the reservations they became dependent on the Indian Agent for distribution of the food and housing guaranteed by the treaty, and the agent also had control of the tribal police. In affect, the agents had virtually unlimited power over the reservations and their residents, and

341

THE HEADWATERS WAR:
Conflict for the Mississippi Headwaters

many used that power to dictate rules of conduct, banning activities of which they personally disapproved; such as the religious practices of the tribe.

While the earlier Supreme Court cases of the 1830s had for years guided the federal government in its dealings with the tribes, beginning in the late 1880s the Supreme Court issued a series of new decisions in cases challenging the power of the federal government. This 'spate' of new cases followed approval by Congress of the Dawes Allotment Act of 1887 (*discussed in detail later*), an Act that that could lead to dismantlement of the reservation system. These decisions more fully defined the 'degree' of sovereignty the tribes retained, and the role of the federal government.

One of the most important of the new decisions affecting the reservations was *United States vs Kagama* in 1902, a case involving a murder on a reservation, where the Court ruled the federal government had 'concurrent' jurisdiction over the reservations along with the tribal government, and hence could enforce laws against crimes even though committed on the reservation. Interestingly, while joint jurisdiction was recognized in the *Kagama* case, many decades later the Supreme Court ruled the tribal government lacked the jurisdiction to try the culprit if a non-Indian. While jurisdiction might be joint, it wasn't necessarily equal. *Kagama* also endorsed the view that the tribes were dependents of the federal government, and the federal government's ability to act for the benefit of the tribe.

A year later, in *Lone Wolf vs Hitchcock,* the Court ruled that the tribes 'were not' independent nations, but were dependents of the federal government in a state of 'pupilage', and that Congress had the unilateral power to abrogate Indian treaties.

In effect, the above two cases confirmed the 1832 case of *Cherokee Nation vs Georgia,* where the Court refused to hear the case, concluding the relationship between the government and the tribes was

THE HEADWATERS WAR:
Conflict for the Mississippi Headwaters

like that of a trustee to its ward. Both cases supported the right of Congress to take actions affecting the tribes if it deemed they were in their best interest.

The above decisions effectively gave the Court's blessing to the Dawes Allotment Act of 1887, which served to dismantle much of the reservation system nationwide by allotting parcels of land on the reservation to individual tribal members, and authorizing sale of the surplus to outsiders.

While there were earlier Acts of Congress affecting the tribes of Minnesota, such as the Civilization Act of 1819, they didn't involve land cessions and restriction to reservations, and for the Ojibwe the final border adjustments for their reservations had been through the Treaty of 1867. Thereafter the later Acts of Congress, particularly the Dawes Allotment Act, served to place constraints on or 'hollow out' those reservations.

The attitude of the government toward Native Americans was no secret, and was clear to those who chose to listen. While the Declaration of Independence declared all men were 'created equal', in listing the complaints against the British King it said:

> *"He has incited domestic insurrections amongst us, and has endeavored to bring on the inhabitants of our frontier, the merciless Indian Savages whose known rules of warfare, is an undistinguished destruction of all ages, sexes, and conditions"*

The above should not come as a surprise. When the Declaration of Independence was signed the French-Indian wars and Pontiac's rebellion were little over a decade in the past, and many of the signers were directly involved in those wars. Further, the above text was not an afterthought slipped in to satisfy some recalcitrant colony, but was also in the initial text submitted by

THE HEADWATERS WAR:
Conflict for the Mississippi Headwaters

Thomas Jefferson who, while known for his liberal views, when Governor of Virginia advocated for extermination of the tribes on its western border; a position he voiced as late as 1801, the year he was elected president. Even with the 1787 Constitution, when residents of a state were counted for purposes of assigning the number of Representatives to Congress, slaves were counted as three-fifths of a person, while Indians weren't counted at all.

And as to George Washington? In 1779, when commander of the revolutionary armies, he dispatched General Sullivan against Iroquois allies of the British with the following orders:

> *"The immediate objects are the total destruction and devastation of their settlements and the capture of as many prisoners of every age and sex as possible . . "*

In the campaign that followed dozens of Iroquois villages were burned and crops destroyed, gaining George Washington the title 'town destroyer' among the Seneca. The attitude of Thomas Jefferson and George Washington to the Indians of the frontier was not unique; to a large extent that reflected the viewpoint of the time.

When the British were in control they had attempted to limit colonial expansion; the Proclamation Line of 1763 defining everything west of the Allegany Mountains as 'tribal lands'; however, the 'land hungry' colonists largely ignored that line, and continued to move over the Allegany Mountains into the area bounded by the Mississippi to the west and the Ohio River to the north. Unable or unwilling to expel these settlers, the Treaty of Fort Stanwix in 1768 redefined tribal lands as that north of the Ohio and west of the Mississippi.

With the 1783 Treaty of Paris officially ending

THE HEADWATERS WAR:
Conflict for the Mississippi Headwaters

the Revolutionary War, the new American government had to face reality; they were no longer a group of 'semi-independent' colonies constrained by the Allegany Mountains, but now had under their jurisdiction the vast area south of the Ohio River between those mountains and the Mississippi; an area filled with powerful native tribes. Further, the weak new United States government was also unable to keep settlers from moving west, or States or other groups from negotiating private treaties, leading to turmoil on the frontier. The colonies were still not completely united, with various areas threatening to secede whenever dissatisfied for some reason. The fledgling national government had attempted to limit this practice with the 1787 Northwest Ordinance, which stated Indian lands could only be taken by use of a treaty agreed to by both parties. However, their control over land-hungry colonists and speculators was limited. Even as late as the 1830s the federal government was unable to stop the state of Georgia from seizing Cherokee land, and only after the War Between the States did a truly strong central government emerge.

The infant government also had been awarded the Northwest Territory, north of the Ohio River, where an even more difficult situation existed; a country considered a tribal sanctuary that the tribes refused to relinquish, leading to a number of confrontations. Adding to the problem was the British refusal to recognize control of the Northwest Territory by the new United States government, even though that area had been awarded to the Colonies by the treaty ending the Revolutionary War. The tribes of the Northwest Territory weren't subdued until their crushing defeat of the allied tribes at the Battle of Fallen Timbers in 1793; but still British interference continued.

In the late 1700s and through the early 1800s Britain often aided the tribes against the fledging United States, and many tribes remained loyal to their former 'white father'. This came to a head when, during the war

345

THE HEADWATERS WAR:
Conflict for the Mississippi Headwaters

of 1812, the British allied themselves with Tecumseh's grand alliance and ravaged the frontier, and only after settlement of that conflict did they withdraw from the Northwest Territory. With defeat of that alliance in 1813 the last hope of the tribes of the Northwest Territory for independence was dead. While many Ojibwe joined the British side, those of Minnesota largely stayed neutral; partly due to the influence of the Ojibwe chief from Leech Lake, Flat Mouth. The area west of Lake Michigan, including Minnesota, remained largely untouched by events in the east.

After settlement of the war of 1812 it was apparent something had to be done about the tribes on the frontier; in the mind of the western world Native Americans were still savages that must be driven out or a way found to assimilate them into western society. Many of the tribes welcomed the idea of assimilation, but in practice when tried it led to many abuses.

One of the first major Acts of Congress to address the issue of assimilation of the tribes was the Civilization Fund Act of 1819; an Act that didn't involve land cessions or boundary changes, but aimed to teach European ways. Four decades had passed since the Declaration of Independence, and the country had grown from thirteen small colonies confined by the Allegany Mountains, and with the additions of the area between the Allegany Mountains and the Mississippi, and the subsequent Louisiana Purchase, had a vastly larger area to govern. Further, just the previous year the United States had arranged for joint occupation of the Oregon Territory with the British. The original small collection of colonies had grown to a nation that vastly exceeded all of Europe in size, and it was filled will many tribes, often at war with each other. While elimination of the tribes was neither possible nor any longer acceptable, something must be done.

The Civilization Fund Act of 1819 took the path of reeducation leading to final assimilation. The Act

THE HEADWATERS WAR:
Conflict for the Mississippi Headwaters

established a fund, to be administered by the Department of Indian Affairs (*created in 1824*), to encourage creation by benevolent societies, such as Indian Christian Missions, of boarding schools for Indian children. At these boarding schools only English was allowed to be spoken and speaking the native language was forbidden, the children were given Christian names, their typically long hair was cut short and they were dressed in clothing typical of white society at the time, and taught the Christian faith. Supposedly voluntary, often coercion by the Indian Agents was involved.

While the Civilization Act of 1819 was worded in terms of providing a benefit to the tribes, the intent was clear. The subsequent treaties establishing reservations and recognition of sovereignty of the tribes were a convenience only; later they would be changed when the need arose. The real goal had become elimination of the tribes by assimilation.

The Civilization Act of 1819 had some success, but it still didn't address the continued existence of the reservations. The Dawes Allotment Act of 1887, which applied to all reservations nationwide unless some prior agreement had been reached, was a major step to force assimilation. Not only was the Dawes Act an attempt to 'force' Native Americans to become farmers by giving each, including minor children, allotments of reservation land, it was a direct challenge to treaty rights.

Under the Dawes Act the reservations would be broken up into individual land allotments, with the head of a family usually allotted 160 acres, while single persons or orphan children received less. These allotments supposedly applied only to land suitable for agriculture, with which land was suitable subject to determination by the Indian Agent. If no land was selected by someone, the Indian Agent made the selection in that persons name.

In its defense, the government did attempt to protect the allotments from unscrupulous outsiders, but

THE HEADWATERS WAR:
Conflict for the Mississippi Headwaters

with limited success. After being allotted to an individual the land was to be held in trust by the government for 25 years for the sole use of the individual or his/her heirs, and during that time could not be sold, liens placed against it, or contracts made affecting the land; after which time full title would be conveyed. Those Native Americans living off the reservation on public land had the right to claim that land as an allotment under the same conditions as those on a reservation. After all allotments were made up to 160 acres of any remaining agricultural land could be sold to 'bona fide' white settlers.

But the Dawes Act went much further. It created tribal membership roles and made citizens those who accepted allotments. Additionally, it provided citizenship to all other Native Americans, as long as they had been born within the confines of the United States and had adapted to what was considered a 'civilized life'. How their life style was determined to be 'civilized' was not defined.

Two years later the Nelson Act of 1889, which applied only to the Minnesota Ojibwe reservations, was a pure land-grab by the timber industry of the rich white pine forests remaining at the headwaters lakes and some of the Lake Superior band reservations. This further 'hollowed out' the reservations by allowing sale to timber interests of non-agricultural land, and restricting future land allotments to Indians to White Earth; logical, since White Earth lacked the stands of white pine coveted by the timber industry.

The land of the Red Lake Ojibwe wasn't covered by either of the above Acts, since it wasn't legally a reservation. In both cases all proceeds of land sold was to be held in trust for the tribes.

After the Dawes and Nelson Acts, what really did those reservations become? While thousands of acres are so designated, what does that really mean? 'Reservation' suggests the land is 'reserved' for Native

THE HEADWATERS WAR:
Conflict for the Mississippi Headwaters

American use, either owned by the tribe or its members, but rarely is that the case. In fact, today Native Americans are in the minority at both the White Earth and Greater Leech Lake reservations, while the tribes or tribal members own less than 10% of the land at the Greater Leech Lake reservation, with not much greater for White Earth. A drive through either reservation shows towns, farms, and businesses much like any other area of Minnesota.

Again, the one exception to the fragmentation of the reservations is Red Lake, which never passed through the hands of the United States. It may even be improper to call it a reservation at all. There land within its boundaries is, with few exceptions, owned by the tribe in common, and the band has authority to determine who may enter or live within its boundaries. Further, for years Red Lake was subject only to federal jurisdiction; although in the 1900s some authority was extended to the state.

Even though the Civilization Act of 1819 and the Dawes Allotment Act of 1887 served to move many Native Americans into the mainstream of American life, many were still considered foreigners in their own land, with the burden to establish they had been born in the United States and lived a 'civilized' life, or that they had accepted a land allotment; something local boards could use to limit voting, like the 'poll tax' limited voting of African Americans in the past. Establishing place of birth for the Ojibwe was a particular problem, since many Ojibwe lived in Canada, and at the time there was free movement across the border.

But times were changing. By the early to mid 20th century Indian boarding schools and the practice of encouraging adoption of Indian children by white families had fallen out of favor, and with the Indian Citizenship Act of 1924 (*Snyder Act*) Native Americans began to be recognized as equal members of American society, without the necessity to establish to some local

THE HEADWATERS WAR:
Conflict for the Mississippi Headwaters

election board that they had been born in the United States and were 'civilized', or that they had accepted a land allotment, before they could vote. Even then it was not really full equality; some restrictions still applied, such as the ban against sale of liquor to Native Americans, which wasn't lifted until 1953.

Given the vote and the protections of the constitution available to others, the wishes of the Native American population could no longer be ignored, but must at least be considered. Rather than the boarding schools, 'mainstreaming' of Indian children became the rule. Still, the Native American culture was too firmly based to extinguish completely, and something had to be done about the existing reservations, where, while many of the residents were American citizens, they were still subject to the arbitrary authority of the government appointed Indian Agents.

Eventually the government realized that, while reeducation and the Dawes Act attempt to turn tribal members into farmers was providing results, there was a hard core within the reservations who continued to resist. This issue was finally addressed by the Indian Reorganization Act of 1934 (*Howard-Wheeler Act*), which, in addition to consolidating many of the scattered or independent reservations, encouraged reservation self government and allowed for return to those new reservation governments any land remaining in government hands after the earlier allotment Acts. The primary affect in Minnesota of the consolidation of reservations authorized by the Reorganization Act was consolidation of the multiple reservations at the headwaters into the single Greater Leech Lake reservation, and decertification of the Sandy Lake band and placing it under the administrative control of the Mille Lacs band.

To support the goal of reservation self government, the Reorganization Act established an overall body to represent the Minnesota Ojibwe (*except*

THE HEADWATERS WAR:
Conflict for the Mississippi Headwaters

those at Red Lake), the Minnesota Chippewa Tribe, with elected members and a constitution, and allowed each reservation to do the same. Rather than being subject to the arbitrary whims of an Indian Agent, each reservation could now establish their own local government, subject only to rules established by the Minnesota Chippewa Tribe and federal laws.

Following the end of World War II pressure began to build for ending much of the 'separation' implied by the fact Native Americans, under the law, were not the same as white citizens. In 1953 Congress passed Public Law 280, which applied in six states, including Minnesota (*Red Lake exempt*), and was optional in others. Under Public Law 280 federal criminal and civil jurisdiction over crimes and civil offences committed on reservations passed to the state, and Indians, on or off the reservations, became subject to the state courts. Tribal jurisdiction over violation of their own set of regulations still applied.

Public Law 280 also allowed a tribe to apply for a return of federal jurisdiction, to be concurrent with the state. In Minnesota, under that clause, the federal government in 2013 reassumed concurrent jurisdiction over major crimes committed on the White Earth reservation, and in 2017 on the Mille Lacs reservation.

But Public Law 280 is also notable for what it 'did not' do; it didn't include making state or county regulations or property taxes apply to Indian-owned reservation land. It also excluded the right of a state to control, by licensing or otherwise, trapping, hunting, or fishing by tribal members on reservation land or on areas of the state where it had been reserved by treaty. Often treaties had reserved this right over broad areas of ceded territory that were now under state or white ownership.

While Public Law 280 removed much of the federal government's direct responsibility for maintaining order on reservations, which it shared with the tribal governments, it didn't relieve it of its trust

THE HEADWATERS WAR:
Conflict for the Mississippi Headwaters

obligations. It remained responsible for providing such resources as housing and medical services, and everything else required under the treaties.

The result of the Reorganization Act and Public Law 280 was that reservations, that once been considered in the minds of many separate nations negotiating with the federal government, now had to be treated like any other community in the state with respect to criminal acts or civil actions. This included sale of liquor; which, if allowed in other communities, must also be allowed on reservations unless banned by the tribal government under their regulations. This effectively ended the ban on sale of liquor to Native Americans off the reservations, and made it optional to the tribal government for sales on the reservation.

In the decades that followed other significant legislation was passed further expanding Native American rights, including the Indian Child Welfare Act, which gave preference in adoptions of Native American children to tribal members, and the American Indian Religious Freedom Act, which guaranteed the right to practice traditional religions. These were following with Acts protecting Indian burial grounds and artifacts; requiring return of many artifacts held by museums or private individuals.

While under the Indian Reorganization Act and Public Act 280 the reservations became separate political entities within a state, that they consisted largely of 'left-over' land after the best land had been given to settlers or other interests limited progress. As farm land it was mostly marginal, the best timber had been logged off, and the reservations lacked assets to build an economy. Additionally they were usually far from large population centers, making it difficult to attract industry. The Indian Gaming Regulation Act of 1988 provided an opening that could at least help solve some of the problems.

The Indian Gaming Regulation Act required that if a state allowed gambling, it must negotiate compacts

THE HEADWATERS WAR:
Conflict for the Mississippi Headwaters

with the tribes to allow similar types of gambling on reservations. Minnesota allowed 'some' of what was considered Class III gambling normally allowed for casinos, and therefore was 'required' to negotiate compacts with the tribes; if they failed to do so the Department of the Interior would do it for them. By 1989 the first compact was approved, soon to be followed by ten others.

Today Indian operated casinos provide at least some support for the reservations, even in sparsely populated parts of the state, and near the larger population centers large Indian casinos thrive. However, since these casinos are exempt from property tax, as is all reservation land, typically some agreement is reached with local authorities to cover the added cost of police and other services provided. However, under the Act each band has much latitude on its use of casino profits; while typically it goes to the tribal government for infrastructure improvements, sometimes large amounts are allocated to individual tribe members.

While there were many treaties, Acts of Congress, and executive orders affecting the Minnesota Ojibwe, those listed below, in addition to the 1854 treaty with the Lake Superior band, had the largest impact on molding the Ojibwe reservation system we see today.

A. Civilization Act of 1819 – established a fund to educate Native American children with the goal of assimilation

B. Treaty of 1855 – establishment of reservations for Mississippi, Pillager, and Winnibigoshish bands of Ojibwe

C. Treaty of 1865 – establishment of a large reservation for the Mississippi band near the Pillager and Winnibigoshish bands' reservations at Leech-Cass-Winnibigoshish

THE HEADWATERS WAR:
Conflict for the Mississippi Headwaters

lakes, in return for vacating the reservations created by the Treaty of 1855.

D. Treaty of 1867 – the Mississippi band reservation near the Pillager and Winnibigoshish band reservations had its boundaries changed, and the large White Earth reservation was added

E. Act of Congress of 1887 (Dawes Allotment Act) –allotted a specific piece of land to each tribe member, and opened the balance of land suitable for agriculture for sale to white settlers. Section 6 of the Act also granted American citizenship to those Native Americans who accepted an allotment, or who had been born in the United States, with the proviso that they had adopted the ways of 'civilized' life.

F. Act of Congress of 1889 (Nelson Act) – allowed timber land as well as agricultural land to be sold to outsiders

G. Indian Citizenship Act of 1924 – made all Native Americans citizens with voting rights

H. Indian Reorganization Act of 1934 (Wheeler-Howard Act) – consolidated reservations, stopped the program of 'allotment' and sale of excess land to non-Indians, and encouraged reservation self-government

I. Public Law 280, 1953 –transferred federal jurisdiction for civil and criminal offenses committed on a reservation to the state, and made Indians, both on and off the reservation, subject to state courtsl

THE HEADWATERS WAR:
Conflict for the Mississippi Headwaters

Because of their significance, some of the above treaties or Acts are attached as an appendix. These are, B) Treaty of 1855. D) Treaty of 1867, E) the Dawes Allotment Act of 1887, G) the Indian Citizenship Act of 1924, and H) the Indian Reorganization Act of 1934.

Item I), above, Public Law 280, is divided into a number of statutes, with 18 U.S.C 1162 and 28 U.S.C. 1360 applying to the six states, including Minnesota, where criminal and civil authority is transferred to the state. Since those statute sections define the current relationship of the state and federal governments with the Minnesota bands and reservations, copies are also included in the Appendix.

Today, 150 years after the last treaty between the government and the Minnesota Ojibwe was signed, the affect of those early treaties remains, and is often the subject of disputes between the tribes and state and local government. For example, in many treaties the Ojibwe retained hunting and fishing rights on the ceded lands, bringing them in conflict with both landowners and state game and fish laws and regulations when they attempted to exercise those rights. The best known example is the shared use of Lake Mille Lacs between the Ojibwe and the state, finally worked out after a long legal battle. As a result the state and the Ojibwe now share fishing rights on Lake Mille Lacs, with each assigned a yearly quota.

And as to the proud Ojibwe who once dominated the region? In the words of George Copway, an Ojibwe turned Christian missionary, who lived from 1818 to 1869 and was a contemporary of many of the great Ojibwe chiefs, who in his 1847 autobiography (4) voiced a lament about his changing world:

> *"The groves, where once my fathers roam'd -*
> *The rivers where the beaver dwelt -*
> *The lakes, where angry waters foam'd -*
> *Their charms, with my fathers, have fled.*

THE HEADWATERS WAR:
Conflict for the Mississippi Headwaters

O! tell me, ye "pale faces," tell,
Where have my proud ancestors gone?
Where smoke curled up from every dale,
To what land have their free spirits flown"
Whose wigwam stood where cities rise;
On whose war-paths the steam-horse flies;
And ships, like mon-e-doos in disguise,
Approach the shore in endless files. "

The above was written by Copway as a young man following his attendance at a missionary school and a trip to the east, where he first saw the great cities with their harbors teaming with ships. If he lived today we could give him an answer to his second stanza lament, *"Where have my proud ancestors gone?"* While some still regard the reservations as their home, many have integrated into American society; in effect, they are all around us.

While it is easy to be nostalgic about days gone by, nostalgia is a bad historian. Life in the 'good old days' was often short and brutal, with frequent tribal warfare resulting in high mortality for young men. In the winter of 1804-1805 Lieutenant Zebulon Pike conducted a census of Ojibwe bands in Northern Minnesota, which showed roughly two women for every man.

Chapter 7 contains a 'battle song' which White Fisher, an Ojibwe chief from La Pointe, made in honor of a particularly bloody battle with the Dakota and Fox in the late 1700s, which is titled *'Waub-o-jeeg's* Battle Song'. Following is the final stanza:

Five winters in hunting we'll spend, we'll spend,
Five winters in hunting we'll spend,
Till our youth, grown to men, we'll to the war
lead again,
And our days like our fathers' will end, will end,
And our days like our fathers' will end.

THE HEADWATERS WAR:
Conflict for the Mississippi Headwaters

Only in five years, when the next generation reached fighting age, would they have enough warriors to again take the warpath. Perhaps that explains the following lament of another Ojibwe, a young warrior on his departure on a campaign at about the time Copway was expressing himself. If a young widow lacked parents to return to, or young men were in short supply, she was often fated for a dim future as second or third wife of some older man.

"Do not weep, do not weep for me, *
Loved women, should I die;
For yourselves alone should you weep!
Poor are you all, and to be pitied:
Ye women, ye are to be pitied!

I seek, I seek our fallen relations;
I go to revenge, revenge the slain,
Our relations fallen and slain,
and our foes, our foes shall lie
Like them, like them shall they lie;
I go to lay them low, lay them low!"

* Petrone, Penny, *First People, First Voice, University of Toronto* Press, 1984, P.2, citing: 'Address of Ojibwe war party on their departure', Anna Jamison, *Winter Studies and Summer Rambles in Canada* (1838; Toronto, Coles Canadiana 1970) III, 223

THE HEADWATERS WAR:
Conflict for the Mississippi Headwaters

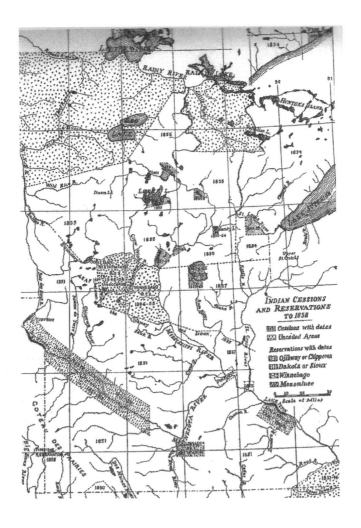

Figure 27: Indian Cessions and Reservations to 1858

THE HEADWATERS WAR:
Conflict for the Mississippi Headwaters

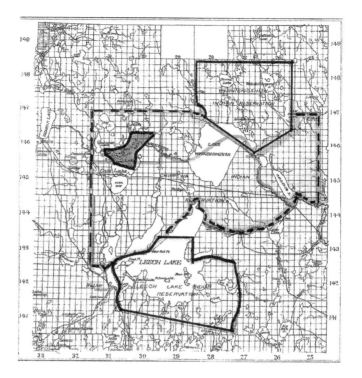

Figure 28: Headwaters Lakes reservations after Treaty of 1867*

> * *The areas bounded by solid lines are reservations established by the treaty of 1855 for the Pillager and Winnibigoshish bands. The dotted lines show additions and adjustments, up to and through the Treaty of 1867, to accommodate Mississippi band members displaced by closure of their reservations.*

THE HEADWATERS WAR:
Conflict for the Mississippi Headwaters

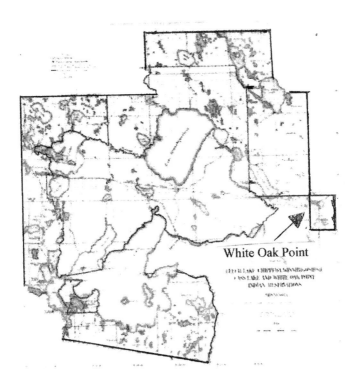

Figure 29: Headwaters Lakes reservations after 1873 addition of White Oak Point*

* The reservations at the headwater lakes as they existed following Executive Order dated October 29, 1873, which added White Oak Point. These are also the boundaries of the Greater Leech Lake Reservation of today

THE HEADWATERS WAR:
Conflict for the Mississippi Headwaters

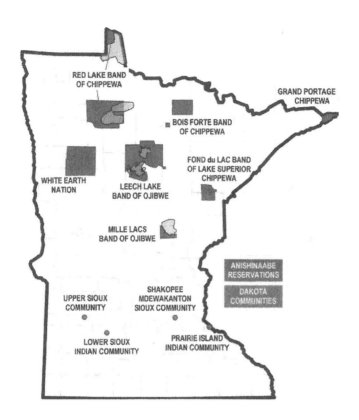

Figure 30: Reservations in Minnesota 2013

THE HEADWATERS WAR:
Conflict for the Mississippi Headwaters

ILLUSTRATION ATTRIBUTIONS

Figure 1: Drainage Basins in Minnesota
Minnesota DNR
Figure 2: Continental Divides
Courtesy of Pfly: http://commons.wikimedia.org/
File: North America-WaterDivides.png
License: https:// creativecommons.org/licenses/by-sa/3.0/deed.en
Figure 3: Nelson River Watershed
Courtesy of Knusser:http://commons.wikimedia.org/
File:Nelsonrivermap.png - License:, https://creativecommons.org/licenses/by-sa/3.0/deed.en
Figure 4: Minnesota Lakes and Rivers
National Atlas, , U.S. Department of the Interior
Figure 5: Mississippi Headwaters
National Atlas, , U.S. Department of the Interior
Figure 6: Big Sandy Lake
by author
Figure 7: Lakes Winnibigoshish & Cut Foot Sioux
Courtesy of Minnesota Department of Natural Resources
Figure 8: Kathio Area of Mille Lac Lake
Courtesy of Firry Floyd: http://commons.wikimedia.org/
File: Lake Mille Area Savanna Soils Wiki Version.pdf
License: https://creativecommons.org/licenses/by-sa/3.0/deed.en
Figure 9: Route of Dakota Raid of 1768
National Atlas, , U.S. Department of the Interior
Figure 10: Minnesota River
Courtesy of Knusser:http://commons.wikimedia.org/
File: Minnesotarivermap.png
License: https://creativecommons.org/licenses/by-sa/3.0/deed.en)
Figure 11: St. Croix Watershed
Courtesy of Knusser:http://commons.wikimedia.org/
File: Stcroixmnwirivermap.png: License:, https://creativecommons.org/licenses/by-sa/2.5/deed.en
Figure 12: West of the Mississippi ....
National Atlas, , U.S. Department of the Interior
Figure13: Treaty of Prairie du Chien Treaty Line
History of Minnesota, by William Watts Folwell, Vol. I, 1st Ed. 1921
Figure 14: Pokegama Lake
Google Earth

362

THE HEADWATERS WAR:
Conflict for the Mississippi Headwaters

Figure 15: Minnesota Territory 1849
Courtesy of CreativeCommons; www.creativecommons.org
File:http://commons.wikimedia.org/wiki/File/Minnesota
territory.PNG : License:, https://
creativecommons.org/licenses/by-sa/2.5/deed.en
Figure 16: Sandy Lake Tragedy Sign
Photograph by author
Figure 17: Chief Hole-in-the-Day the younger
Public Domain
Figure 18: Chief Little Crow IV
Public Domain
Figure 19: Chief Shakopee III
Public Domain
Figure 20: Dakota Chiefs & Villages 1862
A History of Minnesota, Volume II, William Watts
Folwell, published 1924, revised copyright 1961
Figure 21: Sibley Campaigns of 1862
A History of The Dakota or Sioux Indians,
Doane Robinson, 1ˢᵗ published 1905
Figure 22: Fort Ridgely (1862)
Public Domain
Figure 23: Dakota Attack on New Ulm (1862)
Public Domain
Figure 24: The Hanging at Mankato (December, 1862)
Public Domain
Figure 25: Indian Cessions/Reservations to 1858
History of Minnesota, by William Watts Folwell, Vol. I, 1st
Ed. 1921
Figure 26: Headwaters Lakes reservations after Treaty of 1867
1901, Department of Interior
Figure 27: Headwaters Lakes reservations after 1873 addition
of White Oak Point
1916, Department of Interior
Figure 28: Minnesota Indian Reservations 2013
Courtesy of Minnesota Department of Health
Figure 29: Wooden Sandy River Dam, 1895
Courtesy of the Library of Congress
Figure 30: Big Sandy Lake Then & Now
'Cultural Resources Reconnaissance and Survey of Shoreline
of Big Sandy Reservoi'r, 1982, for Army Corp of Engineers,
St. Paul District, contract # DACW37-81-M-2669, G. Gibbon,
Principal Investigator
Documents in Appendix: *U.S. Government, public domain*

THE HEADWATERS WAR:
Conflict for the Mississippi Headwaters

BIBLIOGRAPHY

1 Charles River Editors, *Native American Tribes: The History and Culture of the Chippewa*,

2. Clemmons, Linda M., *"We Will Talk of Nothing Else"*: *Interpretations of the Treaty of 1837*, Great Plains Quarterly Great Plains Studies, University of Nebraska

3. Coffin, Cindy, *Chief Shakopee I,* www.Findagrave.com

4. Copway, George, *"The Life, History, and Travels of Kah-ge-ga-gah-bowh: A Young Indian Chief of the Ojibwe Nation"*, Philadelphia", James Harmstead, No. 40 N. Fourth St, 1847 (reprint, Leopold Classic Library)

5. Diedrich, Mark, *The Chiefs Hole-in-the-Day of the Mississippi Ojibwa,* Coyote Books, 1986

6. Dwyer, Helen, *Ojibwe History and Culture*, Gareth Stevens Publishing, 2005

7. Folwell, William Watts, *A History of Minnesota*, Vol. I, MN Historical Society, 1956 (first published 1921)

8. Folwell, William Watts, *A History of Minnesota*, Vol. II, MN Historical Society, 1961 (first published 1924)

9. Folwell, William Watts, Minnesota, *The North Star State*, Houghton Mifflin Company, The Riverside Press Cambridge, 1908

10. Gibbon, Guy E., *Battle Island*, Minnesota Archaeologist, Vol. 46, No. 1 (1987) – also, *Report AD Ai39725*, for U S. Army Corps of Engineers, 1982

11. Hassrick, Royal B., *The Sioux*, University of Oklahoma Press, 1964

12. Hill, Ruth Beebe, *Hanta Yo*, Warner Books, 1979

13. Laughlin, Marie L., *Myths and Legends of the Sioux*, ----

14. Lund, Dr. Duane, *The Lives and Times of Three Powerful Ojibwe Chiefs: Curly Head, Hole-in-the-Day the elder, and Hole-in-the-Day the younger*,

15. Lund, Dr. Duane, *Minnesota's Chief Flat Mouth of Leech Lake*, National Graphic Communications, 1983

16. Lund, Dr. Duane, *The Indian Wars*, Lund S&R Publications, 2007

17. Mille Lac Lake Indian Museum, *Battle of Kathio*, History Quest, LLC, 2008

18. Minnesota Historical Society, *Ojibwe, Waasa-Inaabidaa, "We Look in All Directions"*, Minnesota Historical Society

THE HEADWATERS WAR:
Conflict for the Mississippi Headwaters

Press
19. Minnesota Historical Society. *Papers of Laurence Taliaferro*
20. Neill, Rev. Edward D, *History of the Ojibways and Their Connection With Fur Traders* (undated manuscript included as addendum of 1974 Ed. of Warren)
21. Nelson, Norvis M. *Historical Highlights of Big Sandy Lake and the Savanna Portage*, 1945
22. Petrone, Penny, *First People, First Voice, University of Toronto* Press, 1984.
23. Pike, Zebulon Mongomery, *An Account of Expeditions to the Sources of the Mississippi, and Through the Western Parts of Louisiana* , C & A Conrad & Co; Somervell & Conrad; Bonasal, Conrad, & Co; and Fielding Lucas, Jr. 1810
24. Radisson, Peter Esprit, *Voyages of Peter Esprit Radisson,* Prince Society, 1885.
25. Robinson, Doan, *A History of the Dakota or Sioux Indians,* Ross & Haines, Vol. I., 1974 (first published 1904)
26. Schoolcraft, Henry Rowe, *Narrative journal of travels through the northwestern regions of the United States . performed as a member of the expedition under Governor Cass in the year 1820* (Albany: E. & E. Hosford, 1821)
27. Schoolcraft, Henry Rowe, *Personal Memoirs of a Residence of Thirty Years with the American Indians on the American Frontier: A.D. 1812 to A.D. 1842*
28. Schoolcraft, Henry Rowe, *The American Indian, Their History, Condition, and Prospects, from Original Notes,* Rochester, Wanzer, Foot, and Co., 1851
29. Shell, James Peery, *In the Ojibway Country: a Story of Early Missions on the Minnesota Frontier,* _____
30. Sultzman, Lee, *Ojibwe History,* http://tolatsga.org/ojib/htmo
31. Syme, Ronald, *The Story of Pierre de la Verendrye: Fur Trader of the North,* William Morrow and Company, 1973
32. Treuer, Anton, *The Assassination of Hole-in-the-Day,* Minnesota Historical Society Press, 2011
33. Treuer, Anton, *Ojibwe in Minnesota*, Minnesota Historical Society Press, 2010
34. Treuer, Anton, *Warrior Nation*: *A History of the Red Lake Ojibwe*, Minnesota Historical Society Press, 2015.

THE HEADWATERS WAR:
Conflict for the Mississippi Headwaters

35. University of Minnesota jointly with the Minnesota Historical Society, 1973; *Land of the Ojibwe,*
36. Wedll, Joycelyn et al. *Against the Tide of American History. The Story of Mille Lacs Anishinabe*, Minnesota Chippewa Tribe (Cass Lake, MN. 1985)
37. Warren, William W., *History of the Ojibway Nation,* Ross & Haines, 1957, 1st Ed. (based on 1853 manuscript)

THE HEADWATERS WAR:
Conflict for the Mississippi Headwaters

APPENDIX

Treaty of 1855

INDIAN AFFAIRS: LAWS AND TREATIES

Vol. II, Treaties

Compiled and edited by Charles J. Kappler. Washington : Government Printing Office, 1904.

Home | Disclaimer & Usage | Table of Contents | Index

TREATY WITH THE CHIPPEWA, 1855.

Feb. 22, 1855. | 10 Stat., 1165. | Ratified Mar. 3, 1855. | Proclaimed Apr. 7, 1855.

Page Images: 685 | 686 | 687 | 688 | 689 | 690

Margin Notes
Cession to the United States.
Reservations for permanent homes.
For the Mississippi bands of Chippewa.
For the Pillager and Lake Winnibigoshish bands.
Reservations may be surveyed and allotted.
Payment to the Mississippi band for the above cessions.
Payment to the Pillager and Lake Winnibigoshish bands for said cessions.
Payment to the Mississippi bands under former treaties may be made in cash.
How the above annuities shall be paid.
Preemption rights in said cession.
Grants of land to mixed bloods.
Laws extended to said reservations.
Roads may be constructed.
Stipulations as to conduct of the Indians.

Page 685

Articles of agreement and convention made and concluded at the city of Washington, this twenty-second day of February, one thousand eight hundred and fifty-five, by

http://digital.library.okstate.edu/kappler/Vol2/treaties/chi0685.htm   9/17/2017

THE HEADWATERS WAR:
Conflict for the Mississippi Headwaters

Treaty of 1855

INDIAN AFFAIRS: LAWS AND TREATIES. Vol. 2, Treaties

Page 2 of 9

George W. Manypenny, commissioner, on the part of the United States, and the following-named chiefs and delegates, representing the Mississippi bands of Chippewa Indians, viz: Pug-o-na-ke-shick, or Hole-in-the-day; Que-we-sans-ish, or Bad Boy; Wand-e-kaw, or Little Hill; I-awe-showe-we-ke-shig, or Crossing Sky; Petud-dunce, or Rat's Liver; Mun-o-min-e-kay-shein, or Rice-Maker; Mah-yah-ge-way-we-durg, or the Chorister; Kay-gwa-daush, or the Attempter; Caw-caug-e-we-goon, or Crow Feather; and Show-baush-king, or He that passes under Everything, and the following-named chiefs and delegates representing the Pillager and Lake Winnibigoshish bands of Chippewa Indians, viz: Aish-ke-bug-e-koshe, or Flat Mouth; Be-sheck-kee, or Buffalo; Nay- bun-a-caush, or Young Man's Son; Maug-e-gaw-bow, or Stepping Ahead; Mi-gi-si, or Eagle, and Kaw-be-mub-bee, or North Star, they being thereto duly authorized by the said bands of Indians respectively.

ARTICLE 1.

The Mississippi, Pillager, and Lake Winnibigoshish bands of Chippewa Indians hereby cede, sell, and convey to the United States all their right, title, and interest in, and to, the lands now owned and claimed by them, in the Territory of Minnesota, and included within the following boundaries, viz: Beginning at a point where the east branch of Snake River crosses the southern boundary-line of the Chippewa country, east of the Mississippi River, as established by the treaty of July twenty-ninth, one thousand eight hundred and thirty-seven, running thence, up the said branch, to its source; thence, nearly north in a straight line, to the mouth of East Savannah River; thence, up the St. Louis River, to the mouth of East Swan River; thence, up said river, to its source; thence, in a straight line, to the most westwardly bend of Vermillion River; thence, northwestwardly, in a straight line, to the first and most considerable bend in the Big Fork River; thence, down said river, to its mouth; thence, down Rainy Lake River, to the mouth of Black River; thence, up that river, to its source; thence, in a straight line, to the northern extremity of Turtle Lake; thence, in a straight line, to the mouth of Wild Rice River; thence, up Red River of the North, to the mouth of Buffalo River; thence, in a straight line, to the southwestern extremity of Otter-Tail Lake; thence, through said lake, to the source of Leaf River; thence down said river, to its junction with Crow Wing River; thence down Crow Wing River, to its junction with the Mississippi River; thence to the commencement on said river of the southern boundary-line of the Chippewa country, as established by the treaty of July twenty-ninth, one thousand eight hundred and thirty-seven; and thence, along said line, to the place of beginning. And the said Indians do further fully and entirely relinquish and convey to the United States, any and all right, title, and

Page 686

interest, of whatsoever nature the same may be, which they may now have in, and to any other lands in the Territory of Minnesota or elsewhere.

ARTICLE 2.

There shall be, and hereby is, reserved and set apart, a sufficient quantity of land for the permanent homes of the said Indians; the lands so reserved and set apart, to be in separate tracts, as follows, viz:
For the Mississippi bands of Chippewa Indians: The first to embrace the following fractional townships, viz: forty-two north, of range twenty-five west; forty-two north, of

http://digital.library.okstate.edu/kappler/Vol2/treaties/chi0685.htm

9/17/2017

THE HEADWATERS WAR:
Conflict for the Mississippi Headwaters

Treaty of 1855

INDIAN AFFAIRS: LAWS AND TREATIES. Vol. 2, Treaties

Page 3 of 9

range twenty-six west; and forty-two and forty-three north, of range twenty-seven west; and, also, the three islands in the southern part of Mille Lac. Second, beginning at a point half a mile east of Rabbit Lake; thence south three miles; thence westwardly, in a straight line, to a point three miles south of the mouth of Rabbit River; thence north to the mouth of said river; thence up the Mississippi River to a point directly north of the place of beginning; thence south to the place of beginning. Third, beginning at a point half a mile southwest from the most southwestwardly point of Gull Lake; thence due south to Crow Wing River; thence down said river, to the Mississippi River; thence up said river to Long Lake Portage; thence, in a straight line, to the head of Gull Lake; thence in a southwestwardly direction, as nearly in a direct line as practicable, but at no point thereof, at a less distance than half a mile from said lake, to the place of beginning. Fourth, the boundaries to be, as nearly as practicable, at right angles, and so as to embrace within them Pokagomon Lake; but nowhere to approach nearer said lake than half a mile therefrom. Fifth, beginning at the mouth of Sandy Lake River; thence south, to a point on an east and west line, two miles south of the most southern point of Sandy Lake; thence east, to a point due south from the mouth of West Savannah River; thence north, to the mouth of said river; thence north to a point on an east and west line, one mile north of the most northern point of Sandy Lake; thence west, to Little Rice River; thence down said river to Sandy Lake River; and thence down said river to the place of beginning. Sixth, to include all the islands in Rice Lake, and also half a section of land on said lake, to include the present gardens of the Indians. Seventh, one section of land for Pug-o-na-ke-shick, or Hole-in-the-day, to include his house and farm; and for which he shall receive a patent in fee-simple. For the Pillager and Lake Winnibigoshish bands, to be in three tracts, to be located and bounded as follows, viz: First, beginning at mouth of Little Boy River; thence up said river to Lake Hassler; thence through the center of said lake to its western extremity; thence in a direct line to the most southern point of Leech Lake; and thence through said lake, so as to include all the islands therein, to the place of beginning. Second, beginning at the point where the Mississippi River leaves Lake Winnibigoshish; thence north, to the head of the first river; thence west, by the head of the next river, to the head of the third river, emptying into said lake; thence down the latter to said lake; and thence in a direct line to the place of beginning. Third, beginning at the mouth of Turtle River; thence up said river to the first lake; thence east, four miles; thence southwardly, in a line parallel with Turtle River, to Cass Lake; and thence, so as to include all the islands in said lake, to the place of beginning; all of which said tracts shall be distinctly designated on the plats of the public surveys. And at such time or times as the President may deem it advisable for the interests and welfare of said Indians, or any of them, he shall cause the said reservation, or such portion or portions thereof as may be necessary, to be surveyed; and assign to each head of a family, or single person over twenty-one years of age, a reasonable quantity of

Page 687

land, in one body, not to exceed eighty acres in any case, for his or their separate use; and he may, at his discretion, as the occupants thereof become capable of managing their business and affairs, issue patents for the tracts so assigned to them, respectively; said tracts to be exempt from taxation, levy, sale, or feiture; and not to be aliened or leased for a longer period than two years, at one time, until otherwise provided for by the legislature of the State in which they may be situate, with the assent of Congress. They shall not be sold, or alienated, in fee, for a period of five years after the date of the patents; and not then without the assent of the President of the United States being first obtained. Prior to the issue of the patents, the President shall make

ittp://digital.library.okstate.edu/kappler/Vol2/treaties/chi0685.htm

9/17/2017

THE HEADWATERS WAR:
Conflict for the Mississippi Headwaters

Treaty of 1855

INDIAN AFFAIRS: LAWS AND TREATIES. Vol. 2, Treaties   Page 4 of 9

such rules and regulations as he may deem necessary and expedient, respecting the disposition of any of said tracts in case of the death of the person or persons to whom they may be assigned, so that the same shall be secured to the families of such deceased person; and should any of the Indians to whom tracts may be assigned thereafter abandon them, the President may make such rules and regulations, in relation to such abandoned tracts, as in his judgment may be necessary and proper.

ARTICLE 3.

In consideration of, and in full compensation for, the cessions made by the said Mississippi, Pillager, and Lake Winnibigoshish bands of Chippewa Indians, in the first article of this agreement, the United States hereby agree and stipulate to pay, expend, and make provision for, the said bands of Indians, as follows, viz: For the Mississippi bands:

Ten thousand dollars ($10,000) in goods, and other useful articles, as soon as practicable after the ratification of this instrument, and after an appropriation shall be made by Congress therefor, to be turned over to the delegates and chiefs for distribution among their people.

Fifty thousand dollars ($50,000) to enable them to adjust and settle their present engagements, so far as the same, on an examination thereof, may be found and decided to be valid and just by the chiefs, subject to the approval of the Secretary of the Interior; and any balance remaining of said sum not required for the above-mentioned purpose shall be paid over to said Indians in the same manner as their annuity money, and in such instalments as the said Secretary may determine; *Provided,* That an amount not exceeding ten thousand dollars ($10,000) of the above sum shall be paid to such full and mixed bloods as the chiefs may direct, for services rendered heretofore to their bands.

Twenty thousand dollars ($20,000) per annum, in money, for twenty years, provided, that two thousand dollars ($2,000) per annum of that sum, shall be paid or expended, as the chiefs may request, for purposes of utility connected with the improvement and welfare of said Indians, subject to the approval of the Secretary of the Interior.

Five thousand dollars ($5,000) for the construction of a road from the mouth of Rum River to Mille Lac, to be expended under the direction of the Commissioner of Indian Affairs.

A reasonable quantity of land, to be determined by the Commissioner of Indian Affairs, to be ploughed and prepared for cultivation in suitable fields, at each of the reservations of the said bands, not exceeding, in the aggregate, three hundred acres for all the reservations, the Indians to make the rails and inclose the fields themselves. For the Pillager and Lake Winnibigoshish bands:

Ten thousand dollars ($10,000) in goods, and other useful articles, as soon as practicable, after the ratification of this agreement, and an appropriation shall be made by Congress therefor; to be turned over to the chiefs and delegates for distribution among their people.

Forty thousand dollars ($40,000) to enable them to adjust and settle their present engagements, so far as the same, on an examination

Page 685

thereof, may be found and decided to be valid and just by the chiefs, subject to the approval of the Secretary of the Interior; and any balance remaining of said sum, not required for that purpose, shall be paid over to said Indians, in the same manner as their annuity money, and in such instalments as the said Secretary may determine;

http://digital.library.okstate.edu/kappler/Vol2/treaties/chi0685.htm   9/17/2017

THE HEADWATERS WAR:
Conflict for the Mississippi Headwaters

Treaty of 1855

INDIAN AFFAIRS: LAWS AND TREATIES. Vol. 2, Treaties   Page 5 of 9

provided that an amount, not exceeding ten thousand dollars ($10,000) of the above sum, shall be paid to such mixed-bloods as the chiefs may direct, for services heretofore rendered to their bands.

Ten thousand six hundred and sixty-six dollars and sixty-six cents ($10,666.66) per annum, in money, for thirty years.

Eight thousand dollars ($8,000) per annum, for thirty years, in such goods as may be requested by the chiefs, and as may be suitable for the Indians, according to their condition and circumstances.

Four thousand dollars ($4,000) per annum, for thirty years, to be paid or expended, as the chiefs may request, for purposes of utility connected with the improvement and welfare of said Indians; subject to the approval of the Secretary of the Interior: *Provided*, That an amount not exceeding two thousand dollars thereof, shall, for a limited number of years, be expended under the direction of the Commissioner of Indian Affairs, for provisions, seeds, and such other articles or things as may be useful in agricultural pursuits.

Such sum as can be usefully and beneficially applied by the United States, annually, for twenty years, and not to exceed three thousand dollars, in any one year, for purposes of education; to be expended under the direction of the Secretary of the Interior.

Three hundred dollars' ($300) worth of powder, per annum, for five years.

One hundred dollars' ($100) worth shot and lead, per annum, for five years.

One hundred dollars' ($100) worth of gilling twine, per annum, for five years.

One hundred dollars' ($100) worth of tobacco, per annum, for five years.

Hire of three laborers at Leech Lake, of two at Lake Winnibigoshish, and of one at Cass Lake, for five years.

Expense of two blacksmiths, with the necessary shop, iron, steel, and tools, for fifteen years.

Two hundred dollars ($200) in grubbing-hoes and tools, the present year.

Fifteen thousand dollars ($15,000) for opening a road from Crow Wing to Leech Lake; to be expended under the direction of the Commissioner of Indian Affairs.

To have ploughed and prepared for cultivation, two hundred acres of land, in ten or more lots, within the reservation at Leech Lake; fifty acres, in four or more lots, within the reservation at Lake Winnibigoshish; and twenty-five acres, in two or more lots within the reservation at Cass Lake: *Provided*, That the Indians shall make the rails and inclose the lots themselves.

A saw-mill, with a portable grist-mill attached thereto, to be established whenever the same shall be deemed necessary and advisable by the Commissioner of Indian Affairs, at such point as he shall think best; and which, together, with the expense of a proper person to take charge of and operate them, shall be continued during ten years: *Provided*, That the cost of all the requisite repairs of the said mills shall be paid by the Indians, out of their own funds.

ARTICLE 4.

The Mississippi bands have expressed a desire to be permitted to employ their own farmers, mechanics, and teachers; and it is therefore agreed that the amounts to which they are now entitled, under former treaties, for purposes of education, for blacksmiths and assistants, shops, tools, iron and steel, and for the employment of farmers and carpenters, shall be paid over to them as their annuities are paid: *Provided, however*, That whenever, in the opinion of the

Page 523

http://digital.library.okstate.edu/kappler/Vol2/treaties/chi0685.htm   9/17/2017

371

THE HEADWATERS WAR:
Conflict for the Mississippi Headwaters

Treaty of 1855

INDIAN AFFAIRS: LAWS AND TREATIES. Vol. 2, Treaties

Commissioner of Indian Affairs, they fail to make proper provision for the above-named purposes, he may retain said amounts, and appropriate them according to his discretion, for their education and improvement.

ARTICLE 5.

The foregoing annuities, in money and goods, shall be paid and distributed as follows: Those due the Mississippi bands, at one of their reservations; and those due the Pillager and Lake Winnibigoshish bands, at Leech Lake; and no part of the said annuities shall ever be taken or applied, in any manner, to or for the payment of the debts or obligations of Indians contracted in their private dealings, as individuals, whether to traders or other persons. And should any of said Indians become intemperate or abandoned, and waste their property, the President may withhold any moneys or goods, due and payable to such, and cause the same to be expended, applied, or distributed, so as to insure the benefit thereof to their families. If, at any time, before the said annuities in money and goods of either of the Indian parties to this convention shall expire, the interests and welfare of said Indians shall, in the opinion of the President, require a different arrangement, he shall have the power to cause the said annuities, instead of being paid over and distributed to the Indians, to be expended or applied to such purposes or objects as may be best calculated to promote their improvement and civilization.

ARTICLE 6.

The missionaries and such other persons as are now, by authority of law, residing in the country ceded by the first article of this agreement, shall each have the privilege of entering one hundred and sixty acres of the said ceded lands, at one dollar and twenty-five cents per acre; said entries not to be made so as to interfere, in any manner, with the laying off of the several reservations herein provided for. And such of the mixed bloods as are heads of families, and now have actual residences and improvements in the ceded country, shall have granted to them, in fee, eighty acres of land, to include their respective improvements.

ARTICLE 7.

The laws which have been or may be enacted by Congress, regulating trade and intercourse with the Indian tribes, to continue and be in force within the several reservations provided for herein; and those portions of said laws which prohibit the introduction, manufacture, use of, and traffic in, ardent spirits, wines, or other liquors, in the Indian country, shall continue and be in force, within the entire boundaries of the country herein ceded to the United States, until otherwise provided by Congress.

ARTICLE 8.

All roads and highways, authorized by law, the lines of which shall be laid through any of the reservations provided for in this convention, shall have the right of way through the same; the fair and just value of such right being paid to the Indians therefor; to be assessed and determined according to the laws in force for the appropriation of lands for such purposes.

ittp://digital.library.okstate.edu/kappler/Vol2/treaties/chi0685.htm 9/17/2017

THE HEADWATERS WAR:
Conflict for the Mississippi Headwaters

Treaty of 1855

NDIAN AFFAIRS: LAWS AND TREATIES. Vol. 2, Treaties

ARTICLE 9.

The said bands of Indians, jointly and severally, obligate and bind themselves not to commit any depredations or wrong upon other Indians, or upon citizens of the United States; to conduct themselves at all times in a peaceable and orderly manner; to submit all difficulties between them and other Indians to the President, and to abide by his decision in regard to the same, and to respect and observe the laws of the United States, so far as the same are to them applicable. And they also stipulate that they will settle down in the peaceful pursuits of life, commence the cultivation of the soil, and appropriate their means to the erection of houses, opening farms, the education of their children, and such other objects of improvement and convenience, as are incident to well-regulated society; and that they will abstain from the use of intoxicating drinks and other vices to which they have been addicted.

Page 690

ARTICLE 10.

This instrument shall be obligatory on the contracting parties as soon as the same shall be ratified by the President and the Senate of the United States.

In testimony whereof the said George W. Manypenny, commissioner as aforesaid, and the said chiefs and delegates of the Mississippi, Pillager and Lake Winnibigoshish bands of Chippewa Indians have hereunto set their hands and seals, at the place and on the day and year hereinbefore written.

George W. Manypenny, commissioner. [L. S.]

Tug-o-na-ke-shick, or Hole in the the Day, his x mark. [L. S.]

Que-we-sans-ish, or Bad Boy, his x mark. [L. S.]

Waud-e-kaw, or Little Hill, his x mark. [L. S.]

I-awe-showe-we-ke-shig, or Crossing Sky, his x mark. [L. S.]

Petud-dunce, or Rat's Liver, his x mark. [L. S.]

Mun-o-min-e-kay-shein, or Rice Maker, his x mark. [L. S.]

Aish-ke-bug-e-koshe, or Flat Mouth, his x mark. [L. S.]

Be-sheck-kee, or Buffalo, his x mark. [L. S.]

Nay-bun-a-caush; or Young Man's Son, his x mark. [L. S.]

Mah-yah-ge-way-we-durg, or The Chorister, his x mark. [L. S.]

Kay-gwa-daush, or The Attempter, his x mark. [L. S.]

Caw-cang-e-we-gwan, or Crow Feather, his x mark. [L. S.]

Show-baush-king, or He that Passeth Under Everything, his x mark. [L. S.]

Chief delegates of the Mississippi bands.

http://digital.library.okstate.edu/kappler/Vol2/treaties/chi0685.htm

THE HEADWATERS WAR:
Conflict for the Mississippi Headwaters

Treaty of 1855

DIAN AFFAIRS: LAWS AND TREATIES. Vol. 2, Treaties

Maug-e-gaw-bow, or Stepping Ahead, his x mark. [L. S.]

Mi-gi-si, or Eagle, his x mark. [L. S.]

Kaw-be-mub-bee, or North Star, his x mark. [L. S.]

Chiefs and delegates of the Pillager and Lake Winnibigoshish bands.

Executed in the presence of—

Henry M. Rice.

Geo. Culver.

D. B. Herriman, Indian agent.

J. E. Fletcher.

John Dowling.

T. A. Warren, United States interpreter.

Paul H. Beaulieu, interpreter.

Edward Ashman, interpreter.

C. H. Beaulieu, interpreter.

Peter Roy, interpreter.

Will P. Ross, Cherokee Nation.

Riley Keys.

Search | OSU Library, Electronic Publishing Center

Produced by the Oklahoma State University Library
URL: http://digital.library.okstate.edu/kappler/

Comments to:

THE HEADWATERS WAR:
Conflict for the Mississippi Headwaters

Treaty of 1867

NDIAN AFFAIRS: LAWS AND TREATIES. Vol. 2, Treaties   Page 1 of 6

INDIAN AFFAIRS: LAWS AND TREATIES

Vol. II, Treaties

Compiled and edited by Charles J. Kappler. Washington : Government Printing Office, 1904.

Home | Disclaimer & Usage | Table of Contents | Index

TREATY WITH THE CHIPPEWA OF THE MISSISSIPPI, 1867.

Mar. 19, 1867. | 16 Stats., 719. | Ratified Apr. 8, 1867. | Proclaimed Apr. 18, 1867.

Page Images: 974 | 975 | 976

Margin Notes
Cession of lands.
Reservation.
Boundaries.
Further reservation.
Land for farming.
Payments for lands ceded.
Schools.
Mills.
Houses.
Cattle, etc.
Agriculture, etc.
Physician, etc.
Provisions and clothing.
No part to any half-breed, etc., except, etc.
Annuities.
Hole-in-the-Day and his heirs.
Land to Min-a-ge-shig and Truman A. Warren.
Reservation to be located.
Survey.

ttp://digital.library.okstate.edu/kappler/Vol2/treaties/chi0974.htm   9/19/2017

THE HEADWATERS WAR:
Conflict for the Mississippi Headwaters

Treaty of 1867

INDIAN AFFAIRS: LAWS AND TREATIES. Vol. 2, Treaties   Page 2 of 6

> Indians having ten acres under cultivation to be entitled to receive a certificate for 40 acres, etc
>
> Land exempt from taxation and not to be alienated, except, etc.
>
> Arrest and punishment of Indians for crimes.

Page 974

Articles of agreement made and concluded at Washington, D. C., this 19th day of March, A. D. 1867, between the United States represented by Louis V. Bogy, special commissioner thereto appointed, William H. Watson, and Joel B. Bassett, United States agent, and the Chippewas of the Mississippi, represented by Que-we-zance, or Hole-in-the-Day, Qui-we-shen-shish, Wau-bon-a-quot, Min-e-do-wob, Mijaw-ke-ke-shik, Shob-osk-kunk, Ka-gway-dosh, Me-no-ke-shick, Way-namee, and O-gub-ay-gwan-ay-aush.

Whereas, by a certain treaty ratified March 20, 1865, between the parties aforesaid, a certain tract of land was, by the second article thereof, reserved and set apart for a home for the said bands of Indians, and by other articles thereof provisions were made for certain moneys to be expended for agricultural improvements for the benefit of said bands: and whereas it has been found that the said reservation is not adapted for agricultural purposes for the use of such of the Indians as desire to devote themselves to such pursuits, while a portion of the bands desire to remain and occupy a part of the aforementioned reservation, and to sell the remainder thereof to the United States: Now, therefore, it is agreed—

ARTICLE 1.

The Chippewas of the Mississippi hereby cede to the United States all their lands in the State of Minnesota, secured to them by the second article of their treaty of March 20, 1865, excepting and reserving therefrom the tract bounded and described as follows, to wit: Commencing at a point on the Mississippi River, opposite the mouth of Wanoman River, as laid down on Sewall's map of Minnesota; thence due north to a point two miles further north than the most northerly point of Lake Winnebagoshish; thence due west to a point two miles west of the most westerly point of Cass Lake; thence south to Kabekona River; thence down said river to Leech Lake; thence along the north shore of Leech lake to its outlet in Leech Lake River; thence down the main channel of said river to its junction with the Mississippi River, and thence down the Mississippi to the place of beginning.

Page 975

And there is further reserved for the said Chippewas out of the land now owned by them such portion of their western outlet as may upon location and survey be found to be within the reservation provided for in the next succeeding section.

ARTICLE 2.

In order to provide a suitable farming region for the said bands there is hereby set apart for their use a tract of land, to be located in a square form as nearly as possible,

http://digital.library.okstate.edu/kappler/Vol2/treaties/chi0974.htm   9/19/2017

THE HEADWATERS WAR:
Conflict for the Mississippi Headwaters

Treaty of 1867

INDIAN AFFAIRS: LAWS AND TREATIES. Vol. 2, Treaties

with lines corresponding to the Government surveys; which reservation shall include White Earth Lake and Rice Lake, and contain thirty-six townships of land: and such portions of the tract herein provided for as shall be found upon actual survey to lie outside of the reservation set apart for the Chippewas of the Mississippi by the second article of the treaty of March 20, 1865, shall be received by them in part consideration for the cession of lands made by this agreement.

ARTICLE 3.

In further consideration for the lands herein ceded, estimated to contain about two million of acres, the United States agree to pay the following sums, to wit: Five thousand dollars for the erection of school buildings upon the reservation provided for in the second article; four thousand dollars each year for ten years, and as long as the President may deem necessary after the ratification of this treaty, for the support of a school or schools upon said reservation; ten thousand dollars for the erection of a saw-mill, with grist-mill attached, on said reservation; five thousand dollars to be expended in assisting in the erection of houses for such of the Indians as shall remove to said reservation.

Five thousand dollars to be expended, with the advice of the chiefs, in the purchase of cattle, horses, and farming utensils, and in making such improvements as are necessary for opening farms upon said reservation.

Six thousand dollars each year for ten years, and as long thereafter as the President may deem proper, to be expended in promoting the progress of the people in agriculture, and assisting them to become self-sustaining by giving aid to those who will labor.

Twelve hundred dollars each year for ten years for the support of a physician, and three hundred each year for ten years for necessary medicines.

Ten thousand dollars to pay for provisions, clothing, or such other articles as the President may determine, to be paid to them immediately on their removal to their new reservation.

ARTICLE 4.

No part of the annuities provided for in this or any former treaty with the Chippewas of the Mississippi bands shall be paid to any half-breed or mixed-blood, except those who actually live with their people upon one of the reservations belonging to the Chippewa Indians.

ARTICLE 5.

It is further agreed that the annuity of $1,000 a year which shall hereafter become due under the provisions of the third article of the treaty with the Chippewas of the Mississippi bands, of August 2, 1847, shall be paid to the chief, Hole-in-the-Day, and to his heirs; and there shall be set apart, by selections to be made in their behalf and reported to the Interior Department by the agent, one half section of land each, upon the Gull Lake reservation, for Min-a-ge-shig and Truman A. Warren, who shall be entitled to patents for the same upon such selections being reported to the Department.

http://digital.library.okstate.edu/kappler/Vol2/treaties/chi0974.htm

9/19/2017

THE HEADWATERS WAR:
Conflict for the Mississippi Headwaters

Treaty of 1867

INDIAN AFFAIRS: LAWS AND TREATIES. Vol. 2, Treaties

ARTICLE 6.

Upon the ratification of this treaty, the Secretary of the Interior shall designate one or more persons who shall, in connection with the agent for the Chippewas in Minnesota, and such of their chiefs, parties to this agreement, as he may deem sufficient, proceed to locate, as near as may be, the reservation set apart by the second article hereof, and designate the places where improvements shall be made, and such portion of the improvements provided for in the fourth

Page 975

article of the Chippewa treaty of May 7, 1864, as the agent may deem necessary and proper, with the approval of the Commissioner of Indian Affairs, may be made upon the new reservation, and the United States will pay the expenses of negotiating this treaty, not to exceed ten thousand dollars.

ARTICLE 7.

As soon as the location of the reservation set apart by the second article hereof shall have been approximately ascertained, and reported to the office of Indian Affairs, the Secretary of the Interior shall cause the same to be surveyed in conformity to the system of Government surveys, and whenever, after such survey, any Indian, of the bands parties hereto, either male or female, shall have ten acres of land under cultivation, such Indian shall be entitled to receive a certificate, showing him to be entitled to the forty acres of land, according to legal subdivision, containing the said ten acres or the greater part thereof, and whenever such Indian shall have an additional ten acres under cultivation, he or she shall be entitled to a certificate for additional forty acres, and so on, until the full amount of one hundred and sixty acres may have been certified to any one Indian; and the land so held by any Indian shall be exempt from taxation and sale for debt, and shall not be alienated except with the approval of the Secretary of the Interior, and in no case to any person not a member of the Chippewa tribe.

ARTICLE 8.

For the purpose of protecting and encouraging the Indians, parties to this treaty, in their efforts to become self-sustaining by means of agriculture, and the adoption of the habits of civilized life, it is hereby agreed that, in case of the commission by any of the said Indians of crimes against life or property, the person charged with such crimes may be arrested, upon the demand of the agent, by the sheriff of the county of Minnesota in which said reservation may be located, and when so arrested may be tried, and if convicted, punished in the same manner as if he were not a member of an Indian tribe.

In testimony whereof, the parties aforementioned, respectively representing the United States and the said Chippewas of the Mississippi, have hereunto set their hands and seals the day and year first above written.

Lewis V. Bogy, special commissioner. [SEAL.]

W. H. Watson. [SEAL.]

http://digital.library.okstate.edu/kappler/Vol2/treaties/chi0974.htm   9/19/2017

THE HEADWATERS WAR:
Conflict for the Mississippi Headwaters

Treaty of 1867

INDIAN AFFAIRS: LAWS AND TREATIES. Vol. 2, Treaties   Page 5 of 6

Joel B. Bassett, U. S. Indian agent. [SEAL.]

Que-we-zance, or Hole-in-the-Day, his x mark. [SEAL.]

Qui-we-shen-shish, his x mark. [SEAL.]

Wau-bon-a-quot, his x mark. [SEAL.]

Min-e-do-wob, his x mark. [SEAL.]

Mi-jaw-ke-ke-shik, his x mark. [SEAL.]

Shob-osh-kunk, his x mark. [SEAL.]

Ka-gway-dosh, his x mark. [SEAL.]

Me-no-ke-shick, his x mark. [SEAL.]

Way-na-mee, his x mark. [SEAL.]

O-gub-ay-gwan-ay-aush, his x mark. [SEAL.]

In presence of—

T. A. Warren, United States interpreter.

Charles E. Mix.

Lewis S. Hayden.

George B. Jonas.

Thos. E. McGraw.

John Johnson.

George Bonga.

*This refers to the treaty of May 7, 1864, proclaimed March 20, 1865, ante p. 862.

Search | OSU Library Electronic Publishing Center

Produced by the Oklahoma State University Library
URL: http://digital.library.okstate.edu/kappler/

Comments to: lib-dig@okstate.edu

THE HEADWATERS WAR:
Conflict for the Mississippi Headwaters

Dawes Allotment Act of 1887

INDIAN AFFAIRS: LAWS AND TREATIES, Vol. 1, Laws   Page 1 of 8

INDIAN AFFAIRS: LAWS AND TREATIES

Dawes Attotmed Act

Vol. I, Laws (Compiled to December 1, 1902)

Compiled and edited by Charles J. Kappler. Washington : Government Printing Office, 1904.

Home | Disclaimer & Usage | Table of Contents | Index

ACTS OF FORTY-NINTH CONGRESS—SECOND SESSION, 1887.
CHAP. 119 | CHAP. 320

Page Images

Chapter 119
Sections 2 | 3 | 4 | 5 | 6 | 7 | 8 | 9 | 10 | 11

Margin Notes	
Chap. 119	President may allot lands.
Sec. 2	Selection of allotments. 19 Opins., 255, 559.
Sec. 2	Improvements.
Sec. 2	Failure to select for four years. Secretary of Interior may select.
Sec. 3	Allotments to be made by special agents, reservation agents. 19 Opins., 14.
Sec. 3	— certificates. 69 Fed. Rep., 886. 64 Fed. Rep., 417.
Sec. 4	Indians not on reservations, etc., may make selection of public lands. 56 Fed. Rep., 855; 72 N. W. Rep., 843; 65 Fed. Rep., 30; 44 N. W. Rep., 471.
Sec. 4	Fees of land officers to be paid from Treasury.
Sec. 5	Patent to issue, holding lands in trust; conveyance after twenty-five years. 1875, Mar. 3., c. 131, s. 15, ante, p. 23. 1889, Feb. 16, c. 172, post, p. 39.

http://digital.library.okstate.edu/kappler/Vol1/HTML_files/SES0033.html 9/20/2017

THE HEADWATERS WAR:
Conflict for the Mississippi Headwaters

Dawes Allotment Act of 1887

INDIAN AFFAIRS: LAWS AND TREATIES. Vol. 1, Laws

	19 Opins., 232. 1901, Mar. 3, c. 832, post, p. 114.
Sec. 5	Contracts, conveyances, etc., before end of twenty-five years void. 1891, Feb. 28, c. 383, s. 1, post, p. 56.
Sec. 5	Laws of descent and partition. 1891, Feb. 18, c. 383, s. 5, post, p. 58.
Sec. 5	Negotiations by Secretary of Interior for purchase of lands not allotted. R. S., 2079.
Sec. 5	Agricultural lands so purchased to be held for actual settlers, if arable. 1891, Mar. 3, c. 561, s. 10, 26 Stat., 1095.
Sec. 5	Patent to issue only to persons taking for homestead.
Sec. 5	Purchase-money to be held in trust for Indians.
Sec. 5	Patents to be recorded free.
Sec. 5	Lands occupied by religious organizations to be confirmed to them.
Sec. 5	In employment of Indians preference to be given, etc. R. S., 2069. 1877, Mar. 3, ch. 101, ante, p. 27. 1880, May 11, ch. 85, ante, p. 28.
Sec. 6	Citizenship to be accorded to allottees and Indians adopting civilized life. R. S., 2119. 1875, Mar. 3, ch. 131, s. 15, ante, p. 23.
Sec. 6	1888, Aug. 9, ch., 818, s. 2, post, p. 38. 64 Fed. Rep., 417. 1901, Mar. 3, ch. 868, post, p. 114. 66 Fed. Rep., 541. 71 Fed. Rep., 576.
Sec. 6	As amended, post, p. 114.
Sec. 7	Secretary of Interior to prescribe rules for use of waters for irrigation.
Sec. 8	Act not to extend to lands of certain tribes.
Sec. 9	Appropriation for surveys.
Sec. 10	Rights of way for railroads, etc., not affected.
Sec. 11	Removal of Southern Utes not affected by act.

{Page 33}

THE HEADWATERS WAR:
Conflict for the Mississippi Headwaters

Dawes Allotment Act of 1887

INDIAN AFFAIRS: LAWS AND TREATIES. Vol. 1, Laws

Chapter 119
Feb. 8, 1887. | 24 Stat., 388.
Page Images

An act to provide for the allotment of lands in severalty to Indians on the various reservations, and to extend the protection of the laws of the United States and the Territories over the Indians, and for other purposes.[a]

---

[a]Special provisions exist in regard to lands in severalty to the following tribes: Stockbridge Munsee, Ottawa and Chippewa of Michigan, Ute, Winnebago, Crow, Omaha, Umatilla, Sac and Fox, Iowa, Sioux, Gros Ventres, Piegan, Blood, Blackfeet, River Crow, Winnebago, Chippewa, Shoshone, Bannock, Sheepeater, Flathead, Ponca, Confederated Wea, Peoria, Kaskaskia, Piankeshaw and Western Miami, Round Valley, Mission, Citizen Band of Pottawatomie, Cheyenne and Arapahoe, Coeur d'Alene, Arickaree, Mandan, Sisseton and Wahpeton bands of Sioux—for reference to which special provisions, see index under title "Allotments;" See also in the index, names of particular tribes.

Be it enacted, &c., [For substitute for section 1, see 1891, Feb. 28, c. 383, s. 1, post, p. 56].

SEC. 2

That all allotments set apart under the provisions of this act shall be selected by the Indians, heads of families selecting for their minor children, and the agents shall select for each orphan child, and in such manner as to embrace the improvements of the Indians making the selection.

Where the improvements of two or more Indians have been made on the same legal subdivision of land, unless they shall otherwise agree, a provisional line may be run dividing said lands between them, and the amount to which each is entitled shall be equalized in the assignment of the remainder of the land to which they are entitled under this act:

Provided, That if any one entitled to an allotment shall fail to make a selection within four years after the President shall direct that allotments may be made on a particular reservation, the Secretary of the Interior may direct the agent of such tribe or band, if such there be, and if there be no agent, then a special agent appointed for that purpose, to make a selection for such Indian, which selection shall be allotted as in cases where selections are made by the Indians, and patents shall issue in like manner.

SEC. 3

That the allotments provided for in this act shall be made by special agents appointed by the President for such purpose, and the agents in charge of the respective reservations on which the allotments are directed to be made, under such rules and regulations as the Secretary of the Interior may from time to time prescribe, and shall be certified by such agents to the Commissioner of Indian Affairs, in duplicate, one copy to be retained in the Indian Office and the other to be transmitted to the Secretary of the Interior for his action, and to be deposited in the General Land Office.

http://digital.library.okstate.edu/kappler/Vol1/HTML_files/SES0033.html   9/20/2017

THE HEADWATERS WAR:
Conflict for the Mississippi Headwaters

Dawes Allotment Act of 1887

INDIAN AFFAIRS: LAWS AND TREATIES. Vol. 1, Laws   Page 4 of 8

SEC. 4

That where any Indian not residing upon a reservation, or for whose tribe no reservation has been provided by treaty, act of Congress or executive order, shall make settlement upon any surveyed or unsurveyed lands of the United States not otherwise appropriated, he or she shall be entitled, upon application to the local land-office for the district in which the lands are located, to have the same allotted to him or her, and to his or her children, in quantities and manner as provided in this act for Indians residing upon reservations; and when such settlement is made upon unsurveyed lands, the grant to such Indians shall be adjusted upon the survey of the lands so as to conform thereto; and patents shall be issued to them for such lands in the manner and with the restrictions as herein provided.

{Page 34}

And the fees to which the officers of such local land-office would have been entitled had such lands been entered under the general laws for the disposition of the public lands shall be paid to them, from any moneys in the Treasury of the United States not otherwise appropriated, upon a statement of an account in their behalf for such fees by the Commissioner of the General Land Office and a certification of such account to the Secretary of the Treasury by the Secretary of the Interior.

SEC. 5

That upon the approval of the allotments provided for in this act by the Secretary of the Interior, he shall cause patents to issue therefor in the name of the allottees, which patents shall be of the legal effect, and declare that the United States does and will hold the land thus allotted for the period of twenty-five years, in trust for the sole use and benefit of the Indian to whom such allotment shall have been made, or, in case of his decease, of his heirs according to the laws of the State or Territory where such land is located, and that at the expiration of said period the United States will convey the same by patent to said Indian, or his heirs as aforesaid, in fee, discharged of said trust and free of all charge or incumbrance whatsoever: Provided, That the President of the United States may in any case in his discretion extend the period.

And if any conveyance shall be made of the lands set apart and allotted as herein provided, or any contract made touching the same, before the expiration of the time above mentioned, such conveyance or contract shall be absolutely null and void:

Provided, That the law of descent and partition in force in the State or Territory where such lands are situate shall apply thereto after patents therefor have been executed and delivered, except as herein otherwise provided; and the laws of the State of Kansas regulating the descent and partition of real estate shall, so far as practicable, apply to all lands in the Indian Territory which may be allotted in severalty under the provisions of this act:

And provided further, That at any time after lands have been allotted to all the Indians of any tribe as herein provided, or sooner if in the opinion of the President it shall be for the best interests of said tribe, it shall be lawful for the Secretary of the Interior to negotiate with such Indian tribe for the purchase and release by said tribe, in conformity with the treaty or statute under which such reservation is held, of such portions of its reservation not allotted as such tribe shall, from time to time, consent to sell, on such terms and conditions as shall be considered just and equitable between

http://digital.library.okstate.edu/kappler/Vol1/HTML_files/SES0033.html   9/20/2017

THE HEADWATERS WAR:
Conflict for the Mississippi Headwaters

Dawes Allotment Act of 1887

NDIAN AFFAIRS: LAWS AND TREATIES. Vol. 1, Laws   Page 5 of 8

the United States and said tribe of Indians, which purchase shall not be complete until ratified by Congress, and the form and manner of executing such release shall also be prescribed by Congress:

Provided however, That all lands adapted to agriculture, with or without irrigation so sold or released to the United States by any Indian tribe shall be held by the United States for the sole purpose of securing homes to actual settlers and shall be disposed of by the United States to actual and bona fide settlers only in tracts not exceeding one hundred and sixty acres to any one person, on such terms as Congress shall prescribe, subject to grants which Congress may make in aid of education:

And provided further, That no patents shall issue therefor except to the person so taking the same as and for a homestead, or his heirs, and after the expiration of five years occupancy thereof as such homestead; and any conveyance of said lands so taken as a homestead, or any contract touching the same, or lien thereon, created prior to the date of such patent, shall be null and void.

And the sums agreed to be paid by the United States as purchase money for any portion of any such reservation shall be held in the Treasury of the United States for the sole use of the tribe or tribes

(Page 36)

of Indians to whom such reservations belonged; and the same, with interest thereon at three per cent per annum, shall be at all times subject to appropriation by Congress for the education and civilization of such tribe or tribes of Indians or the members thereof.

The patents aforesaid shall be recorded in the General Land Office, and afterward delivered, free of charge, to the allottee entitled thereto.

And if any religious society or other organization is now occupying any of the public lands to which this act is applicable, for religious or educational work among the Indians, the Secretary of the Interior is hereby authorized to confirm such occupation to such society or organization, in quantity not exceeding one hundred and sixty acres in any one tract, so long as the same shall be so occupied, on such terms as he shall deem just; but nothing herein contained shall change or alter any claim of such society for religious or educational purposes heretofore granted by law.

And hereafter in the employment of Indian police, or any other employes in the public service among any of the Indian tribes or bands affected by this act, and where Indians can perform the duties required, those Indians who have availed themselves of the provisions of this act and become citizens of the United States shall be preferred.

SEC. 6

That upon the completion of said allotments and the patenting of the lands to said allottees, each and every member of the respective bands or tribes of Indians to whom allotments have been made shall have the benefit of and be subject to the laws, both civil and criminal, of the State or Territory in which they may reside; and no Territory shall pass or enforce any law denying any such Indian within its jurisdiction the equal protection of the law.

And every Indian born within the territorial limits of the United States to whom allotments shall have been made under the provisions of this act, or under any law or

http://digital.library.okstate.edu/kappler/Vol1/HTML_files/SES0033.html   9/20/2017

THE HEADWATERS WAR:
Conflict for the Mississippi Headwaters

Dawes Allotment Act of 1887

INDIAN AFFAIRS: LAWS AND TREATIES. Vol. 1, Laws

treaty, and every Indian born within the territorial limits of the United States who has voluntarily taken up, within said limits, his residence separate and apart from any tribe of Indians therein, and has adopted the habits of civilized life, [*and every Indian in Indian Territory,*] is hereby declared to be a citizen of the United States, and is entitled to all the rights, privileges, and immunities of such citizens, whether said Indian has been or not, by birth or otherwise, a member of any tribe of Indians within the territorial limits of the United States without in any manner impairing or otherwise affecting the right of any such Indian to tribal or other property.

SEC. 7

That in cases where the use of water for irrigation is necessary to render the lands within any Indian reservation available for agricultural purposes, the Secretary of the Interior be, and he is hereby, authorized to prescribe such rules and regulations as he may deem necessary to secure a just and equal distribution thereof among the Indians residing upon any such reservations; and no other appropriation or grant of water by any riparian proprietor shall be authorized or permitted to the damage of any other riparian proprietor.

SEC. 8

That the provision of this act shall not extend to the territory occupied by the Cherokees, Creeks, Choctaws, Chickasaws, Seminoles, and Osage, Miamies and Peorias, and Sacs and Foxes, in the Indian Territory, nor to any of the reservations of the Seneca Nation of New York Indians in the State of New York, nor to that strip of territory in the State of Nebraska adjoining the Sioux Nation on the south added by executive order.[o]

[o]The provisions of this act are extended to the Wea, Peoria, Kaskaskia, Piankeshaw, and Western Miami tribes by act of 1889, March 2, ch. 422 (post, p. 344).

SEC. 9

That for the purpose of making the surveys and resurveys mentioned in section two of this act, there be, and hereby is, appro-

[Page 36]

priated, out of any moneys in the Treasury not otherwise appropriated, the sum of one hundred thousand dollars, to be repaid proportionally out of the proceeds of the sales of such land as may be acquired from the Indians under the provisions of this act.

SEC. 10

That nothing in this act contained shall be so construed as to affect the right and power of congress to grant the right of way through any lands granted to an Indian, or a tribe of Indians, for railroads or other highways, or telegraph lines, for the public use, or to condemn such lands to public uses, upon making just compensation.

SEC. 11

That nothing in this act shall be so construed as to prevent the removal of the Southern Ute Indians from their present reservation in Southwestern Colorado to a

http://digital.library.okstate.edu/kappler/Vol1/HTML_files/SES0033.html 9/20/2017

THE HEADWATERS WAR:
Conflict for the Mississippi Headwaters

Dawes Allotment Act of 1887

INDIAN AFFAIRS: LAWS AND TREATIES. Vol. 1, Laws

new reservation by and with the consent of a majority of the adult male members of said tribe. [*February 8, 1887.*]

Search | OSU Library Digitization Center

Produced by the Oklahoma State University Library, 1999-2000
Generous support provided by The Coca-Cola Foundation, Atlanta, GA
URL: http://digital.library.okstate.edu/kappler/

Comments to: lib-dig@okstate.edu

THE HEADWATERS WAR:
Conflict for the Mississippi Headwaters

Indian Citizenship Act of 1924

INDIAN AFFAIRS: LAWS AND TREATIES. Vol. IV, Laws

INDIAN AFFAIRS: LAWS AND TREATIES

Vol. IV, Laws   {Compiled to March 4, 1927}

Compiled and edited by Charles J. Kappler. Washington : Government Printing Office, 1929.

Home | Disclaimer & Usage | Table of Contents | Index

PART VI.

Page Images

INDIAN CITIZENSHIP

By the act of June 2, 1924 (43 Stat. 253, ante, 420), Congress conferred citizenship upon all noncitizen Indians born within the territorial limits of the United States. The text of the act follows:

> *Be it enacted by the Senate and House of Representatives of the United States of America in Congress assembled,* That all noncitizen Indians born within the territorial limits of the United States be, and they are hereby, declared to be citizens of the United States: *Provided,* That the granting of such citizenship shall not in any manner impair or otherwise affect the right of any Indian to tribal or other property.

Indians who are otherwise eligible to vote may not be denied that right because of their race. Their right in this respect is protected by the fifteenth amendment to the Constitution of the United States, which says:

> The right of citizens of the United States to vote shall not be denied or abridged by the United States or by any State on account of race, color, or previous condition of servitude.

In order to exercise the right of suffrage, Indians must of course comply with the conditions equally required of other voters, and may be denied the privilege of voting if they fail to comply with the requirements of the law as to registration, payment of poll tax, or do not meet the educational or other qualifications for electors, etc., as provided by the State laws.

http://digital.library.okstate.edu/kappler/Vol4/html_files/v4p1165.html   10/8/2017

THE HEADWATERS WAR:
Conflict for the Mississippi Headwaters

Indian Citizenship Act of 1924

INDIAN AFFAIRS: LAWS AND TREATIES. Vol. IV, Laws   Page 2 of 4

It will be observed that the act provides that the granting of such citizenship shall not in any manner impair or otherwise affect the right of any Indian to tribal or other property. Therefore, the restrictions upon the trust property—real or personal—of Indians are not removed by the passage of this act. Questions relative to the control or management of trust property are, therefore, not changed by the act but are to be handled on their own merits as heretofore.

Prior to the passage of the act of June 2, 1924, about two-thirds of the Indians of the United States were already citizens. There were a number of different provisions of law by which or under which Indians became citizens previous to June 2, 1924. Some of the most important ways of their attaining citizenship were as follows:

1. *Treaty Provision.*—In some of the treaties or agreements with certain tribes of Indians provision was made whereby Indians desiring to become citizens might become such by complying with certain prescribed formalities somewhat similar to those required of aliens. For example, see Articles 13, 17, and 28 of the Treaty of February 23, 1867, with various bands or tribes of Indians. (15 Stat. 513, vol. 2, 960.)

2. *Allotment under the Act of February 8, 1887.*—In the act of February 8, 1887 (24 Stat. 388, vol. 1, 33-38), Congress provided for the allotment of land to the Indians in severalty and in section 6 thereof declared that Indians so allotted should become citizens of the United States and of the State in which they reside. (See the language of the Act.)

3. *Issuance of Patent in Fee Simple.*—In the Act of May 8, 1906 (34 Stat. 182, vol. 3, 181), Congress amended the Act of February 8, 1887, so as to postpone citizenship of Indians thereafter allotted until after a patent in fee simple had been issued to said Indians. Provision was also made whereby patent in fee might be issued by the Secretary of the Interior to competent Indians before the expiration of the twenty-five-year trust period. Therefore Indians whose trust patents are dated subsequent to May 8, 1906, and who have also received their patents in fee simple have become citizens under said act of May 8, 1906.

4. *Adopting Habits of Civilized Life.*—Section 6 of the Act of February 8, 1887, both before and after its amendment of May 8, 1906, *provided:*

That every Indian born within the territorial limits of the United States who has voluntarily taken up within said limits his residence, separate and apart from any tribe of Indians therein, and has adopted the habits of civilized life is hereby declared to be a citizen of the United States, and is entitled to all the rights, privileges, and immunities of such citizens, whether said Indian has been

Page 1166

or not, by birth or otherwise, a member of any tribe of Indians within the territorial limits of the United States, without in any manner impairing or otherwise affecting the rights of any such Indian to tribal or other property.

5. *Minor Children.*—The Solicitor of the Interior Department has held that where Indian parents became citizens upon allotment, their minor children became citizens with them, and that children born subsequent thereto were born to citizenship.

http://digital.library.okstate.edu/kappler/Vol4/html_files/v4p1165.html   10/8/2017

THE HEADWATERS WAR:
Conflict for the Mississippi Headwaters

Indian Citizenship Act of 1924

INDIAN AFFAIRS: LAWS AND TREATIES. Vol. IV, Laws

6. *Citizenship by Birth.*—(a) An Indian child born in the United States of citizen Indian parents is born to citizenship. (b) Legitimate children born of an Indian woman and a white citizen father are born to citizenship.

7. *Soldiers and Sailors.*—Congress in the act of November 6, 1919, ante 232, provided that Indian soldiers and sailors who served in the recent World War and who have been honorably discharged might be granted citizenship by courts of competent jurisdiction. (Indian Office Circulars, Nos. 1587 and 1618.)

8. *Marriage.*—The act of August 9, 1888 (25 Stat. 392, vol. 1, 38), provided that Indian women who married citizens of the United States thereby became citizens of the United States. This provision is apparently inconsistent with the act of September 22, 1922 (42 Stat. 1020), and would probably be held to have been repealed by the latter act, though not specifically mentioned therein. Marriages coming within the act of August 9, 1888, and consummated before the passage of the act of September 22, 1922, would not of course be affected by the later act.

9. *Special Act of Congress.*—Sometimes Congress makes provision for a particular tribe of Indians or a particular group of Indians to become citizens. For instance:

(a) In the act of March 3, 1901 (31 Stat. 1447, vol. 1, 114), provision was made for the extension of citizenship to the Indians in the "Indian Territory" by amending section 6 of the act of February 8, 1887 (24 Stat. 388, vol. 1, 33). It should be observed, however, that in the act of May 8, 1906 (34 Stat. 182, vol. 3, 181), amending said section 6, the language, "and every Indian in the Indian Territory," was not included.

(b) In the act of March 3, 1921 (41 Stat. 1249-50, ante, 317), citizenship was extended to all members of the Osage tribe of Indians.

The above is not intended to be a complete list of the acts of Congress involving the citizenship of Indians, as there are a number of other laws including those affecting particular tribes, but it is believed the foregoing list or statement is sufficient to give a general idea of the main principles or rules that were involved in the determination of whether or not a particular Indian was a citizen prior to the act of June 2, 1924, *supra.*

Search | OSU Library Electronic Publishing Center

Produced by the Oklahoma State University Library
URL: http://digital.library.okstate.edu/kappler/

Comments to: lib-dig@okstate.edu

THE HEADWATERS WAR:
Conflict for the Mississippi Headwaters

Indian Reorganization Act of 1934

Wheeler-Howard Act, June 18, 1934
(The Indian Reorganization Act)

--An Act to conserve and develop Indian lands and resources; to extend to Indians the right to form bussiness and other organizations; to establish a credit system for Indians; to grant certain rights of home rule to Indians; to provide for vocational education for Indians; and for other purposes.

BE IT ENACTED *by the Senate and House of Representatives of the United States of America in Congress assembled,* That hereafter no land of any Indian reservation, created or set apart by treaty or agreement with the Indians, Act of Congress, Executive order, purchase, or otherwise, shall be allotted in severalty to any Indian.

Sec. 2. The existing periods of trust placed upon any Indian lands and any restriction on alienation thereof are hereby extended and continued until otherwise directed by Congress.

Sec. 3. The Secretary of the Interior, if he shall find it to be in the public interest, is hereby authorized to restore to tribal ownership the remaining surplus lands of any Indian reservation heretofore opened, or authorized to be opened, to sale, or any other form of disposal by Presidential proclamation, or by any of the public land laws of the United States; Provided, however, That valid rights or claims of any persons to any·lands so withdrawn existing on the date of the withdrawal shall not be affected by this Act: Provided further, That this section shall not apply to lands within any reclamation project heretofore authorized in any Indian reservation:*Provided further,* That this section shall not apply to lands within any reclamation project heretofore authorized in any Indian reservation: *Provided further,* That the order of the Department of the interior signed, dated, and approved by Honorable Ray Lyman Wilbur, as Secretary of the Interior, on October 28, 1932, temporarily withdrawing lands of the Papago Indian Reservation in Arizona from all forms of mineral entry or claim under the public land mining laws is hereby revoked and rescinded, and the lands of the said Papago Indian Reservation are hereby restored to exploration and location, under the existing mining laws of the United States, in accordance with the express terms and provisions declared and set forth in the Executive orders establishing said Papago Indian Reservation: *Provided further,* That the damages shall be paid to the Papago Tribe for loss of any improvements of any land located for mining in such a sum as may be determined by the Secretary of the Interior but not exceed the cost of said improvements: *Provided further,* That a yearly rental not to exceed five cents per acre shall be paid to the Papago Indian Tribe: *Provided further,* That in the event that any person or persons, partnership, corporation, or association, desires a mineral patent, according to the mining laws of the United States, he or they shall first deposit in the treasury of the United States to the credit of the Papago Tribe the sum of $1.00 per acre in lieu of annual rental, as

THE HEADWATERS WAR:
Conflict for the Mississippi Headwaters

Indian Reorganization Act of 1934

hereinbefore provided, to compensate for the loss or occupancy of the lands withdrawn by the requirements of mining operations: *Provided further*, That patentee shall also pay into the Treasury of the United States to the credit of the Papago Tribe damages for the loss of improvements not heretofore said in such a sum as may be determined by the Secretary of the Interior, but not to exceed the cost thereof; the payment of $1.00 per acre for surface use to be refunded to patentee in the event that the patent is not required.

Nothing herein contained shall restrict the granting or use of permits for easements or rights-of-way; or ingress or egress over the lands for all proper and lawful purposes; and nothing contained therein, except as expressly provided, shall be construed as authority by the Secretary of the Interior, or any other person, to issue or promulgate a rule or regulation in conflict with the Executive order of February 1, 1917, creating the Papago Indian Reservation in Arizona or the Act of February 21, 1931 (46 Stat. 1202).

Sec. 4. Except as herein provided, no sale, devise, gift, exchange or other transfer of restricted Indian lands or of shares in the assets of any Indian tribe or corporation organized hereunder, shall be made or approved: *Provided, however*, That such lands or interests may, with the approval of the Secretary of the Interior, be sold, devised, or otherwise transferred to the Indian tribe in which the lands or shares are located or from which the shares were derived or to a successor corporation; and in all instances such lands or interests shall descend or be devised, in accordance with the then existing laws of the State, or Federal laws where applicable, in which said lands are located or in which the subject matter of the corporation is located, to any member of such tribe or of such corporation or any heirs of such member: *Provided further*, That the Secretary of the Interior may authorize voluntary exchanges of lands of equal value and the voluntary exchange of shares of equal value whenever such exchange, in his judgement, is expedient and beneficial for or compatible with the proper consolidation of Indian lands and for the benefit of cooperative organizations.

Sec. 5. The Secretary of the Interior is hereby authorized, in his discretion, to acquire through purchase, relinquishment, gift, exchange, or assignment, any interest in lands, water rights or surface rights to lands, within or without existing reservations, including trust or otherwise restricted allotments whether the allottee be living or deceased, for the purpose of providing lands for Indians.

For the acquisition of such lands, interests in lands, water rights, and surface rights, and for expenses incident to such acquisition, there is hereby authorized to be appropriated, out of any funds in the Treasury not otherwise appropriated, a sum not to exceed $2,000,000 in any one fiscal year: *Provided*, That no part of such funds shall be used to acquire additional land outside of the exterior boundaries of Navajo

THE HEADWATERS WAR:
Conflict for the Mississippi Headwaters

Indian Reorganization Act of 1934

Indian Reservation for the Navajo Indians in Arizona and New Mexico, in the event that the proposed Navajo boundary extension measures how pending in congress and embodied in the bills (S. 2531 and H.R. 8927) to define the exterior boundaries of the Navajo Indian Reservation in Arizona, and for other purposes, and the bills (S. 2531 and H.R. 8982) to define the exterior boundaries of the Navajo Indian Reservation in New Mexico and for other purposes, or similar legislation, become law.

The unexpended balances of any appropriations made pursuant to this section shall remain available until expended.

Title to any lands or rights acquired pursuant to this Act shall be taken in the name of the United States in trust for the Indian tribe or individual Indian for which the land is acquired, and such lands or rights shall be exempt from State and local taxation.

Sec. 6. The Secretary of the Interior is directed to make rules and regulations for the operation and management of Indian forestry units on the principle of sustained-yield management, to restrict the number of livestock grazed on Indian range units to the estimated carrying capacity of such ranges, and to promulgate such other rules and regulations as may be necessary to protect the range from deterioration, to prevent soil erosion, to assure full utilization of the range, and like purposes.

Sec. 7. The Secretary of the Interior is hereby authorized to proclaim new Indian reservations on lands acquired pursuant to any authority conferred by this Act, or to add such lands to existing reservations: *Provided*, That lands added to existing reservations shall be designated for the exclusive use of Indians entitled by enrollment or by tribal membership to residence at such reservations shall be designated for the exclusive use of Indians entitled by enrollment or by tribal membership to residence at such reservations.

Sec. 8. Nothing contained in this Act shall be construed to relate to Indian holdings of allotments or homesteads upon the public domain outside of the geographic boundaries of any Indian reservation now existing or established hereafter.

Sec. 9. There is hereby authorized to be appropriated, out of any funds in the Treasury not otherwise appropriated, such sums as may be necessary, but not to exceed $250,000 in any fiscal year, to be expended at the order of the Secretary of the Interior, in defraying the expenses of organizing Indian chartered corporations or other organizations created under this Act.

Sec. 10. There is hereby authorized to be appropriated, out of any funds in the Treasury not otherwise appropriated, the sum of $10,000,000 to be established as a

THE HEADWATERS WAR:
Conflict for the Mississippi Headwaters

Indian Reorganization Act of 1934

revolving fund from which the Secretary of the Interior, under such rules and regulations as he may prescribe, may make loans to Indian chartered corporations for the purpose of promoting the economic development of such tribes and of their members, and may defray the expenses of administering such loans. Repayment of amounts loaned under this authorization shall be credited to the revolving fund and shall be available for the purposes for which the fund is established. A report shall be made annually to Congress of transactions under this authorization.

Sec. 11. There is hereby authorized to be appropriated, out of any funds in the United States Treasury not otherwise appropriated, a sum not to exceed $250,000 annually, together with any unexpended balances of previous appropriations made pursuant to this section, for loans to Indians for the payment of tuition and other expenses in recognized vocational and trade schools: *Provided,* That not more than $50,000 of such sum shall be available for loans to Indian students in high schools and colleges. Such loans shall be reimbursable under rules established by the Commissioner of Indian Affairs.

Sec. 12. The Secretary of the Interior is directed to establish standards of health, age, character, experience, knowledge, and ability for Indians who maybe appointed, without regard to civil-service laws, to the various positions maintained, now or hereafter, by the Indian office, in the administrations functions or services affecting any Indian tribe. Such qualified Indians shall hereafter have the preference to appointment to vacancies in any such positions.

Sec. 13. The provisions of this Act shall not apply to any of the Territories, colonies, or insular possessions of the United States, except that sections 9, 10, 11, 12, and 16 shall apply to the Territory of Alaska: *Provided,* That Sections 2, 4, 7, 16, 17, and 18 of this Act shall not apply to the following named Indian tribes, together with members of other tribes affiliated with such named located in the State of Oklahoma, as follows: Cheyenne, Arapaho, Apache, Comanche, Kiowa, Caddo, Delaware, Wichita, Osage, Kaw, Otoe, Tonkawa, Pawnee, Ponca, Shawnee, Ottawa, Quapaw, Seneca, Wyandotte, Iowa, Sac and Fox, Kickapoo, Pottawatomi, Cherokee, Chickasaw, Choctaw, Creek, and Seminole. Section 4 of this Act shall not apply to the Indians of the Klamath Reservation in Oregon.

Sec. 14. The Secretary of the Interior is hereby directed to continue the allowance of the articles enumerated in section 17 of the Act of March 2, 1889 (25 Stat.L. 891), or their commuted cash value under the Act of June 10, 1886 (29 Stat.L. 334), to all Sioux Indians who would be eligible, but for the provisions of this Act, to receive allotments of lands in severalty under section 19 of the Act of May 29, 1908 (25 (35) Stat.L. 451), or under any prior Act, and who have the prescribed status of the head of a family or single person over the age of eighteen years, and his approval shall be final and conclusive, claims therefor to be paid as formerly from the permanent

THE HEADWATERS WAR:
Conflict for the Mississippi Headwaters

Indian Reorganization Act of 1934

appropriation made by said section 17 and carried on the books of the Treasury for this purpose. No person shall receive in his own right more than one allowance of the benefits, and application must be made and approved during the lifetime of the allotee or the right shall lapse. Such benefits shall continue to be paid upon such reservation until such time as the lands available therein for allotment at the time of the passage of this Act would have been exhausted by the award to each person receiving such benefits of an allotment of eighty acres of such land.

Sec. 15. Nothing in this Act shall be construed to impair or prejudice any claim or suit of any Indian tribe against the United States. It is hereby declared to be the intent of Congress that no expenditures for the benefit of Indians made out of appropriations authorized by this Act shall be considered as offsets in any suit brought to recover upon any claim of such Indians against the United States.

Sec. 16. Any Indian tribe, or tribes, residing on the same reservation, shall have the right to organize for its common welfare, and may adopt an appropriate constitution and bylaws, which shall become effective when ratified by a majority vote of the adult members of the tribe, or of the adult Indians residing on such reservation, as the case may be, at a special election authorized by the Secretary of the Interior under such rules and regulations as he may prescribe. Such constitution and bylaws when ratified as aforesaid and approved by the Secretary of the Interior shall be revocable by an election open to the same voters and conducted in the same manner as hereinabove provided. Amendments to the constitution and bylaws may be ratified and approved by the Secretary in the same manner as the original constitution and bylaws.

In addition to all powers vested in any Indian tribe or tribal council by existing law, the constitution adopted by said tribe shall also vest in such tribe or its tribal council the following rights and powers: To employ legal counsel, the choice of counsel and fixing of fees to be subject to the approval of the Secretary of the Interior; to prevent the sale, disposition, lease, or encumbrance of tribal lands, interests in lands, or other tribal assets without the consent of the tribe; and to negotiate with the Federal, State, and local Governments. The Secretary of the Interior shall advise such tribe or its tribal council of all appropriation estimates or Federal projects for the benefit of the tribe prior to the submission of such estimates to the Bureau of the Budget and the Congress.

Sec. 17. The Secretary of the Interior may, upon petition by at least one-third of the adult Indians, issue a charter of incorporation to such tribe: *Provided,* That such charter shall not become operative until ratified at a special election by a majority vote of the adult Indians living on the reservation. Such charter may convey to the incorporated tribe the power to purchase, take by gift, or bequest, or otherwise, own, hold, manage, operate, and dispose of property of every description, real and

THE HEADWATERS WAR:
Conflict for the Mississippi Headwaters

Indian Reorganization Act of 1934

personal, including the power to purchase restricted Indian lands and to issue in exchange therefor interests in corporate property, and such further powers as may be incidental to the conduct of corporate business, not inconsistent with law, but no authority shall be granted to sell, mortgage, or lease for a period exceeding ten years any of the land included in the limits of the reservation. Any charter so issued shall not be revoked or surrendered except by Act of Congress.

Sec. 18. This Act shall not apply to any reservation wherein a majority of the adult Indians, voting at a special election duly called by the Secretary of the Interior, shall vote against it application. It shall be the duty of the Secretary of the Interior, within one year after the passage and approval of this Act, to call such an election, which election shall be held by secret ballot upon thirty days' notice.

Sec. 19. The term "Indian" as used in this Act shall include all persons of Indian descent who are members of any recognized Indian tribe now under Federal jurisdiction, and all person who are descendants of such members who were, on June 1, 1934, residing within the present boundaries of any reservation, and shall further include all other persons of one-half or more Indian blood. For the purposes of this Act, Eskimos and other aboriginal peoples of Alaska shall be considered Indians. The term "tribe" wherever used in this Act shall be construed to refer to any Indian tribe, organized band, pueblo, or the Indians residing on one reservation. The words "adult Indians" wherever used in this Act shall be construed to refer to Indians who have attained the age of twenty-one years.

THE HEADWATERS WAR:
Conflict for the Mississippi Headwaters

Statutes Codifying Public Law 280

Cornell Law School

U.S. Code › Title 18 › Part I › Chapter 53 › § 1162

18 U.S. Code § 1162 - State jurisdiction over offenses committed by or against Indians in the Indian country

(a) Each of the States or Territories listed in the following table shall have jurisdiction over offenses committed by or against Indians in the areas of Indian country listed opposite the name of the State or Territory to the same extent that such State or Territory has jurisdiction over offenses committed elsewhere within the State or Territory, and the criminal laws of such State or Territory shall have the same force and effect within such Indian country as they have elsewhere within the State or Territory:

State or Territory of	Indian country affected
Alaska	All Indian country within the State, except that on Annette Islands, the Metlakatla Indian community may exercise jurisdiction over offenses committed by Indians in the same manner in which such jurisdiction may be exercised by Indian tribes in Indian country over which State jurisdiction has not been extended.
California . .	All Indian country within the State.
Minnesota .	All Indian country within the State, except the Red Lake Reservation.
Nebraska . .	All Indian country within the State.
Oregon. . . .	All Indian country within the State, except the Warm Springs Reservation.
Wisconsin .	All Indian country within the State.

(b) Nothing in this section shall authorize the alienation, encumbrance, or taxation of any real or personal property, including water rights, belonging to any Indian or any Indian tribe, band, or community that is held in trust by the United States or is subject to a restriction against alienation imposed by the United States; or shall authorize regulation of the use of such property in a manner inconsistent with any Federal treaty, agreement, or statute or with any regulation made pursuant thereto; or shall deprive any Indian or any Indian tribe, band, or community of any right, privilege, or immunity afforded under Federal treaty, agreement, or statute with respect to hunting, trapping, or fishing or the control, licensing, or regulation thereof.

THE HEADWATERS WAR:
Conflict for the Mississippi Headwaters

Statutes Codifying Public Law 280

(c) The provisions of sections 1152 and 1153 of this chapter shall not be applicable within the areas of Indian country listed in subsection (a) of this section as areas over which the several States have exclusive jurisdiction.

(d) Notwithstanding subsection (c), at the request of an Indian tribe, and after consultation with and consent by the Attorney General—

(1) sections 1152 and 1153 shall apply in the areas of the Indian country of the Indian tribe; and

(2) jurisdiction over those areas shall be concurrent among the Federal Government, State governments, and, where applicable, tribal governments.

(Added Aug. 15, 1953, ch. 505, § 2, 67 Stat. 588; amended Aug. 24, 1954, ch. 910, § 1, 68 Stat. 795; Pub. L. 85–615, § 1, Aug. 8, 1958, 72 Stat. 545; Pub. L. 91–523, §§ 1, 2, Nov. 25, 1970, 84 Stat. 1358; Pub. L. 111–211, title II, § 221(b), July 29, 2010, 124 Stat. 2272.)

LII has no control over and does not endorse any external Internet site that contains links to or references LII.

About LII

Contact us

Advertise here

Help

Terms of use

Privacy

THE HEADWATERS WAR:
Conflict for the Mississippi Headwaters

Statutes Codifying Public Law 280

Cornell Law School

U.S. Code › Title 28 › Part IV › Chapter 85 › § 1360

28 U.S. Code § 1360 - State civil jurisdiction in actions to which Indians are parties

(a) Each of the States listed in the following table shall have jurisdiction over civil causes of action between Indians or to which Indians are parties which arise in the areas of Indian country listed opposite the name of the State to the same extent that such State has jurisdiction over other civil causes of action, and those civil laws of such State that are of general application to private persons or private property shall have the same force and effect within such Indian country as they have elsewhere within the State:

State of   Indian country affected
Alaska . . . All Indian country within the State.
California . All Indian country within the State.
Minnesota All Indian country within the State, except the Red Lake Reservation.
Nebraska . All Indian country within the State.
Oregon. . . All Indian country within the State, except the Warm Springs Reservation.
Wisconsin. All Indian country within the State.

(b) Nothing in this section shall authorize the alienation, encumbrance, or taxation of any real or personal property, including water rights, belonging to any Indian or any Indian tribe, band, or community that is held in trust by the United States or is subject to a restriction against alienation imposed by the United States; or shall authorize regulation of the use of such property in a manner inconsistent with any Federal treaty, agreement, or statute or with any regulation made pursuant thereto; or shall confer jurisdiction upon the State to adjudicate, in probate proceedings or otherwise, the ownership or right to possession of such property or any interest therein.

(c) Any tribal ordinance or custom heretofore or hereafter adopted by an Indian tribe, band, or community in the exercise of any authority which it may possess shall, if not inconsistent with any applicable civil law of the State, be given full force and effect in the determination of civil causes of action pursuant to this section.

(Added Aug. 15, 1953, ch. 505, § 4, 67 Stat. 589; amended Aug. 24, 1954, ch. 910, § 2, 68 Stat. 795; Pub. L. 85–615, § 2, Aug. 8, 1958, 72 Stat. 545; Pub. L. 95–598, title II, § 239, Nov. 6, 1978, 92 Stat. 2668; Pub. L. 98–353, title I, § 110, July 10, 1984, 98 Stat. 342.)

LII has no control over and does not endorse any external Internet site that contains links to or references LII.

About LII

Made in the USA
Middletown, DE
05 February 2018